THE MADAME MORA'S CORSETS

A MARVEL OF COMFORT AND ELEGANCE !

Their popularity has induced many imitations, which are frauds, high at any price. Buy only the genuine, stamped Madame Mora's. Sold by all leading dealers with this GUARANTEE: that if not perfectly satisfactory upon trial the money will be refunded.

L. KRAUS & CO., Manufacturers, Birmingham, Conn.

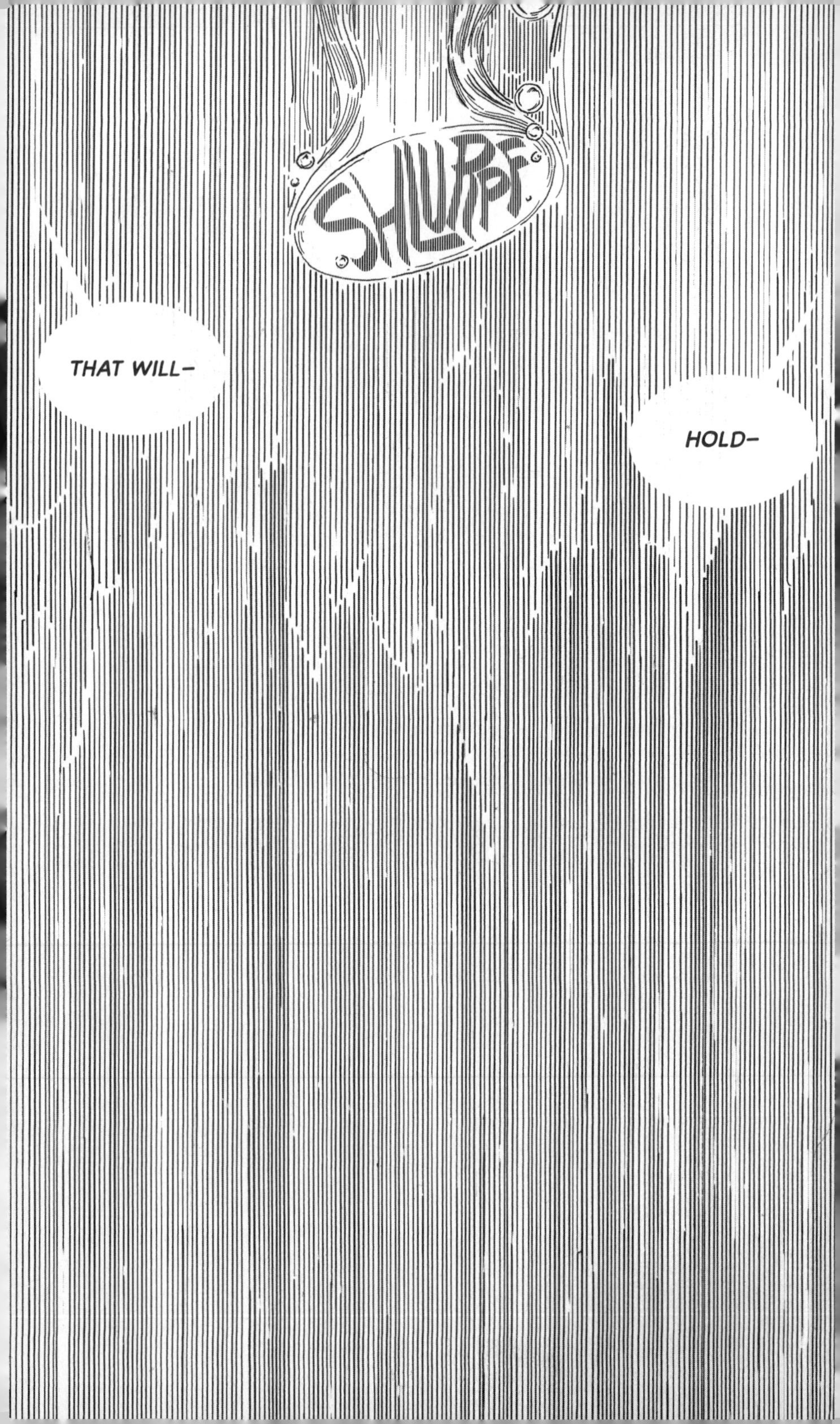
SHLLRPP
THAT WILL–
HOLD–

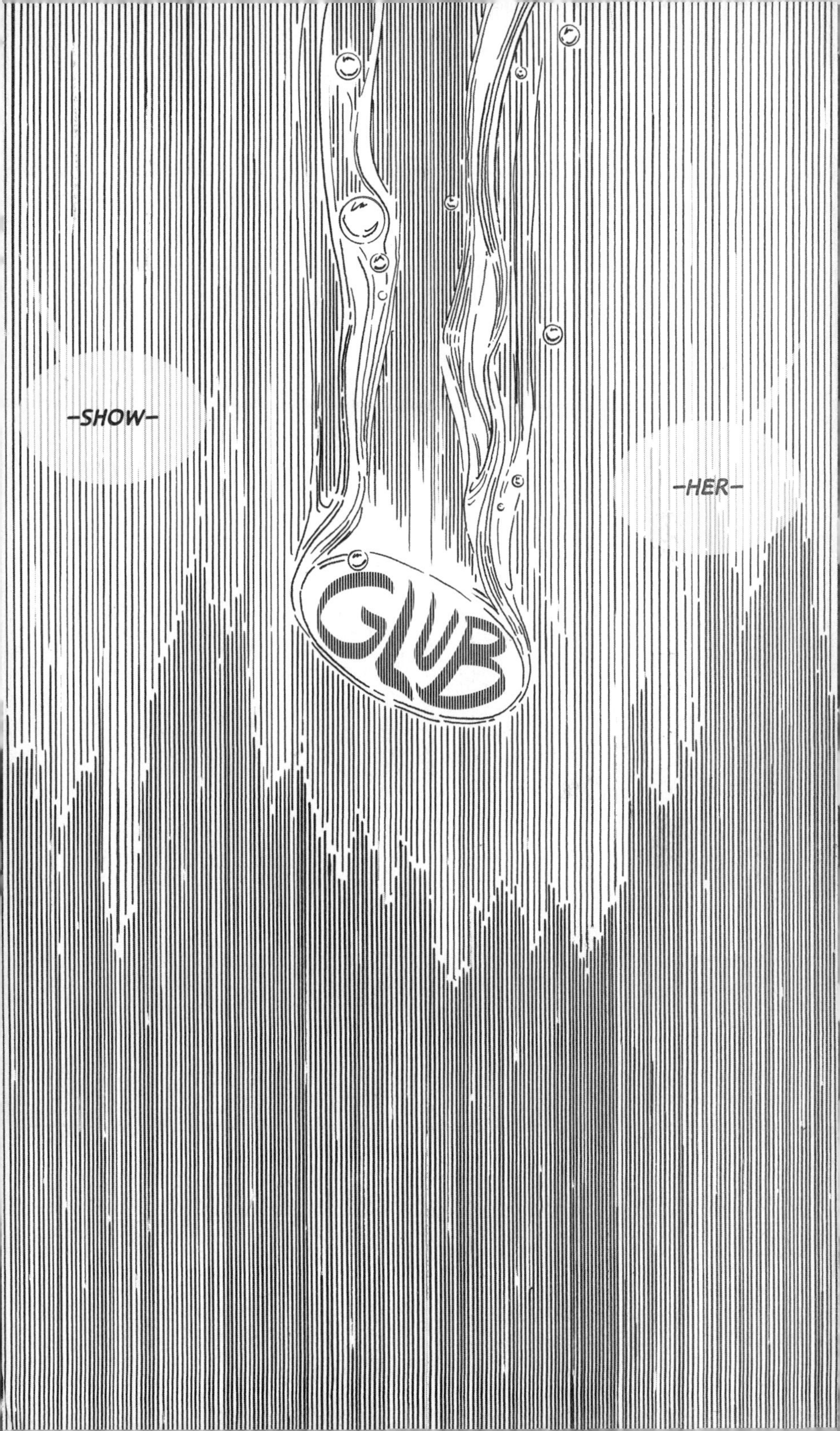
-SHOW-
-HER-
GUB

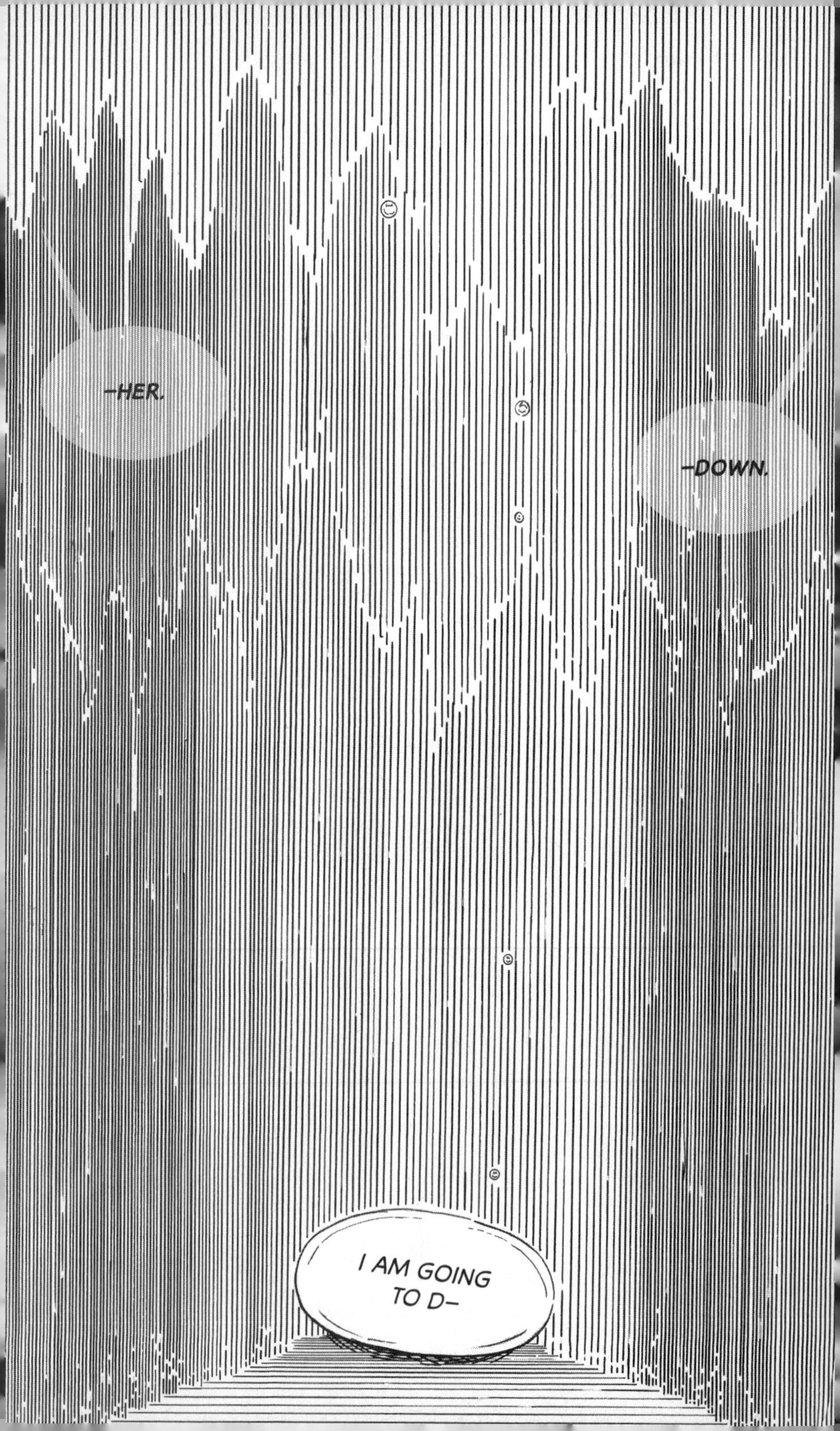
–HER.
–DOWN.
I AM GOING
TO D–

TEN DAYS
IN A
MAD-HOUSE

WRITTEN BY **BRAD RICCA**

ILLUSTRATED BY **COURTNEY SIEH**

ADAPTED FROM THE WORK OF **NELLIE BLY**

GALLERY 13

New York   London   Toronto   Sydney   New Delhi

Gallery 13
An Imprint of Simon & Schuster, Inc.
1230 Avenue of the Americas
New York, NY 10020

First Gallery 13 trade paperback edition
April 2022

GALLERY 13 and colophon are trademarks of Simon &
Schuster, Inc.

For information about special discounts for bulk
purchases, please contact Simon & Schuster
Special Sales at 1-866-506-1949 or
business@simonandschuster.com

The Simon & Schuster Speakers Bureau can bring
authors to your live event. For more information or to book
an event contact the Simon & Schuster Speakers Bureau at
1-866-248-3049 or visit our website at
www.simonspeakers.com.

Manufactured in the United States of America

10   9   8   7   6   5   4   3   2   1

Library of Congress Cataloging-in-Publication Data is
available.

ISBN 978-1-9821-4065-6
ISBN 978-1-9821-4066-3 (ebook)

PART I

• A DELICATE MISSION •

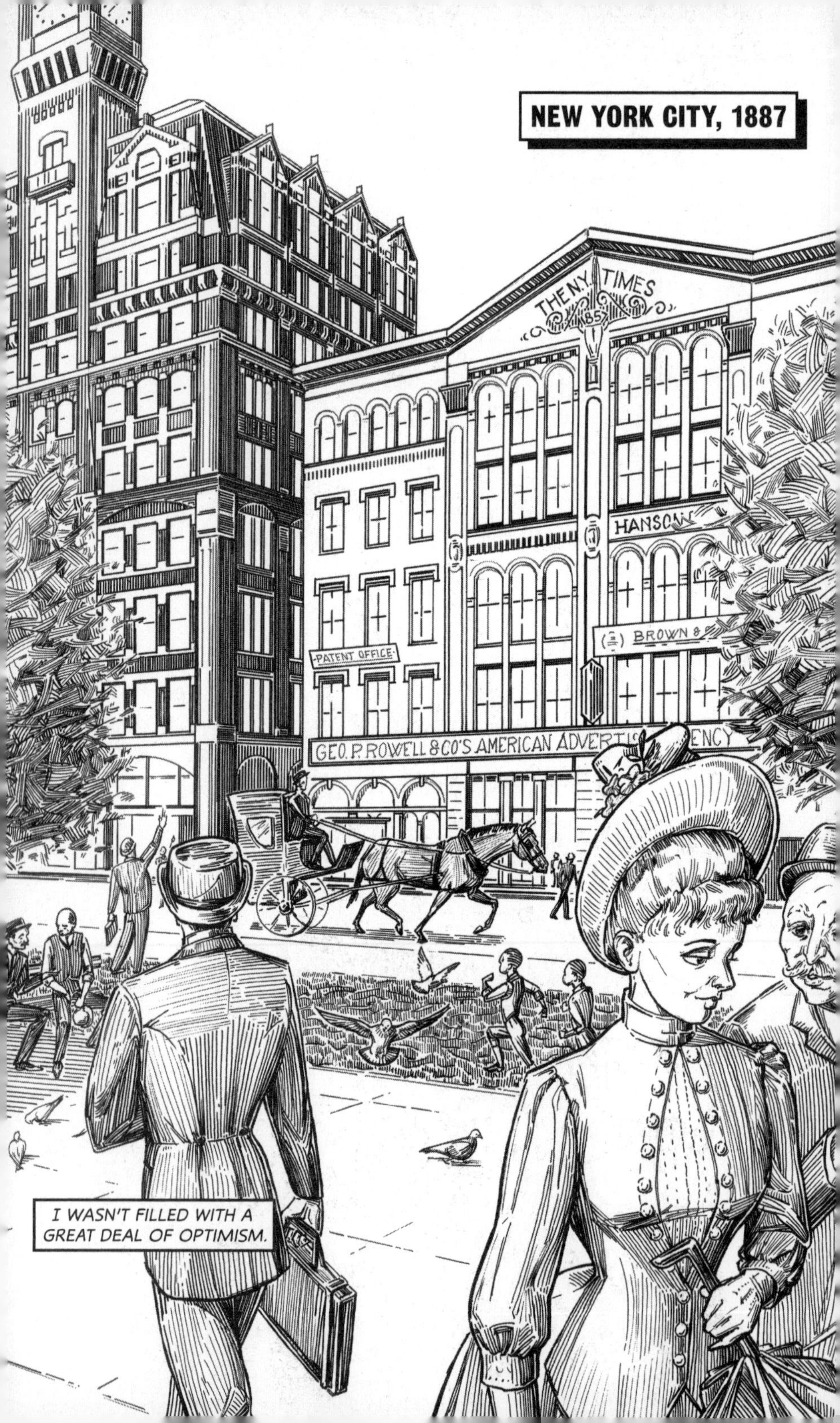
NEW YORK CITY, 1887
THE N.Y. TIMES
HANSON
PATENT OFFICE
BROWN &
I WASN'T FILLED WITH A GREAT DEAL OF OPTIMISM.

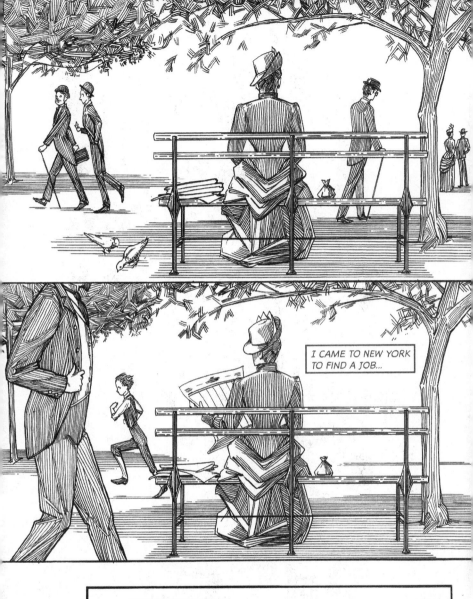

I CAME TO NEW YORK TO FIND A JOB...

...AS A REPORTER.

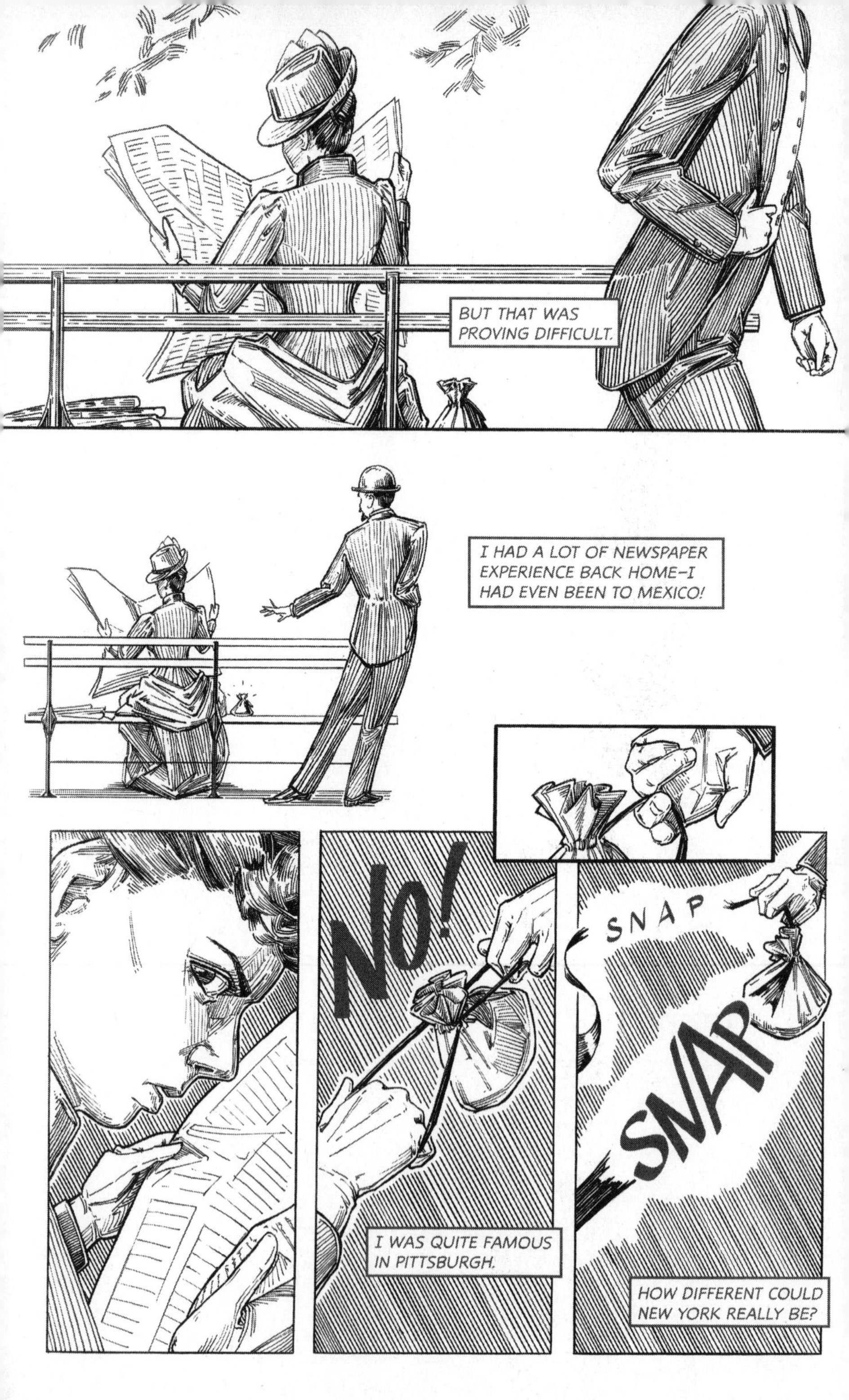
BUT THAT WAS PROVING DIFFICULT.
I HAD A LOT OF NEWSPAPER EXPERIENCE BACK HOME—I HAD EVEN BEEN TO MEXICO!
NO!
I WAS QUITE FAMOUS IN PITTSBURGH.
SNAP
SNAP
HOW DIFFERENT COULD NEW YORK REALLY BE?

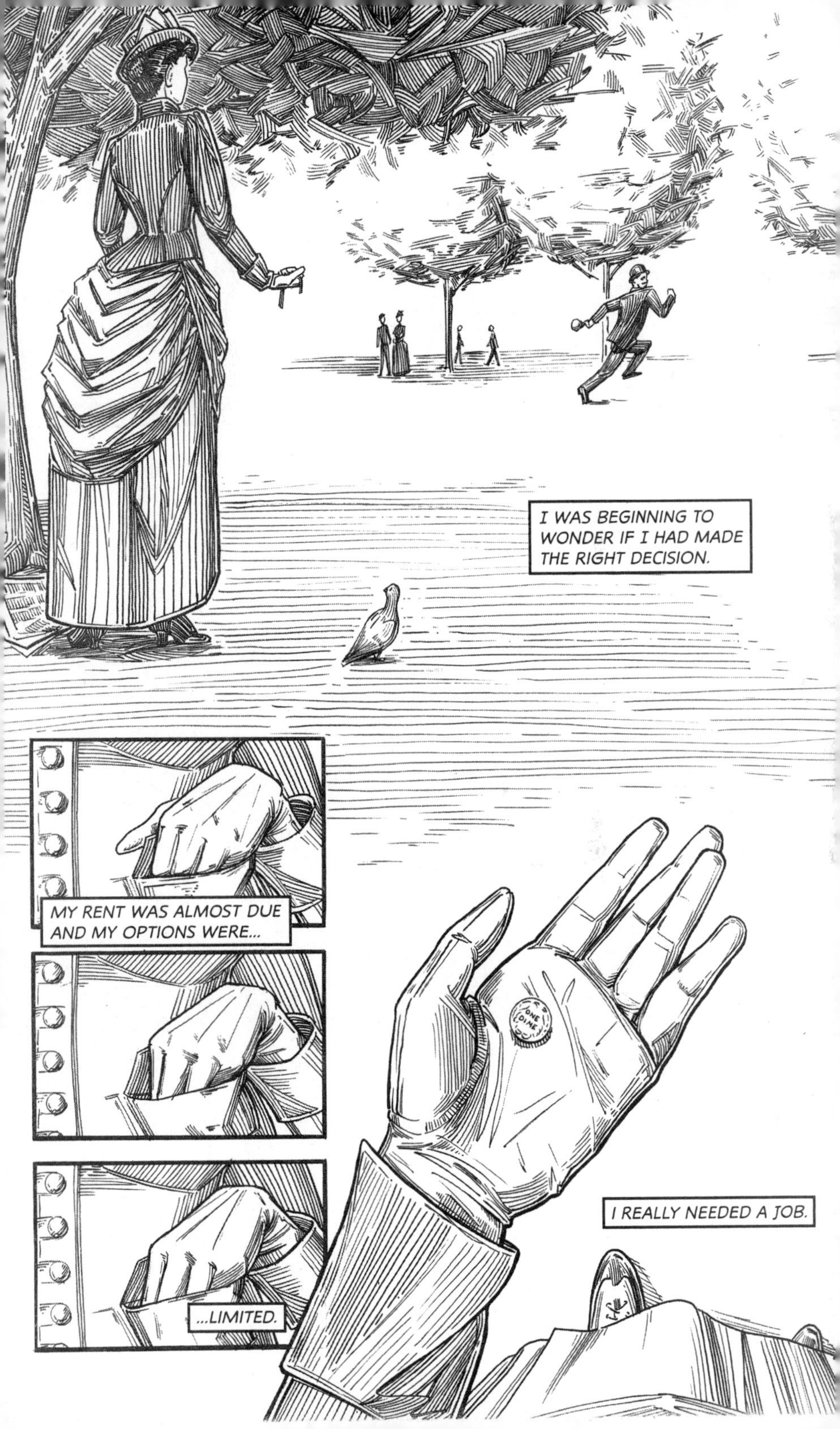
I WAS BEGINNING TO WONDER IF I HAD MADE THE RIGHT DECISION.
MY RENT WAS ALMOST DUE AND MY OPTIONS WERE...
...LIMITED.
ONE DIME
I REALLY NEEDED A JOB.

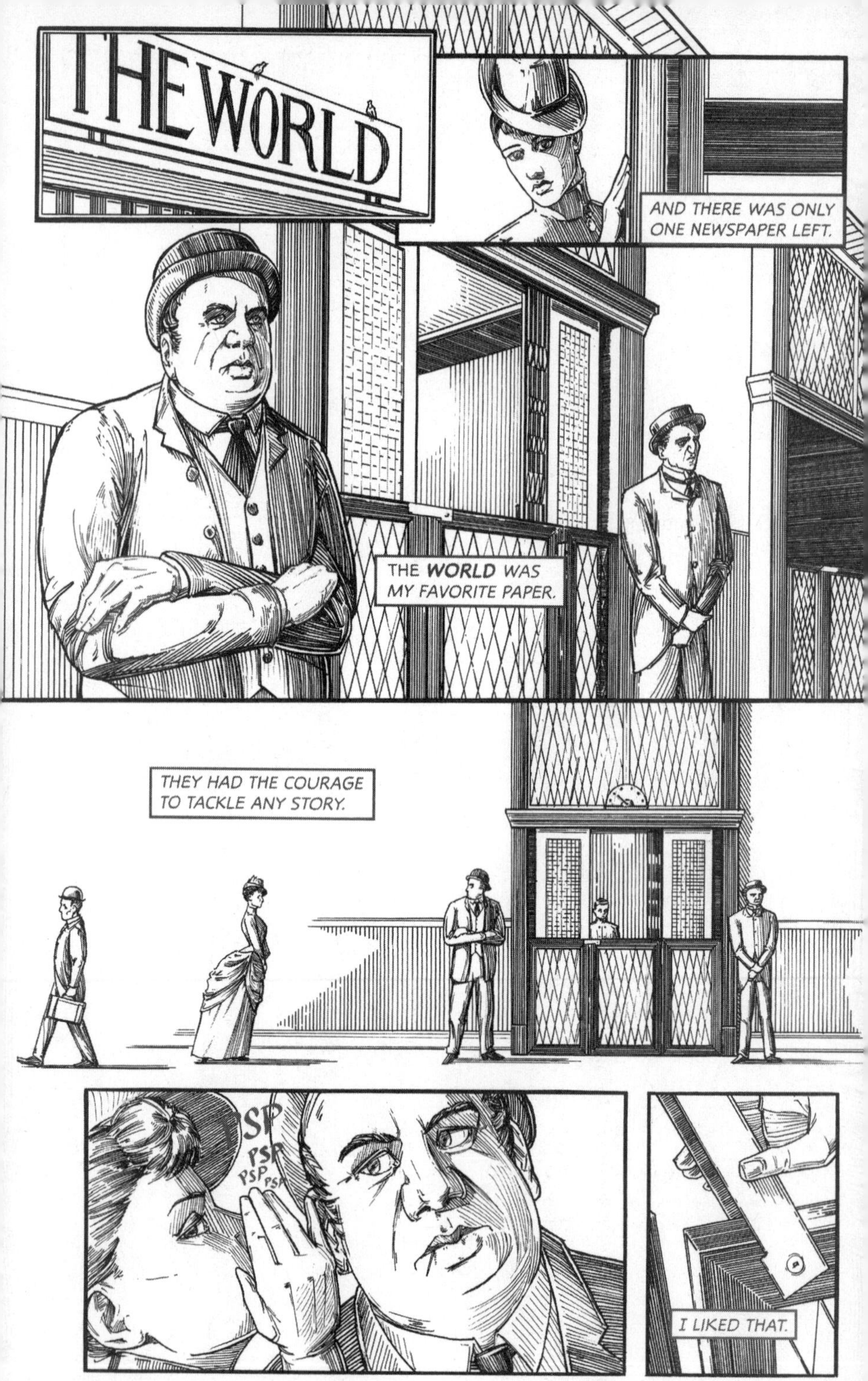
THE WORLD
AND THERE WAS ONLY ONE NEWSPAPER LEFT.
THE WORLD WAS MY FAVORITE PAPER.
THEY HAD THE COURAGE TO TACKLE ANY STORY.
PSP PSP PSP PSP PSP
I LIKED THAT.

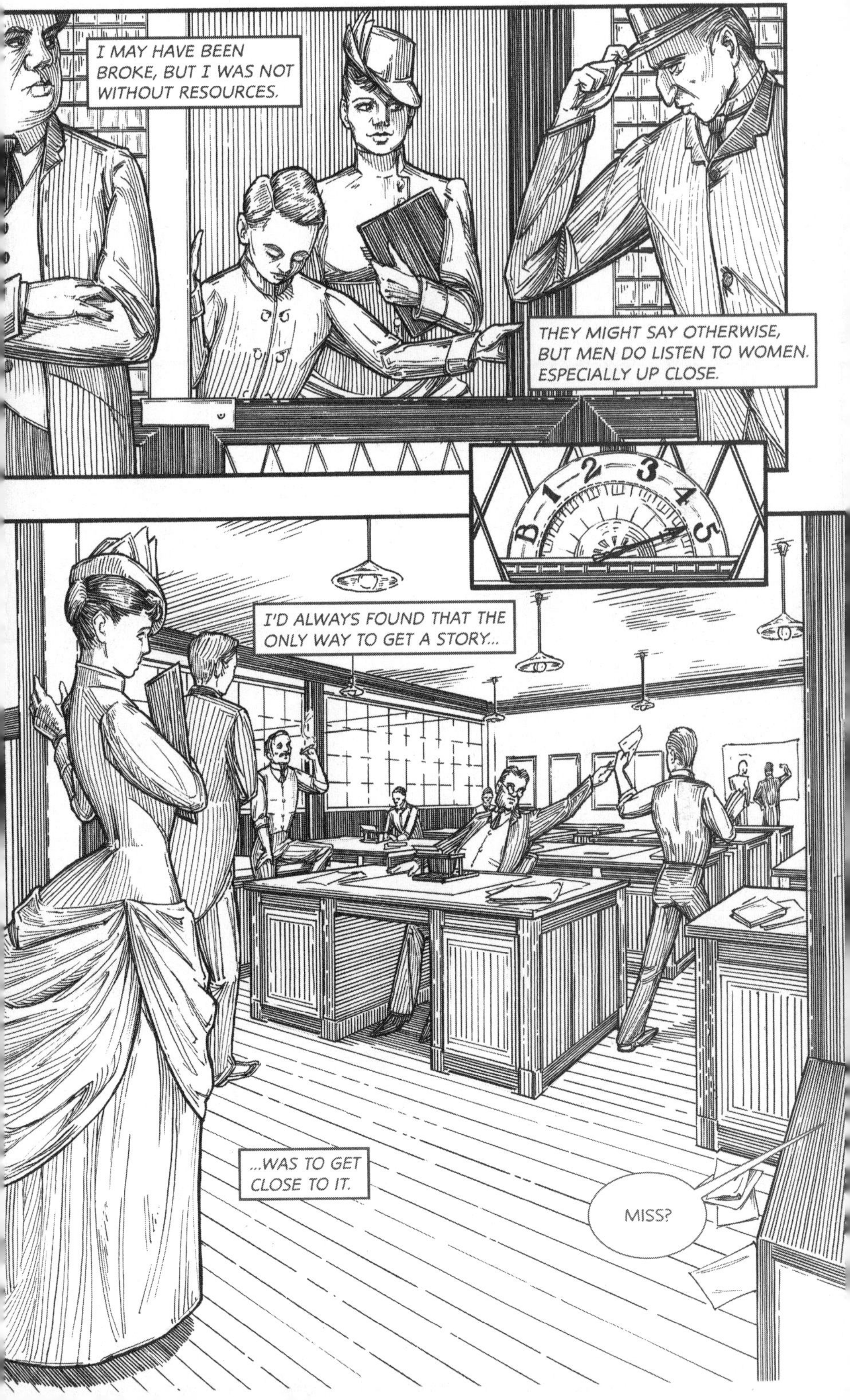
I MAY HAVE BEEN BROKE, BUT I WAS NOT WITHOUT RESOURCES.
THEY MIGHT SAY OTHERWISE, BUT MEN DO LISTEN TO WOMEN. ESPECIALLY UP CLOSE.
B 1 2 3 4 5
I'D ALWAYS FOUND THAT THE ONLY WAY TO GET A STORY...
...WAS TO GET CLOSE TO IT.
MISS?

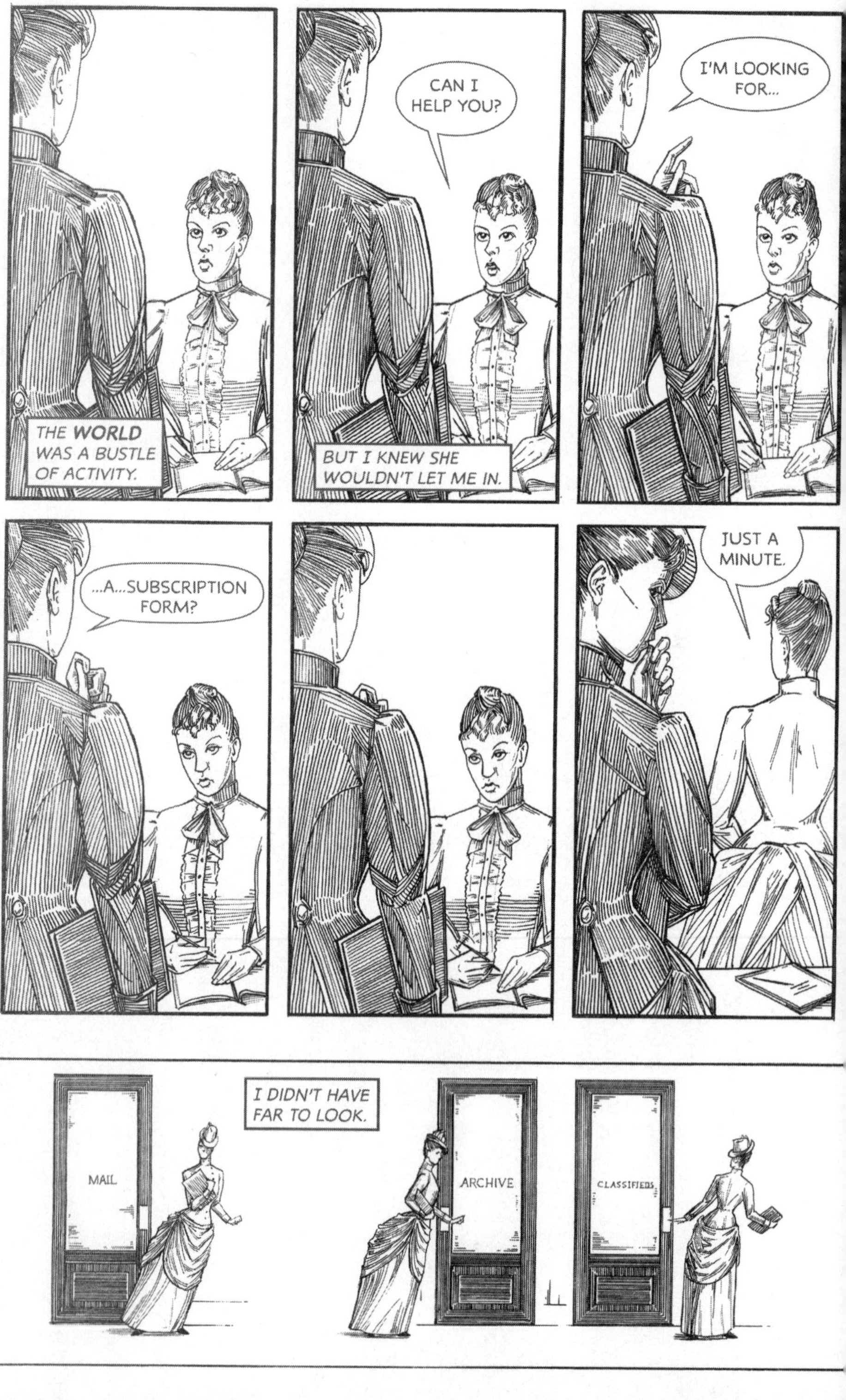
THE **WORLD** WAS A BUSTLE OF ACTIVITY.
CAN I HELP YOU?
BUT I KNEW SHE WOULDN'T LET ME IN.
I'M LOOKING FOR...
...A...SUBSCRIPTION FORM?
JUST A MINUTE.
I DIDN'T HAVE FAR TO LOOK.
MAIL
ARCHIVE
CLASSIFIEDS

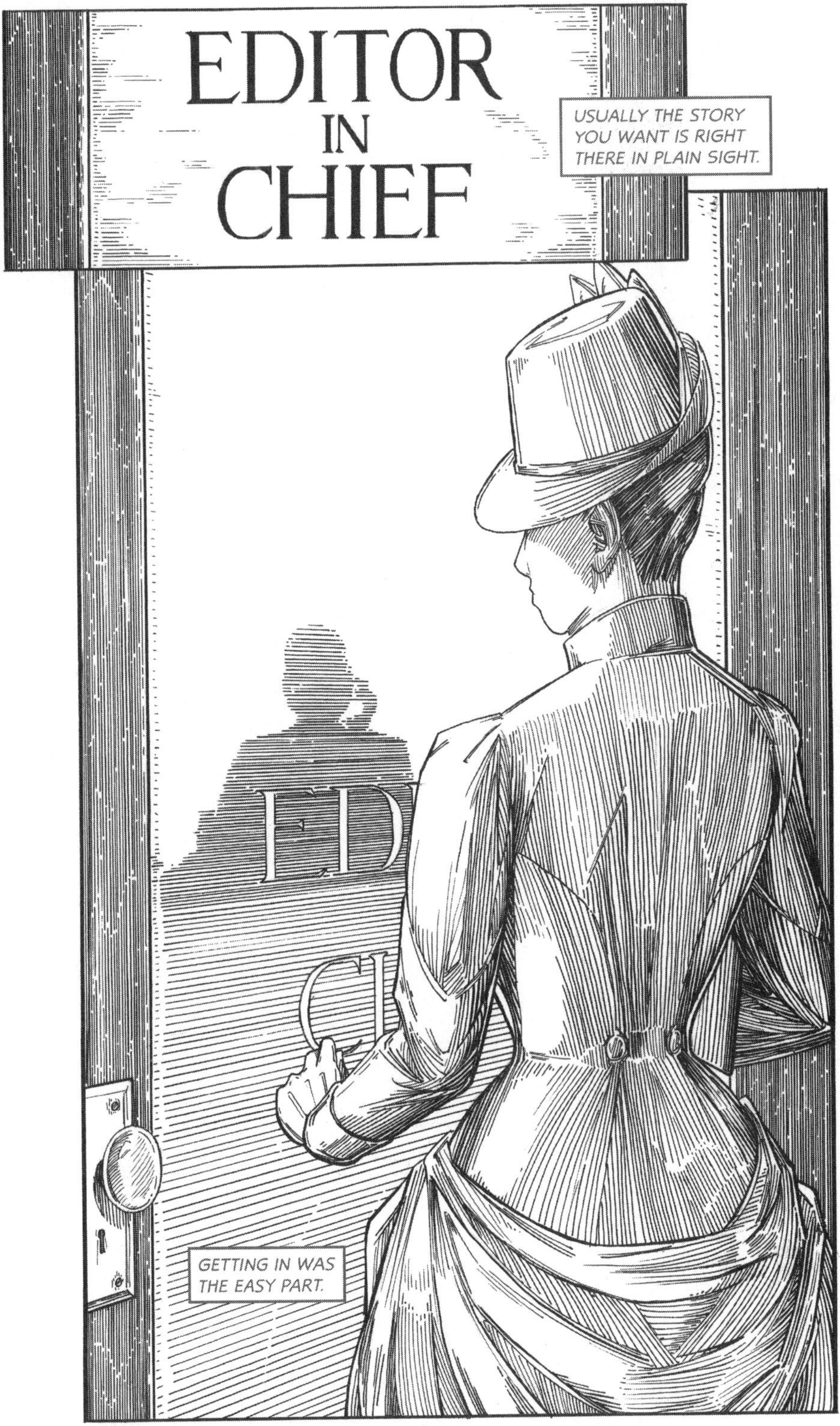

EDITOR IN CHIEF
USUALLY THE STORY YOU WANT IS RIGHT THERE IN PLAIN SIGHT.
GETTING IN WAS THE EASY PART.

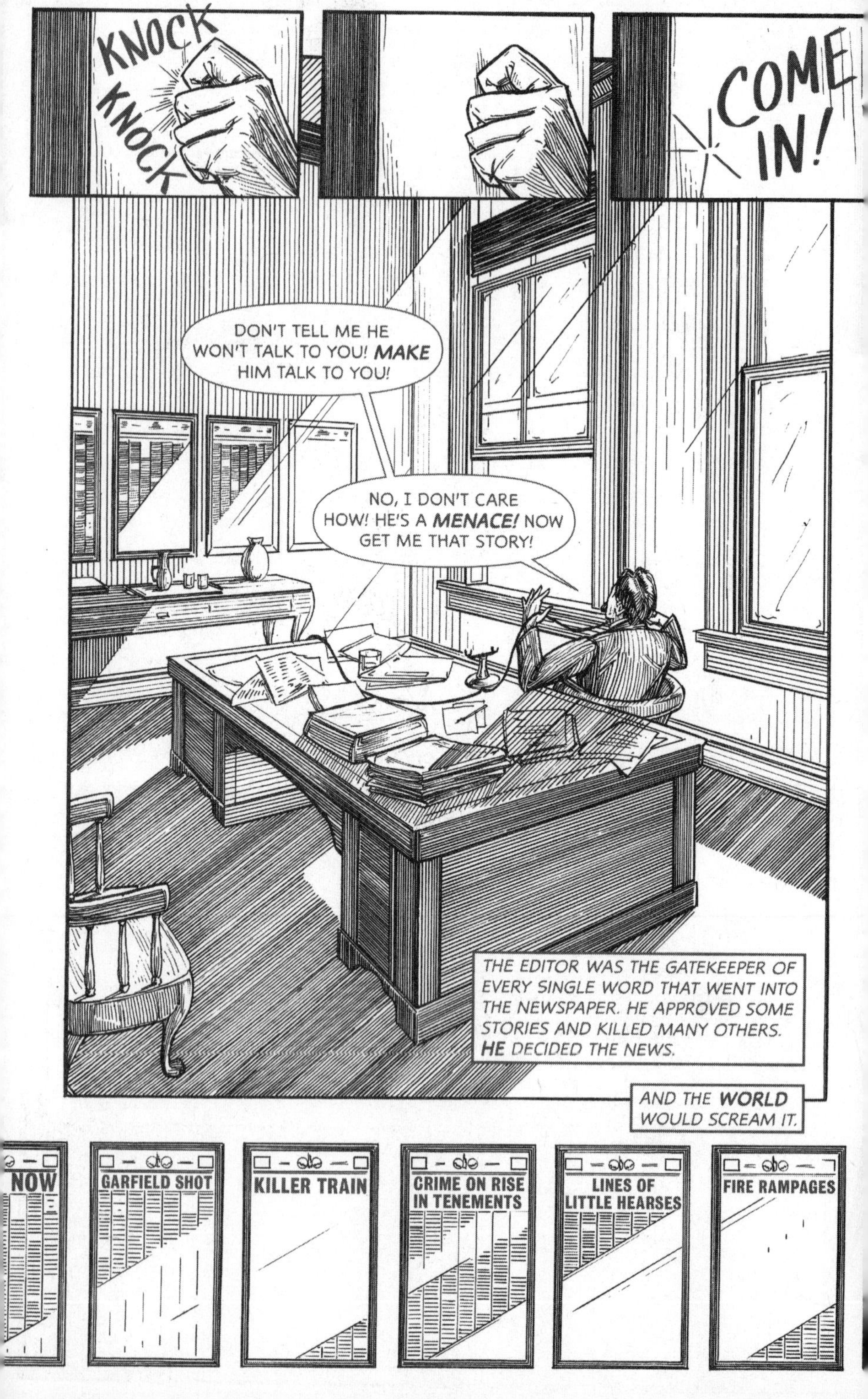
KNOCK KNOCK
COME IN!
DON'T TELL ME HE WON'T TALK TO YOU! MAKE HIM TALK TO YOU!
NO, I DON'T CARE HOW! HE'S A MENACE! NOW GET ME THAT STORY!
THE EDITOR WAS THE GATEKEEPER OF EVERY SINGLE WORD THAT WENT INTO THE NEWSPAPER. HE APPROVED SOME STORIES AND KILLED MANY OTHERS. HE DECIDED THE NEWS.
AND THE WORLD WOULD SCREAM IT.
NOW
GARFIELD SHOT
KILLER TRAIN
CRIME ON RISE IN TENEMENTS
LINES OF LITTLE HEARSES
FIRE RAMPAGES

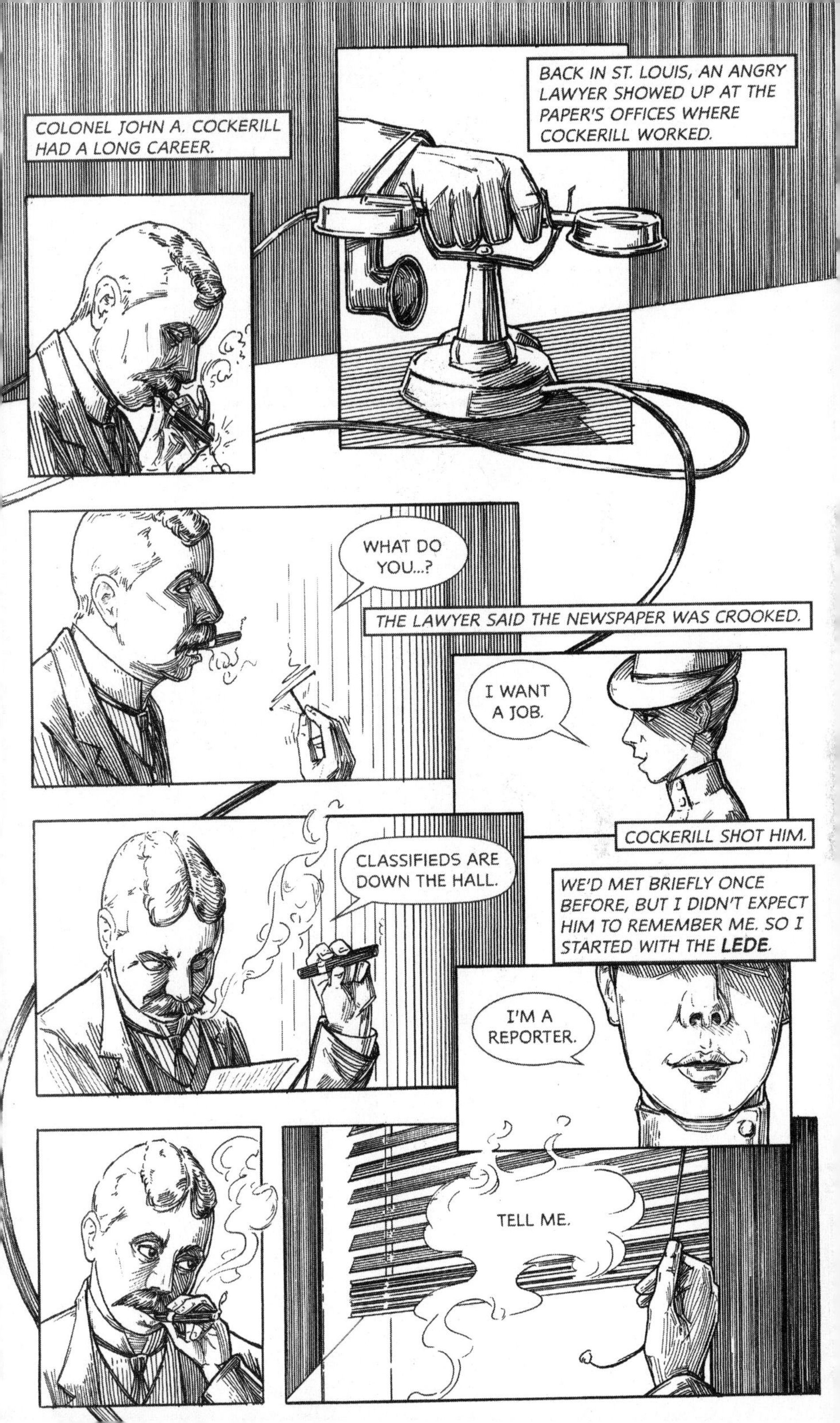
COLONEL JOHN A. COCKERILL HAD A LONG CAREER.
BACK IN ST. LOUIS, AN ANGRY LAWYER SHOWED UP AT THE PAPER'S OFFICES WHERE COCKERILL WORKED.
THE LAWYER SAID THE NEWSPAPER WAS CROOKED.
COCKERILL SHOT HIM.
WHAT DO YOU...?
I WANT A JOB.
CLASSIFIEDS ARE DOWN THE HALL.
WE'D MET BRIEFLY ONCE BEFORE, BUT I DIDN'T EXPECT HIM TO REMEMBER ME. SO I STARTED WITH THE **LEDE**.
I'M A REPORTER.
TELL ME.

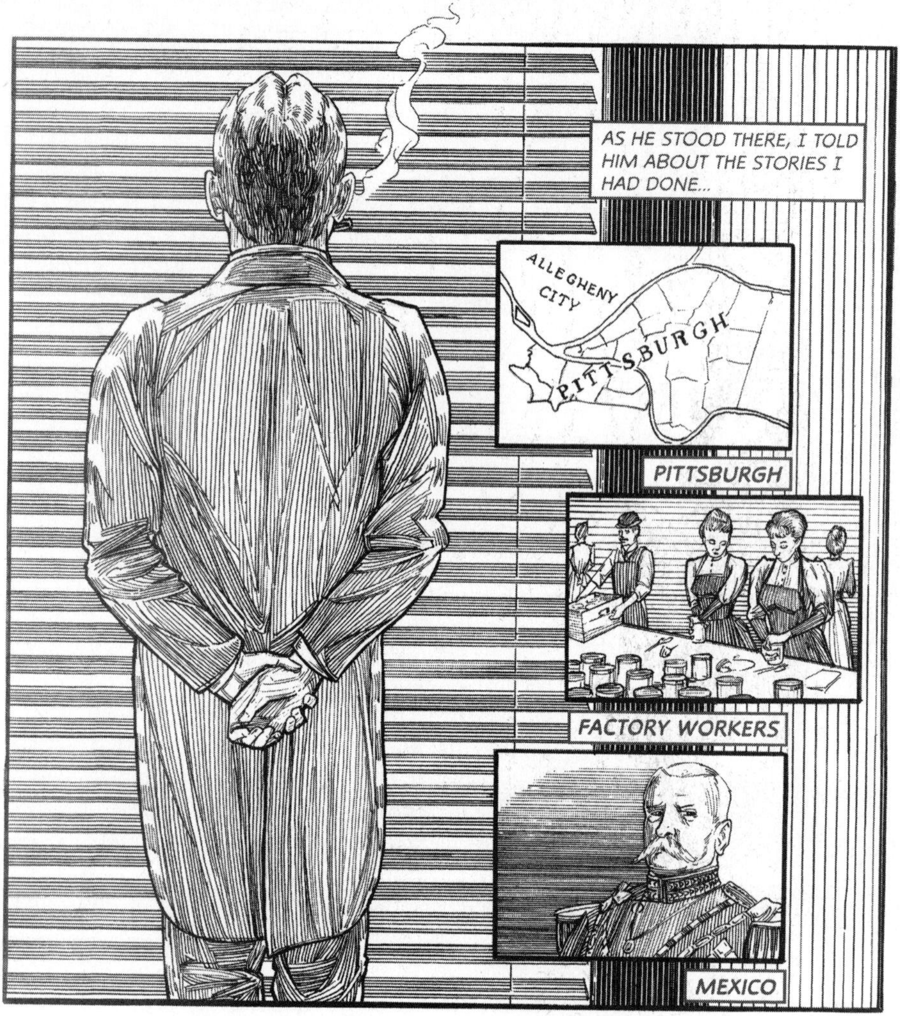

AS HE STOOD THERE, I TOLD HIM ABOUT THE STORIES I HAD DONE...
ALLEGHENY CITY
PITTSBURGH
PITTSBURGH
FACTORY WORKERS
MEXICO

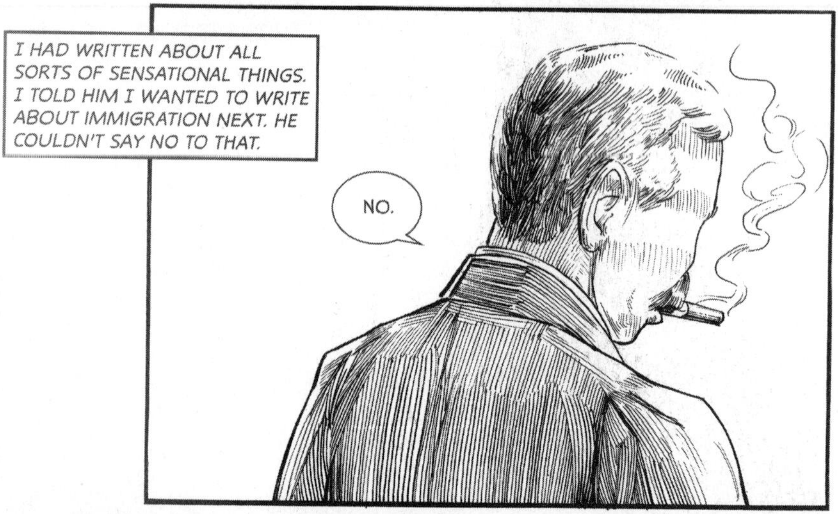

I HAD WRITTEN ABOUT ALL SORTS OF SENSATIONAL THINGS. I TOLD HIM I WANTED TO WRITE ABOUT IMMIGRATION NEXT. HE COULDN'T SAY NO TO THAT.
NO.

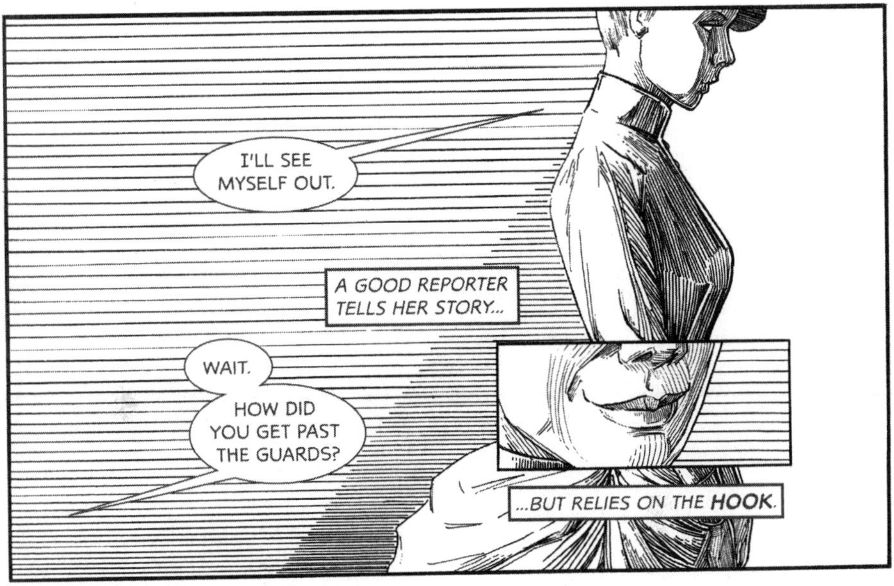
I'LL SEE MYSELF OUT.
A GOOD REPORTER TELLS HER STORY...
WAIT.
HOW DID YOU GET PAST THE GUARDS?
...BUT RELIES ON THE **HOOK**.

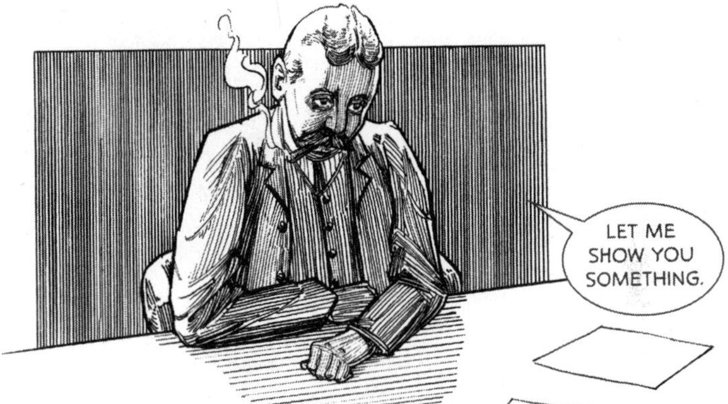
LET ME SHOW YOU SOMETHING.

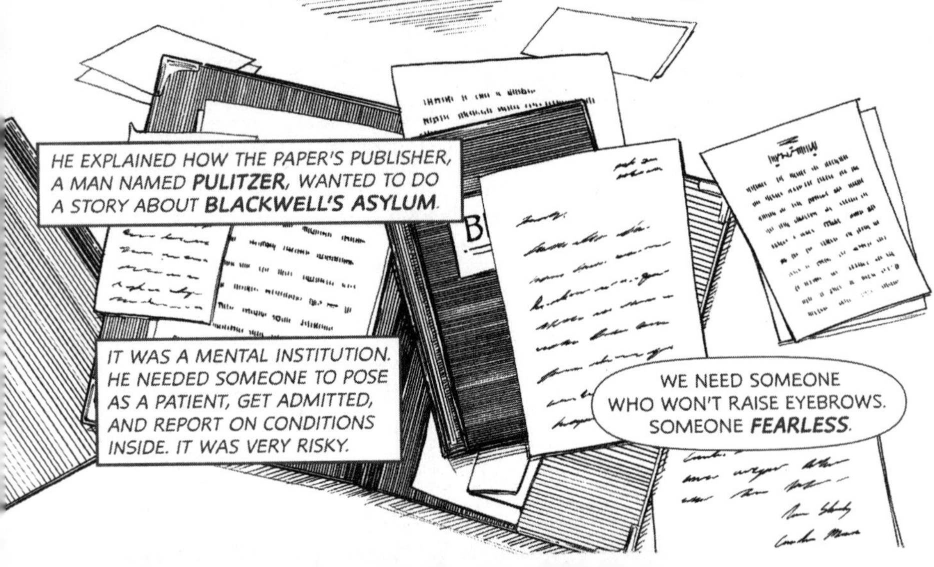
HE EXPLAINED HOW THE PAPER'S PUBLISHER, A MAN NAMED **PULITZER**, WANTED TO DO A STORY ABOUT **BLACKWELL'S ASYLUM**.
IT WAS A MENTAL INSTITUTION. HE NEEDED SOMEONE TO POSE AS A PATIENT, GET ADMITTED, AND REPORT ON CONDITIONS INSIDE. IT WAS VERY RISKY.
WE NEED SOMEONE WHO WON'T RAISE EYEBROWS. SOMEONE ***FEARLESS***.

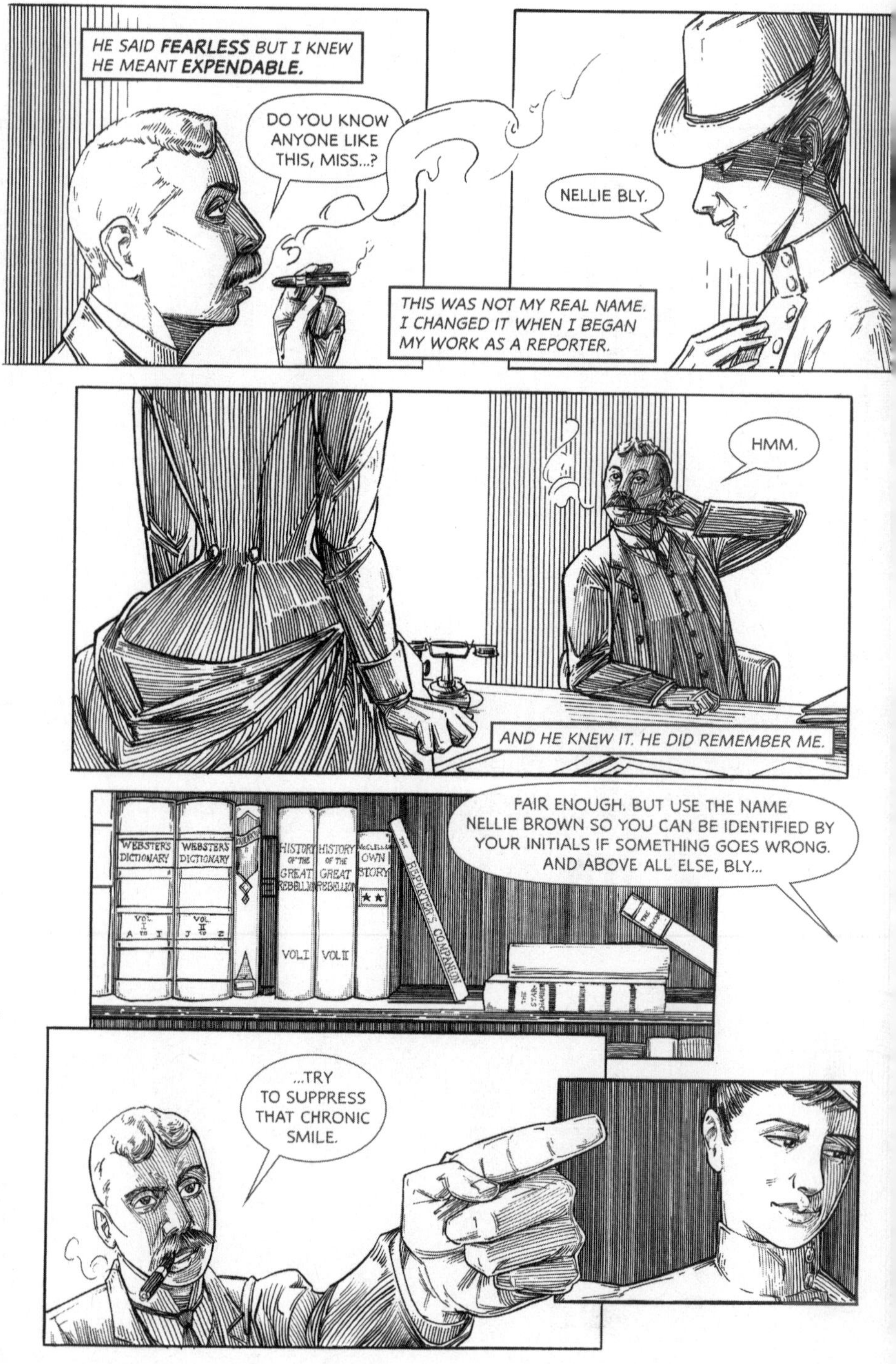
HE SAID **FEARLESS** BUT I KNEW HE MEANT **EXPENDABLE.**
DO YOU KNOW ANYONE LIKE THIS, MISS...?
NELLIE BLY.
THIS WAS NOT MY REAL NAME. I CHANGED IT WHEN I BEGAN MY WORK AS A REPORTER.
HMM.
AND HE KNEW IT. HE DID REMEMBER ME.
WEBSTER'S DICTIONARY
WEBSTER'S DICTIONARY
HISTORY OF THE GREAT REBELLION
HISTORY OF THE GREAT REBELLION
OWN STORY
THE REPORTER'S COMPANION
FAIR ENOUGH. BUT USE THE NAME NELLIE BROWN SO YOU CAN BE IDENTIFIED BY YOUR INITIALS IF SOMETHING GOES WRONG. AND ABOVE ALL ELSE, BLY...
...TRY TO SUPPRESS THAT CHRONIC SMILE.

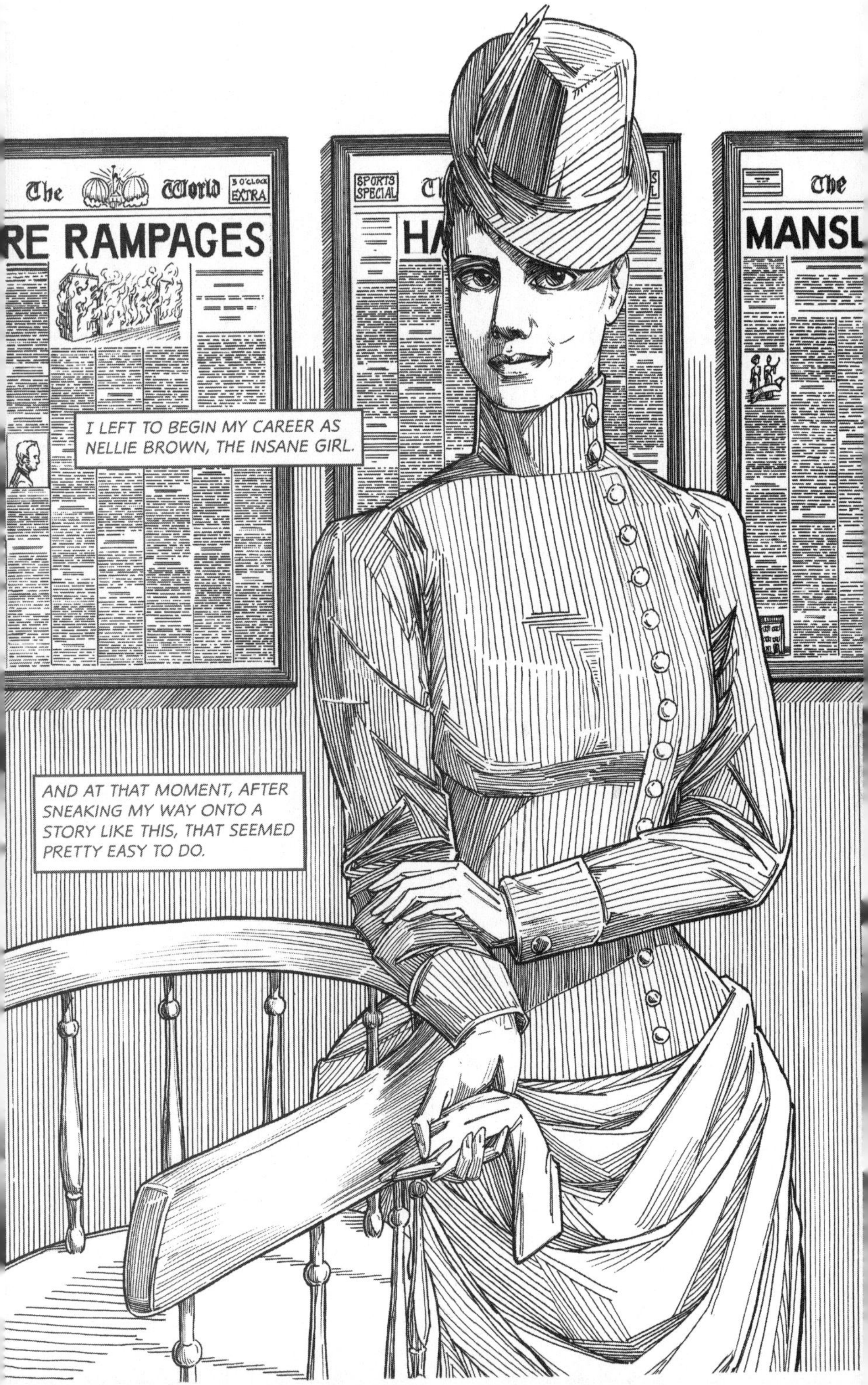

The World
3 O'CLOCK EXTRA
RE RAMPAGES
SPORTS SPECIAL
HA
The
MANSL
I LEFT TO BEGIN MY CAREER AS NELLIE BROWN, THE INSANE GIRL.
AND AT THAT MOMENT, AFTER SNEAKING MY WAY ONTO A STORY LIKE THIS, THAT SEEMED PRETTY EASY TO DO.

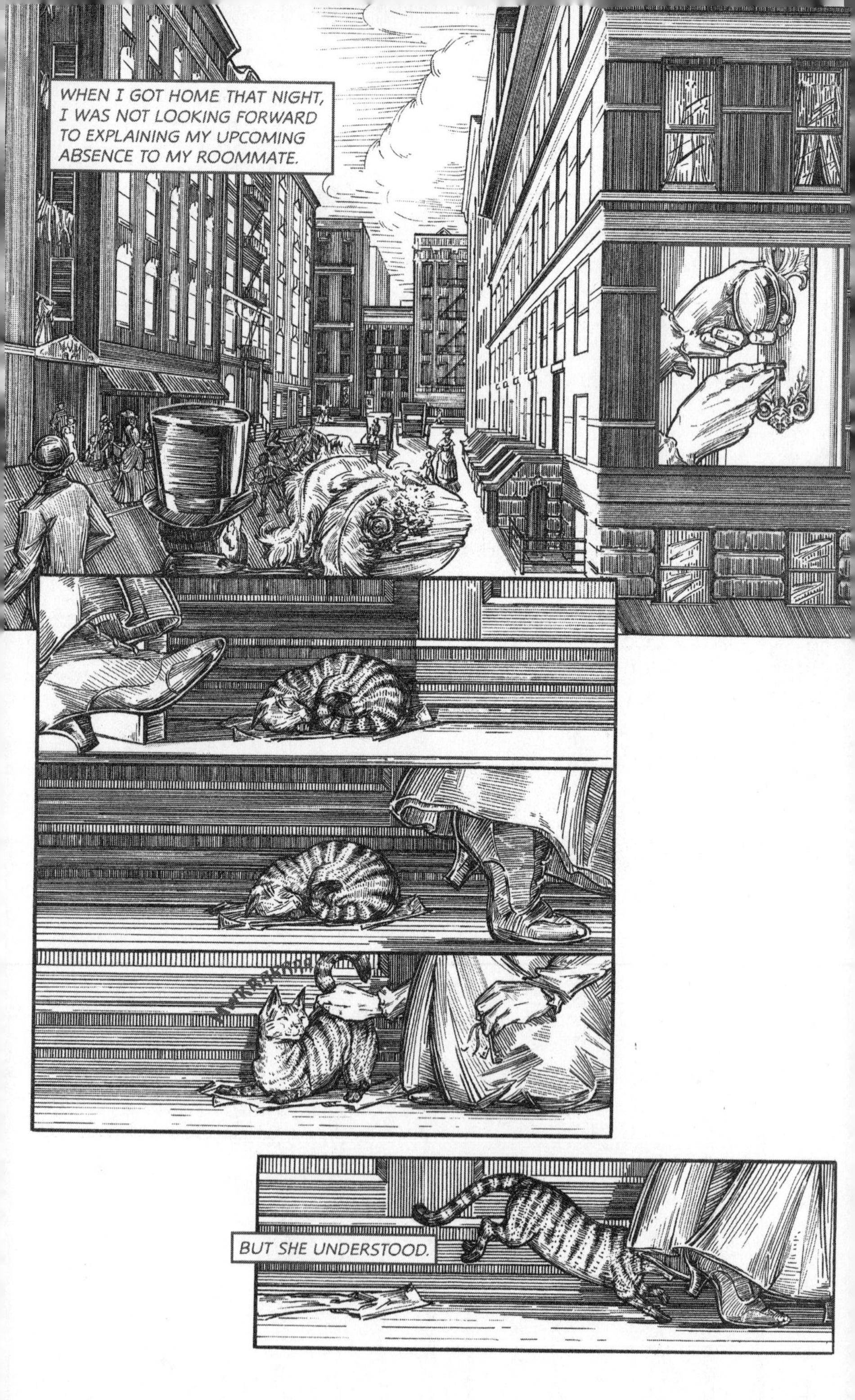
WHEN I GOT HOME THAT NIGHT, I WAS NOT LOOKING FORWARD TO EXPLAINING MY UPCOMING ABSENCE TO MY ROOMMATE.
BUT SHE UNDERSTOOD.

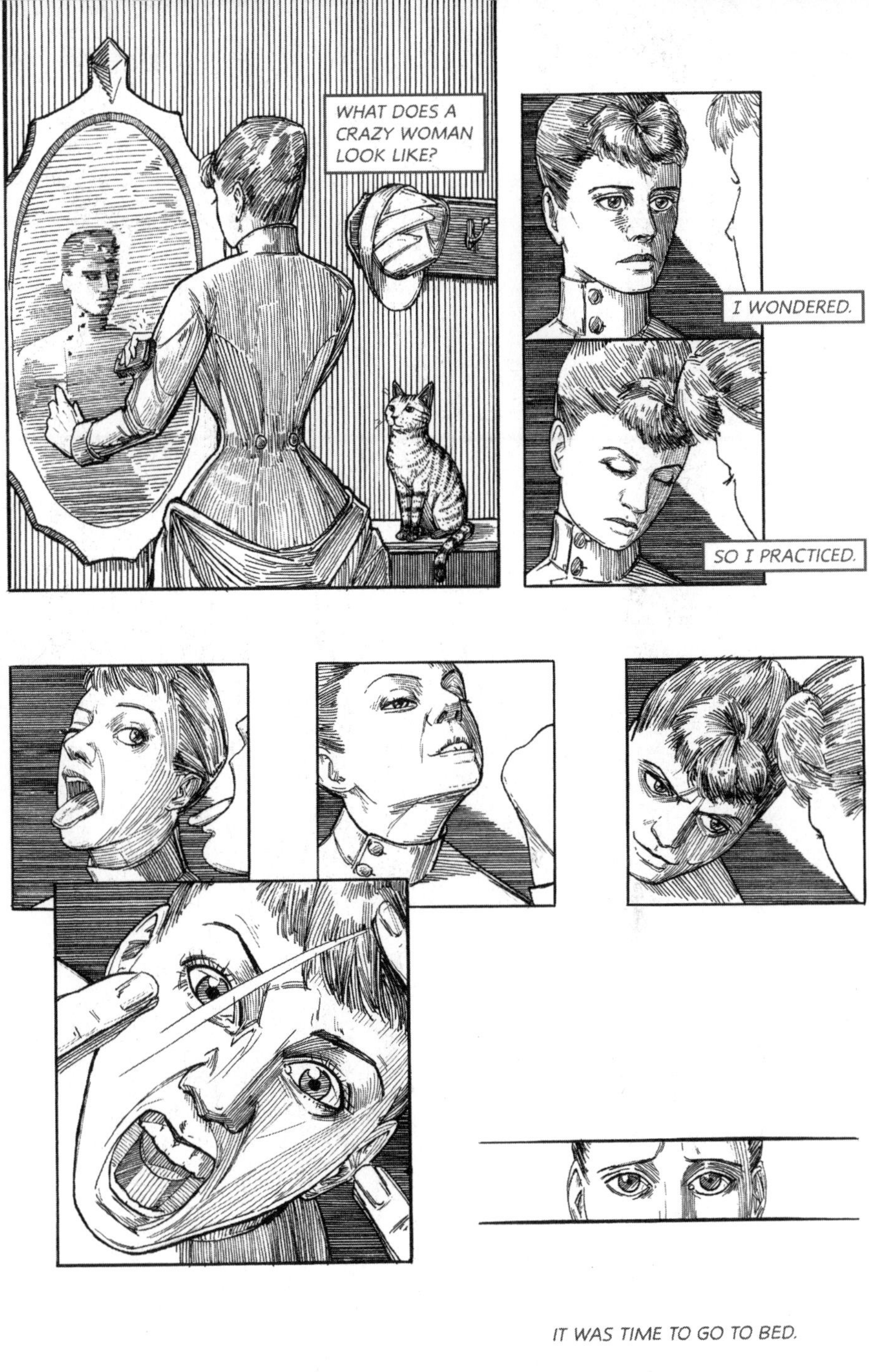
WHAT DOES A CRAZY WOMAN LOOK LIKE?
I WONDERED.
SO I PRACTICED.
IT WAS TIME TO GO TO BED.

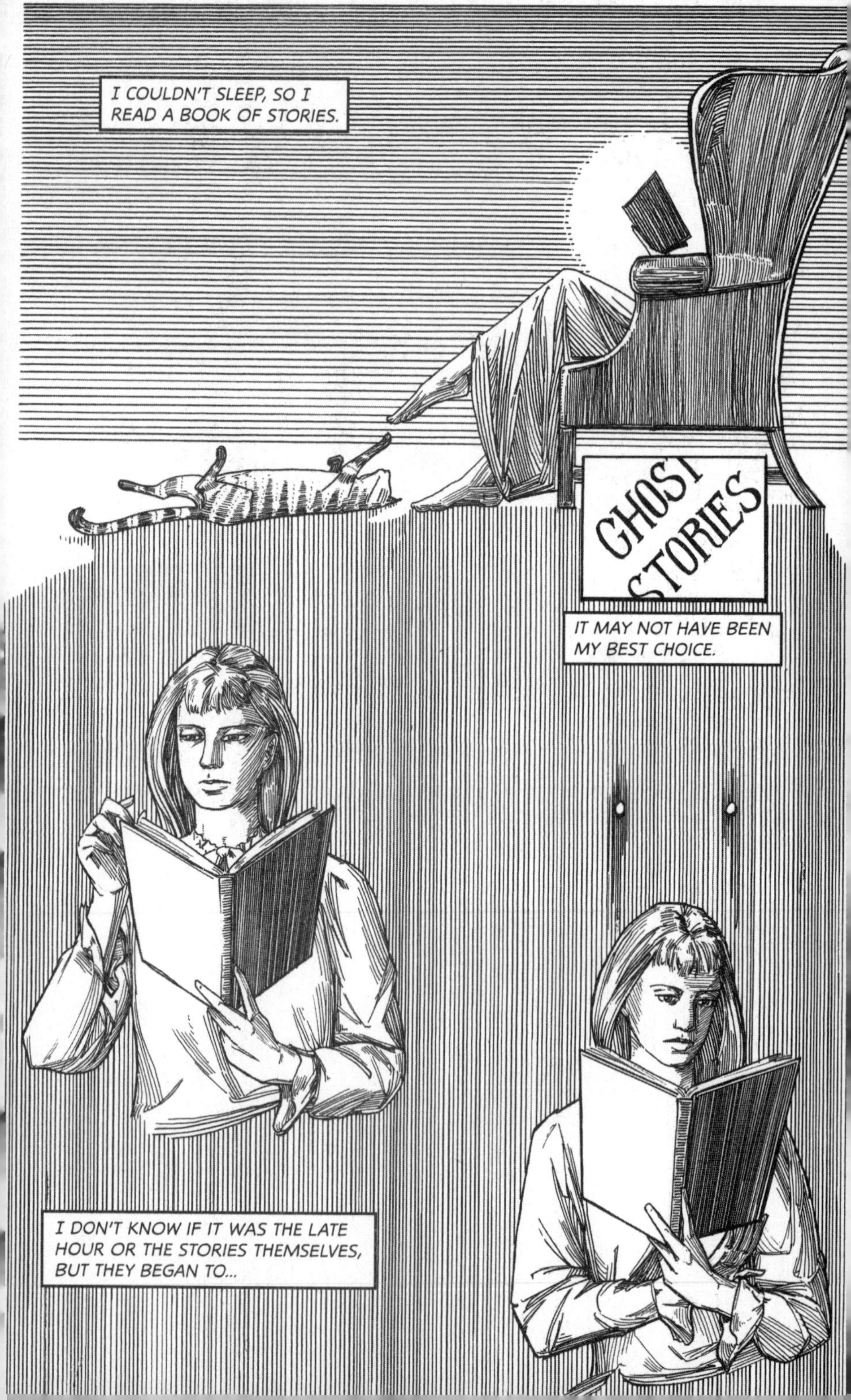
I COULDN'T SLEEP, SO I READ A BOOK OF STORIES.
GHOST STORIES
IT MAY NOT HAVE BEEN MY BEST CHOICE.
I DON'T KNOW IF IT WAS THE LATE HOUR OR THE STORIES THEMSELVES, BUT THEY BEGAN TO...

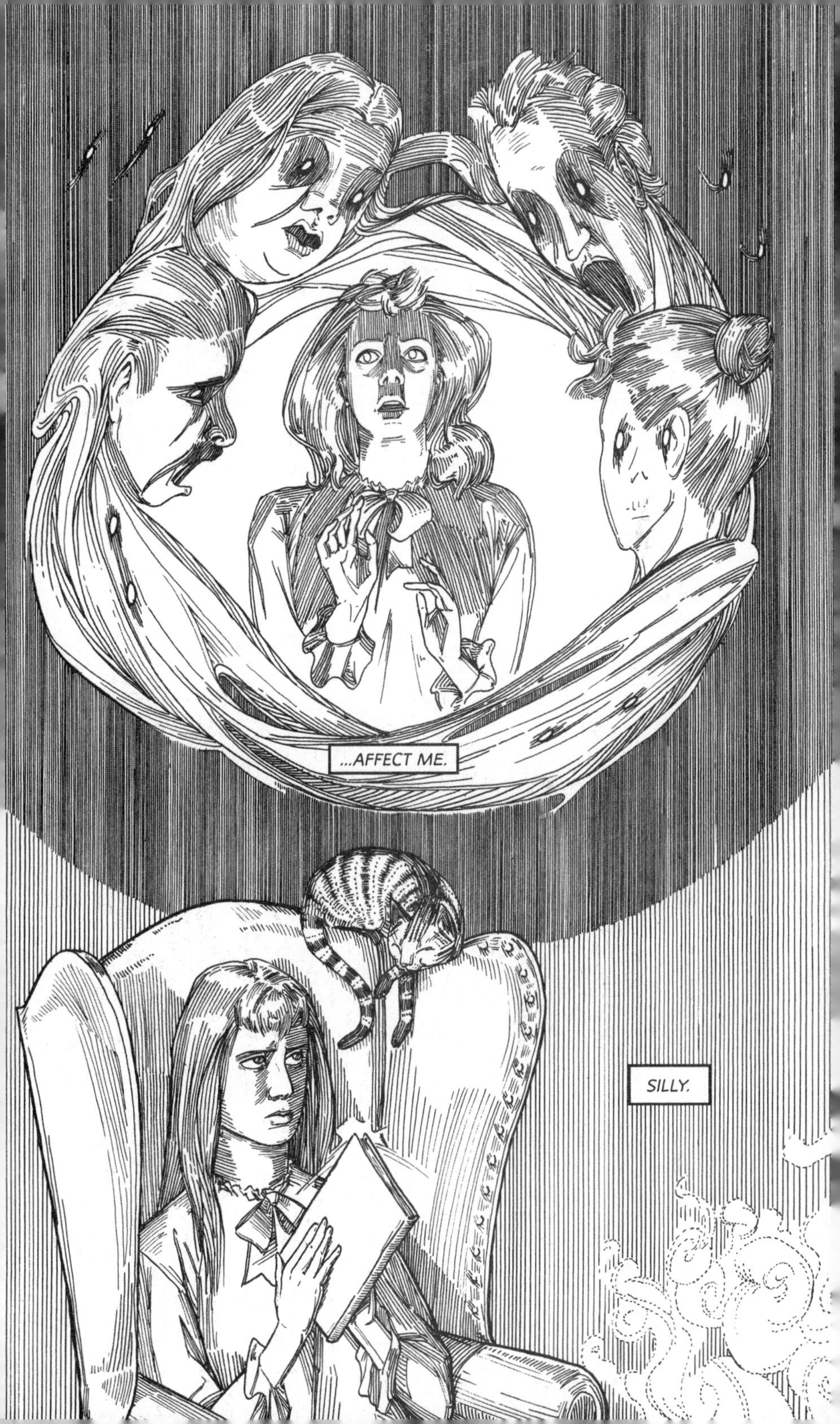
...AFFECT ME.
SILLY.

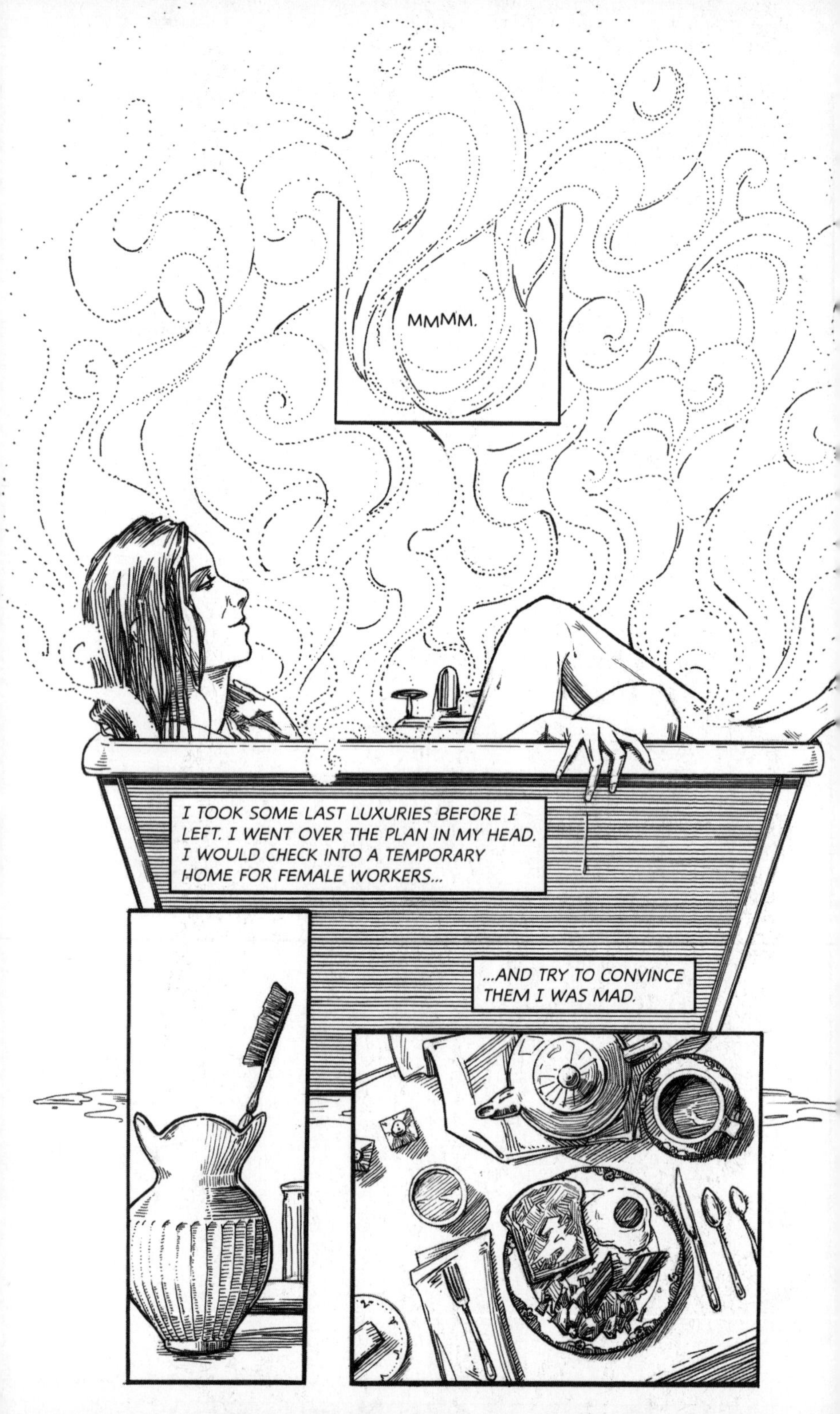
MMMM.
I TOOK SOME LAST LUXURIES BEFORE I LEFT. I WENT OVER THE PLAN IN MY HEAD. I WOULD CHECK INTO A TEMPORARY HOME FOR FEMALE WORKERS...
...AND TRY TO CONVINCE THEM I WAS MAD.

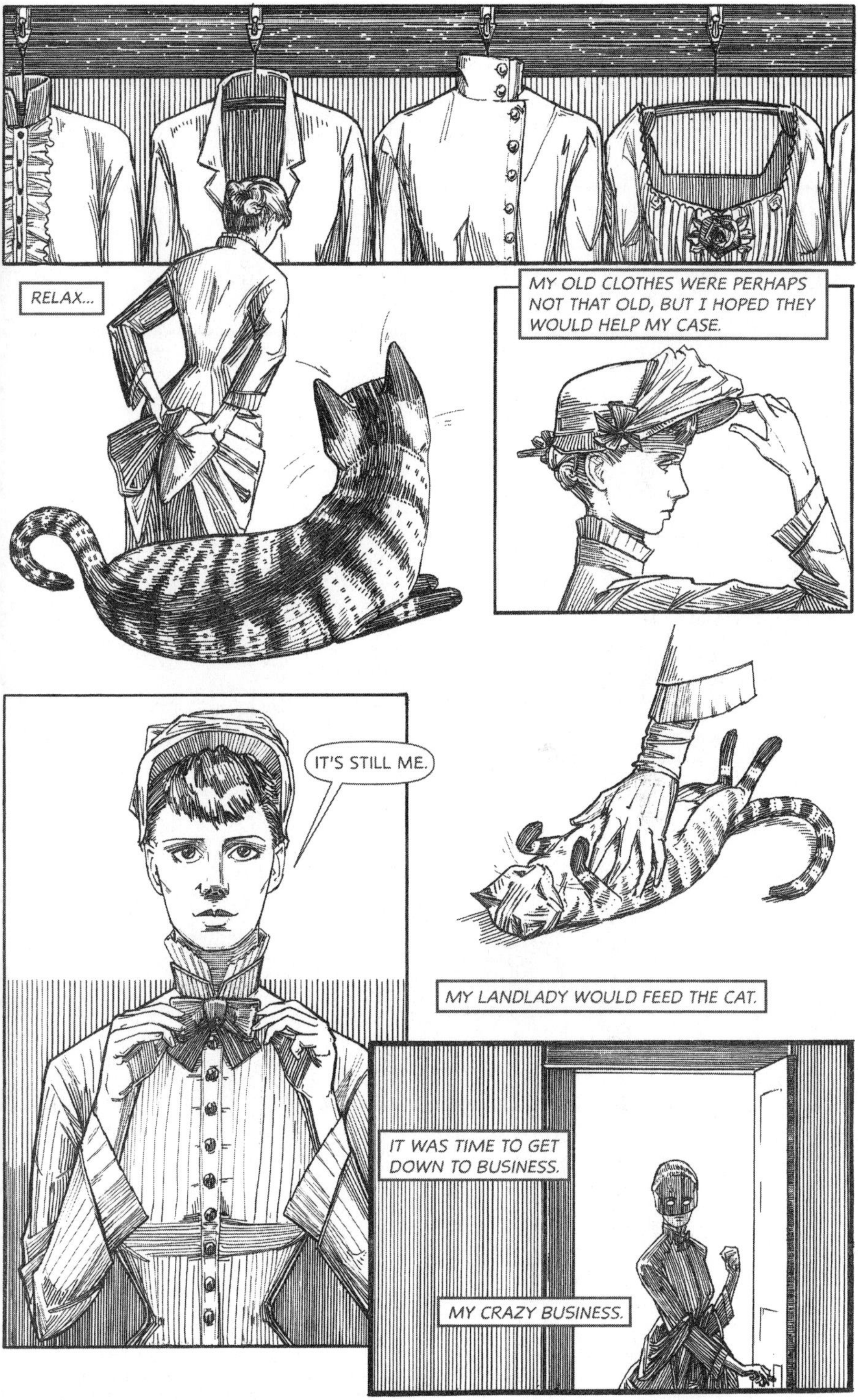
RELAX...
MY OLD CLOTHES WERE PERHAPS NOT THAT OLD, BUT I HOPED THEY WOULD HELP MY CASE.
IT'S STILL ME.
MY LANDLADY WOULD FEED THE CAT.
IT WAS TIME TO GET DOWN TO BUSINESS.
MY CRAZY BUSINESS.

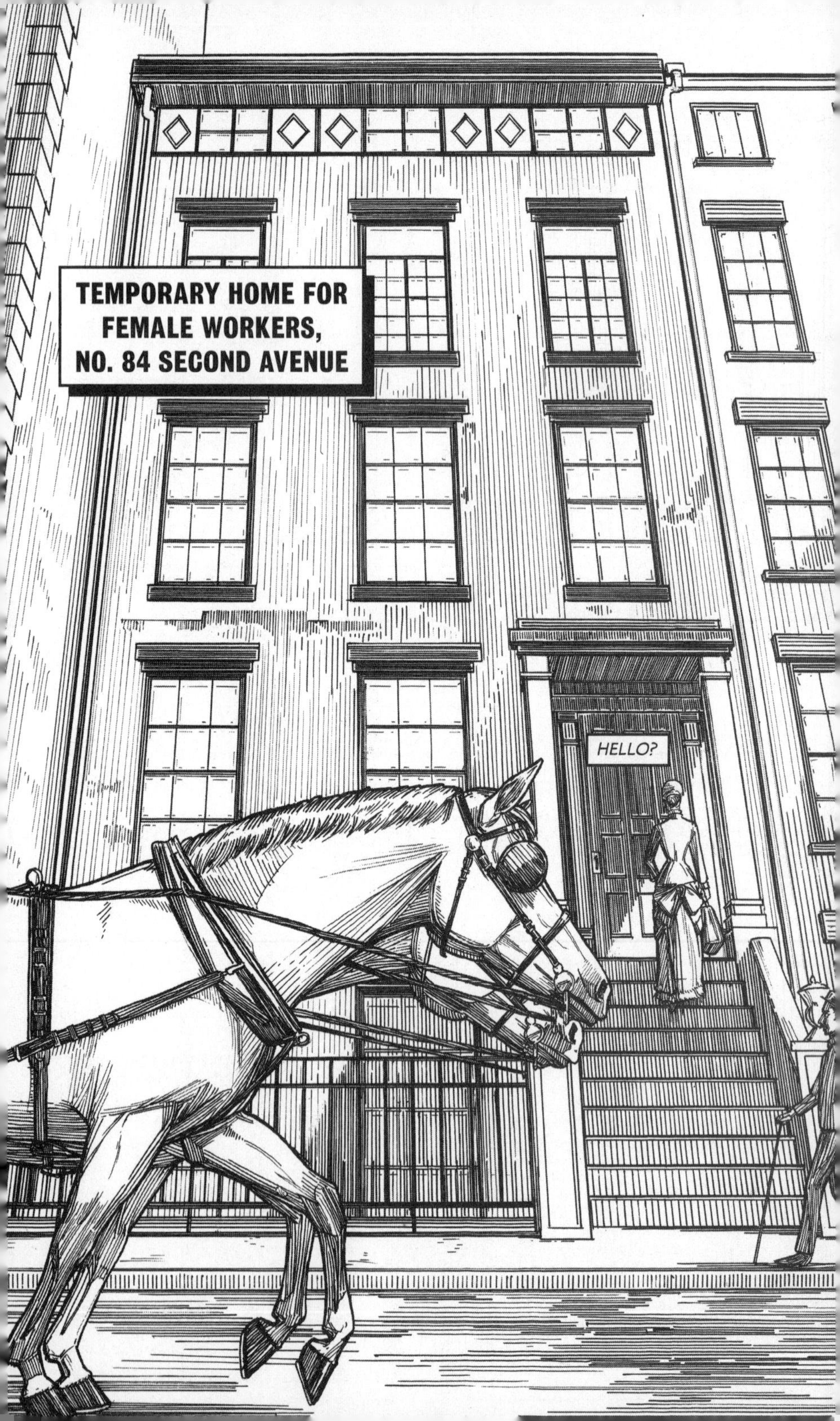
TEMPORARY HOME FOR FEMALE WORKERS, NO. 84 SECOND AVENUE
HELLO?

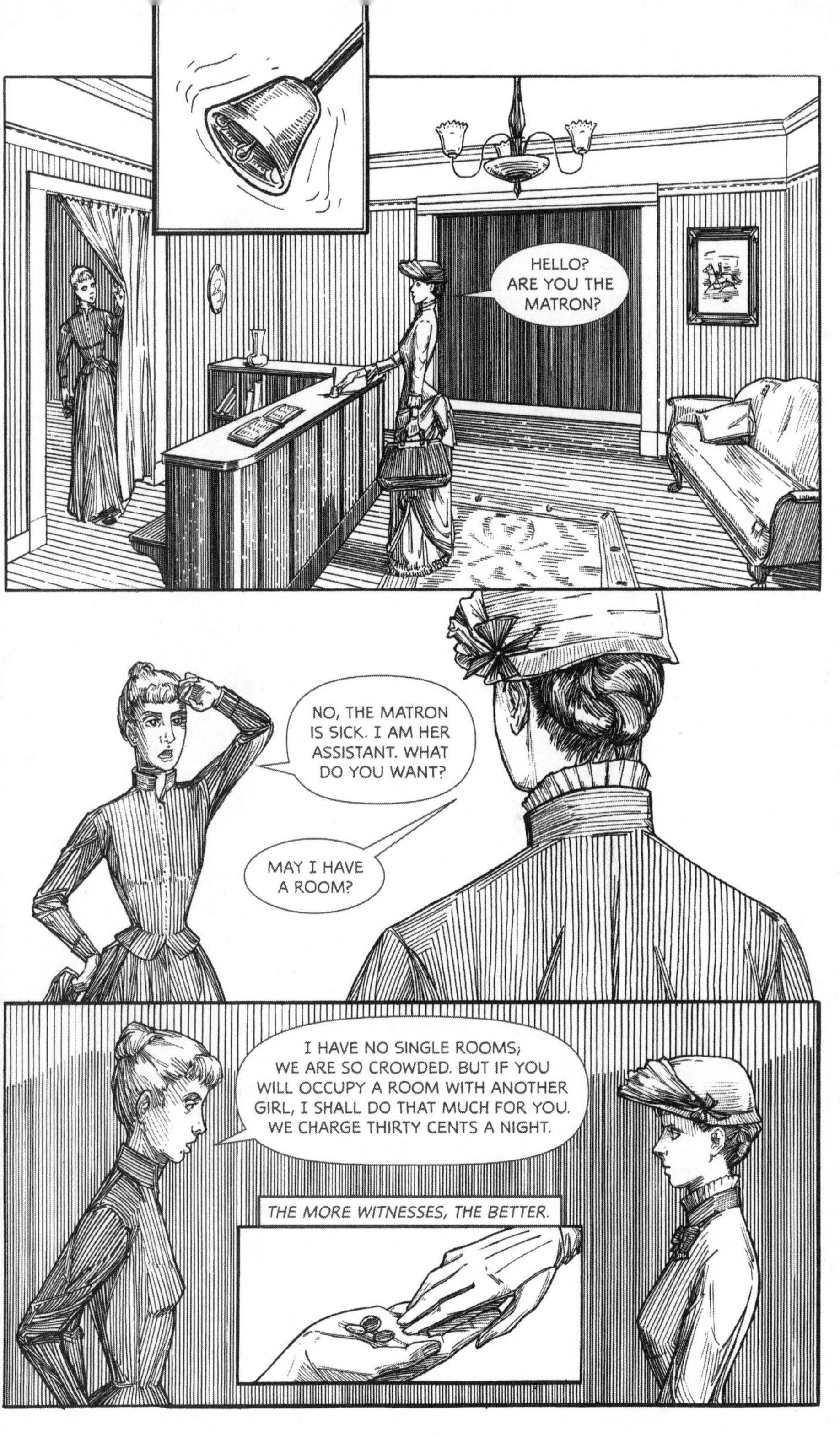
HELLO? ARE YOU THE MATRON?
NO, THE MATRON IS SICK. I AM HER ASSISTANT. WHAT DO YOU WANT?
MAY I HAVE A ROOM?
I HAVE NO SINGLE ROOMS; WE ARE SO CROWDED. BUT IF YOU WILL OCCUPY A ROOM WITH ANOTHER GIRL, I SHALL DO THAT MUCH FOR YOU. WE CHARGE THIRTY CENTS A NIGHT.
THE MORE WITNESSES, THE BETTER.

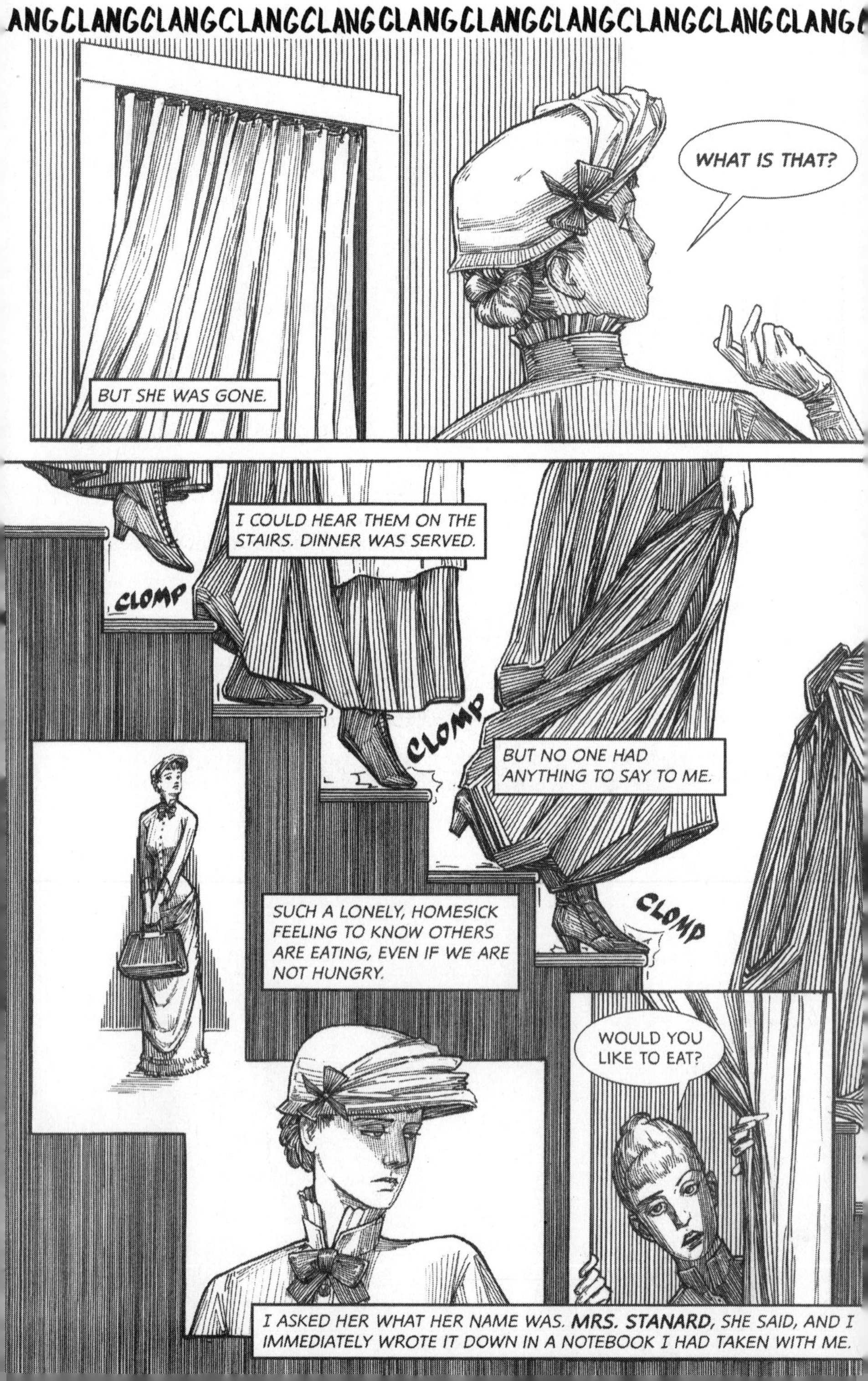
ANGCLANGCLANGCLANGCLANGCLANGCLANGCLANGCLANGCLANGCLANG
BUT SHE WAS GONE.
WHAT IS THAT?
I COULD HEAR THEM ON THE STAIRS. DINNER WAS SERVED.
CLOMP
CLOMP
BUT NO ONE HAD ANYTHING TO SAY TO ME.
CLOMP
SUCH A LONELY, HOMESICK FEELING TO KNOW OTHERS ARE EATING, EVEN IF WE ARE NOT HUNGRY.
WOULD YOU LIKE TO EAT?
I ASKED HER WHAT HER NAME WAS. MRS. STANARD, SHE SAID, AND I IMMEDIATELY WROTE IT DOWN IN A NOTEBOOK I HAD TAKEN WITH ME.

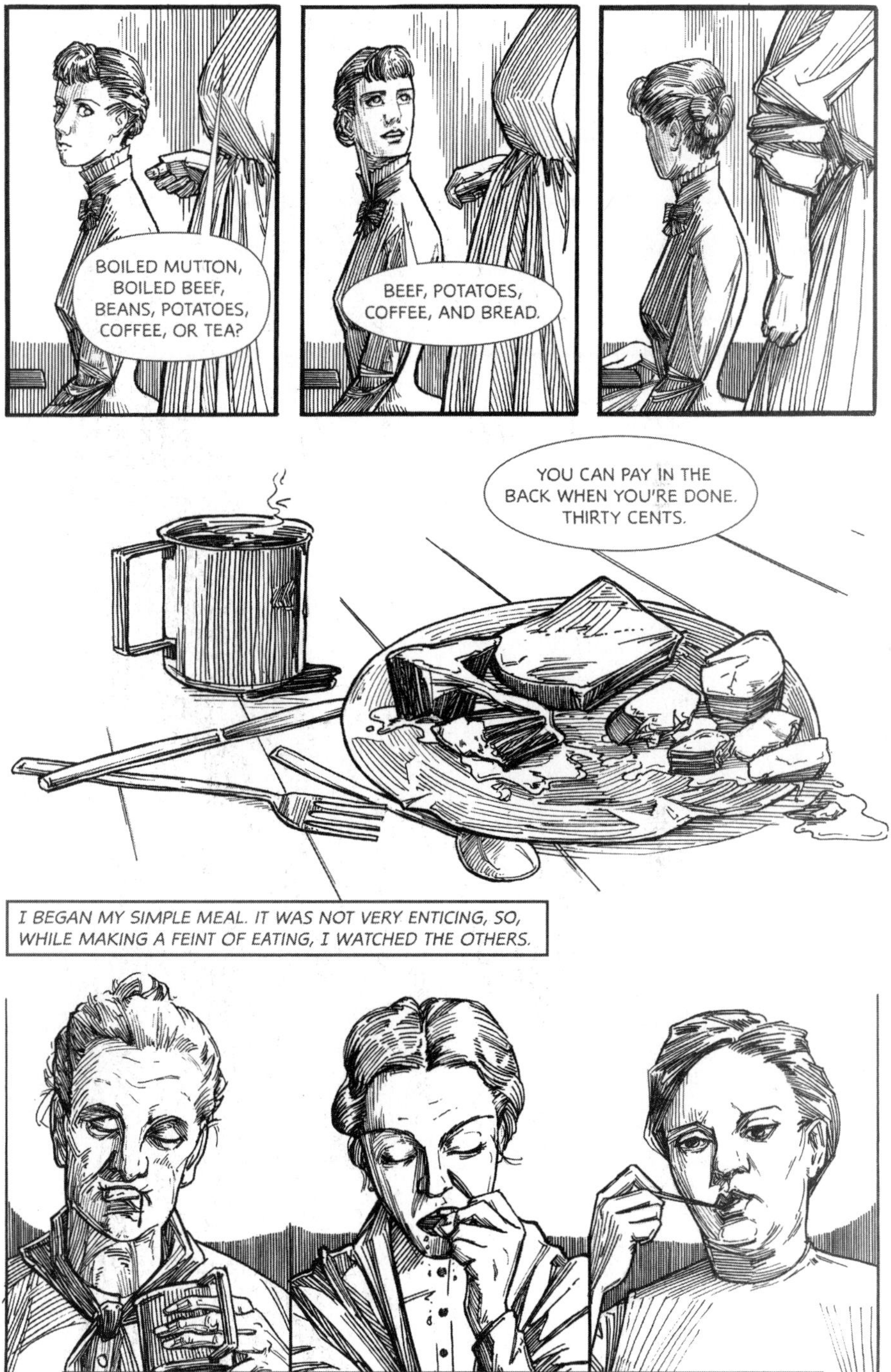

BOILED MUTTON, BOILED BEEF, BEANS, POTATOES, COFFEE, OR TEA?
BEEF, POTATOES, COFFEE, AND BREAD.
YOU CAN PAY IN THE BACK WHEN YOU'RE DONE. THIRTY CENTS.
I BEGAN MY SIMPLE MEAL. IT WAS NOT VERY ENTICING, SO, WHILE MAKING A FEINT OF EATING, I WATCHED THE OTHERS.
I HAVE OFTEN MORALIZED ON THE REPULSIVE FORM CHARITY ALWAYS ASSUMES! HERE WAS A HOME FOR DESERVING WOMEN AND YET WHAT A MOCKERY THE NAME WAS.

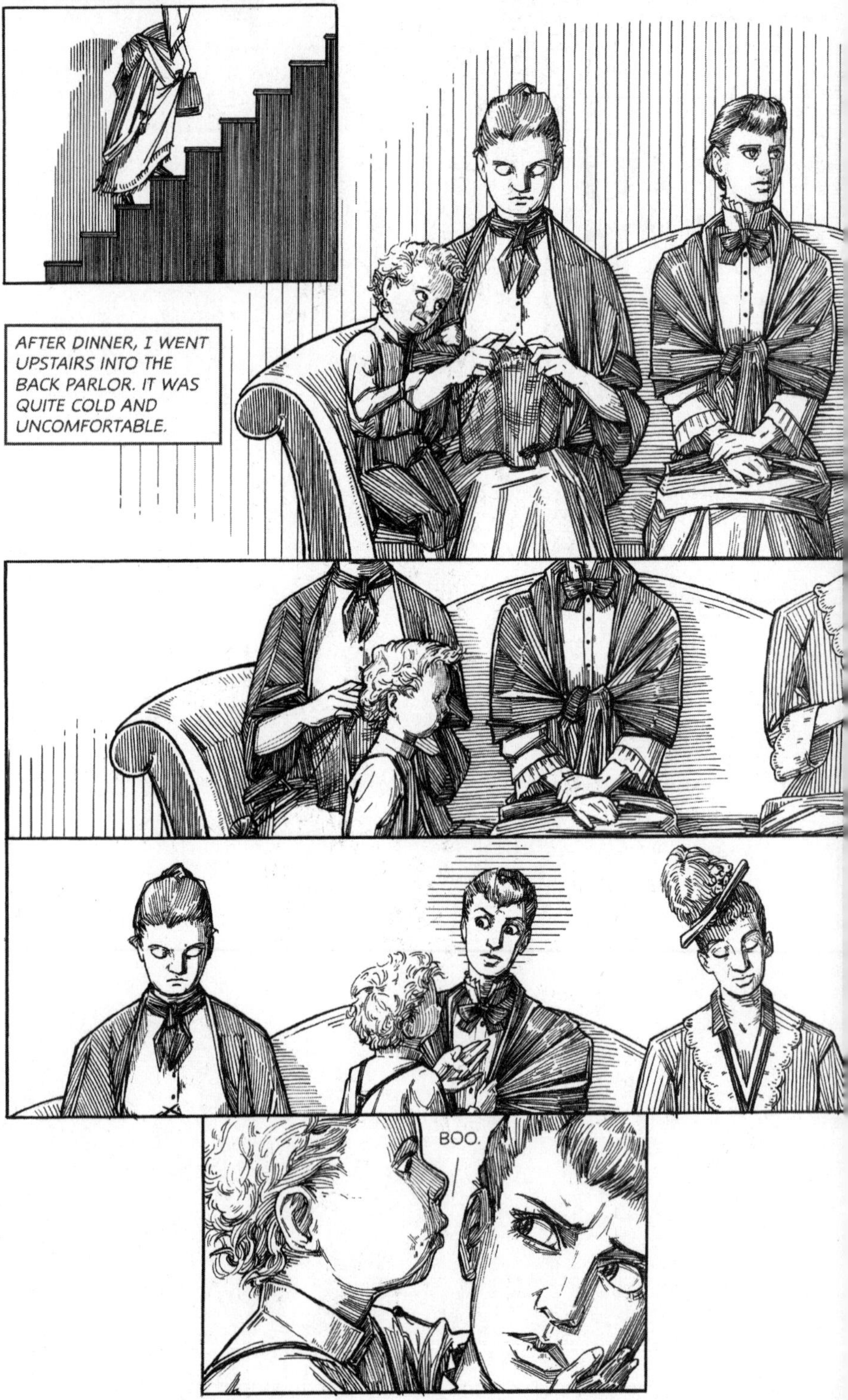
AFTER DINNER, I WENT UPSTAIRS INTO THE BACK PARLOR. IT WAS QUITE COLD AND UNCOMFORTABLE.
BOO.

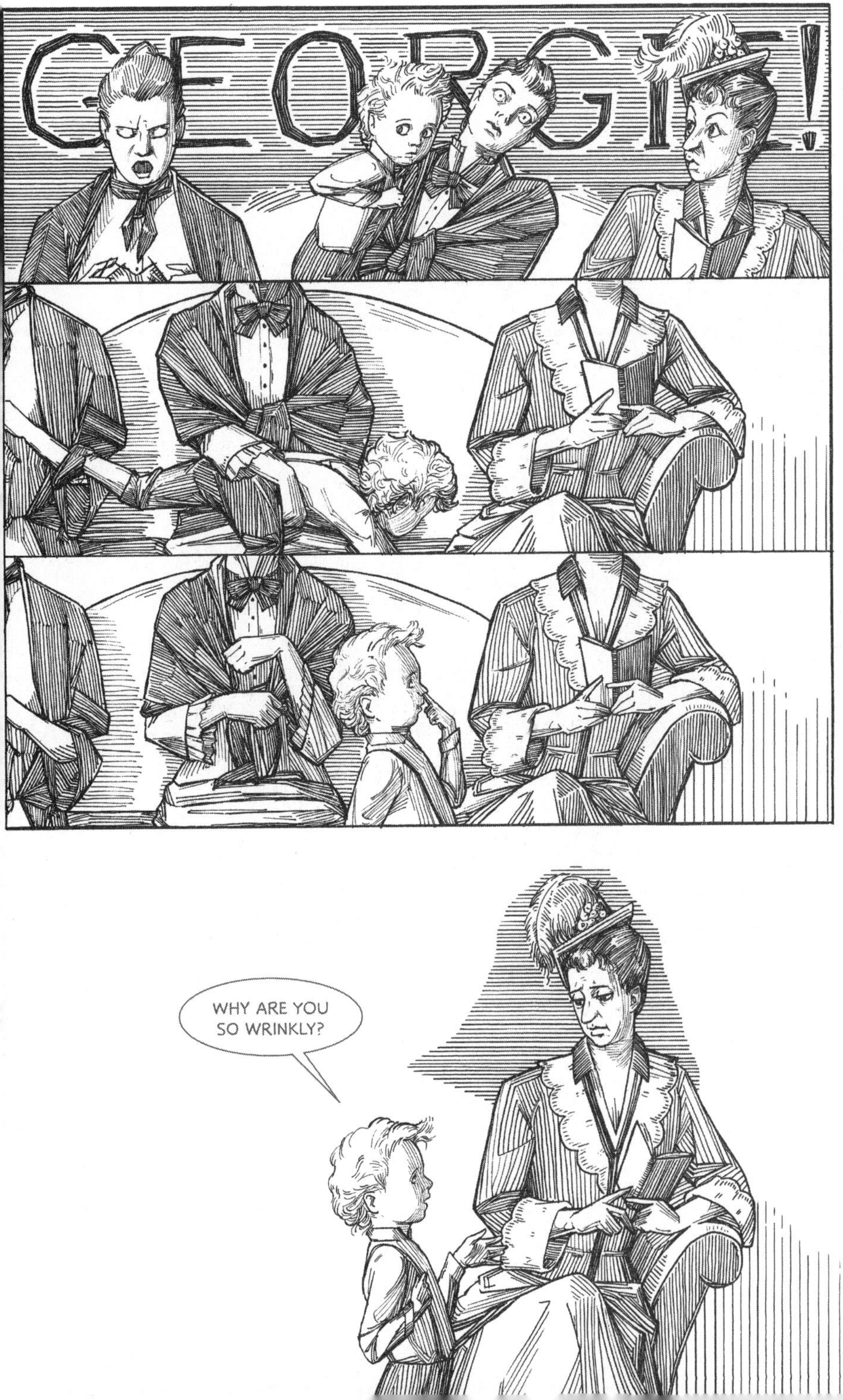
GEORGIE!
WHY ARE YOU SO WRINKLY?

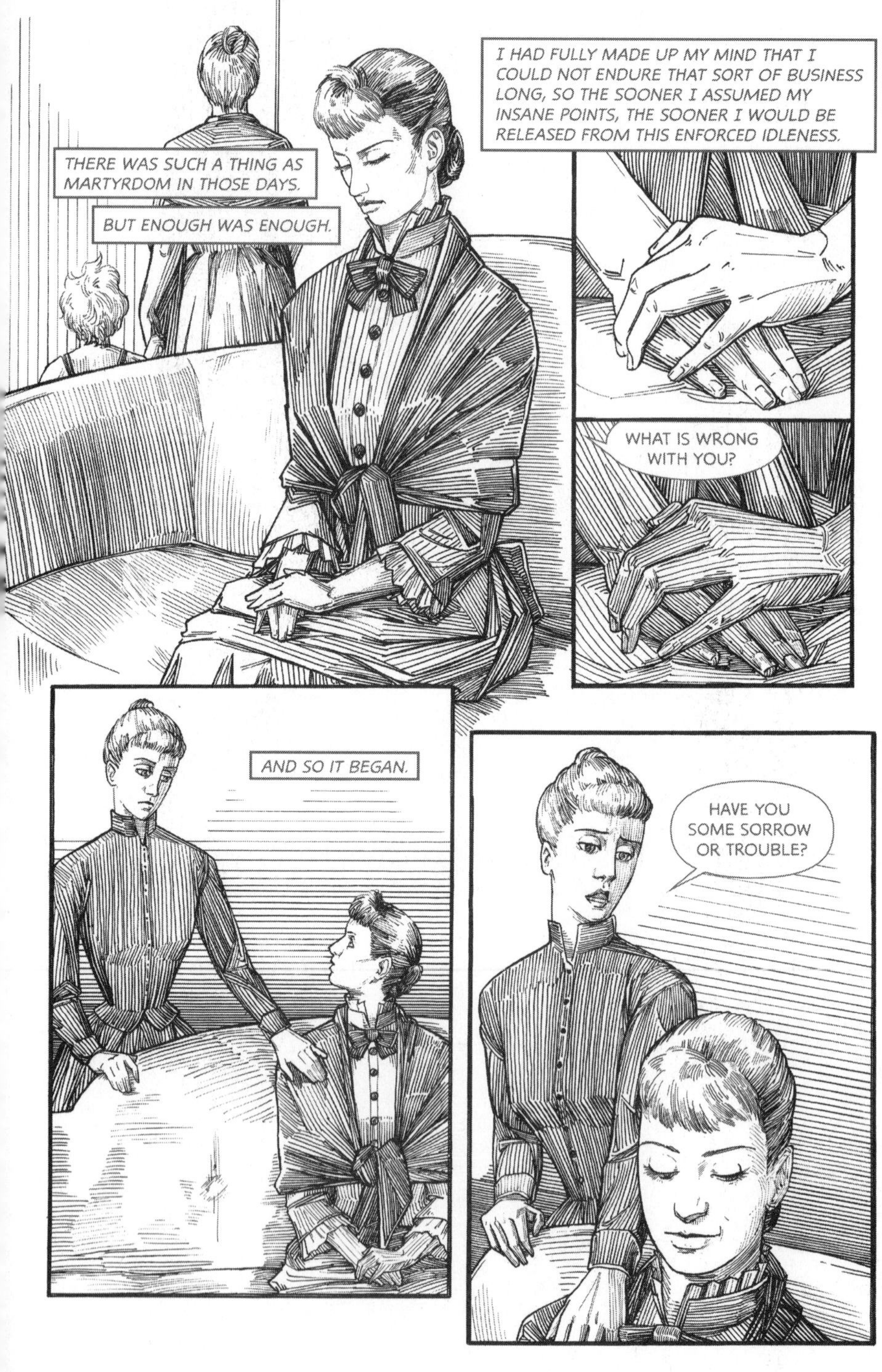
THERE WAS SUCH A THING AS MARTYRDOM IN THOSE DAYS.
BUT ENOUGH WAS ENOUGH.
I HAD FULLY MADE UP MY MIND THAT I COULD NOT ENDURE THAT SORT OF BUSINESS LONG, SO THE SOONER I ASSUMED MY INSANE POINTS, THE SOONER I WOULD BE RELEASED FROM THIS ENFORCED IDLENESS.
WHAT IS WRONG WITH YOU?
AND SO IT BEGAN.
HAVE YOU SOME SORROW OR TROUBLE?

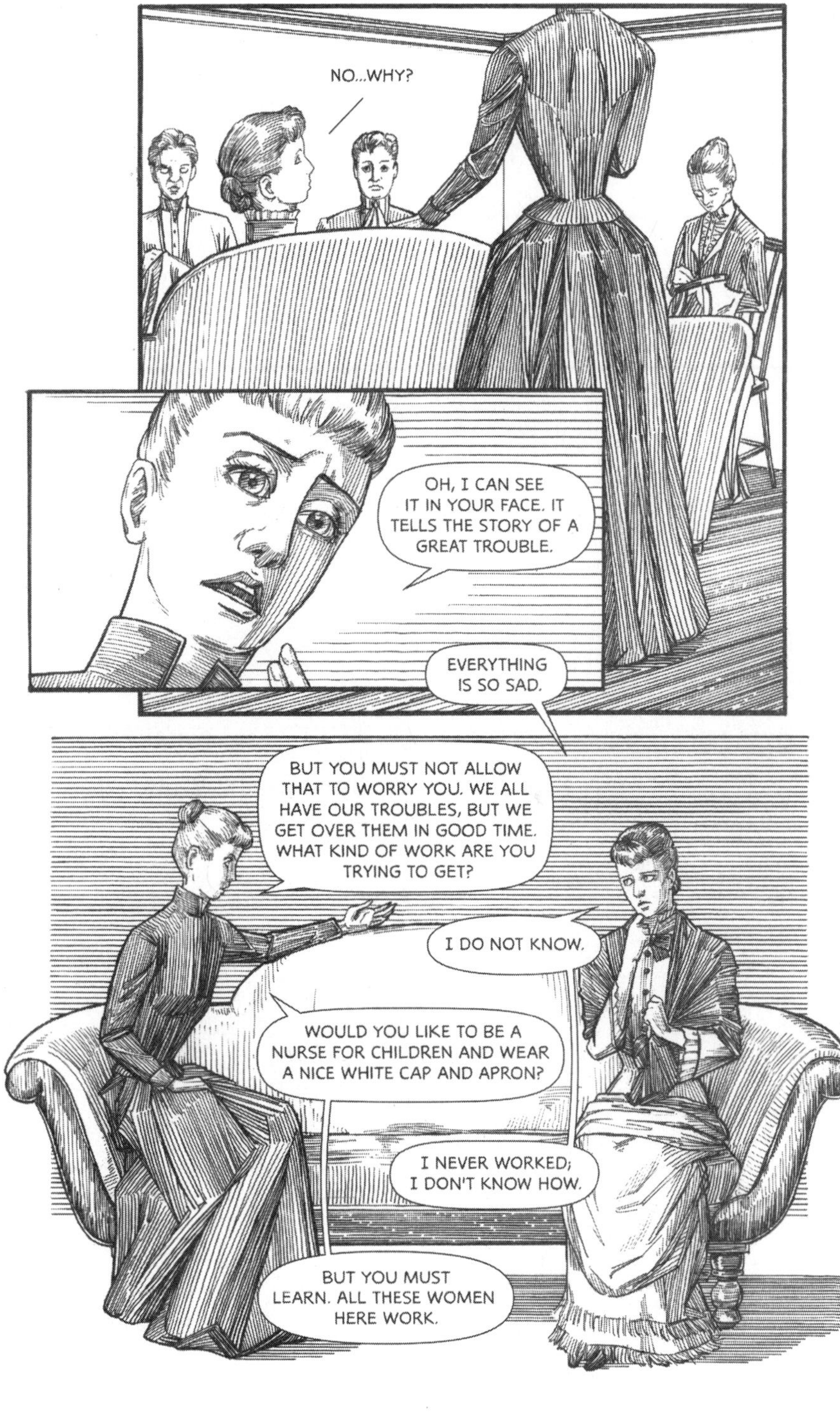
NO...WHY?
OH, I CAN SEE IT IN YOUR FACE. IT TELLS THE STORY OF A GREAT TROUBLE.
EVERYTHING IS SO SAD.
BUT YOU MUST NOT ALLOW THAT TO WORRY YOU. WE ALL HAVE OUR TROUBLES, BUT WE GET OVER THEM IN GOOD TIME. WHAT KIND OF WORK ARE YOU TRYING TO GET?
I DO NOT KNOW.
WOULD YOU LIKE TO BE A NURSE FOR CHILDREN AND WEAR A NICE WHITE CAP AND APRON?
I NEVER WORKED; I DON'T KNOW HOW.
BUT YOU MUST LEARN. ALL THESE WOMEN HERE WORK.

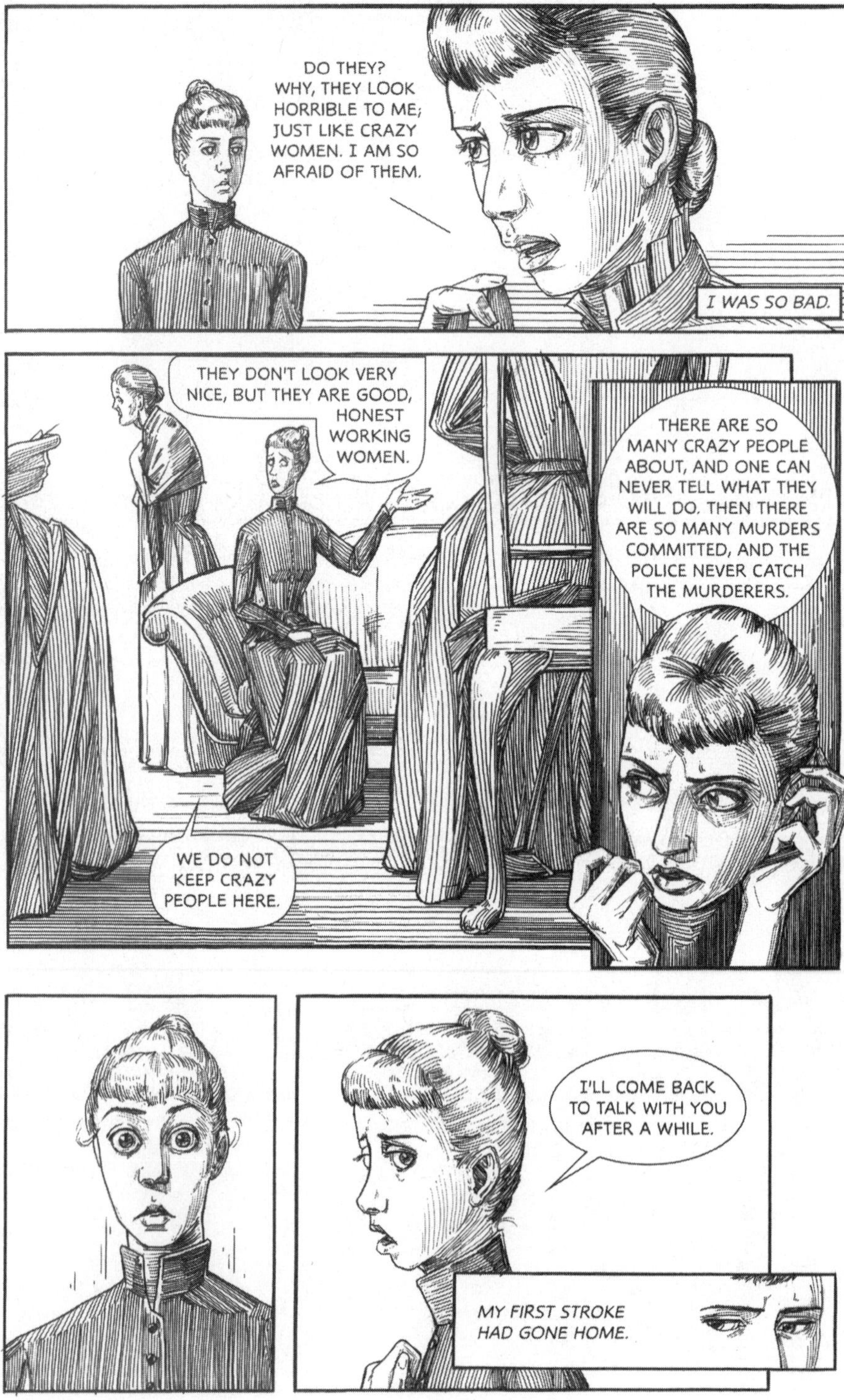
DO THEY? WHY, THEY LOOK HORRIBLE TO ME; JUST LIKE CRAZY WOMEN. I AM SO AFRAID OF THEM.
I WAS SO BAD.
THEY DON'T LOOK VERY NICE, BUT THEY ARE GOOD, HONEST WORKING WOMEN.
WE DO NOT KEEP CRAZY PEOPLE HERE.
THERE ARE SO MANY CRAZY PEOPLE ABOUT, AND ONE CAN NEVER TELL WHAT THEY WILL DO. THEN THERE ARE SO MANY MURDERS COMMITTED, AND THE POLICE NEVER CATCH THE MURDERERS.
I'LL COME BACK TO TALK WITH YOU AFTER A WHILE.
MY FIRST STROKE HAD GONE HOME.

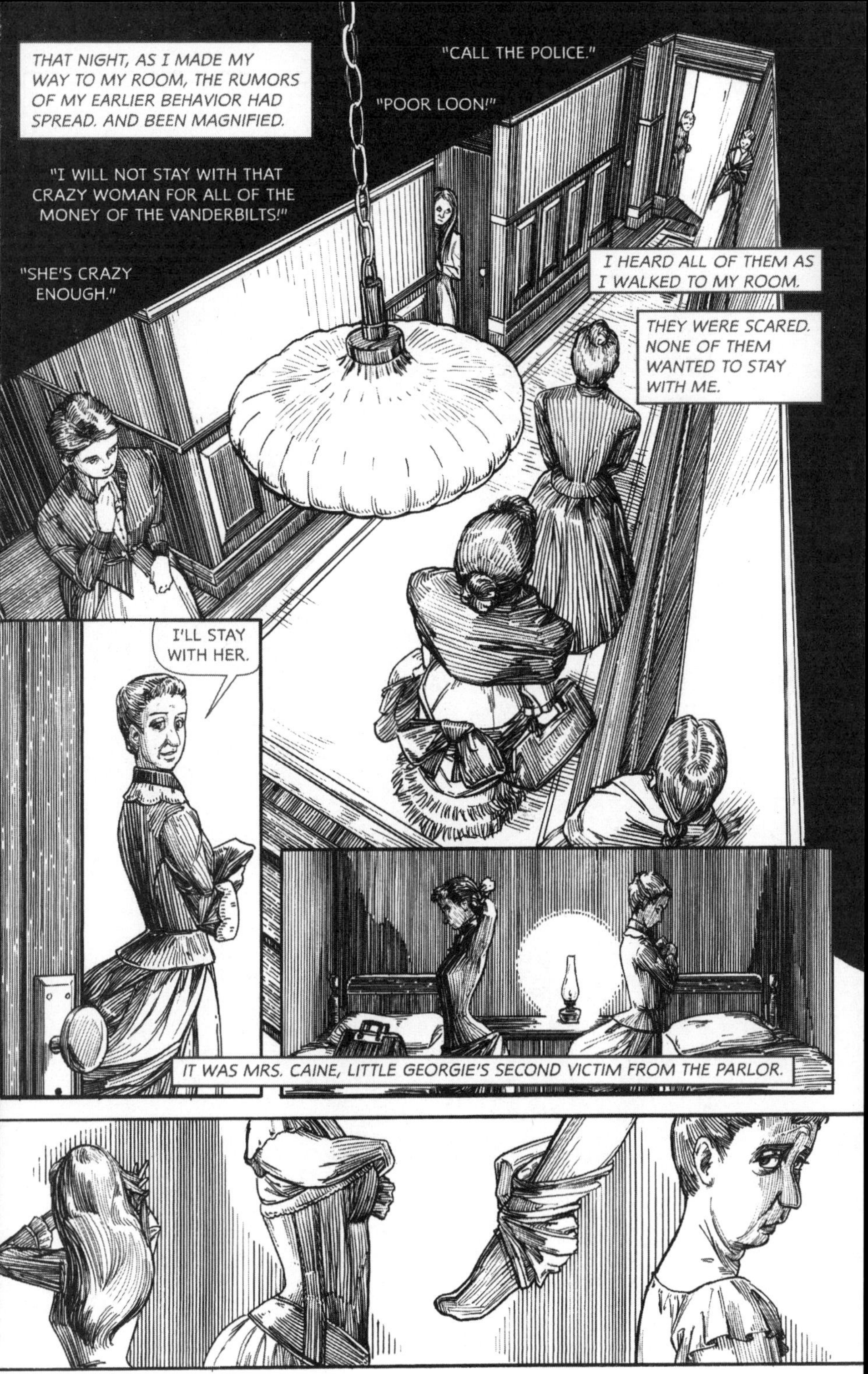
THAT NIGHT, AS I MADE MY WAY TO MY ROOM, THE RUMORS OF MY EARLIER BEHAVIOR HAD SPREAD. AND BEEN MAGNIFIED.
"CALL THE POLICE."
"POOR LOON!"
"I WILL NOT STAY WITH THAT CRAZY WOMAN FOR ALL OF THE MONEY OF THE VANDERBILTS!"
"SHE'S CRAZY ENOUGH."
I HEARD ALL OF THEM AS I WALKED TO MY ROOM.
THEY WERE SCARED. NONE OF THEM WANTED TO STAY WITH ME.
I'LL STAY WITH HER.
IT WAS MRS. CAINE, LITTLE GEORGIE'S SECOND VICTIM FROM THE PARLOR.

SHE TRIED TO INDUCE ME TO LIE DOWN, BUT I WAS AFRAID TO DO THIS.

I KNEW THAT IF I ONCE GAVE WAY I SHOULD FALL ASLEEP AND DREAM AS PLEASANTLY AND PEACEFULLY AS A CHILD. I SHOULD, TO USE A SLANG EXPRESSION, BE LIABLE TO "GIVE MYSELF DEAD AWAY."

SO I INSISTED ON SITTING ON THE SIDE OF THE BED AND STARING BLANKLY AT VACANCY.

MY POOR COMPANION WAS PUT INTO A WRETCHED STATE OF UNHAPPINESS. EVERY FEW MOMENTS, SHE WOULD RISE UP TO LOOK AT ME. SHE TOLD ME THAT MY EYES SHONE TERRIBLY BRIGHTLY AND THEN BEGAN TO QUESTION ME, ASKING ME WHERE I HAD LIVED, HOW LONG I HAD BEEN IN NEW YORK, WHAT I HAD BEEN DOING, AND MANY THINGS BESIDES. TO ALL HER QUESTIONINGS, I HAD BUT ONE RESPONSE— I TOLD HER THAT I HAD FORGOTTEN EVERYTHING, THAT EVER SINCE MY HEADACHE HAD COME ON I COULD NOT REMEMBER.

POOR SOUL! HOW CRUELLY I TORTURED HER, AND WHAT A KIND HEART SHE HAD!

EEEEEEEEEEEEEEEEEEEEEEEEEEEEE !!!

WE HEARD A TERRIBLE SCREAM. MRS. CAINE WENT TO INVESTIGATE.

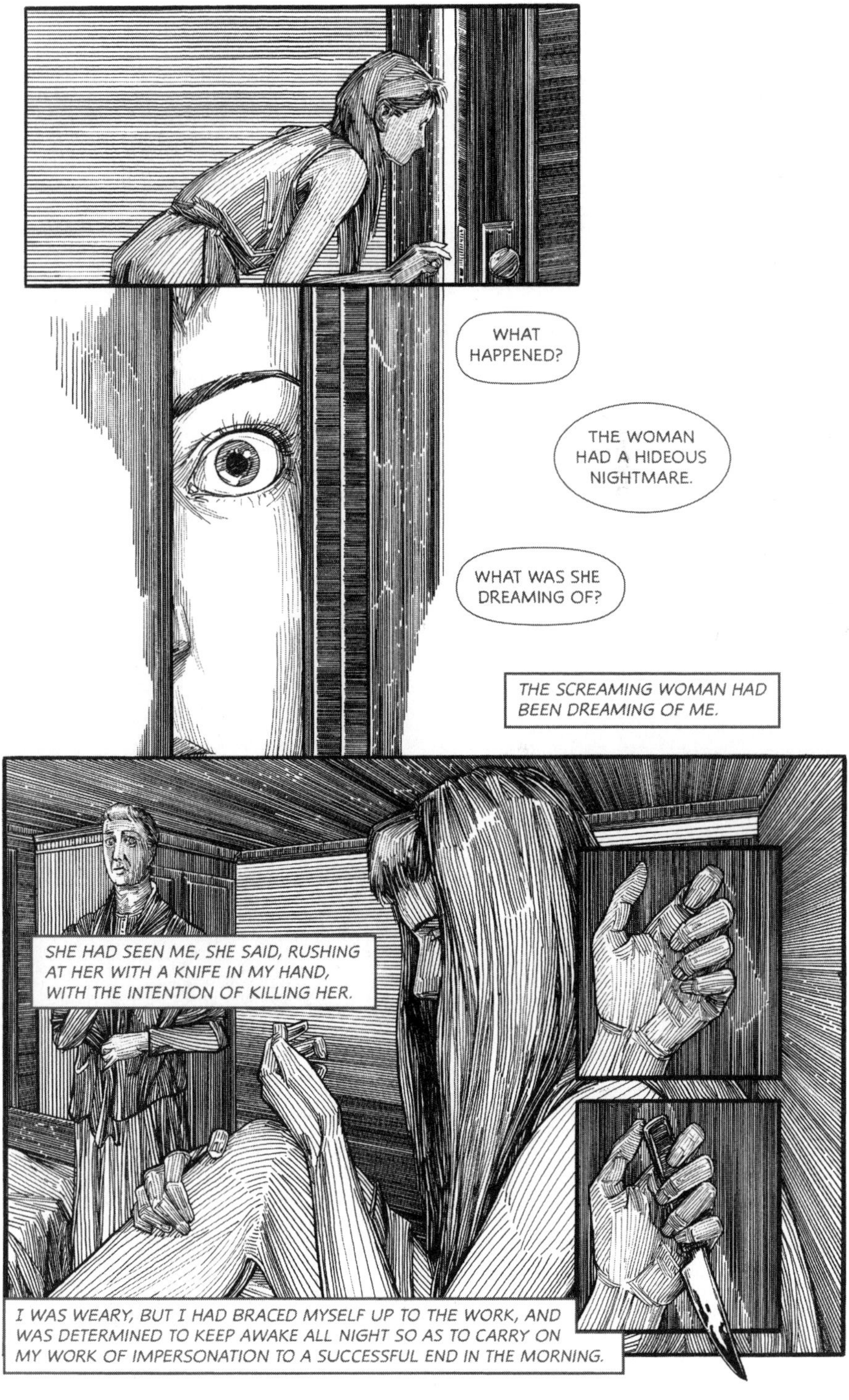
WHAT HAPPENED?
THE WOMAN HAD A HIDEOUS NIGHTMARE.
WHAT WAS SHE DREAMING OF?
THE SCREAMING WOMAN HAD BEEN DREAMING OF ME.
SHE HAD SEEN ME, SHE SAID, RUSHING AT HER WITH A KNIFE IN MY HAND, WITH THE INTENTION OF KILLING HER.
I WAS WEARY, BUT I HAD BRACED MYSELF UP TO THE WORK, AND WAS DETERMINED TO KEEP AWAKE ALL NIGHT SO AS TO CARRY ON MY WORK OF IMPERSONATION TO A SUCCESSFUL END IN THE MORNING.

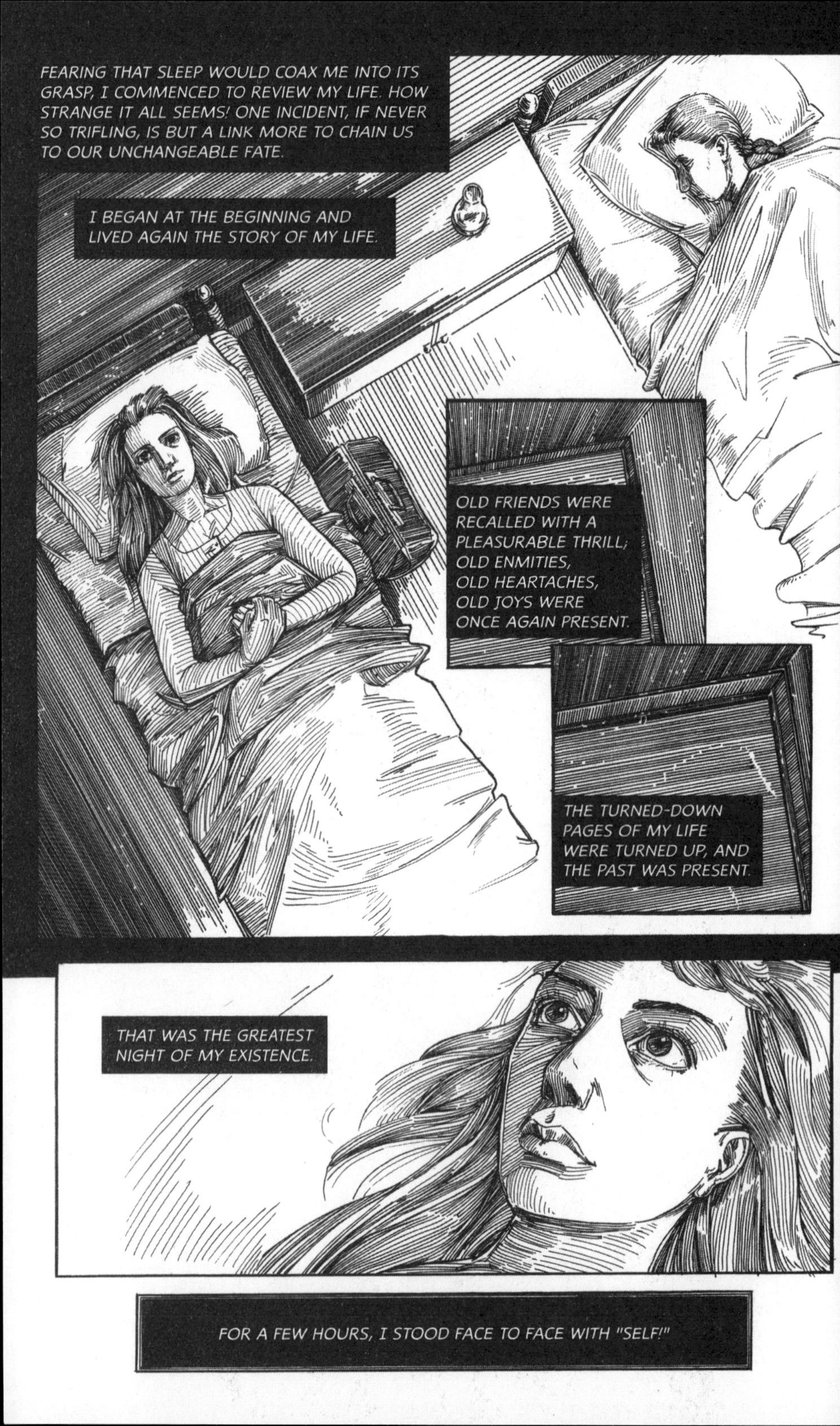
FEARING THAT SLEEP WOULD COAX ME INTO ITS GRASP, I COMMENCED TO REVIEW MY LIFE. HOW STRANGE IT ALL SEEMS! ONE INCIDENT, IF NEVER SO TRIFLING, IS BUT A LINK MORE TO CHAIN US TO OUR UNCHANGEABLE FATE.
I BEGAN AT THE BEGINNING AND LIVED AGAIN THE STORY OF MY LIFE.
OLD FRIENDS WERE RECALLED WITH A PLEASURABLE THRILL; OLD ENMITIES, OLD HEARTACHES, OLD JOYS WERE ONCE AGAIN PRESENT.
THE TURNED-DOWN PAGES OF MY LIFE WERE TURNED UP, AND THE PAST WAS PRESENT.
THAT WAS THE GREATEST NIGHT OF MY EXISTENCE.
FOR A FEW HOURS, I STOOD FACE TO FACE WITH "SELF!"

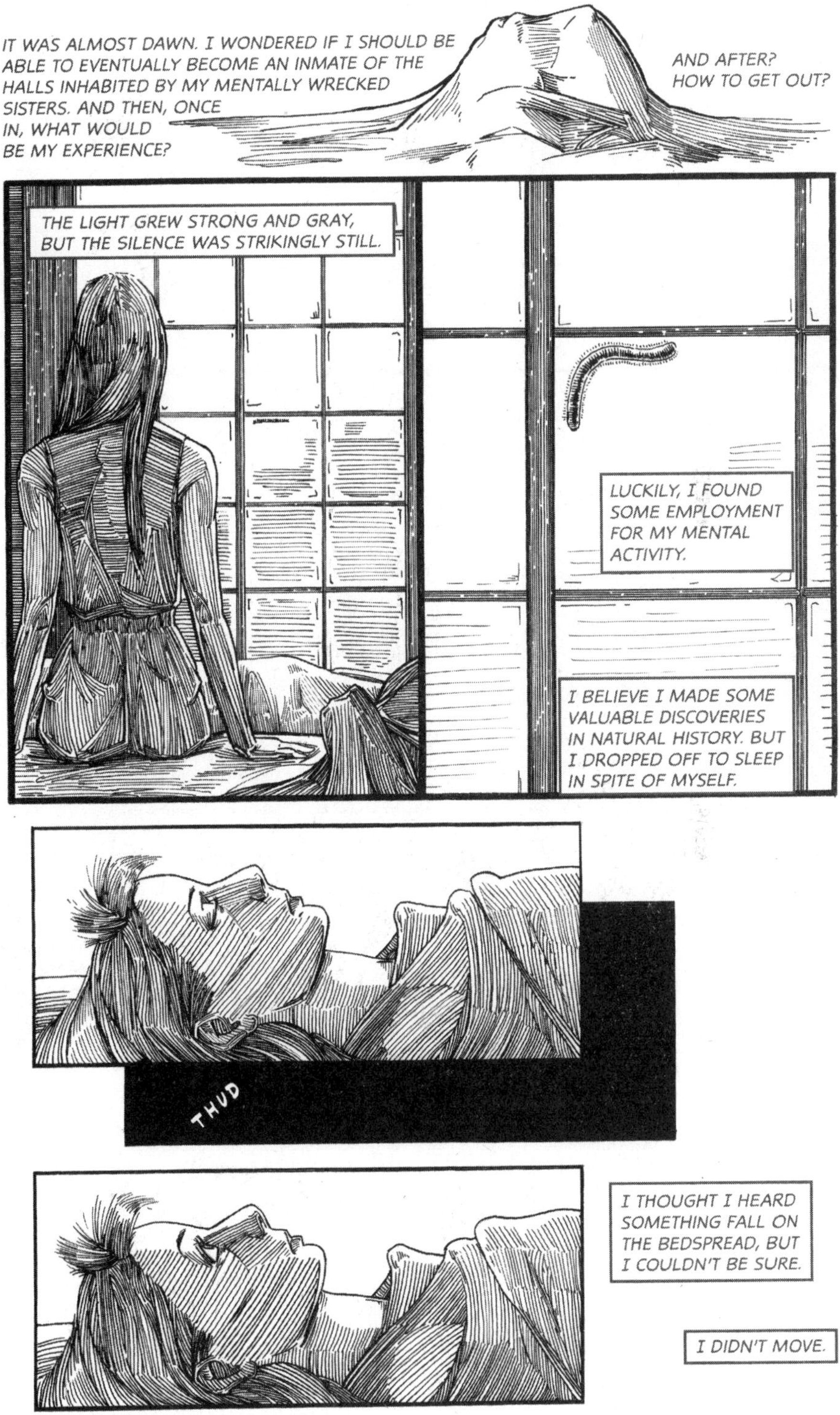
IT WAS ALMOST DAWN. I WONDERED IF I SHOULD BE ABLE TO EVENTUALLY BECOME AN INMATE OF THE HALLS INHABITED BY MY MENTALLY WRECKED SISTERS. AND THEN, ONCE IN, WHAT WOULD BE MY EXPERIENCE?
AND AFTER? HOW TO GET OUT?
THE LIGHT GREW STRONG AND GRAY, BUT THE SILENCE WAS STRIKINGLY STILL.
LUCKILY, I FOUND SOME EMPLOYMENT FOR MY MENTAL ACTIVITY.
I BELIEVE I MADE SOME VALUABLE DISCOVERIES IN NATURAL HISTORY. BUT I DROPPED OFF TO SLEEP IN SPITE OF MYSELF.
THUD
I THOUGHT I HEARD SOMETHING FALL ON THE BEDSPREAD, BUT I COULDN'T BE SURE.
I DIDN'T MOVE.

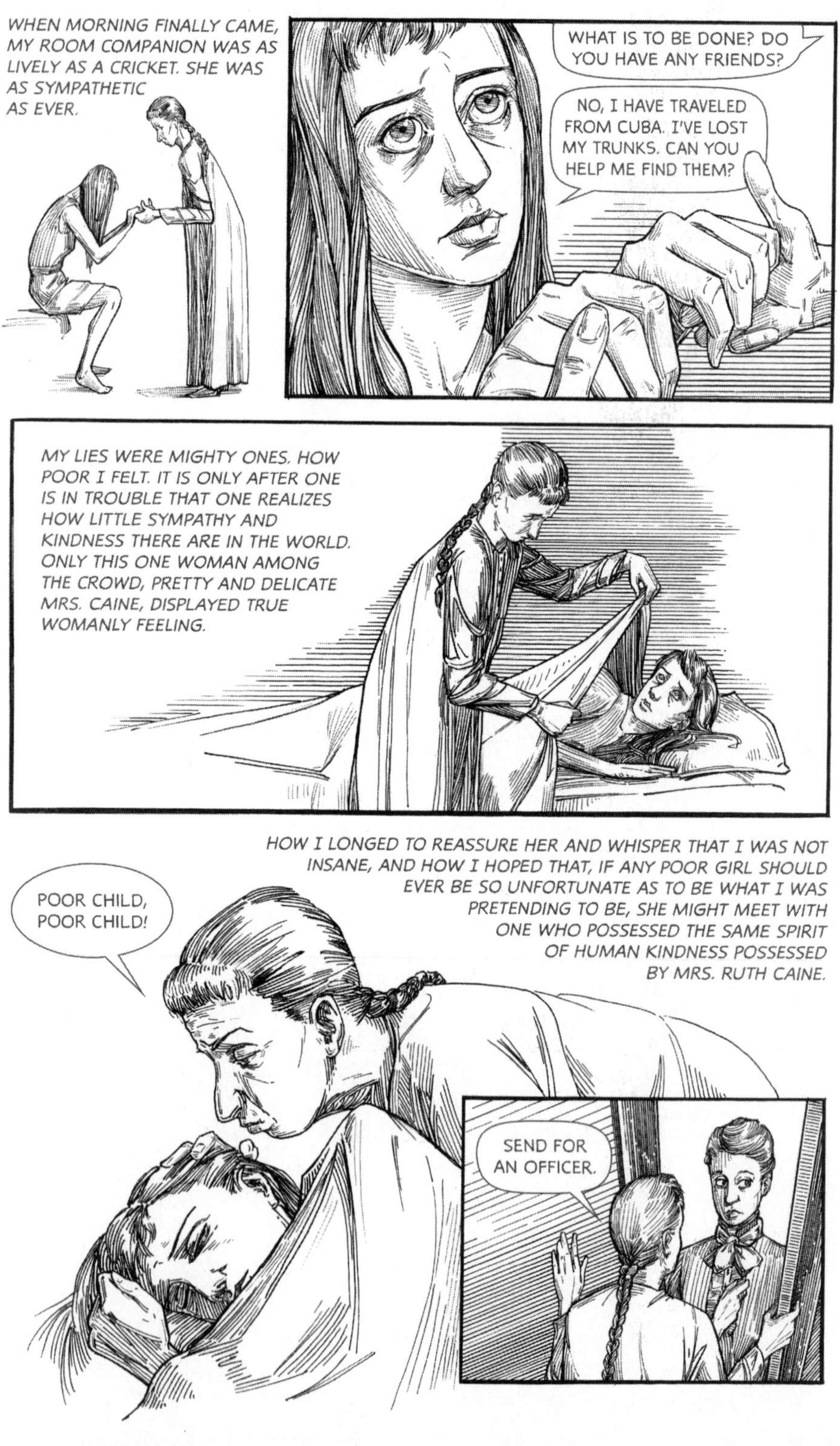
WHEN MORNING FINALLY CAME, MY ROOM COMPANION WAS AS LIVELY AS A CRICKET. SHE WAS AS SYMPATHETIC AS EVER.
WHAT IS TO BE DONE? DO YOU HAVE ANY FRIENDS?
NO, I HAVE TRAVELED FROM CUBA. I'VE LOST MY TRUNKS. CAN YOU HELP ME FIND THEM?
MY LIES WERE MIGHTY ONES. HOW POOR I FELT. IT IS ONLY AFTER ONE IS IN TROUBLE THAT ONE REALIZES HOW LITTLE SYMPATHY AND KINDNESS THERE ARE IN THE WORLD. ONLY THIS ONE WOMAN AMONG THE CROWD, PRETTY AND DELICATE MRS. CAINE, DISPLAYED TRUE WOMANLY FEELING.
HOW I LONGED TO REASSURE HER AND WHISPER THAT I WAS NOT INSANE, AND HOW I HOPED THAT, IF ANY POOR GIRL SHOULD EVER BE SO UNFORTUNATE AS TO BE WHAT I WAS PRETENDING TO BE, SHE MIGHT MEET WITH ONE WHO POSSESSED THE SAME SPIRIT OF HUMAN KINDNESS POSSESSED BY MRS. RUTH CAINE.
POOR CHILD, POOR CHILD!
SEND FOR AN OFFICER.

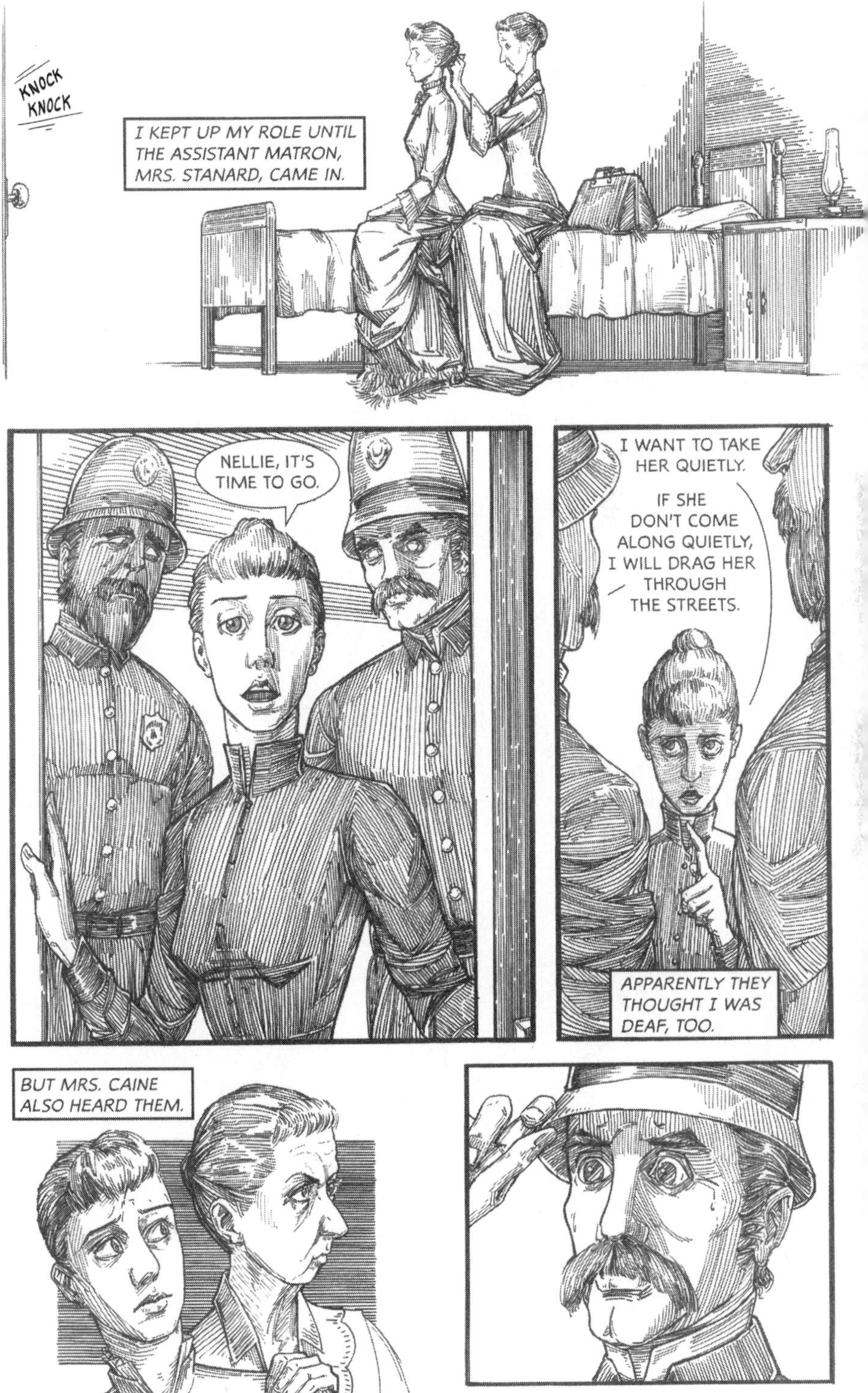
KNOCK KNOCK
I KEPT UP MY ROLE UNTIL THE ASSISTANT MATRON, MRS. STANARD, CAME IN.
NELLIE, IT'S TIME TO GO.
I WANT TO TAKE HER QUIETLY.
IF SHE DON'T COME ALONG QUIETLY, I WILL DRAG HER THROUGH THE STREETS.
APPARENTLY THEY THOUGHT I WAS DEAF, TOO.
BUT MRS. CAINE ALSO HEARD THEM.

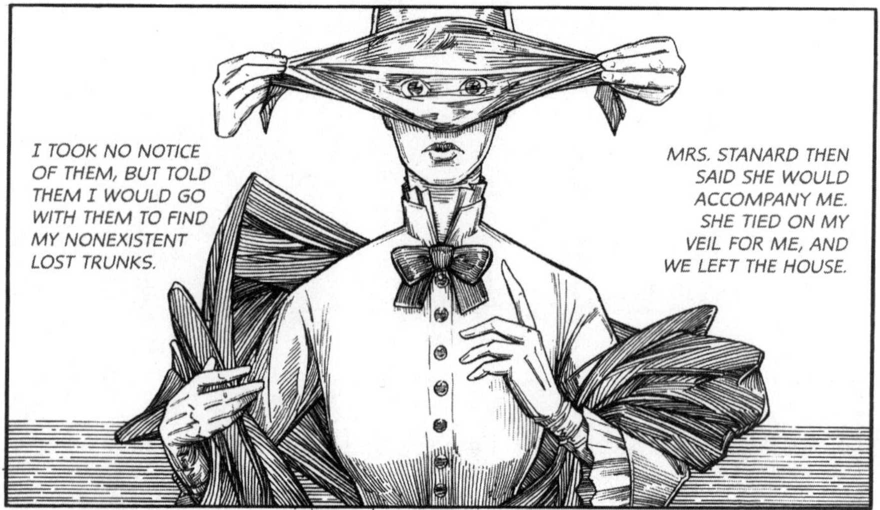
I TOOK NO NOTICE OF THEM, BUT TOLD THEM I WOULD GO WITH THEM TO FIND MY NONEXISTENT LOST TRUNKS.
MRS. STANARD THEN SAID SHE WOULD ACCOMPANY ME. SHE TIED ON MY VEIL FOR ME, AND WE LEFT THE HOUSE.

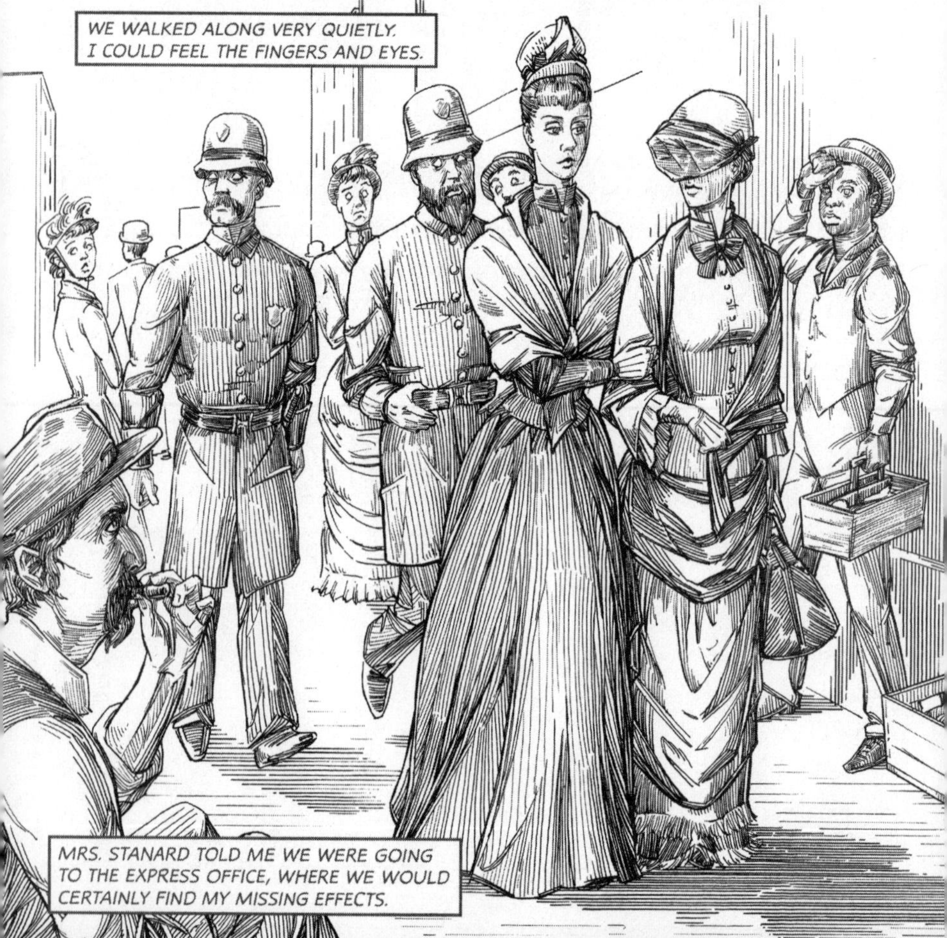
WE WALKED ALONG VERY QUIETLY. I COULD FEEL THE FINGERS AND EYES.
MRS. STANARD TOLD ME WE WERE GOING TO THE EXPRESS OFFICE, WHERE WE WOULD CERTAINLY FIND MY MISSING EFFECTS.

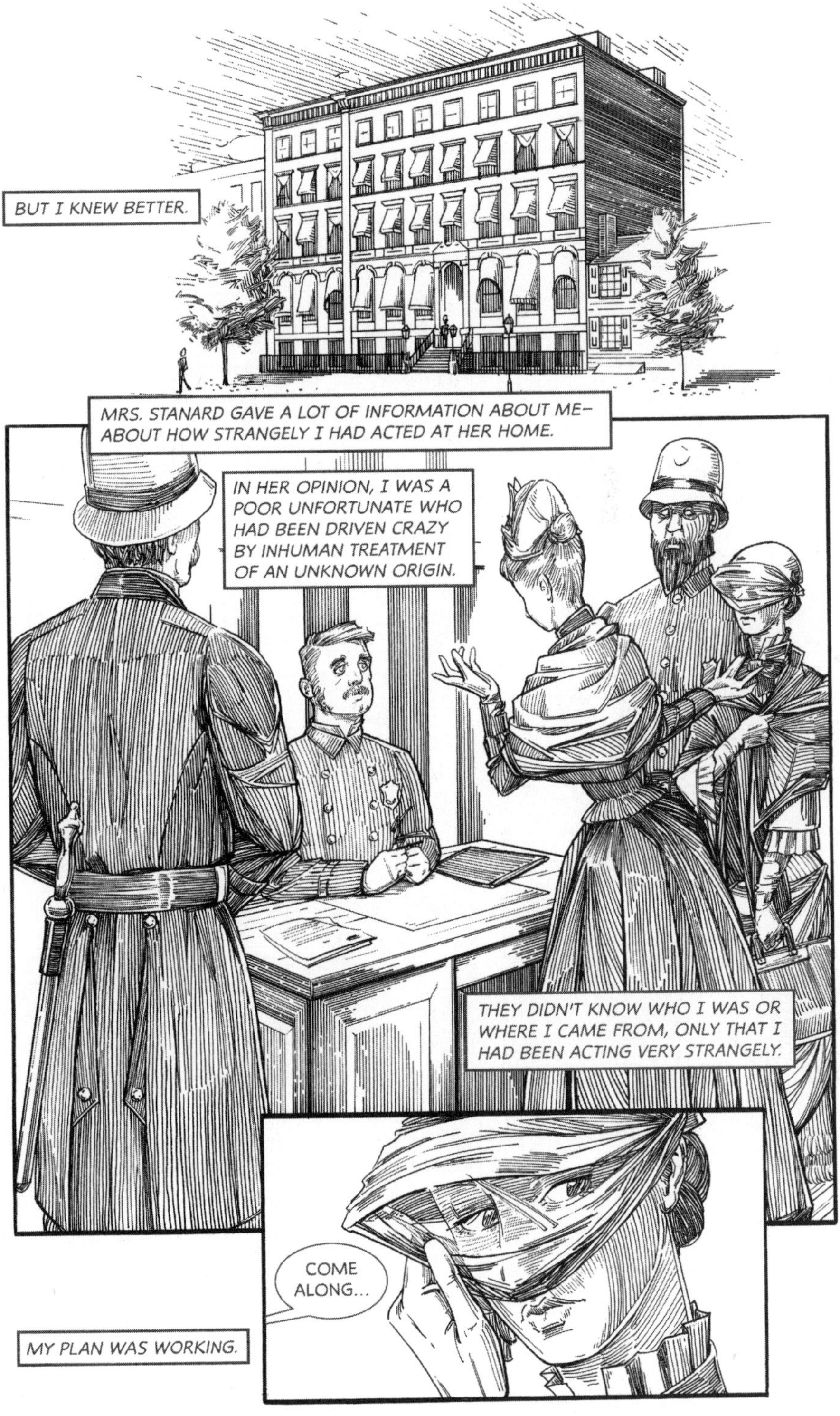
BUT I KNEW BETTER.
MRS. STANARD GAVE A LOT OF INFORMATION ABOUT ME—ABOUT HOW STRANGELY I HAD ACTED AT HER HOME.
IN HER OPINION, I WAS A POOR UNFORTUNATE WHO HAD BEEN DRIVEN CRAZY BY INHUMAN TREATMENT OF AN UNKNOWN ORIGIN.
THEY DIDN'T KNOW WHO I WAS OR WHERE I CAME FROM, ONLY THAT I HAD BEEN ACTING VERY STRANGELY.
COME ALONG...
MY PLAN WAS WORKING.

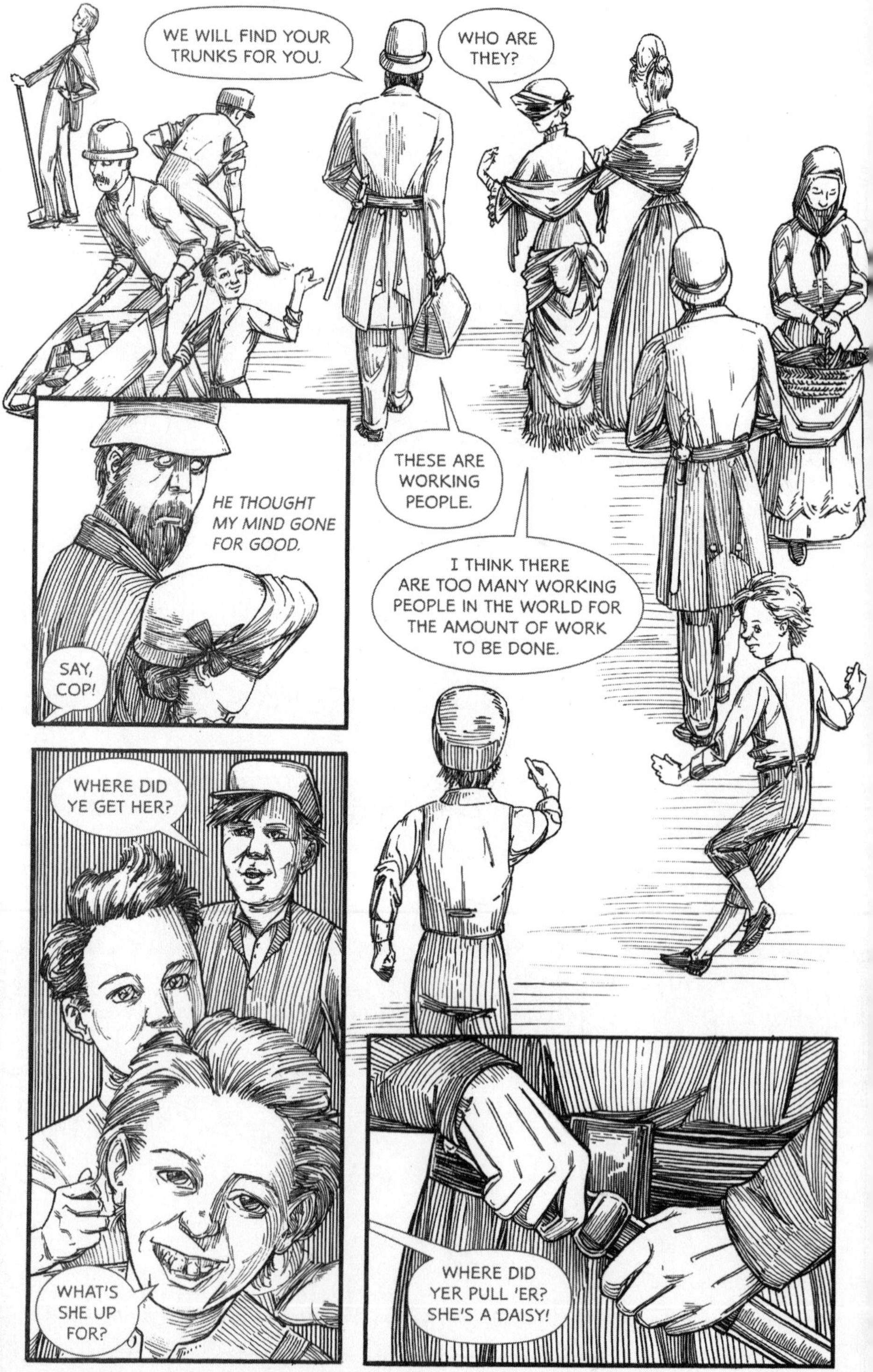
WE WILL FIND YOUR TRUNKS FOR YOU.
WHO ARE THEY?
THESE ARE WORKING PEOPLE.
I THINK THERE ARE TOO MANY WORKING PEOPLE IN THE WORLD FOR THE AMOUNT OF WORK TO BE DONE.
HE THOUGHT MY MIND GONE FOR GOOD.
SAY, COP!
WHERE DID YE GET HER?
WHAT'S SHE UP FOR?
WHERE DID YER PULL 'ER? SHE'S A DAISY!

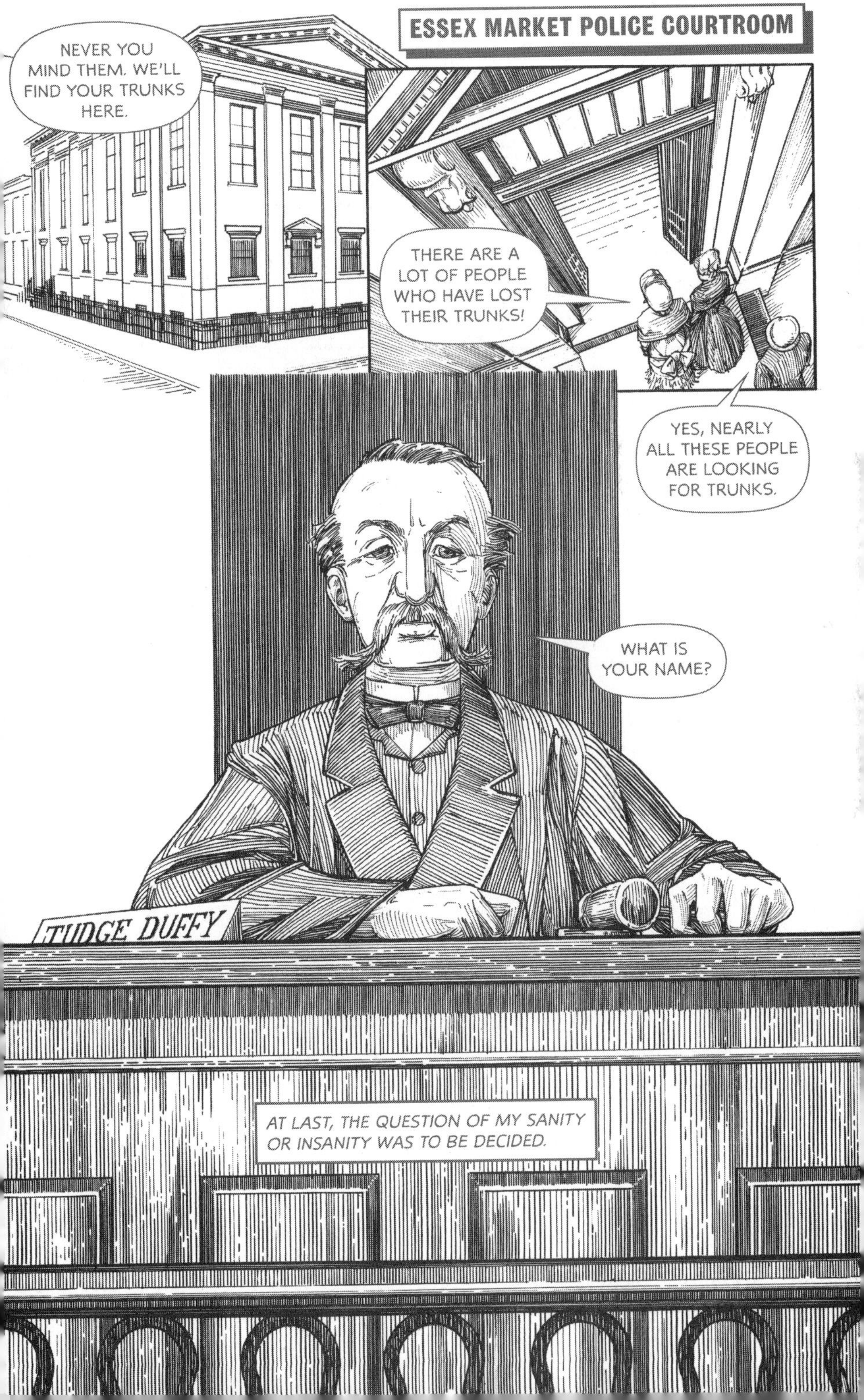
ESSEX MARKET POLICE COURTROOM
NEVER YOU MIND THEM. WE'LL FIND YOUR TRUNKS HERE.
THERE ARE A LOT OF PEOPLE WHO HAVE LOST THEIR TRUNKS!
YES, NEARLY ALL THESE PEOPLE ARE LOOKING FOR TRUNKS.
WHAT IS YOUR NAME?
JUDGE DUFFY
AT LAST, THE QUESTION OF MY SANITY OR INSANITY WAS TO BE DECIDED.

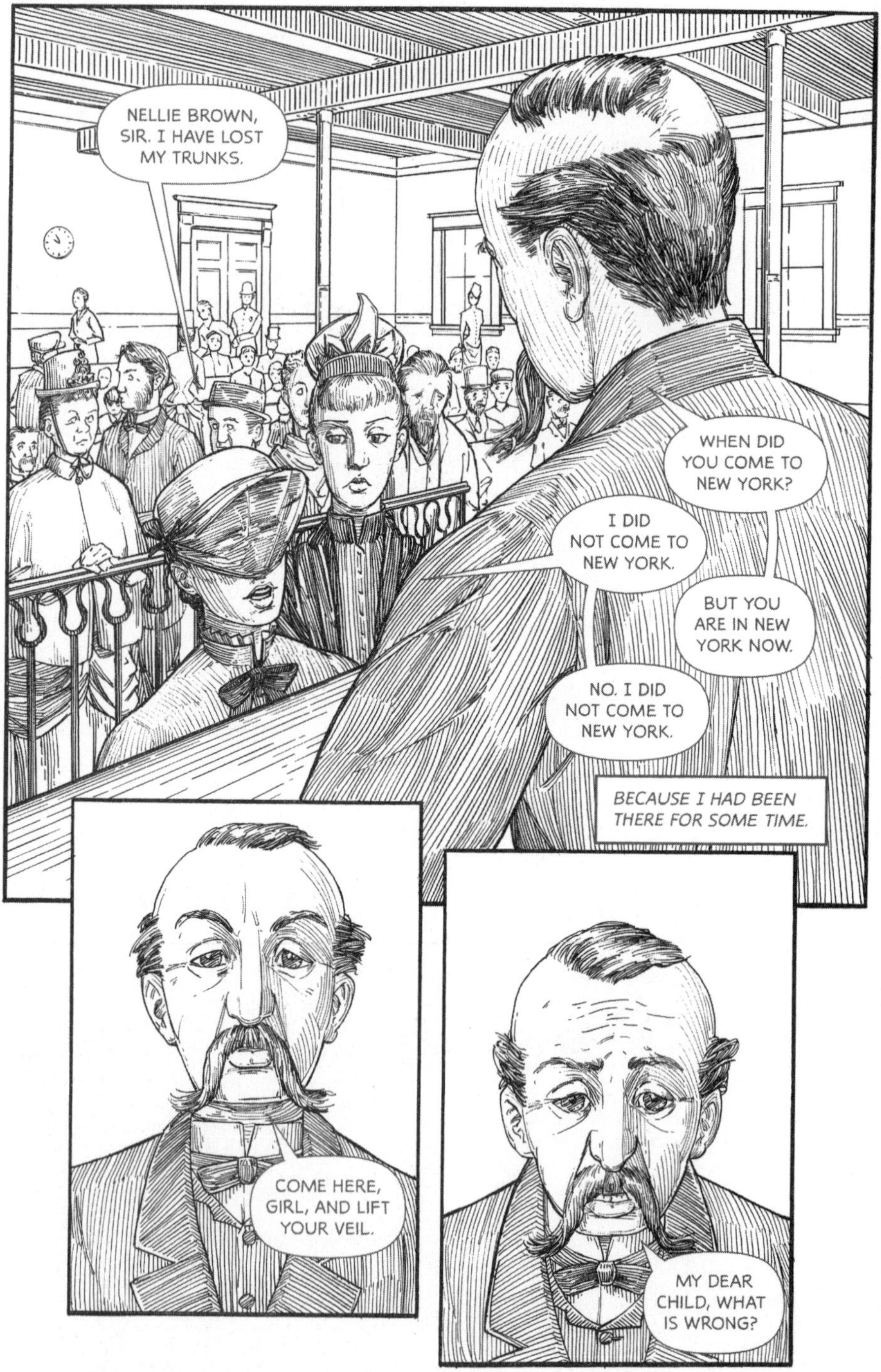

NELLIE BROWN, SIR. I HAVE LOST MY TRUNKS.
WHEN DID YOU COME TO NEW YORK?
I DID NOT COME TO NEW YORK.
BUT YOU ARE IN NEW YORK NOW.
NO. I DID NOT COME TO NEW YORK.
BECAUSE I HAD BEEN THERE FOR SOME TIME.
COME HERE, GIRL, AND LIFT YOUR VEIL.
MY DEAR CHILD, WHAT IS WRONG?

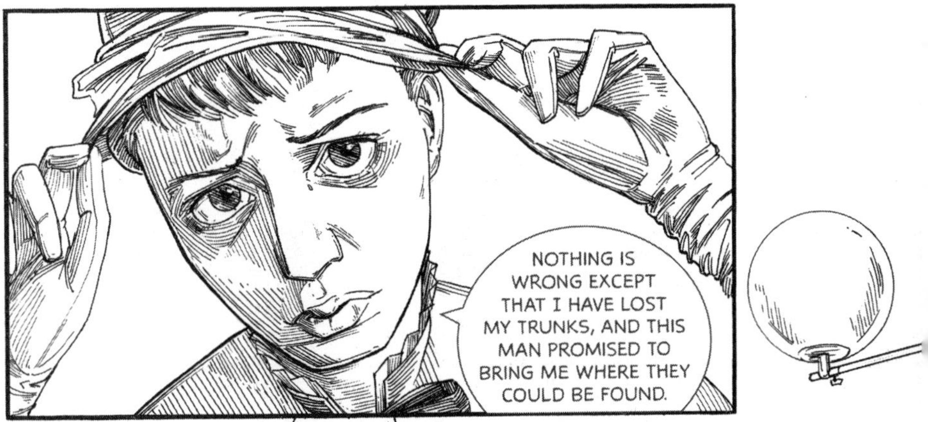
NOTHING IS WRONG EXCEPT THAT I HAVE LOST MY TRUNKS, AND THIS MAN PROMISED TO BRING ME WHERE THEY COULD BE FOUND.

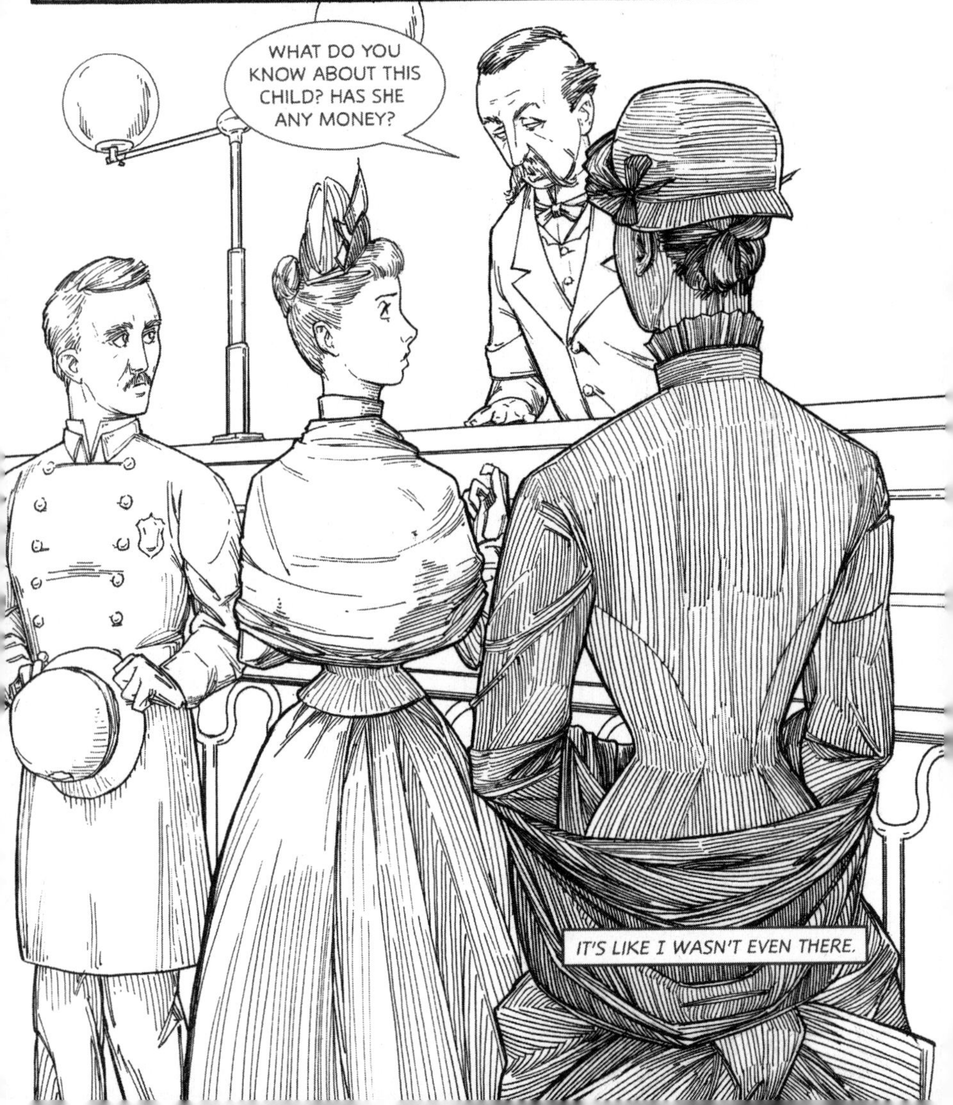
WHAT DO YOU KNOW ABOUT THIS CHILD? HAS SHE ANY MONEY?
IT'S LIKE I WASN'T EVEN THERE.

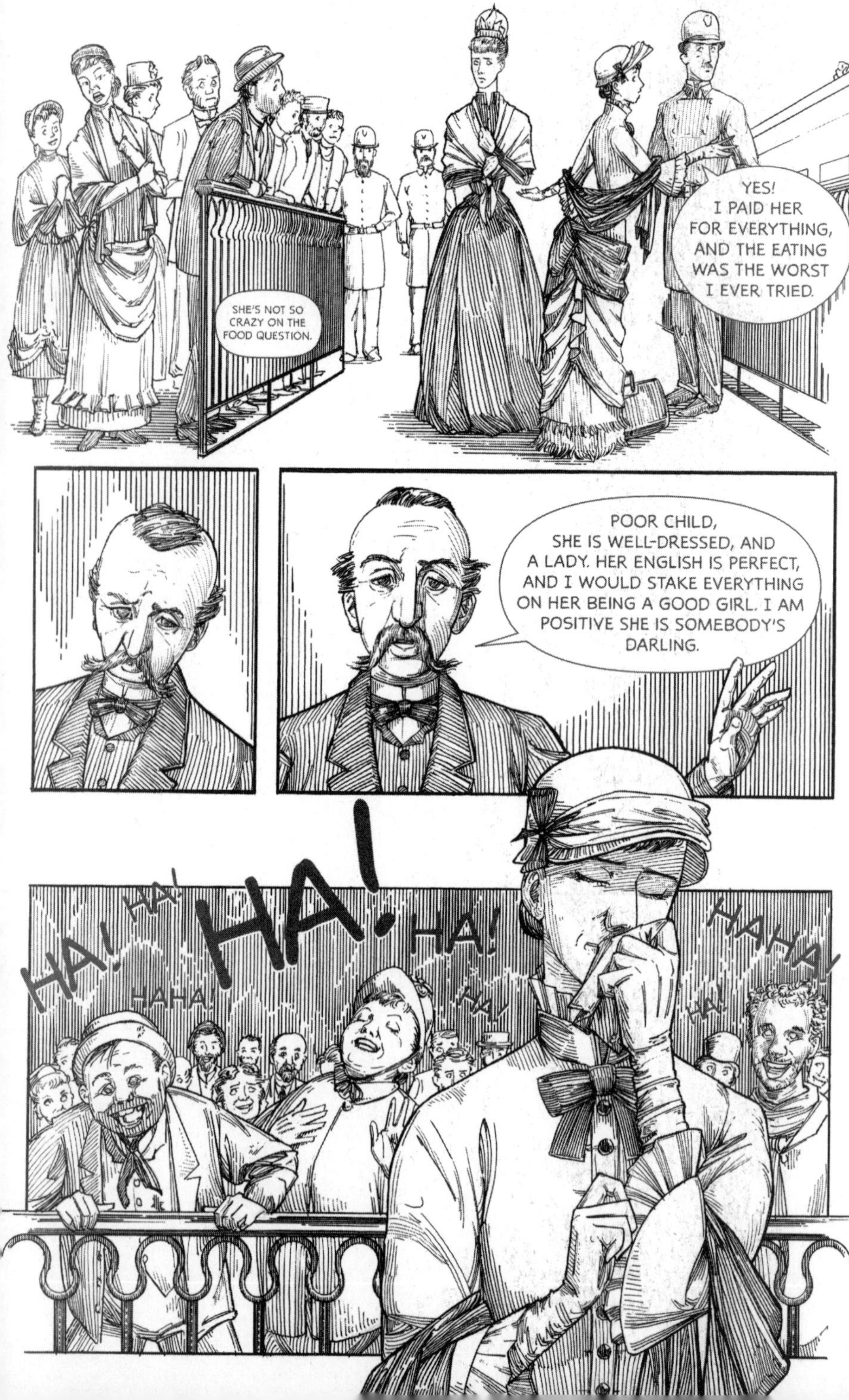

SHE'S NOT SO CRAZY ON THE FOOD QUESTION.
YES! I PAID HER FOR EVERYTHING, AND THE EATING WAS THE WORST I EVER TRIED.
POOR CHILD, SHE IS WELL-DRESSED, AND A LADY. HER ENGLISH IS PERFECT, AND I WOULD STAKE EVERYTHING ON HER BEING A GOOD GIRL. I AM POSITIVE SHE IS SOMEBODY'S DARLING.
HA!
HA!
HA!
HA!
HAHA!
HAHA!

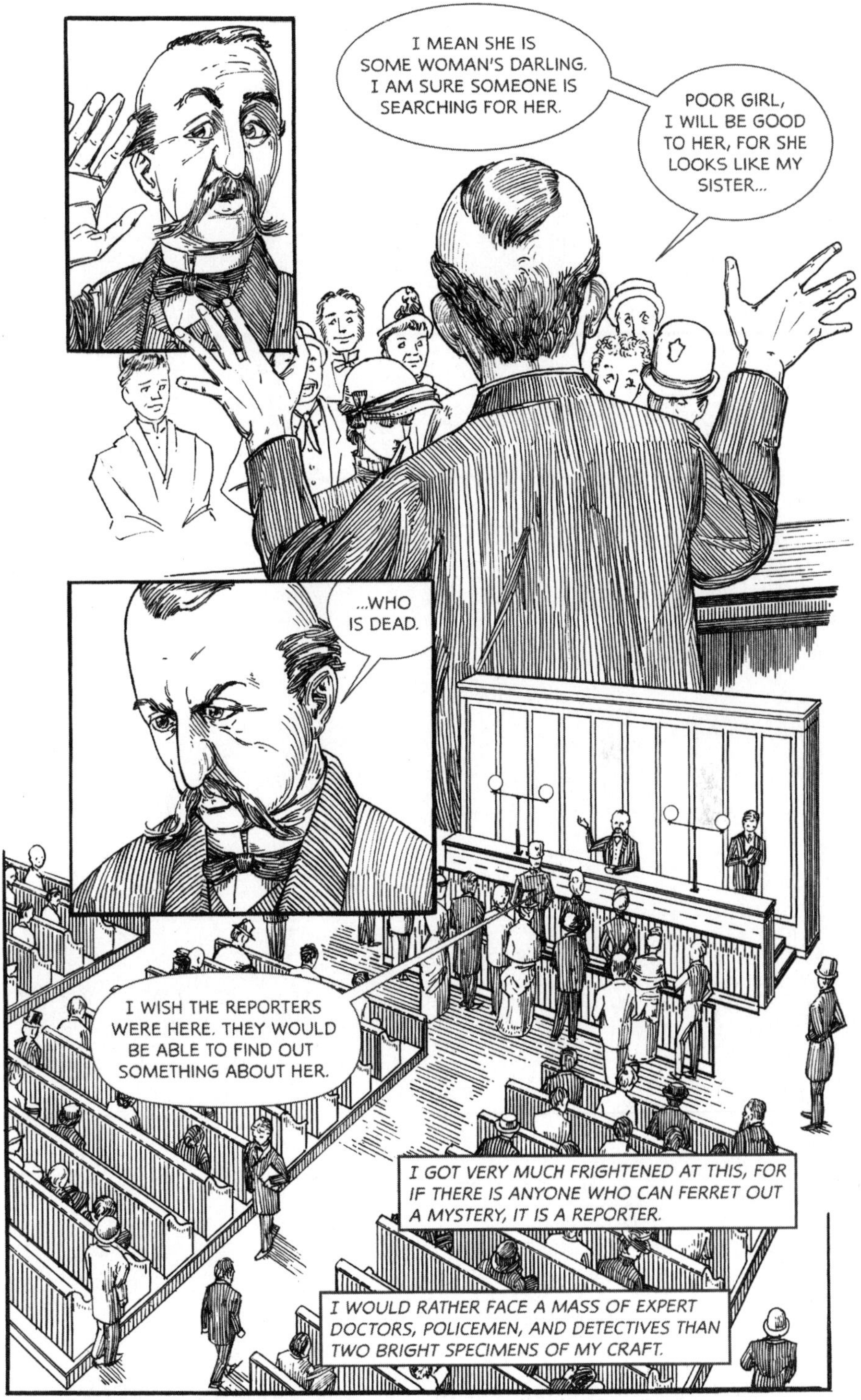
I MEAN SHE IS SOME WOMAN'S DARLING. I AM SURE SOMEONE IS SEARCHING FOR HER.
POOR GIRL, I WILL BE GOOD TO HER, FOR SHE LOOKS LIKE MY SISTER...
...WHO IS DEAD.
I WISH THE REPORTERS WERE HERE. THEY WOULD BE ABLE TO FIND OUT SOMETHING ABOUT HER.
I GOT VERY MUCH FRIGHTENED AT THIS, FOR IF THERE IS ANYONE WHO CAN FERRET OUT A MYSTERY, IT IS A REPORTER.
I WOULD RATHER FACE A MASS OF EXPERT DOCTORS, POLICEMEN, AND DETECTIVES THAN TWO BRIGHT SPECIMENS OF MY CRAFT.

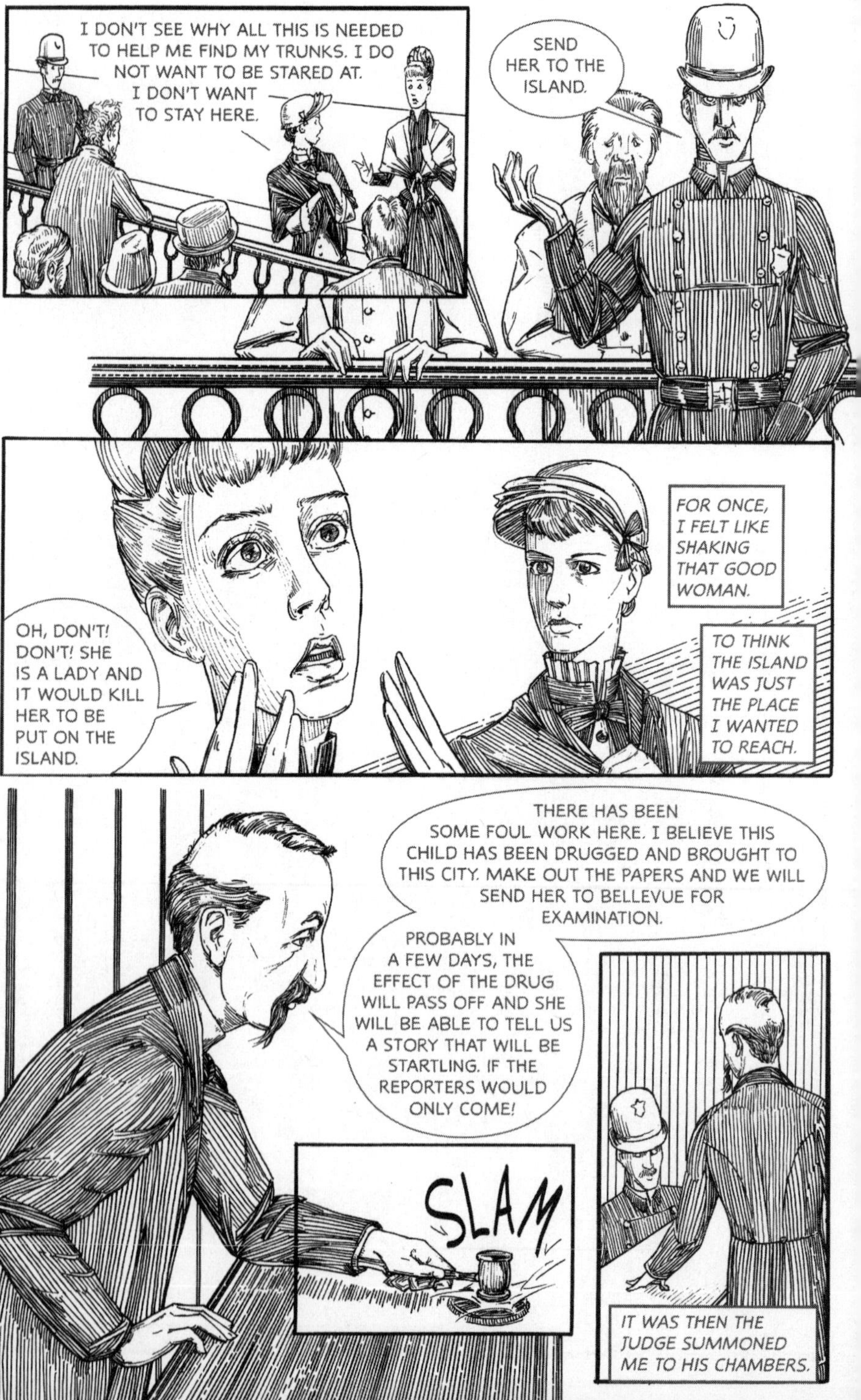
I DON'T SEE WHY ALL THIS IS NEEDED TO HELP ME FIND MY TRUNKS. I DO NOT WANT TO BE STARED AT. I DON'T WANT TO STAY HERE.
SEND HER TO THE ISLAND.
OH, DON'T! DON'T! SHE IS A LADY AND IT WOULD KILL HER TO BE PUT ON THE ISLAND.
FOR ONCE, I FELT LIKE SHAKING THAT GOOD WOMAN.
TO THINK THE ISLAND WAS JUST THE PLACE I WANTED TO REACH.
THERE HAS BEEN SOME FOUL WORK HERE. I BELIEVE THIS CHILD HAS BEEN DRUGGED AND BROUGHT TO THIS CITY. MAKE OUT THE PAPERS AND WE WILL SEND HER TO BELLEVUE FOR EXAMINATION.
PROBABLY IN A FEW DAYS, THE EFFECT OF THE DRUG WILL PASS OFF AND SHE WILL BE ABLE TO TELL US A STORY THAT WILL BE STARTLING. IF THE REPORTERS WOULD ONLY COME!
SLAM
IT WAS THEN THE JUDGE SUMMONED ME TO HIS CHAMBERS.

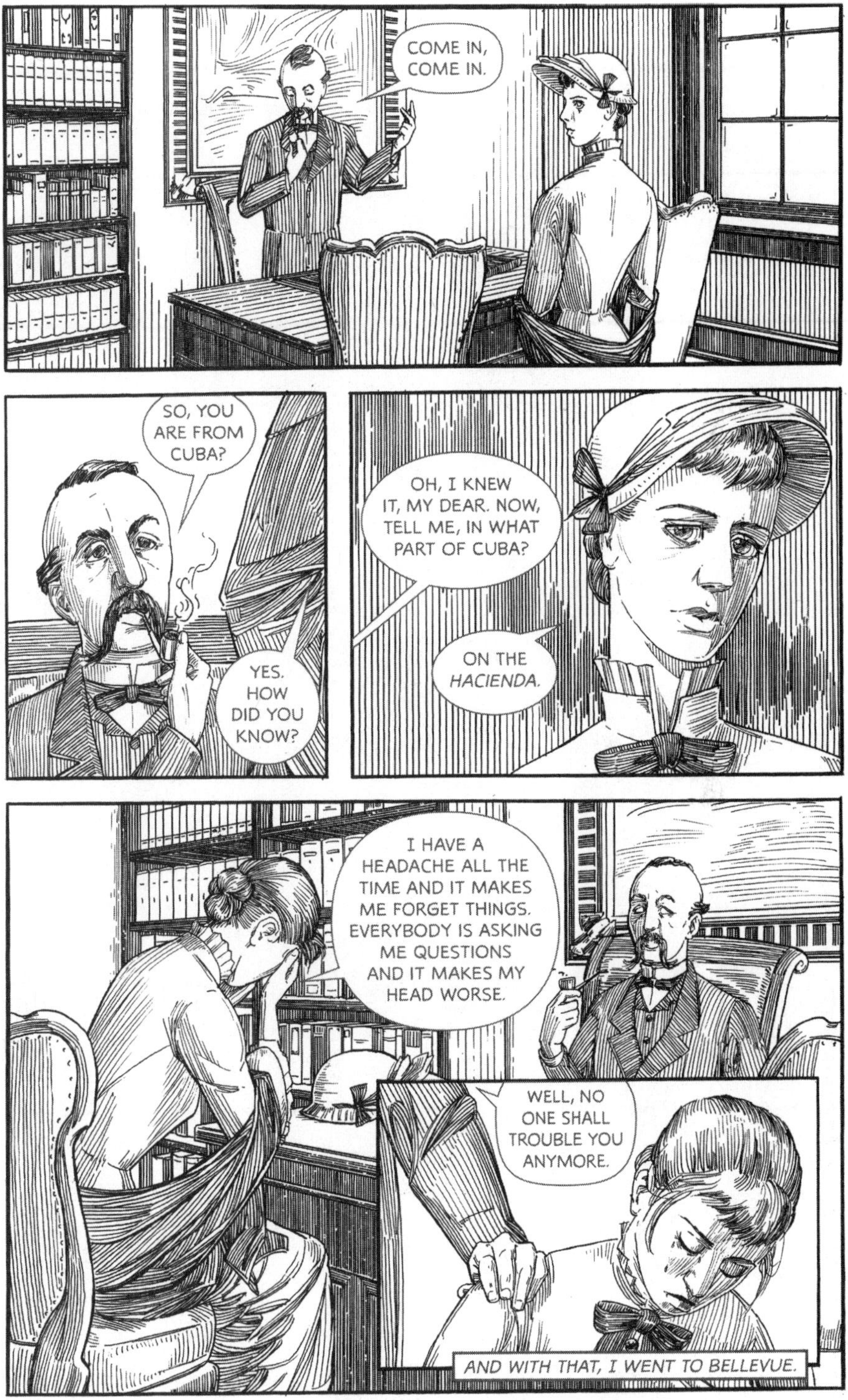
COME IN, COME IN.
SO, YOU ARE FROM CUBA?
YES. HOW DID YOU KNOW?
OH, I KNEW IT, MY DEAR. NOW, TELL ME, IN WHAT PART OF CUBA?
ON THE *HACIENDA*.
I HAVE A HEADACHE ALL THE TIME AND IT MAKES ME FORGET THINGS. EVERYBODY IS ASKING ME QUESTIONS AND IT MAKES MY HEAD WORSE.
WELL, NO ONE SHALL TROUBLE YOU ANYMORE.
AND WITH THAT, I WENT TO BELLEVUE.

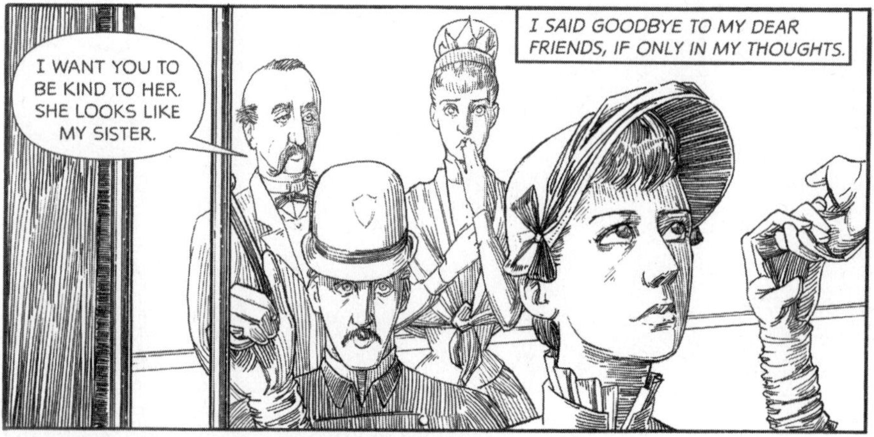
I SAID GOODBYE TO MY DEAR FRIENDS, IF ONLY IN MY THOUGHTS.
I WANT YOU TO BE KIND TO HER. SHE LOOKS LIKE MY SISTER.

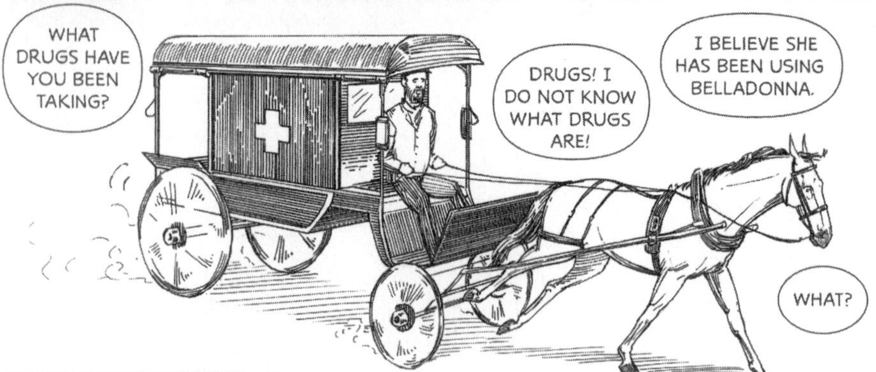
WHAT DRUGS HAVE YOU BEEN TAKING?
DRUGS! I DO NOT KNOW WHAT DRUGS ARE!
I BELIEVE SHE HAS BEEN USING BELLADONNA.
WHAT?

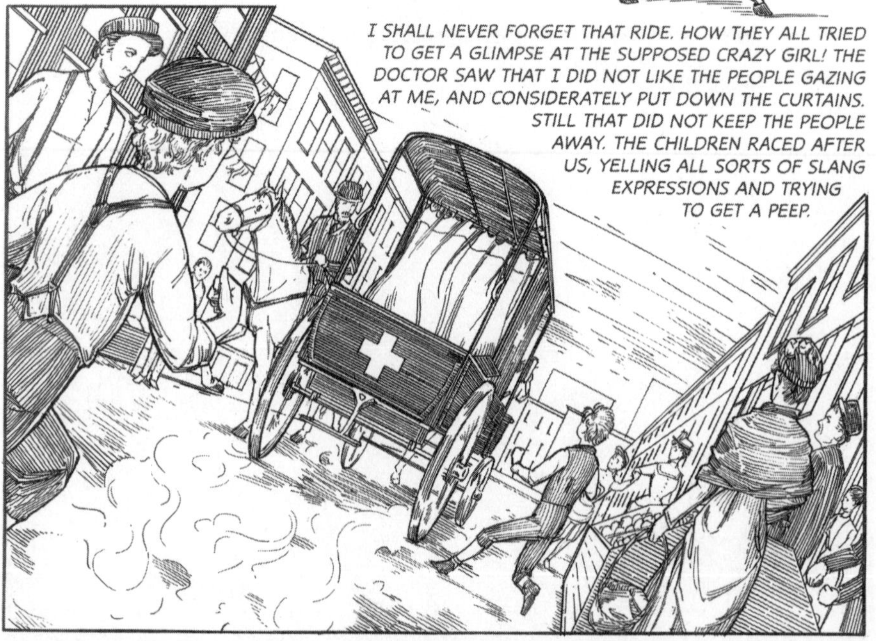
I SHALL NEVER FORGET THAT RIDE. HOW THEY ALL TRIED TO GET A GLIMPSE AT THE SUPPOSED CRAZY GIRL! THE DOCTOR SAW THAT I DID NOT LIKE THE PEOPLE GAZING AT ME, AND CONSIDERATELY PUT DOWN THE CURTAINS. STILL THAT DID NOT KEEP THE PEOPLE AWAY. THE CHILDREN RACED AFTER US, YELLING ALL SORTS OF SLANG EXPRESSIONS AND TRYING TO GET A PEEP.

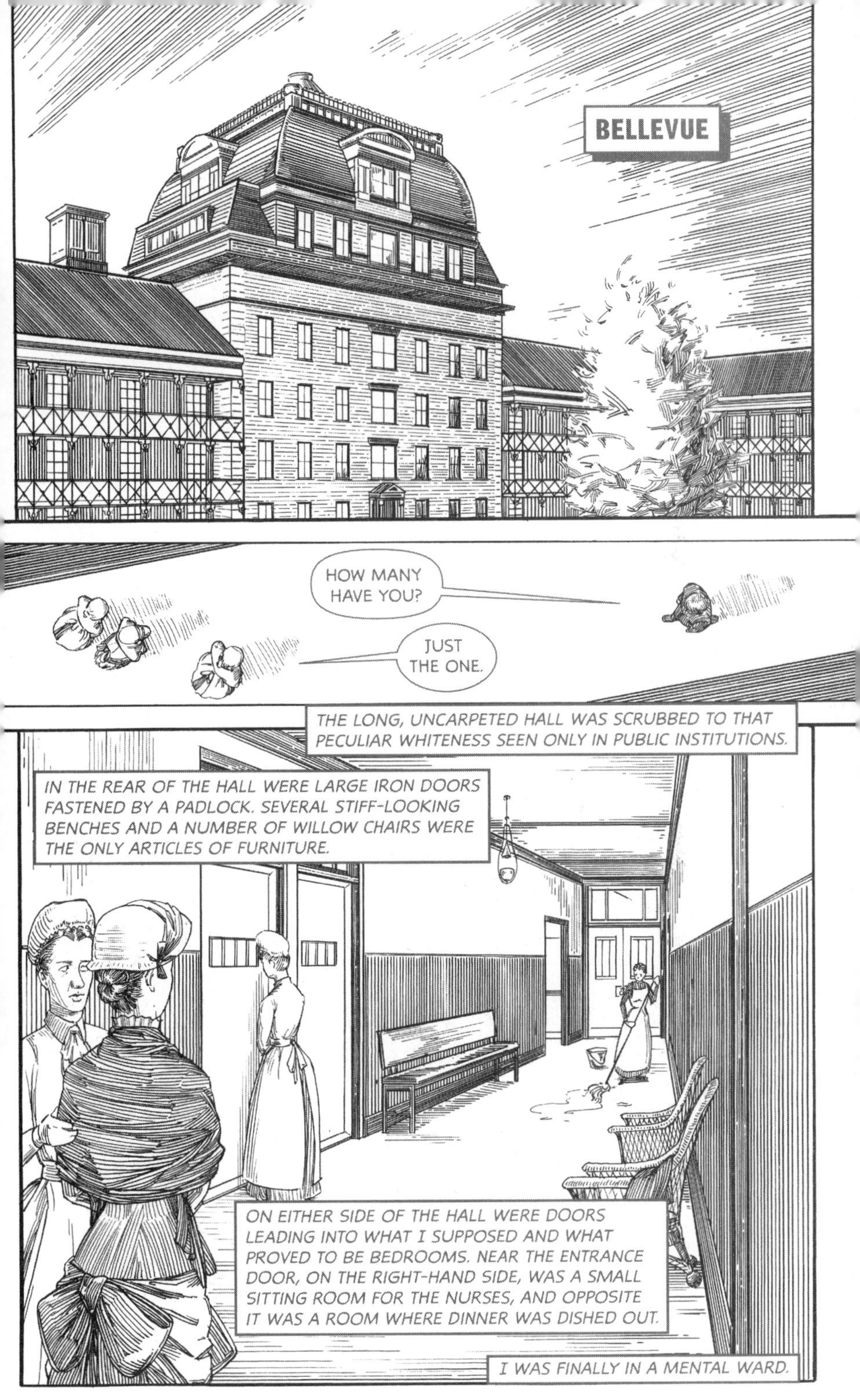
BELLEVUE
HOW MANY HAVE YOU?
JUST THE ONE.
THE LONG, UNCARPETED HALL WAS SCRUBBED TO THAT PECULIAR WHITENESS SEEN ONLY IN PUBLIC INSTITUTIONS.
IN THE REAR OF THE HALL WERE LARGE IRON DOORS FASTENED BY A PADLOCK. SEVERAL STIFF-LOOKING BENCHES AND A NUMBER OF WILLOW CHAIRS WERE THE ONLY ARTICLES OF FURNITURE.
ON EITHER SIDE OF THE HALL WERE DOORS LEADING INTO WHAT I SUPPOSED AND WHAT PROVED TO BE BEDROOMS. NEAR THE ENTRANCE DOOR, ON THE RIGHT-HAND SIDE, WAS A SMALL SITTING ROOM FOR THE NURSES, AND OPPOSITE IT WAS A ROOM WHERE DINNER WAS DISHED OUT.
I WAS FINALLY IN A MENTAL WARD.

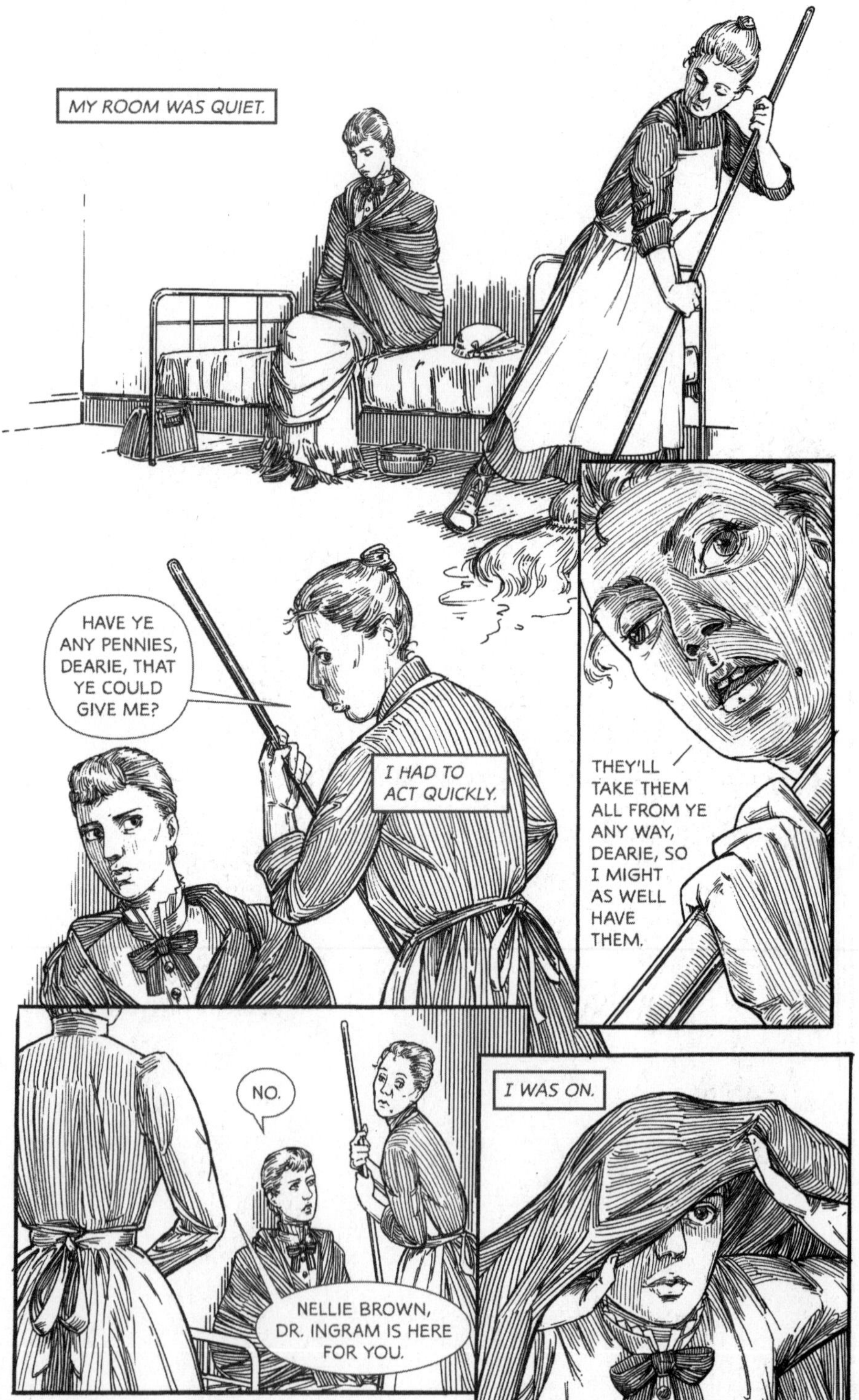
MY ROOM WAS QUIET.
HAVE YE ANY PENNIES, DEARIE, THAT YE COULD GIVE ME?
I HAD TO ACT QUICKLY.
THEY'LL TAKE THEM ALL FROM YE ANY WAY, DEARIE, SO I MIGHT AS WELL HAVE THEM.
NO.
NELLIE BROWN, DR. INGRAM IS HERE FOR YOU.
I WAS ON.

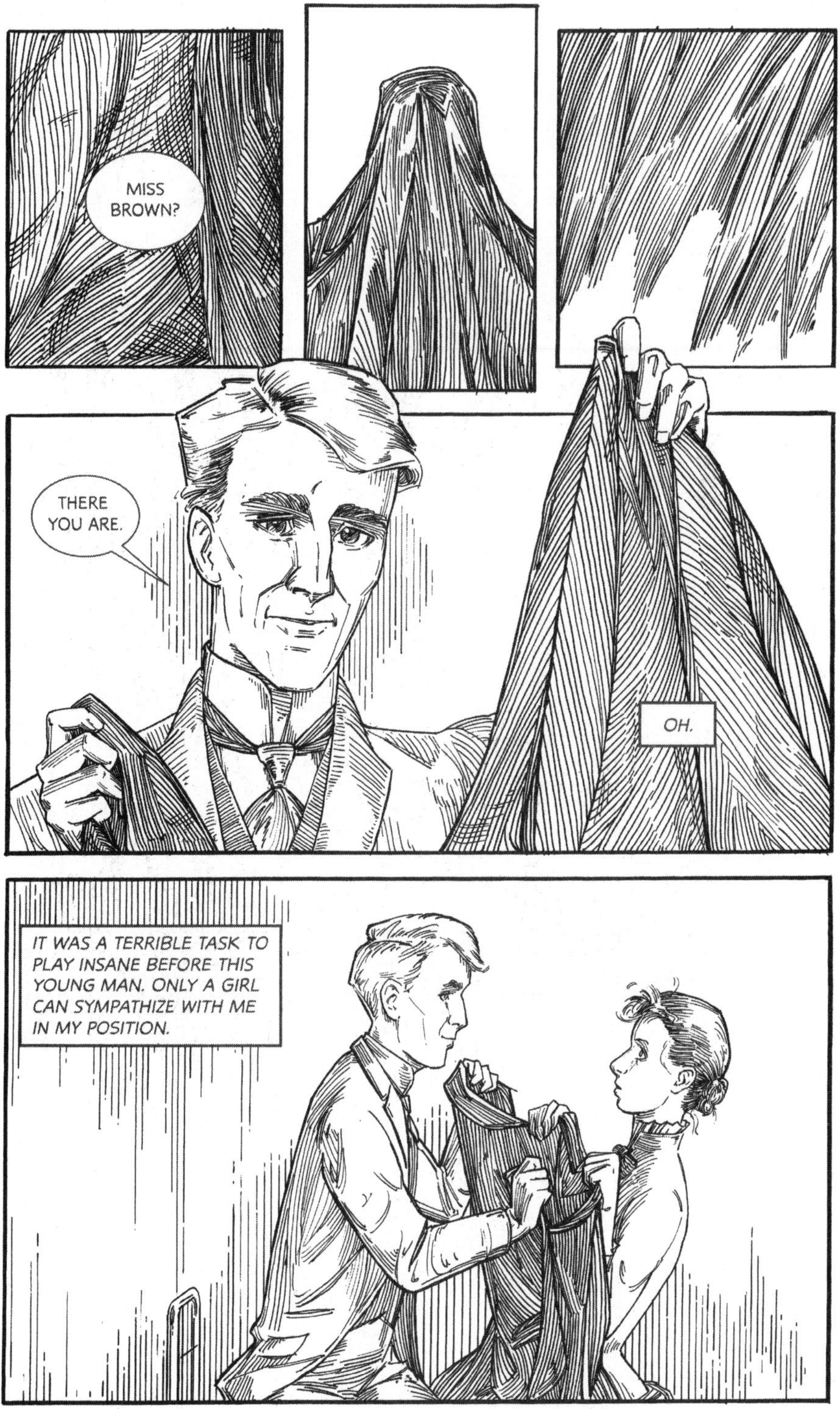
MISS BROWN?
THERE YOU ARE.
OH.
IT WAS A TERRIBLE TASK TO PLAY INSANE BEFORE THIS YOUNG MAN. ONLY A GIRL CAN SYMPATHIZE WITH ME IN MY POSITION.

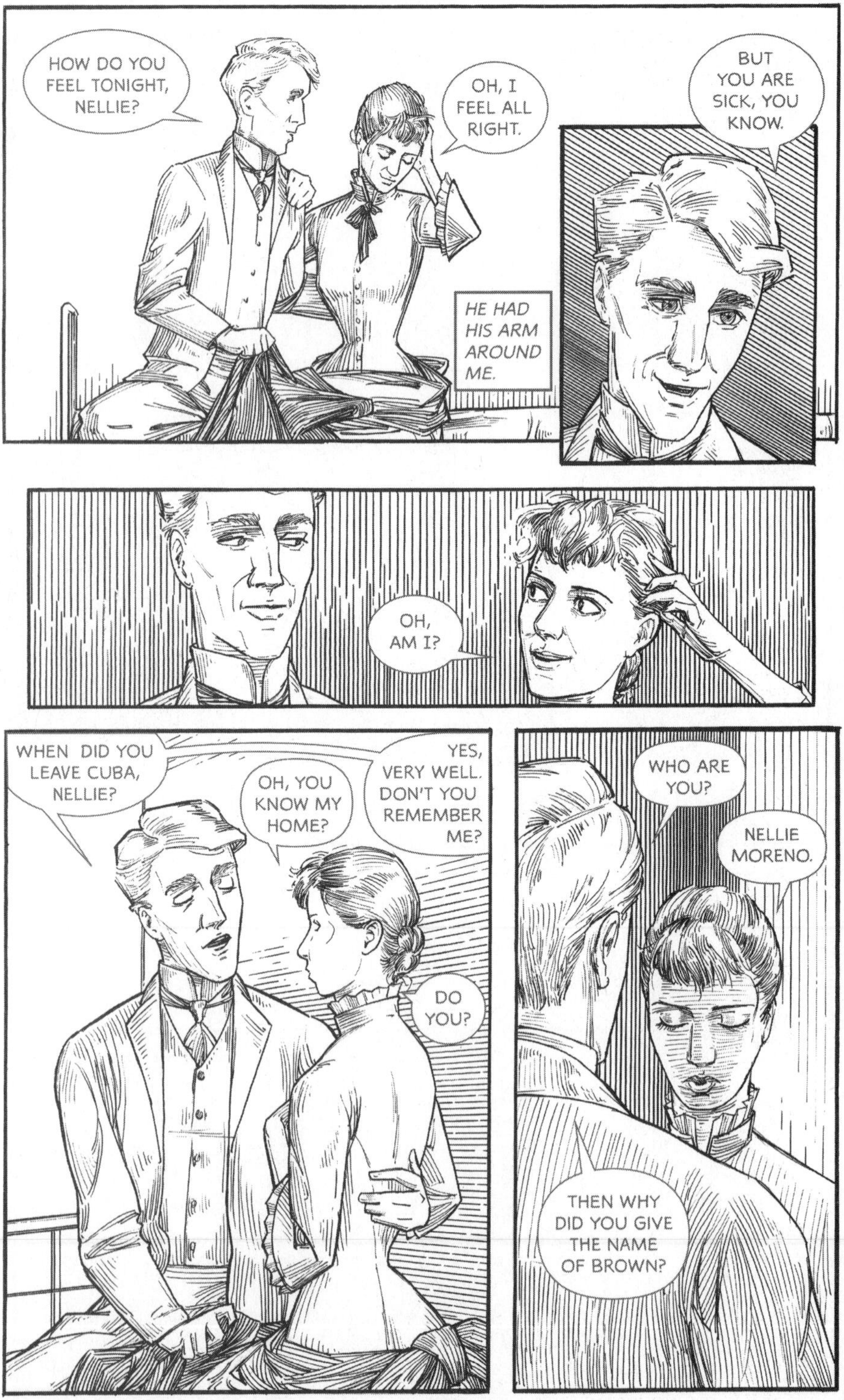
HOW DO YOU FEEL TONIGHT, NELLIE?
OH, I FEEL ALL RIGHT.
HE HAD HIS ARM AROUND ME.
BUT YOU ARE SICK, YOU KNOW.
OH, AM I?
WHEN DID YOU LEAVE CUBA, NELLIE?
OH, YOU KNOW MY HOME?
YES, VERY WELL. DON'T YOU REMEMBER ME?
DO YOU?
WHO ARE YOU?
NELLIE MORENO.
THEN WHY DID YOU GIVE THE NAME OF BROWN?

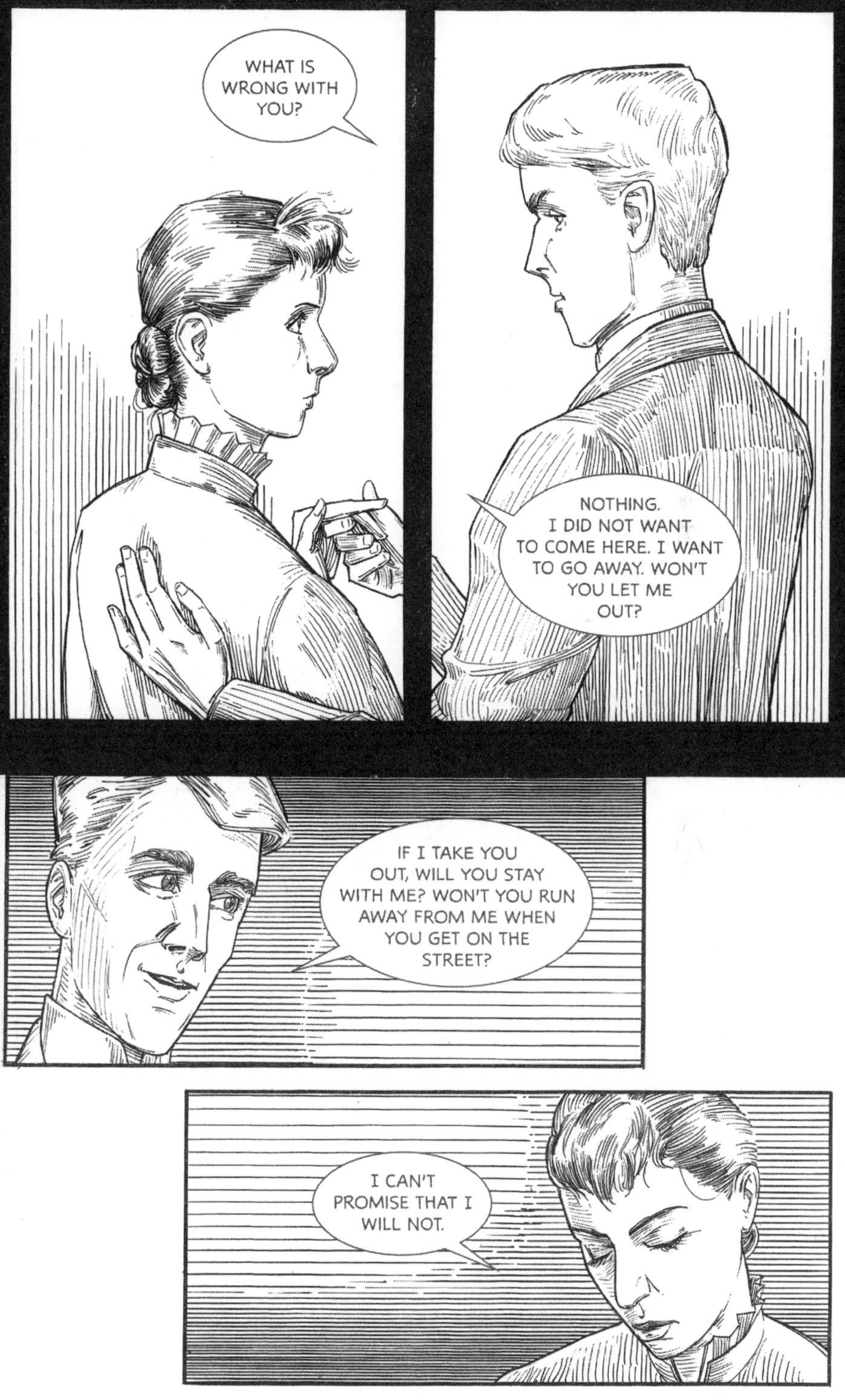
WHAT IS WRONG WITH YOU?
NOTHING. I DID NOT WANT TO COME HERE. I WANT TO GO AWAY. WON'T YOU LET ME OUT?
IF I TAKE YOU OUT, WILL YOU STAY WITH ME? WON'T YOU RUN AWAY FROM ME WHEN YOU GET ON THE STREET?
I CAN'T PROMISE THAT I WILL NOT.

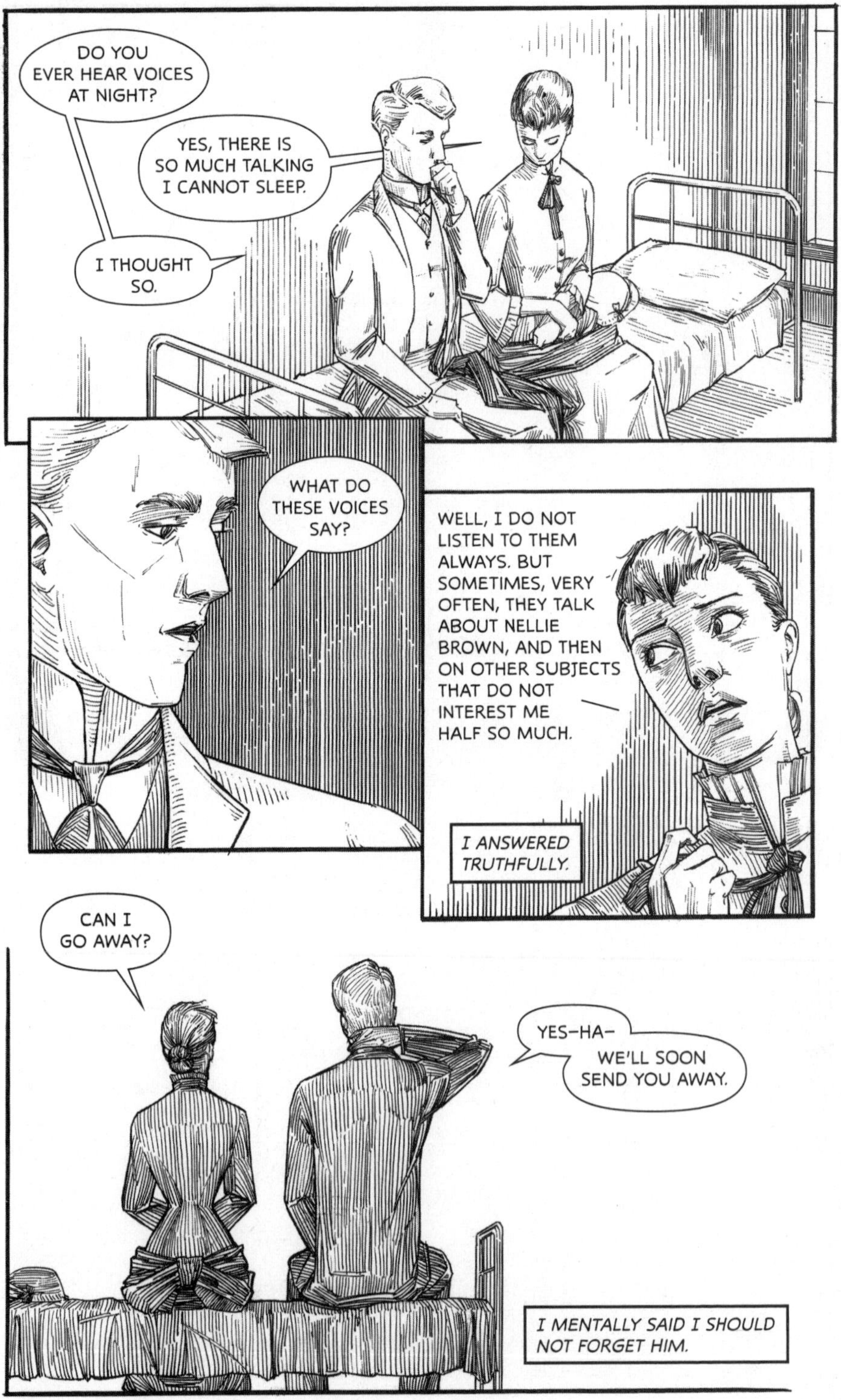
DO YOU EVER HEAR VOICES AT NIGHT?
YES, THERE IS SO MUCH TALKING I CANNOT SLEEP.
I THOUGHT SO.
WHAT DO THESE VOICES SAY?
WELL, I DO NOT LISTEN TO THEM ALWAYS. BUT SOMETIMES, VERY OFTEN, THEY TALK ABOUT NELLIE BROWN, AND THEN ON OTHER SUBJECTS THAT DO NOT INTEREST ME HALF SO MUCH.
I ANSWERED TRUTHFULLY.
CAN I GO AWAY?
YES–HA–
WE'LL SOON SEND YOU AWAY.
I MENTALLY SAID I SHOULD NOT FORGET HIM.

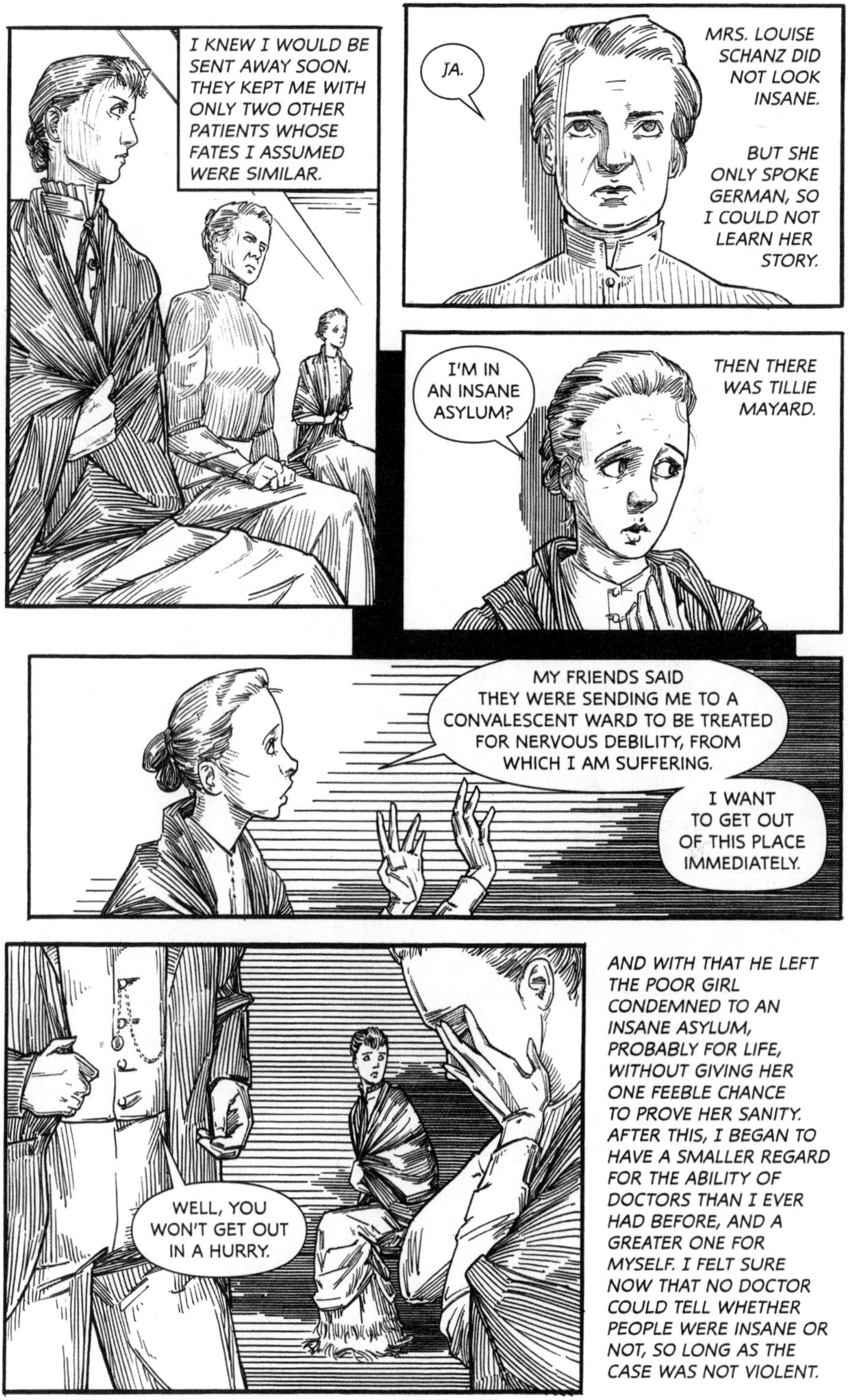
I KNEW I WOULD BE SENT AWAY SOON. THEY KEPT ME WITH ONLY TWO OTHER PATIENTS WHOSE FATES I ASSUMED WERE SIMILAR.
MRS. LOUISE SCHANZ DID NOT LOOK INSANE.
JA.
BUT SHE ONLY SPOKE GERMAN, SO I COULD NOT LEARN HER STORY.
THEN THERE WAS TILLIE MAYARD.
I'M IN AN INSANE ASYLUM?
MY FRIENDS SAID THEY WERE SENDING ME TO A CONVALESCENT WARD TO BE TREATED FOR NERVOUS DEBILITY, FROM WHICH I AM SUFFERING.
I WANT TO GET OUT OF THIS PLACE IMMEDIATELY.
WELL, YOU WON'T GET OUT IN A HURRY.
AND WITH THAT HE LEFT THE POOR GIRL CONDEMNED TO AN INSANE ASYLUM, PROBABLY FOR LIFE, WITHOUT GIVING HER ONE FEEBLE CHANCE TO PROVE HER SANITY. AFTER THIS, I BEGAN TO HAVE A SMALLER REGARD FOR THE ABILITY OF DOCTORS THAN I EVER HAD BEFORE, AND A GREATER ONE FOR MYSELF. I FELT SURE NOW THAT NO DOCTOR COULD TELL WHETHER PEOPLE WERE INSANE OR NOT, SO LONG AS THE CASE WAS NOT VIOLENT.

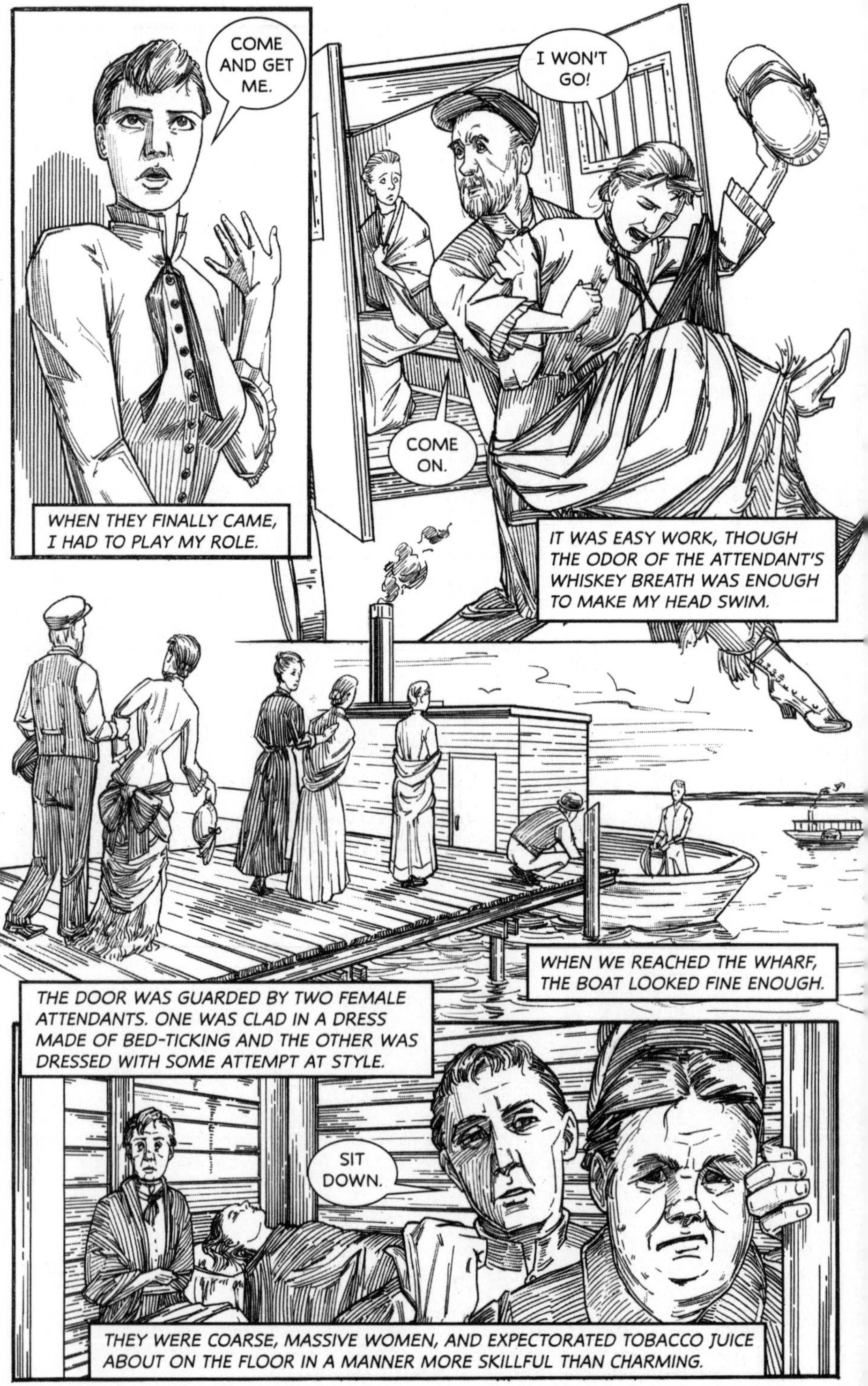
COME AND GET ME.
WHEN THEY FINALLY CAME, I HAD TO PLAY MY ROLE.
I WON'T GO!
COME ON.
IT WAS EASY WORK, THOUGH THE ODOR OF THE ATTENDANT'S WHISKEY BREATH WAS ENOUGH TO MAKE MY HEAD SWIM.
WHEN WE REACHED THE WHARF, THE BOAT LOOKED FINE ENOUGH.
THE DOOR WAS GUARDED BY TWO FEMALE ATTENDANTS. ONE WAS CLAD IN A DRESS MADE OF BED-TICKING AND THE OTHER WAS DRESSED WITH SOME ATTEMPT AT STYLE.
SIT DOWN.
THEY WERE COARSE, MASSIVE WOMEN, AND EXPECTORATED TOBACCO JUICE ABOUT ON THE FLOOR IN A MANNER MORE SKILLFUL THAN CHARMING.

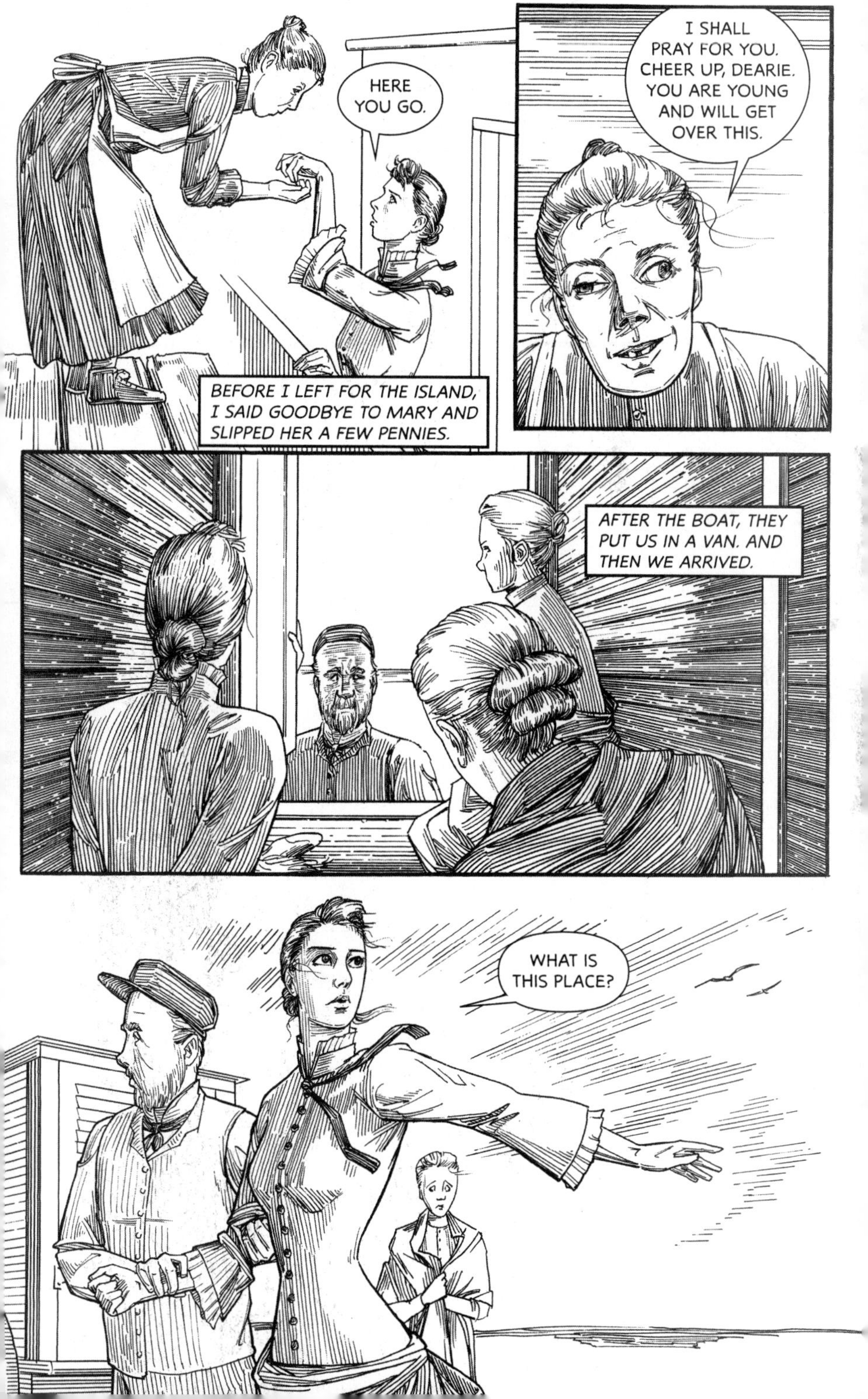
HERE YOU GO.
BEFORE I LEFT FOR THE ISLAND, I SAID GOODBYE TO MARY AND SLIPPED HER A FEW PENNIES.
I SHALL PRAY FOR YOU. CHEER UP, DEARIE. YOU ARE YOUNG AND WILL GET OVER THIS.
AFTER THE BOAT, THEY PUT US IN A VAN. AND THEN WE ARRIVED.
WHAT IS THIS PLACE?

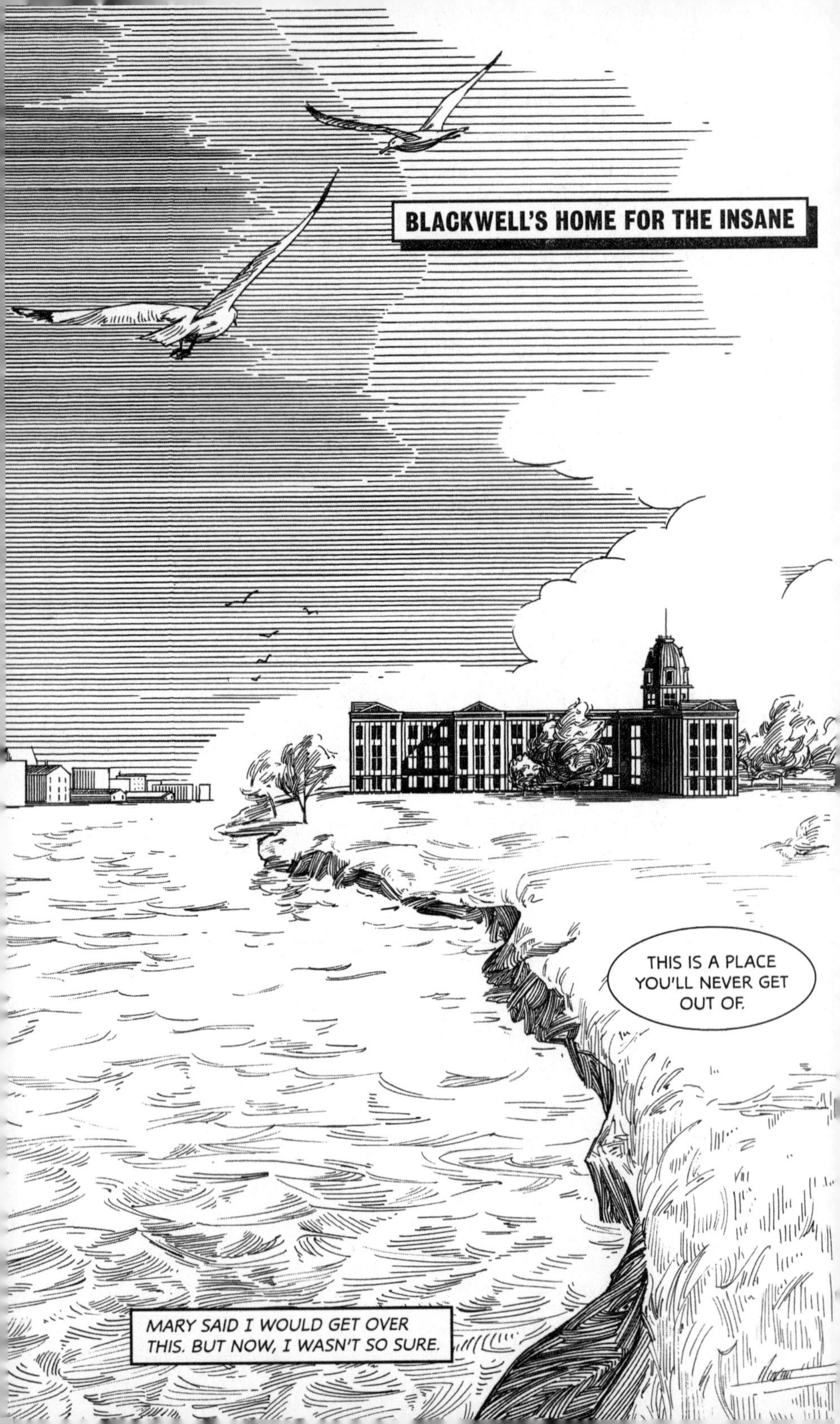
BLACKWELL'S HOME FOR THE INSANE
THIS IS A PLACE YOU'LL NEVER GET OUT OF.
MARY SAID I WOULD GET OVER THIS. BUT NOW, I WASN'T SO SURE.

PART II

◆ INSIDE THE MAD-HOUSE ◆

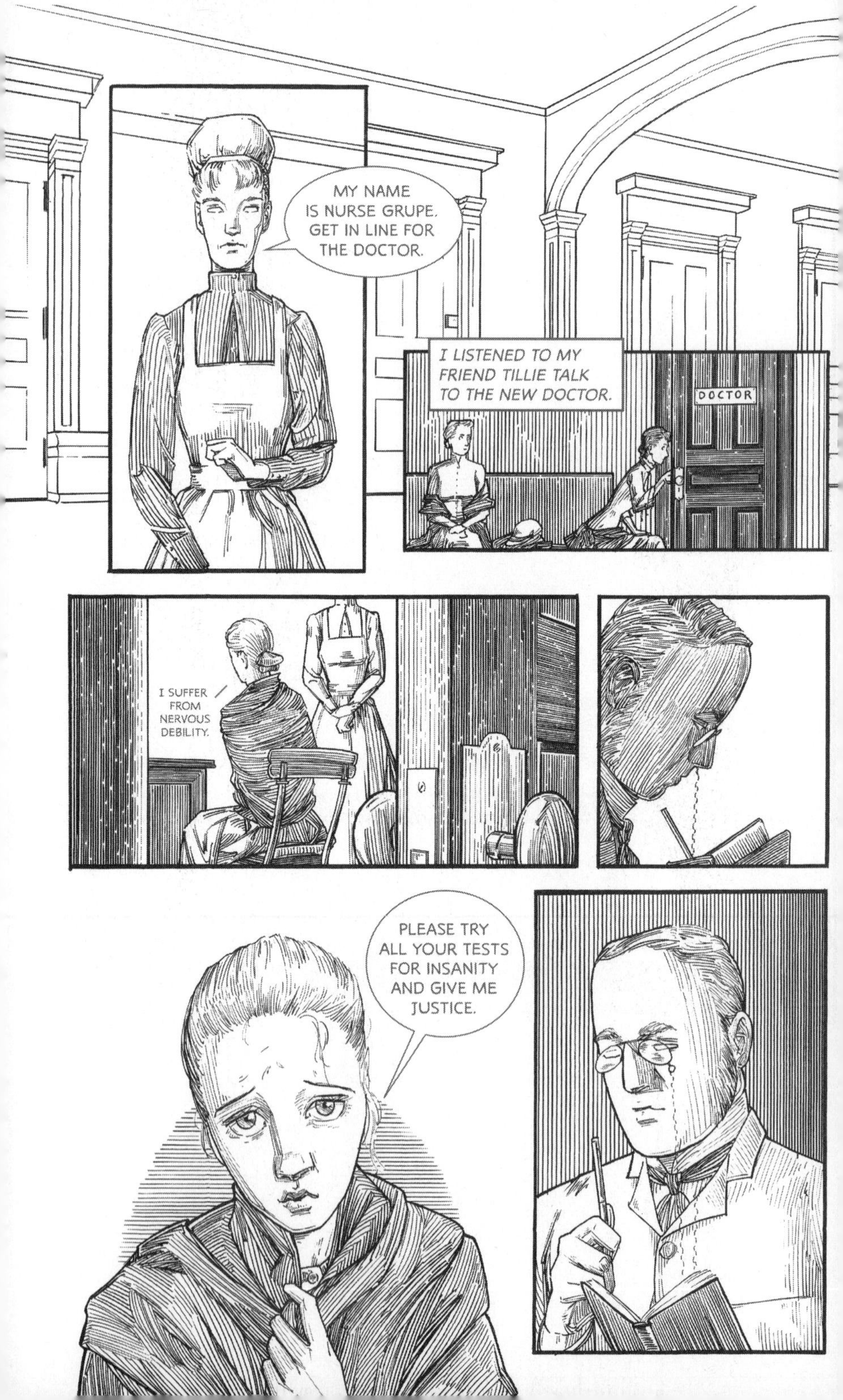
MY NAME IS NURSE GRUPE. GET IN LINE FOR THE DOCTOR.
I LISTENED TO MY FRIEND TILLIE TALK TO THE NEW DOCTOR.
DOCTOR
I SUFFER FROM NERVOUS DEBILITY.
PLEASE TRY ALL YOUR TESTS FOR INSANITY AND GIVE ME JUSTICE.

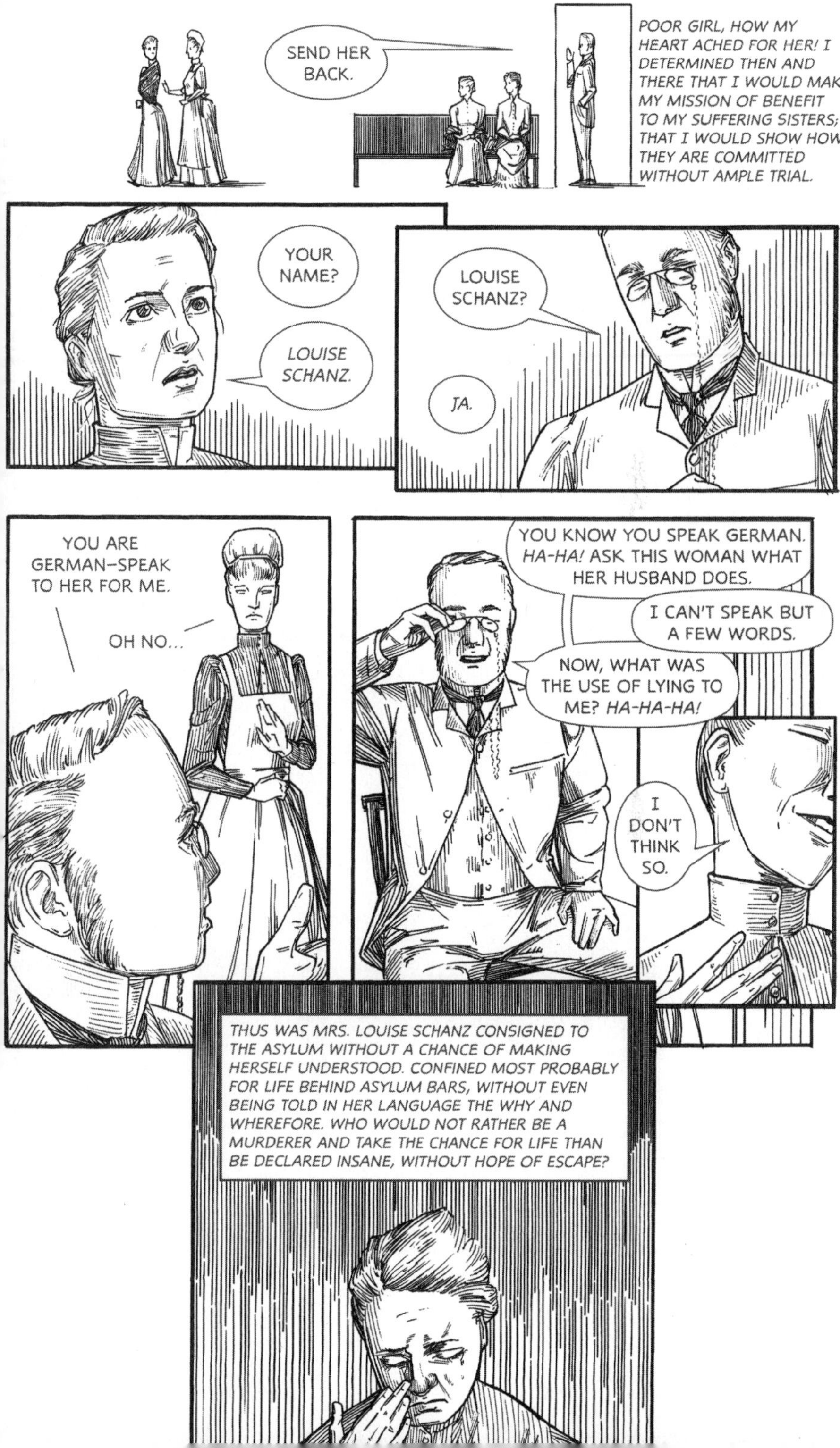
SEND HER BACK.
POOR GIRL, HOW MY HEART ACHED FOR HER! I DETERMINED THEN AND THERE THAT I WOULD MAKE MY MISSION OF BENEFIT TO MY SUFFERING SISTERS; THAT I WOULD SHOW HOW THEY ARE COMMITTED WITHOUT AMPLE TRIAL.
YOUR NAME?
LOUISE SCHANZ.
LOUISE SCHANZ?
JA.
YOU ARE GERMAN—SPEAK TO HER FOR ME.
OH NO...
YOU KNOW YOU SPEAK GERMAN. HA-HA! ASK THIS WOMAN WHAT HER HUSBAND DOES.
I CAN'T SPEAK BUT A FEW WORDS.
NOW, WHAT WAS THE USE OF LYING TO ME? HA-HA-HA!
I DON'T THINK SO.
THUS WAS MRS. LOUISE SCHANZ CONSIGNED TO THE ASYLUM WITHOUT A CHANCE OF MAKING HERSELF UNDERSTOOD. CONFINED MOST PROBABLY FOR LIFE BEHIND ASYLUM BARS, WITHOUT EVEN BEING TOLD IN HER LANGUAGE THE WHY AND WHEREFORE. WHO WOULD NOT RATHER BE A MURDERER AND TAKE THE CHANCE FOR LIFE THAN BE DECLARED INSANE, WITHOUT HOPE OF ESCAPE?

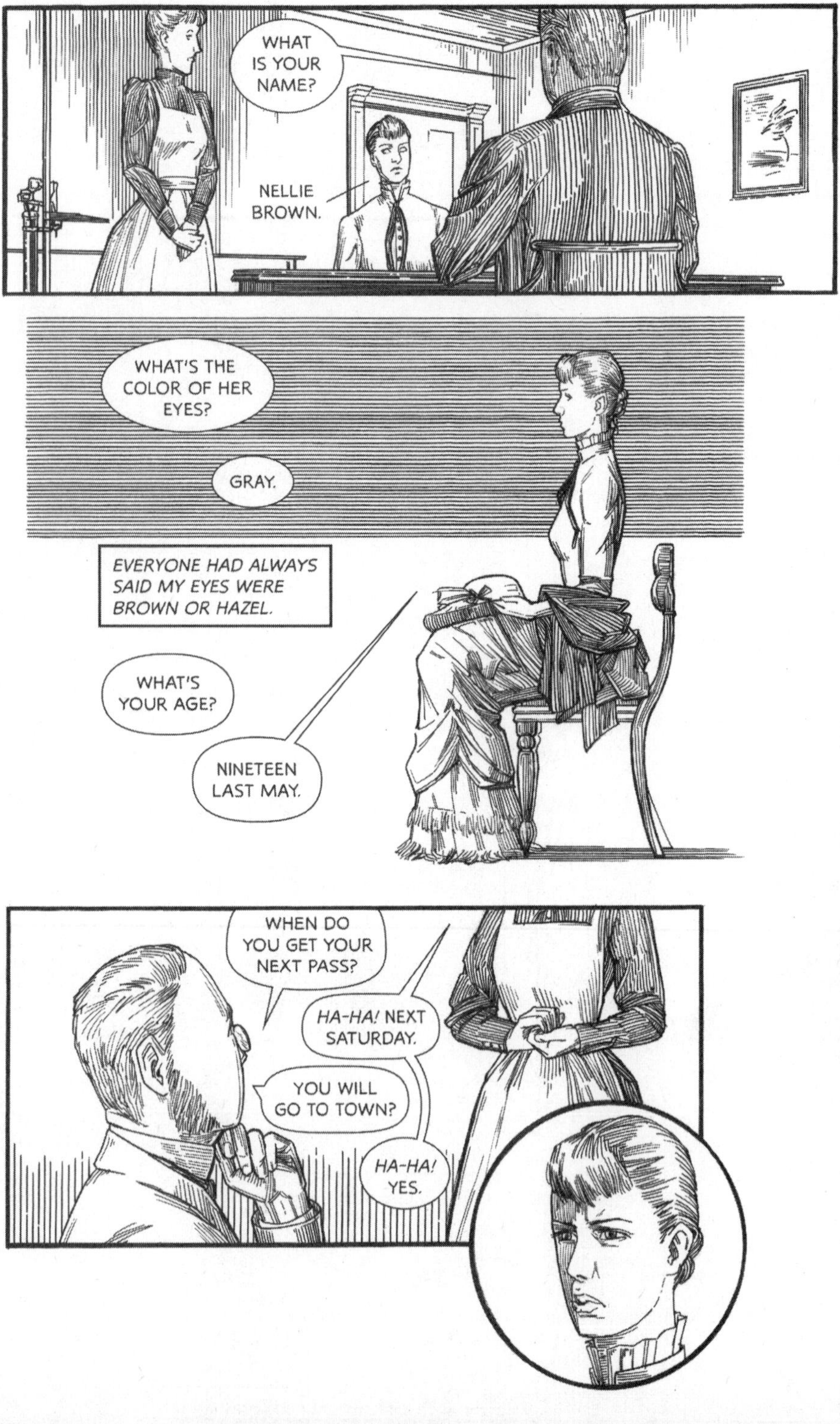
WHAT IS YOUR NAME?
NELLIE BROWN.
WHAT'S THE COLOR OF HER EYES?
GRAY.
EVERYONE HAD ALWAYS SAID MY EYES WERE BROWN OR HAZEL.
WHAT'S YOUR AGE?
NINETEEN LAST MAY.
WHEN DO YOU GET YOUR NEXT PASS?
HA-HA! NEXT SATURDAY.
YOU WILL GO TO TOWN?
HA-HA! YES.

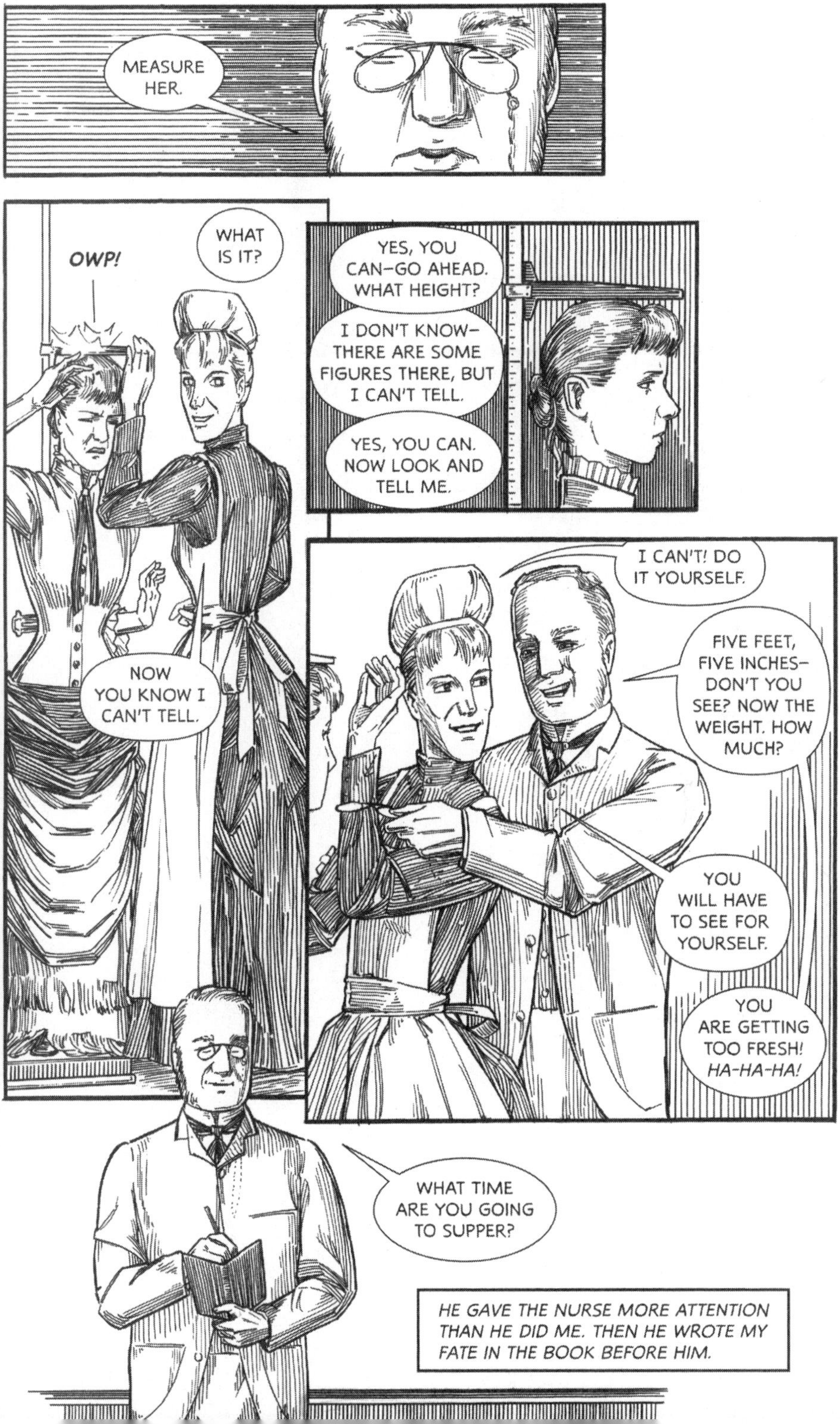
MEASURE HER.
WHAT IS IT?
OWP!
NOW YOU KNOW I CAN'T TELL.
YES, YOU CAN—GO AHEAD. WHAT HEIGHT?
I DON'T KNOW—THERE ARE SOME FIGURES THERE, BUT I CAN'T TELL.
YES, YOU CAN. NOW LOOK AND TELL ME.
I CAN'T! DO IT YOURSELF.
FIVE FEET, FIVE INCHES—DON'T YOU SEE? NOW THE WEIGHT. HOW MUCH?
YOU WILL HAVE TO SEE FOR YOURSELF.
YOU ARE GETTING TOO FRESH! *HA-HA-HA!*
WHAT TIME ARE YOU GOING TO SUPPER?
HE GAVE THE NURSE MORE ATTENTION THAN HE DID ME. THEN HE WROTE MY FATE IN THE BOOK BEFORE HIM.

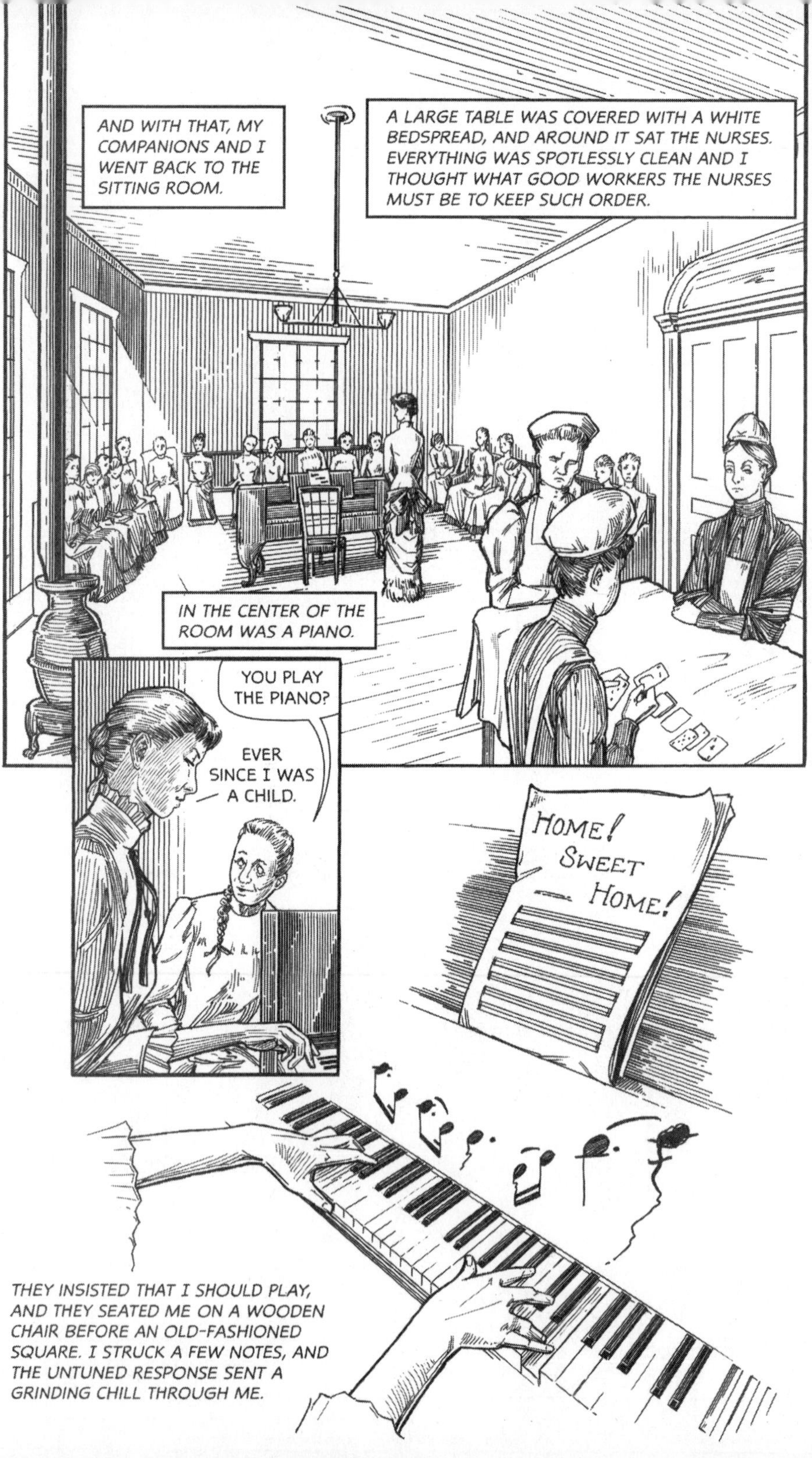
AND WITH THAT, MY COMPANIONS AND I WENT BACK TO THE SITTING ROOM.
A LARGE TABLE WAS COVERED WITH A WHITE BEDSPREAD, AND AROUND IT SAT THE NURSES. EVERYTHING WAS SPOTLESSLY CLEAN AND I THOUGHT WHAT GOOD WORKERS THE NURSES MUST BE TO KEEP SUCH ORDER.
IN THE CENTER OF THE ROOM WAS A PIANO.
YOU PLAY THE PIANO?
EVER SINCE I WAS A CHILD.
HOME! SWEET HOME!
THEY INSISTED THAT I SHOULD PLAY, AND THEY SEATED ME ON A WOODEN CHAIR BEFORE AN OLD-FASHIONED SQUARE. I STRUCK A FEW NOTES, AND THE UNTUNED RESPONSE SENT A GRINDING CHILL THROUGH ME.

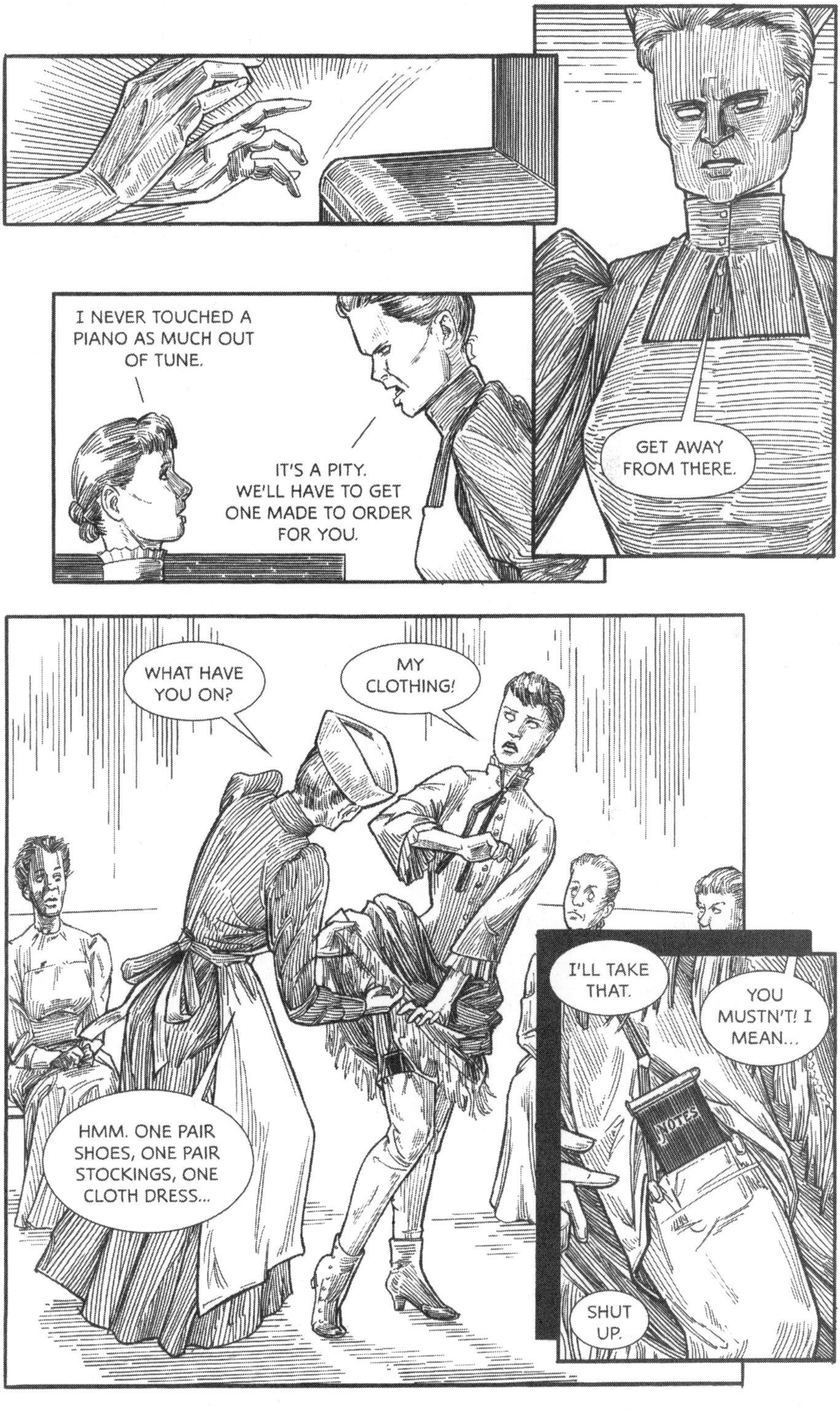
GET AWAY FROM THERE.
I NEVER TOUCHED A PIANO AS MUCH OUT OF TUNE.
IT'S A PITY. WE'LL HAVE TO GET ONE MADE TO ORDER FOR YOU.
WHAT HAVE YOU ON?
MY CLOTHING!
HMM. ONE PAIR SHOES, ONE PAIR STOCKINGS, ONE CLOTH DRESS...
I'LL TAKE THAT.
YOU MUSTN'T! I MEAN...
NOTES
SHUT UP.

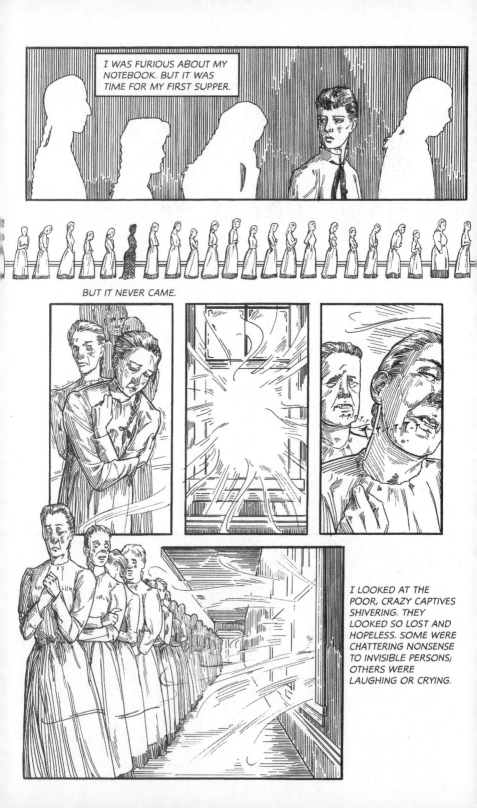

I WAS FURIOUS ABOUT MY NOTEBOOK. BUT IT WAS TIME FOR MY FIRST SUPPER.

BUT IT NEVER CAME.

I LOOKED AT THE POOR, CRAZY CAPTIVES SHIVERING. THEY LOOKED SO LOST AND HOPELESS. SOME WERE CHATTERING NONSENSE TO INVISIBLE PERSONS; OTHERS WERE LAUGHING OR CRYING.

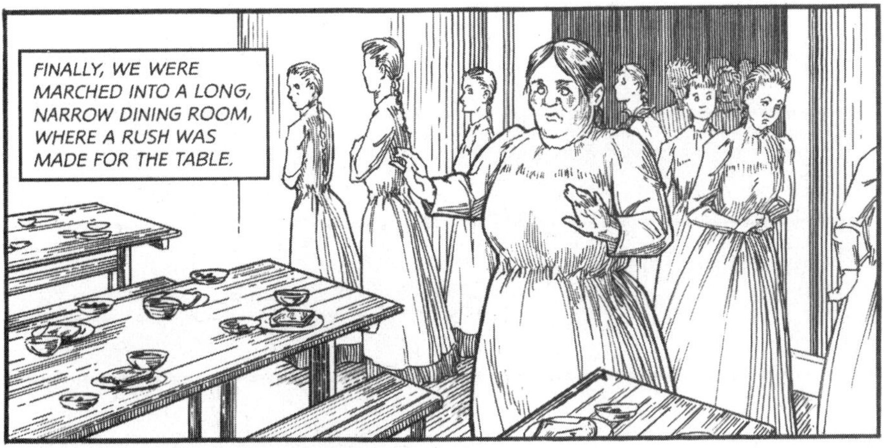
FINALLY, WE WERE MARCHED INTO A LONG, NARROW DINING ROOM, WHERE A RUSH WAS MADE FOR THE TABLE.

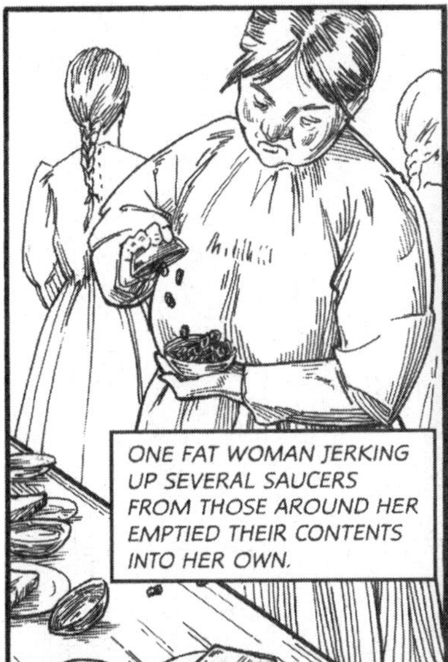
ONE FAT WOMAN JERKING UP SEVERAL SAUCERS FROM THOSE AROUND HER EMPTIED THEIR CONTENTS INTO HER OWN.

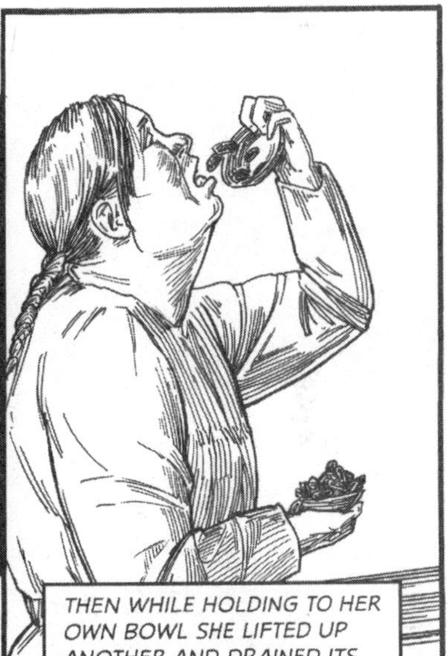
THEN WHILE HOLDING TO HER OWN BOWL SHE LIFTED UP ANOTHER AND DRAINED ITS CONTENTS AT ONE GULP.

PLACED CLOSE TOGETHER ALL ALONG THE TABLE WERE LARGE DRESSING BOWLS FILLED WITH A PINKISH-LOOKING STUFF WHICH THE PATIENTS CALLED TEA. BY EACH BOWL WAS LAID A PIECE OF BREAD, CUT THICK AND BUTTERED. A SMALL SAUCER CONTAINING FIVE PRUNES ACCOMPANIED THE BREAD. I WAS SO AMUSED AT HER SUCCESSFUL GRABBINGS THAT WHEN I LOOKED AT MY OWN SHARE THE WOMAN OPPOSITE, WITHOUT SO MUCH AS A BY YOUR LEAVE, GRABBED MY BREAD AND LEFT ME WITHOUT ANY.

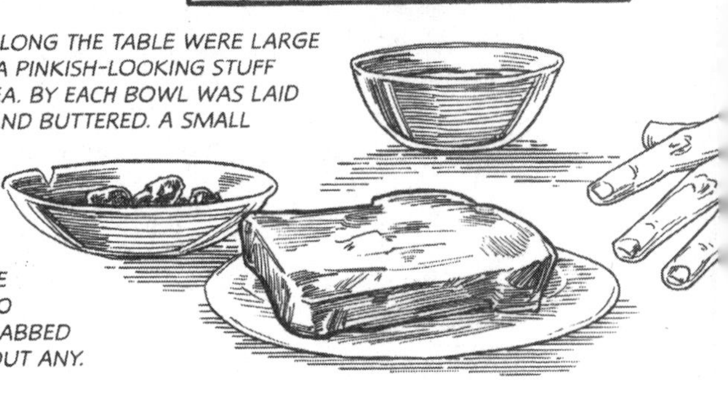

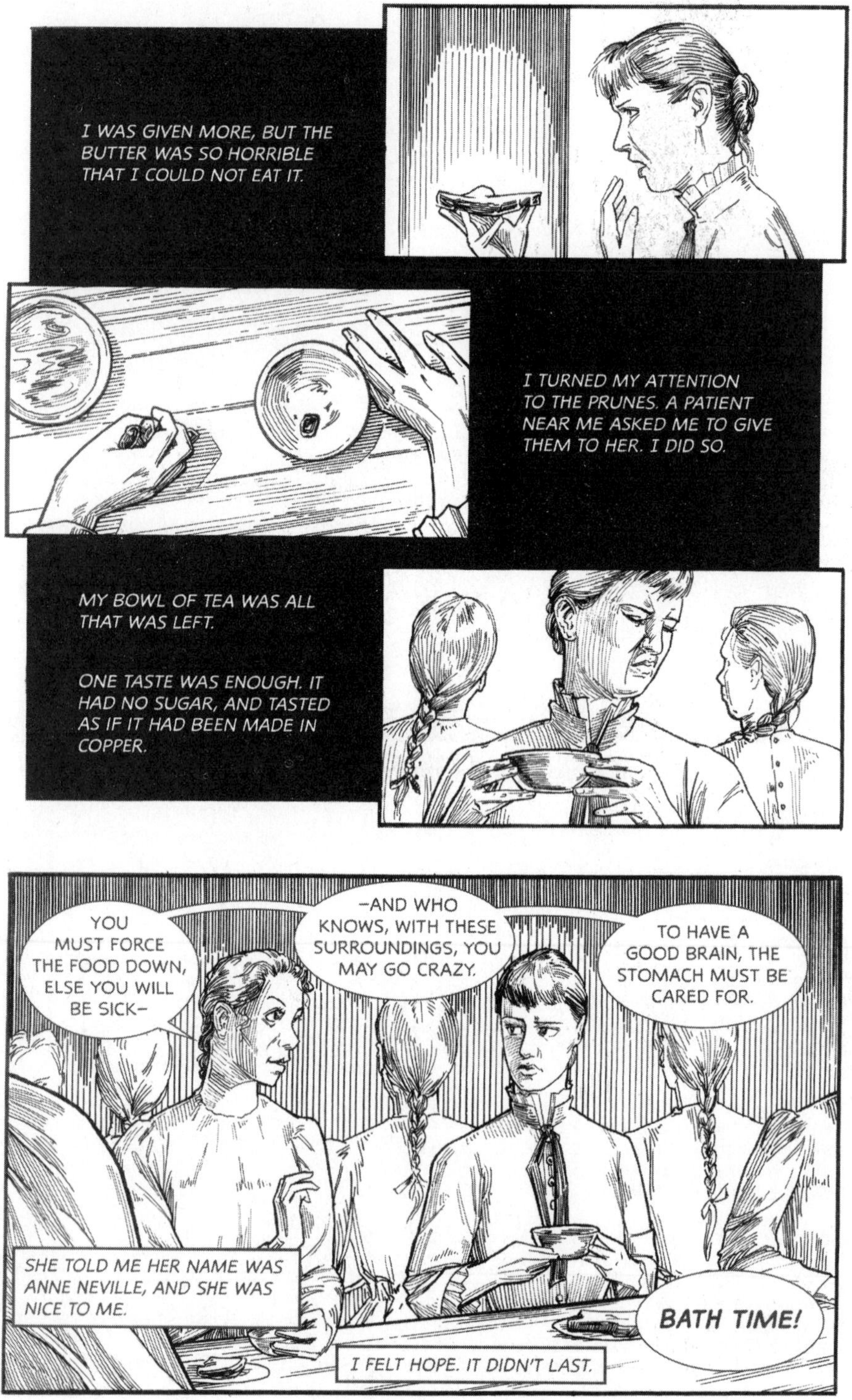
I WAS GIVEN MORE, BUT THE BUTTER WAS SO HORRIBLE THAT I COULD NOT EAT IT.
I TURNED MY ATTENTION TO THE PRUNES. A PATIENT NEAR ME ASKED ME TO GIVE THEM TO HER. I DID SO.
MY BOWL OF TEA WAS ALL THAT WAS LEFT.
ONE TASTE WAS ENOUGH. IT HAD NO SUGAR, AND TASTED AS IF IT HAD BEEN MADE IN COPPER.
YOU MUST FORCE THE FOOD DOWN, ELSE YOU WILL BE SICK–
–AND WHO KNOWS, WITH THESE SURROUNDINGS, YOU MAY GO CRAZY.
TO HAVE A GOOD BRAIN, THE STOMACH MUST BE CARED FOR.
SHE TOLD ME HER NAME WAS ANNE NEVILLE, AND SHE WAS NICE TO ME.
I FELT HOPE. IT DIDN'T LAST.
BATH TIME!

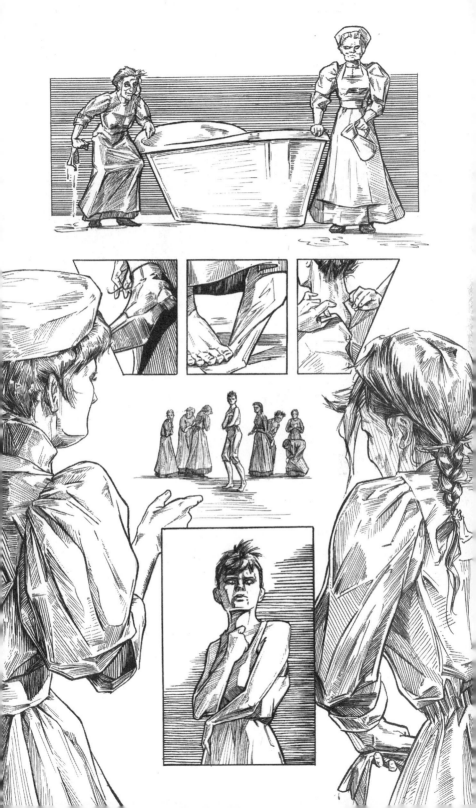

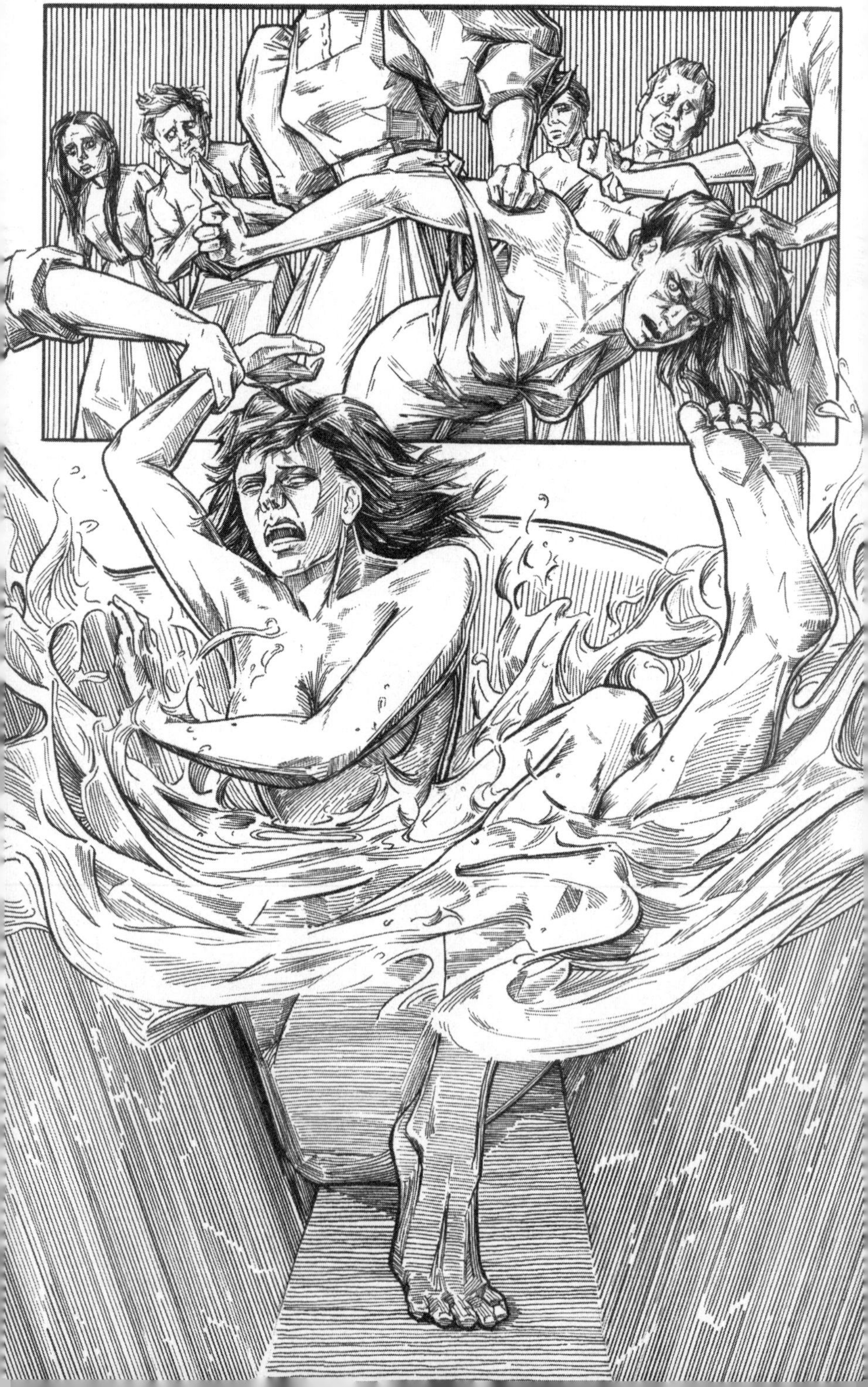

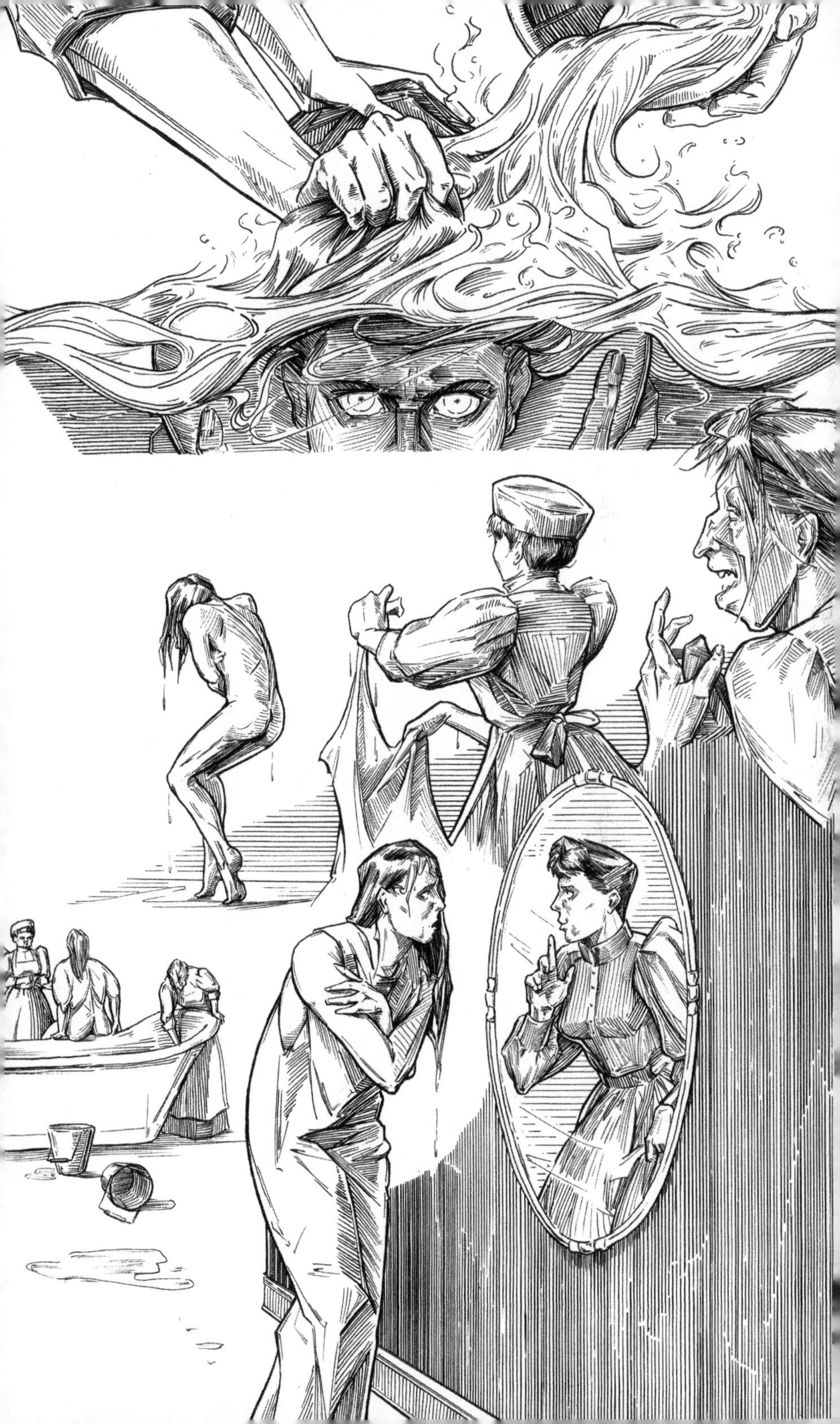

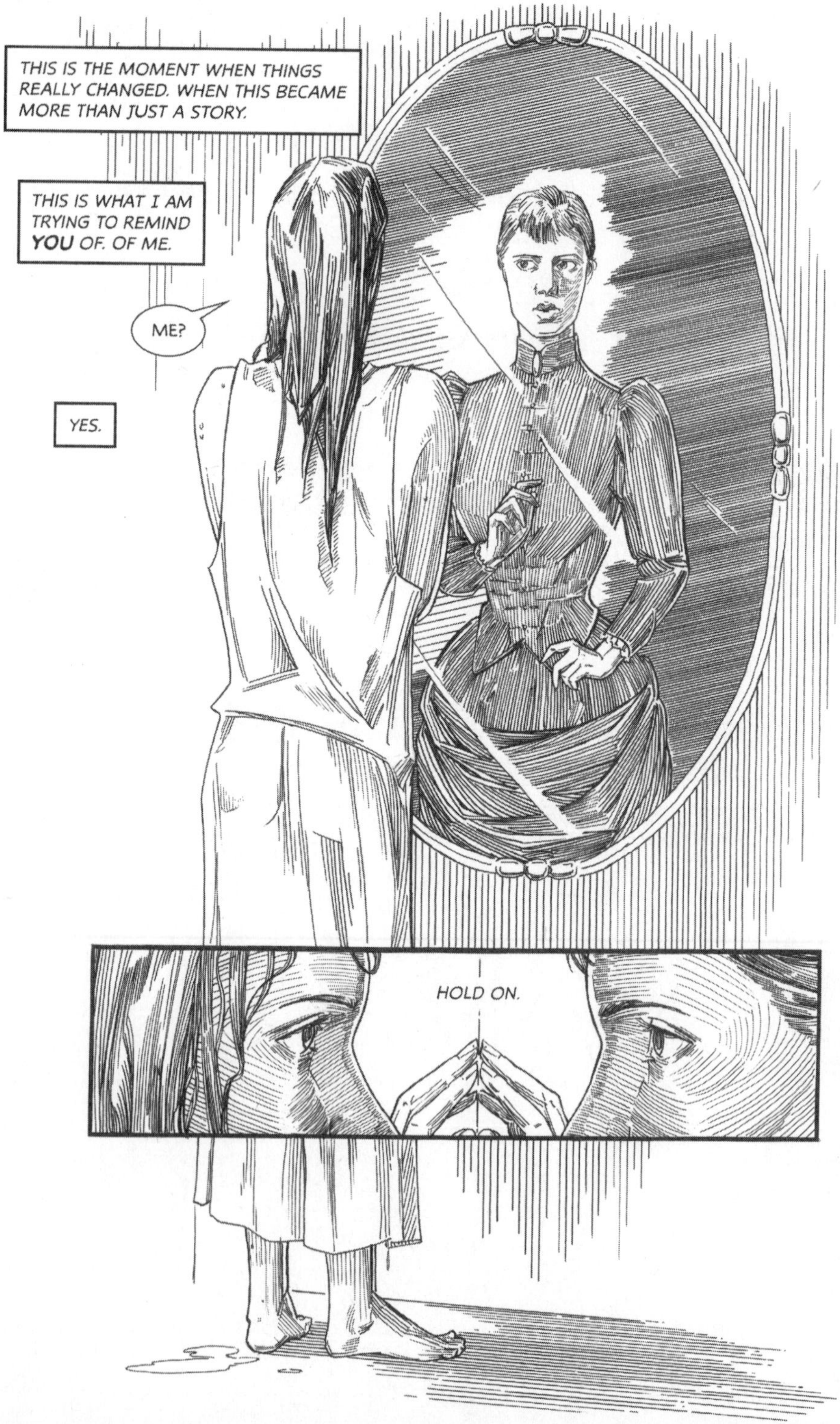
THIS IS THE MOMENT WHEN THINGS REALLY CHANGED. WHEN THIS BECAME MORE THAN JUST A STORY.
THIS IS WHAT I AM TRYING TO REMIND YOU OF. OF ME.
ME?
YES.
HOLD ON.

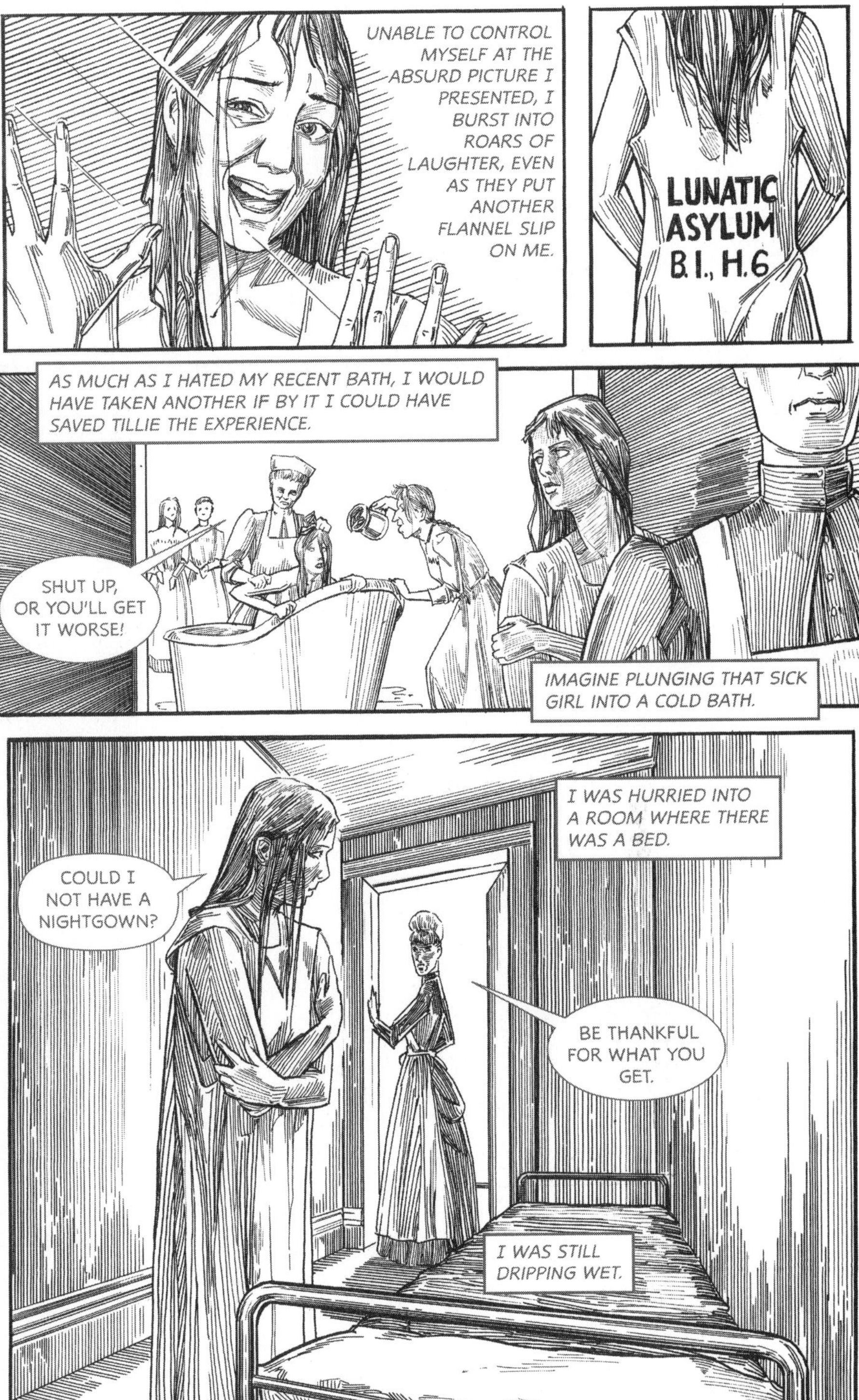
UNABLE TO CONTROL MYSELF AT THE ABSURD PICTURE I PRESENTED, I BURST INTO ROARS OF LAUGHTER, EVEN AS THEY PUT ANOTHER FLANNEL SLIP ON ME.
LUNATIC ASYLUM B.I., H.6
AS MUCH AS I HATED MY RECENT BATH, I WOULD HAVE TAKEN ANOTHER IF BY IT I COULD HAVE SAVED TILLIE THE EXPERIENCE.
SHUT UP, OR YOU'LL GET IT WORSE!
IMAGINE PLUNGING THAT SICK GIRL INTO A COLD BATH.
I WAS HURRIED INTO A ROOM WHERE THERE WAS A BED.
COULD I NOT HAVE A NIGHTGOWN?
BE THANKFUL FOR WHAT YOU GET.
I WAS STILL DRIPPING WET.

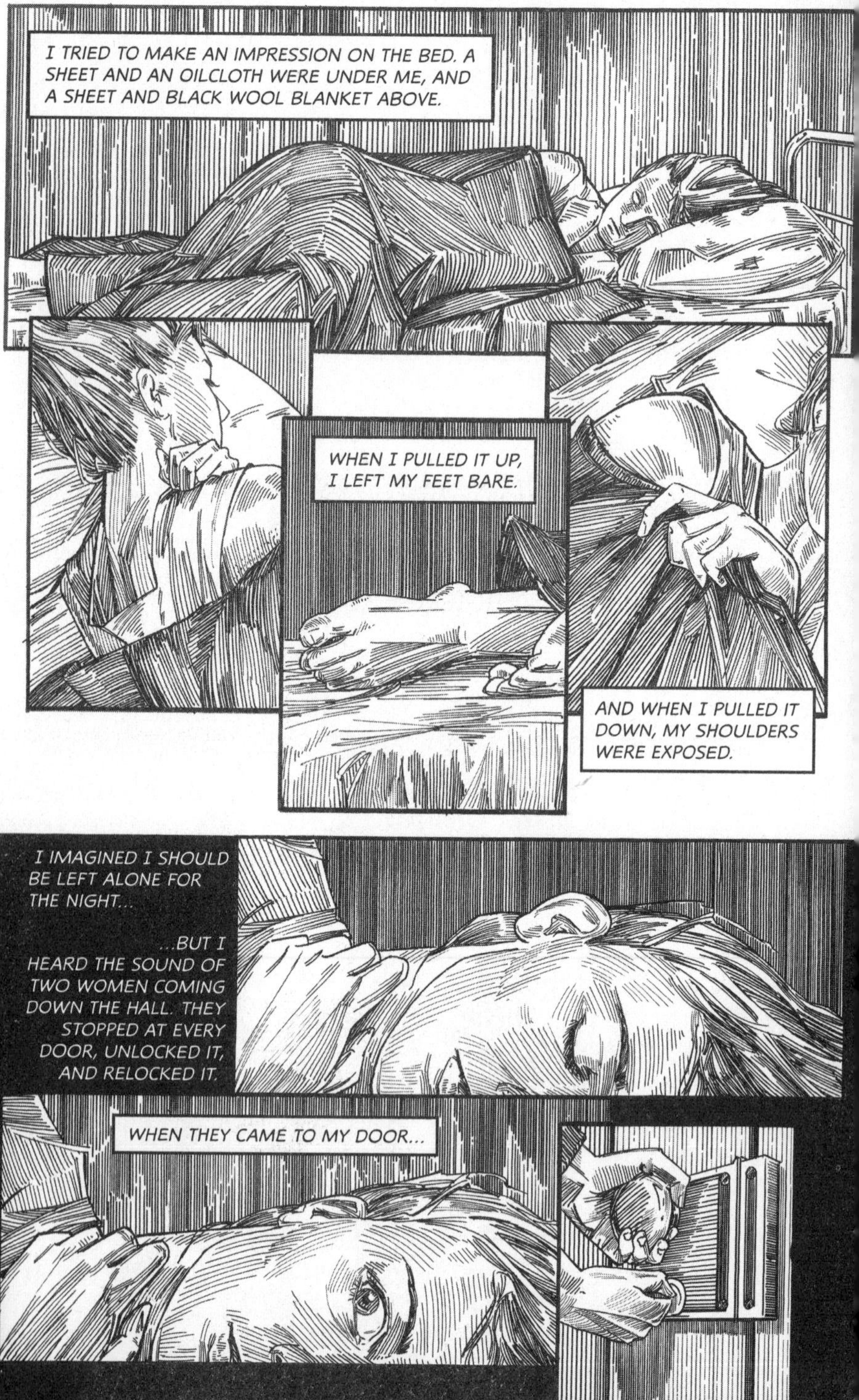
I TRIED TO MAKE AN IMPRESSION ON THE BED. A SHEET AND AN OILCLOTH WERE UNDER ME, AND A SHEET AND BLACK WOOL BLANKET ABOVE.
WHEN I PULLED IT UP, I LEFT MY FEET BARE.
AND WHEN I PULLED IT DOWN, MY SHOULDERS WERE EXPOSED.
I IMAGINED I SHOULD BE LEFT ALONE FOR THE NIGHT...
...BUT I HEARD THE SOUND OF TWO WOMEN COMING DOWN THE HALL. THEY STOPPED AT EVERY DOOR, UNLOCKED IT, AND RELOCKED IT.
WHEN THEY CAME TO MY DOOR...

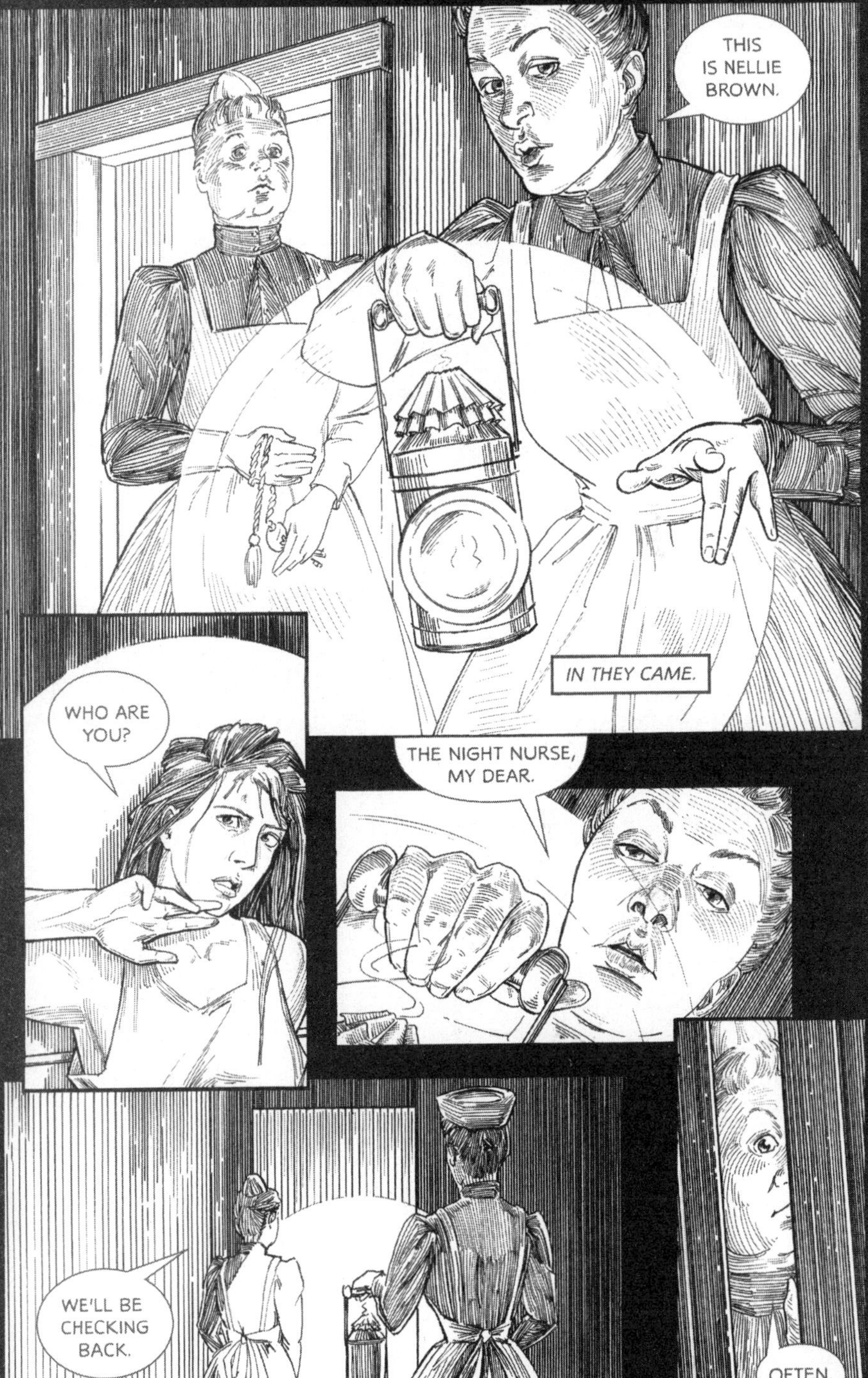
THIS IS NELLIE BROWN.
IN THEY CAME.
WHO ARE YOU?
THE NIGHT NURSE, MY DEAR.
WE'LL BE CHECKING BACK.
OFTEN.

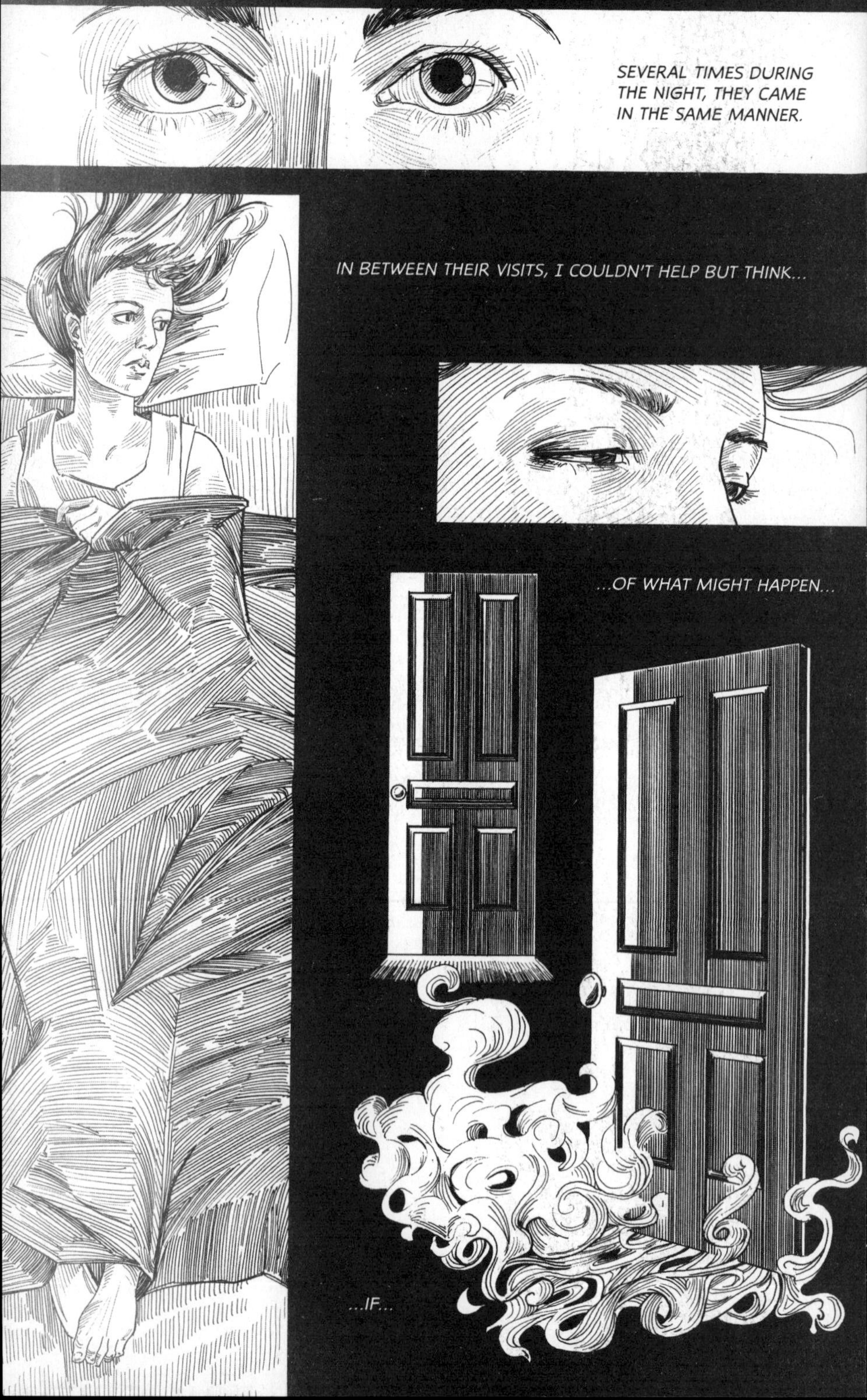
SEVERAL TIMES DURING THE NIGHT, THEY CAME IN THE SAME MANNER.
IN BETWEEN THEIR VISITS, I COULDN'T HELP BUT THINK...
...OF WHAT MIGHT HAPPEN...
...IF...

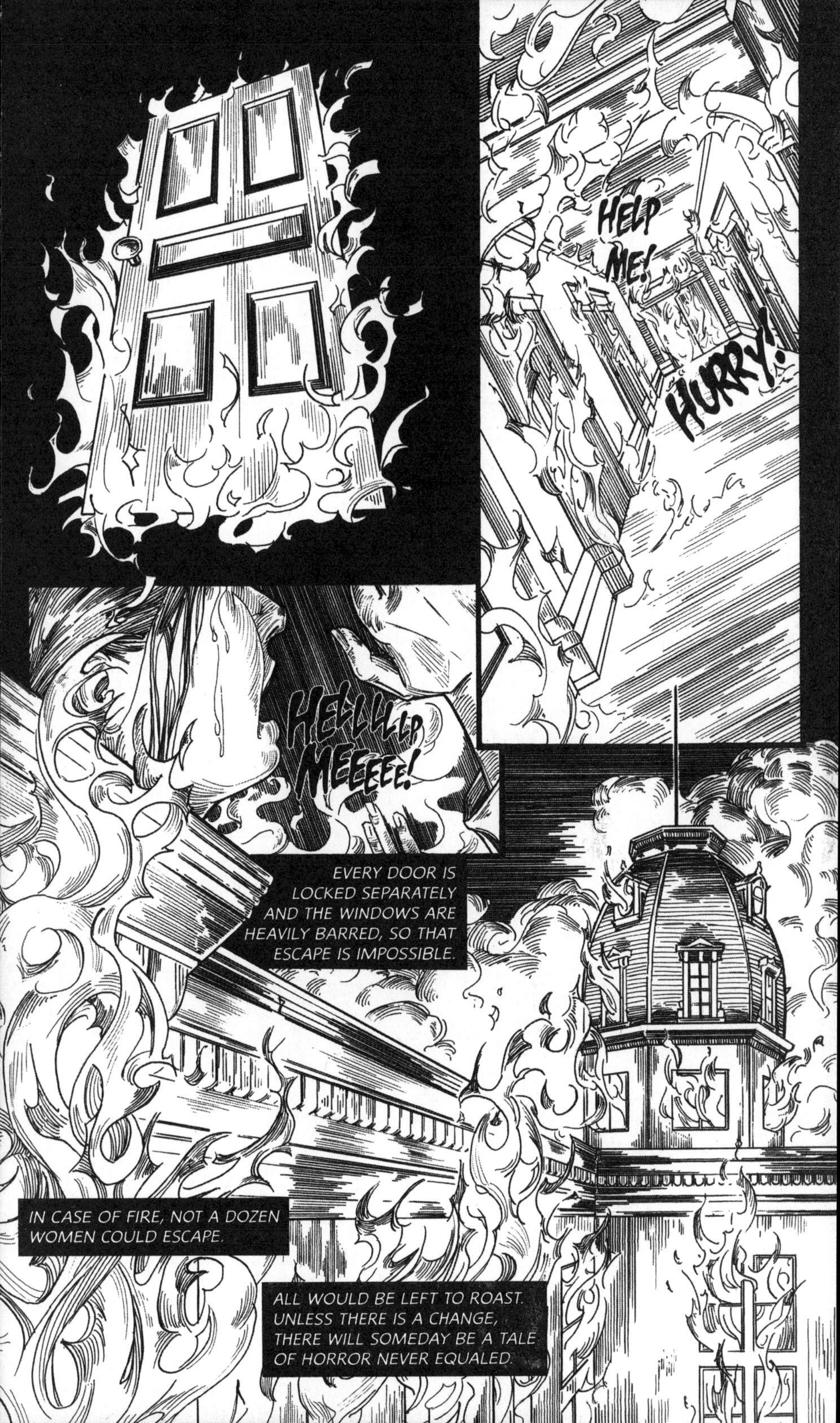
HELP ME!
HURRY!
HELLLLP MEEEEE!
EVERY DOOR IS LOCKED SEPARATELY AND THE WINDOWS ARE HEAVILY BARRED, SO THAT ESCAPE IS IMPOSSIBLE.
IN CASE OF FIRE, NOT A DOZEN WOMEN COULD ESCAPE.
ALL WOULD BE LEFT TO ROAST. UNLESS THERE IS A CHANGE, THERE WILL SOMEDAY BE A TALE OF HORROR NEVER EQUALED.

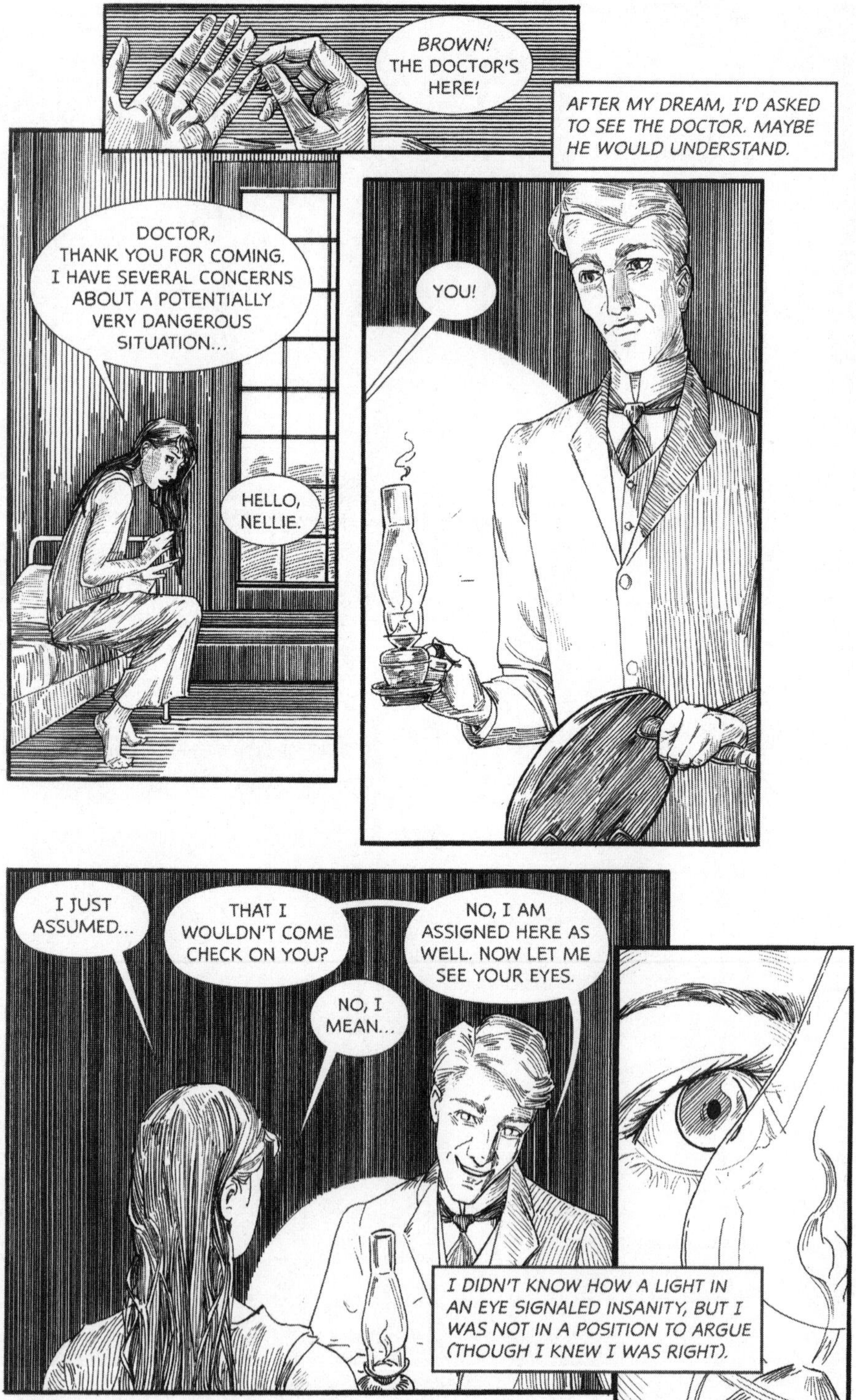
BROWN! THE DOCTOR'S HERE!
AFTER MY DREAM, I'D ASKED TO SEE THE DOCTOR. MAYBE HE WOULD UNDERSTAND.
DOCTOR, THANK YOU FOR COMING. I HAVE SEVERAL CONCERNS ABOUT A POTENTIALLY VERY DANGEROUS SITUATION...
HELLO, NELLIE.
YOU!
I JUST ASSUMED...
THAT I WOULDN'T COME CHECK ON YOU?
NO, I MEAN...
NO, I AM ASSIGNED HERE AS WELL. NOW LET ME SEE YOUR EYES.
I DIDN'T KNOW HOW A LIGHT IN AN EYE SIGNALED INSANITY, BUT I WAS NOT IN A POSITION TO ARGUE (THOUGH I KNEW I WAS RIGHT).

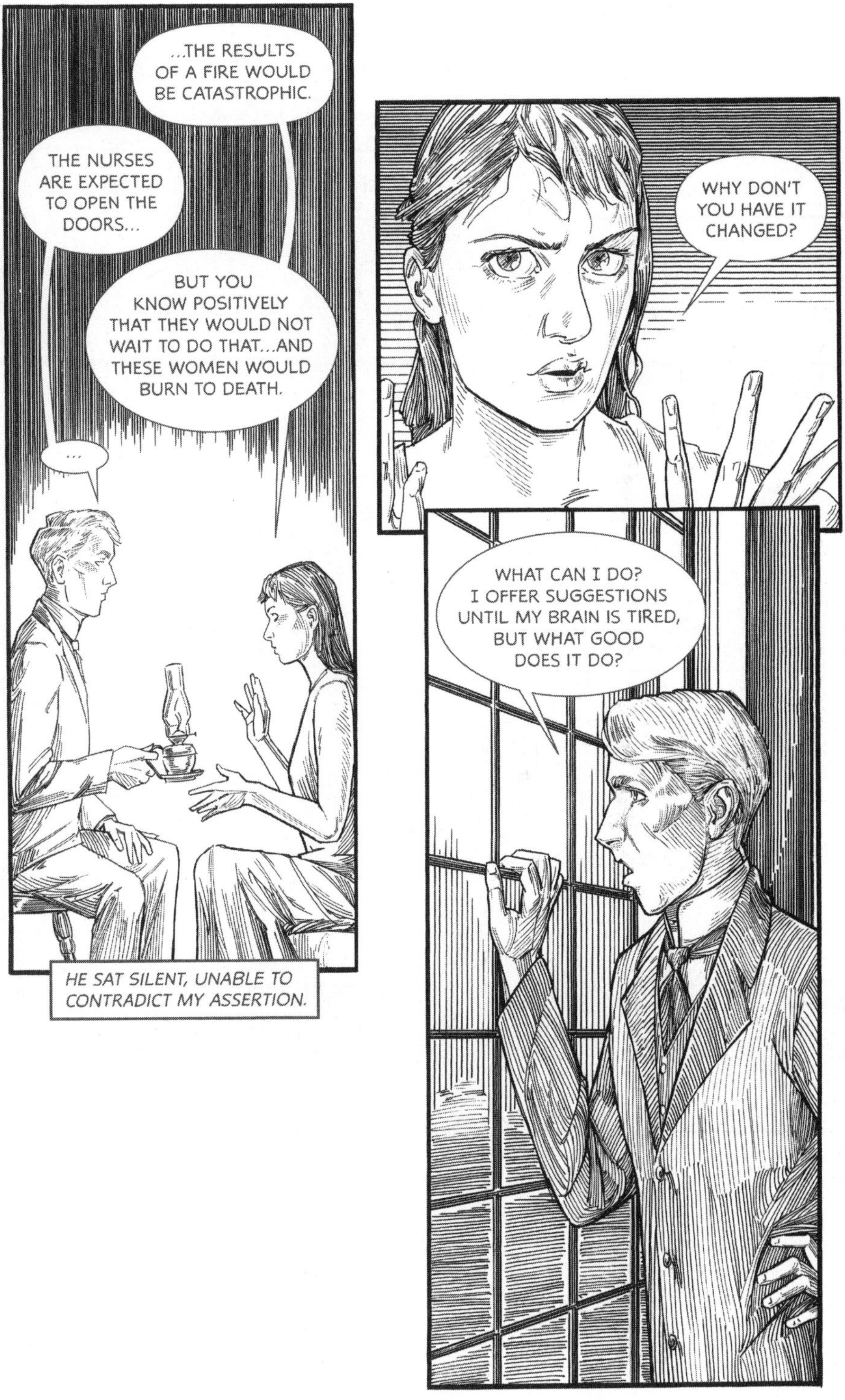
...THE RESULTS OF A FIRE WOULD BE CATASTROPHIC.
THE NURSES ARE EXPECTED TO OPEN THE DOORS...
BUT YOU KNOW POSITIVELY THAT THEY WOULD NOT WAIT TO DO THAT...AND THESE WOMEN WOULD BURN TO DEATH.
...
HE SAT SILENT, UNABLE TO CONTRADICT MY ASSERTION.
WHY DON'T YOU HAVE IT CHANGED?
WHAT CAN I DO? I OFFER SUGGESTIONS UNTIL MY BRAIN IS TIRED, BUT WHAT GOOD DOES IT DO?

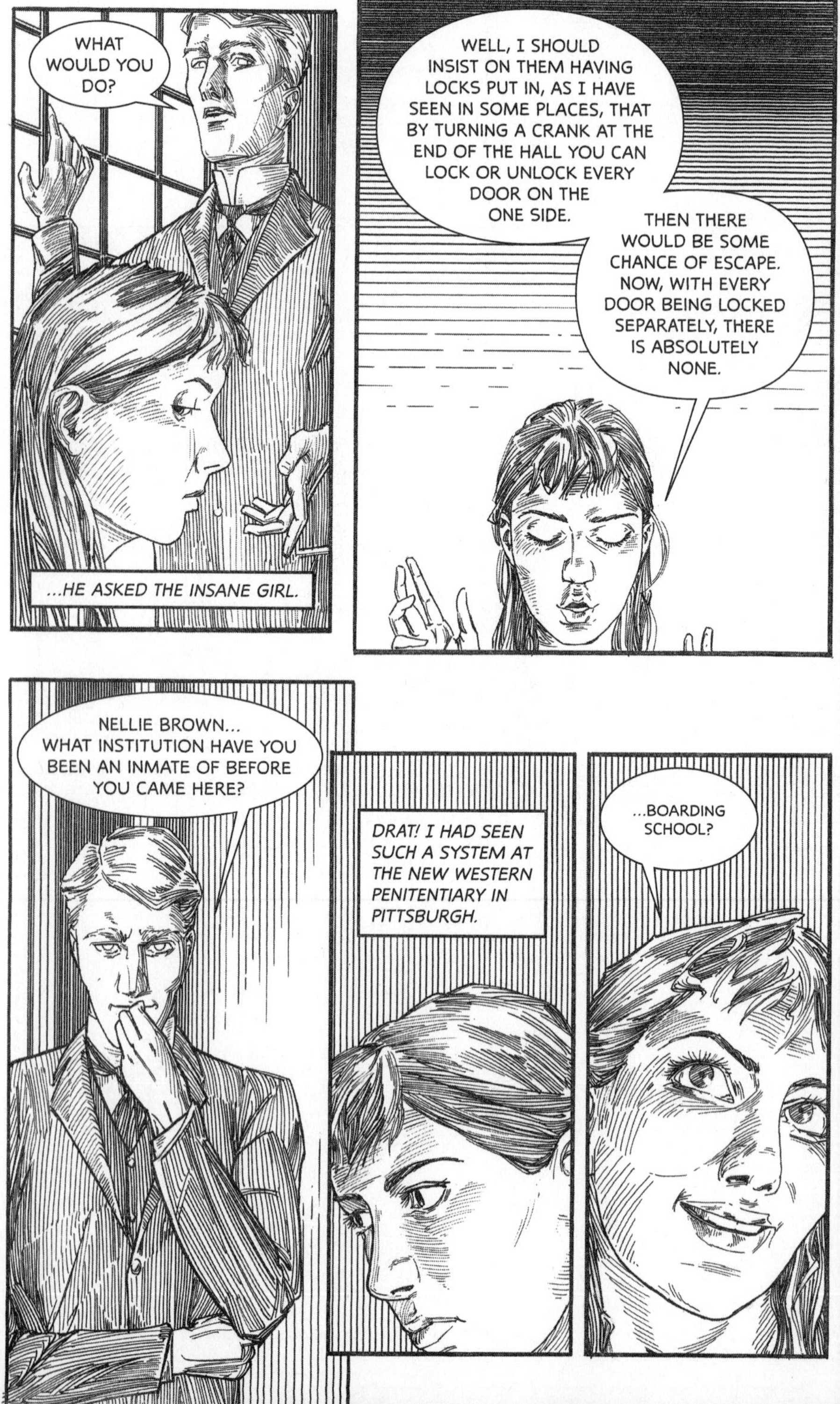
WHAT WOULD YOU DO?
...HE ASKED THE INSANE GIRL.
WELL, I SHOULD INSIST ON THEM HAVING LOCKS PUT IN, AS I HAVE SEEN IN SOME PLACES, THAT BY TURNING A CRANK AT THE END OF THE HALL YOU CAN LOCK OR UNLOCK EVERY DOOR ON THE ONE SIDE.
THEN THERE WOULD BE SOME CHANCE OF ESCAPE. NOW, WITH EVERY DOOR BEING LOCKED SEPARATELY, THERE IS ABSOLUTELY NONE.
NELLIE BROWN... WHAT INSTITUTION HAVE YOU BEEN AN INMATE OF BEFORE YOU CAME HERE?
DRAT! I HAD SEEN SUCH A SYSTEM AT THE NEW WESTERN PENITENTIARY IN PITTSBURGH.
...BOARDING SCHOOL?

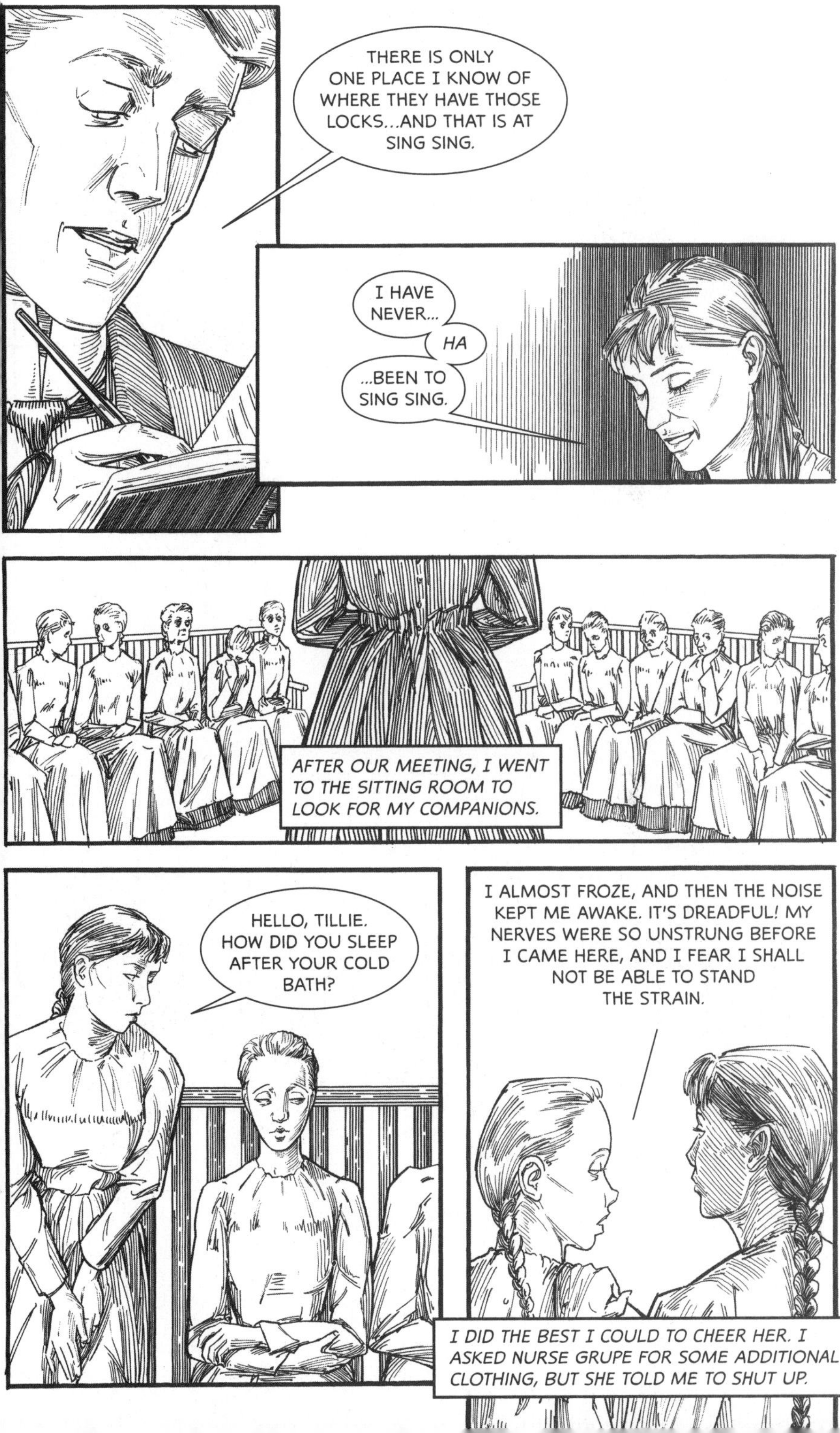
THERE IS ONLY ONE PLACE I KNOW OF WHERE THEY HAVE THOSE LOCKS...AND THAT IS AT SING SING.
I HAVE NEVER...
HA
...BEEN TO SING SING.
AFTER OUR MEETING, I WENT TO THE SITTING ROOM TO LOOK FOR MY COMPANIONS.
HELLO, TILLIE. HOW DID YOU SLEEP AFTER YOUR COLD BATH?
I ALMOST FROZE, AND THEN THE NOISE KEPT ME AWAKE. IT'S DREADFUL! MY NERVES WERE SO UNSTRUNG BEFORE I CAME HERE, AND I FEAR I SHALL NOT BE ABLE TO STAND THE STRAIN.
I DID THE BEST I COULD TO CHEER HER. I ASKED NURSE GRUPE FOR SOME ADDITIONAL CLOTHING, BUT SHE TOLD ME TO SHUT UP.

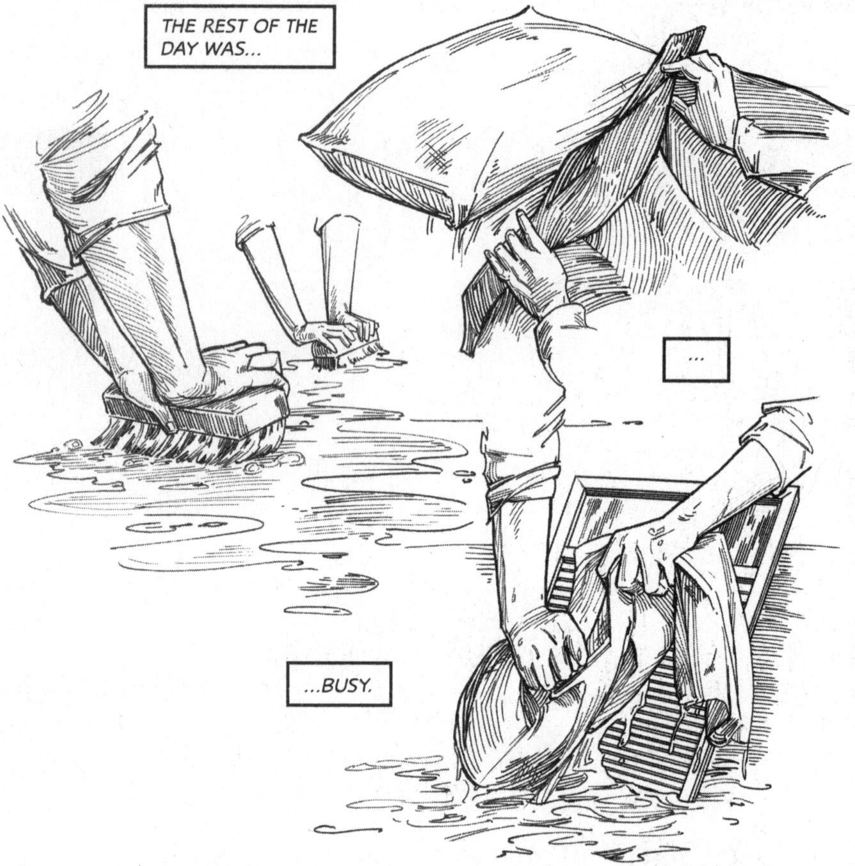
THE REST OF THE DAY WAS...
...
...BUSY.

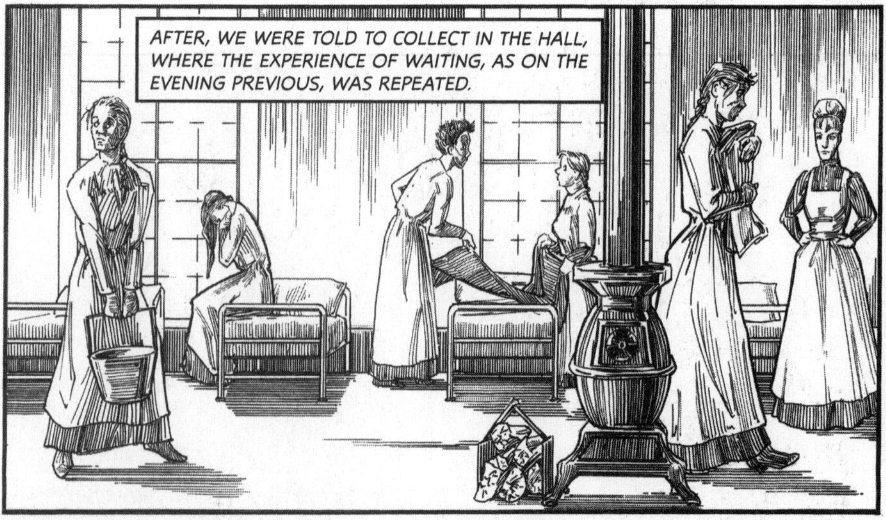
AFTER, WE WERE TOLD TO COLLECT IN THE HALL, WHERE THE EXPERIENCE OF WAITING, AS ON THE EVENING PREVIOUS, WAS REPEATED.

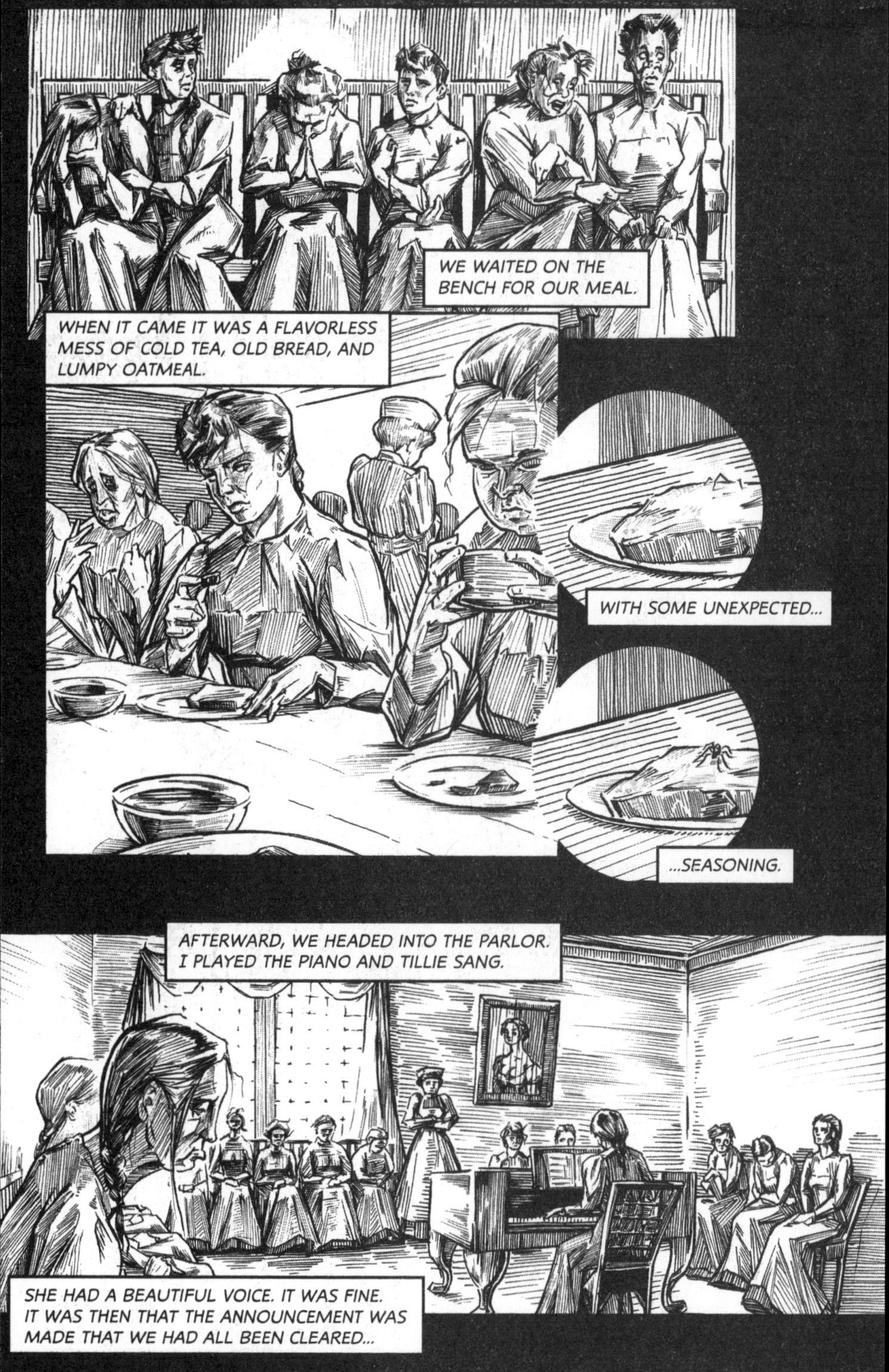
WE WAITED ON THE BENCH FOR OUR MEAL.
WHEN IT CAME IT WAS A FLAVORLESS MESS OF COLD TEA, OLD BREAD, AND LUMPY OATMEAL.
WITH SOME UNEXPECTED...
...SEASONING.
AFTERWARD, WE HEADED INTO THE PARLOR. I PLAYED THE PIANO AND TILLIE SANG.
SHE HAD A BEAUTIFUL VOICE. IT WAS FINE. IT WAS THEN THAT THE ANNOUNCEMENT WAS MADE THAT WE HAD ALL BEEN CLEARED...

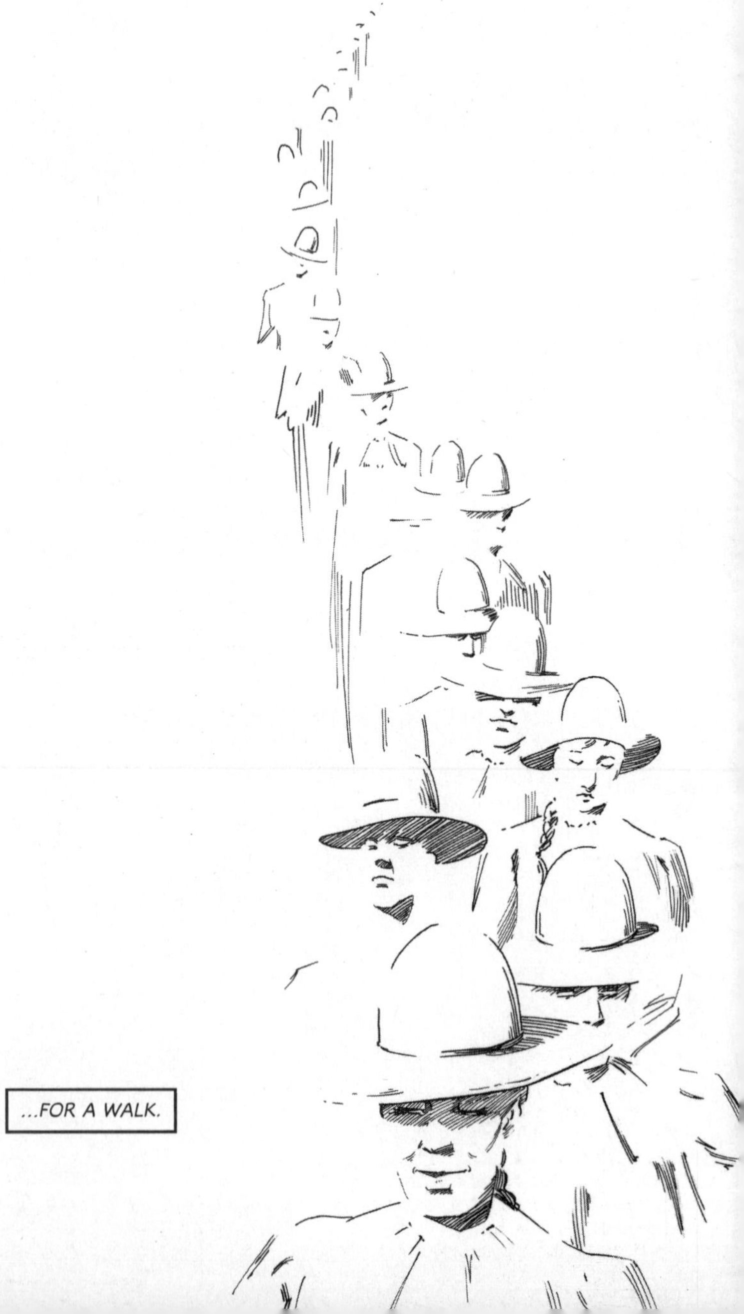
...FOR A WALK.

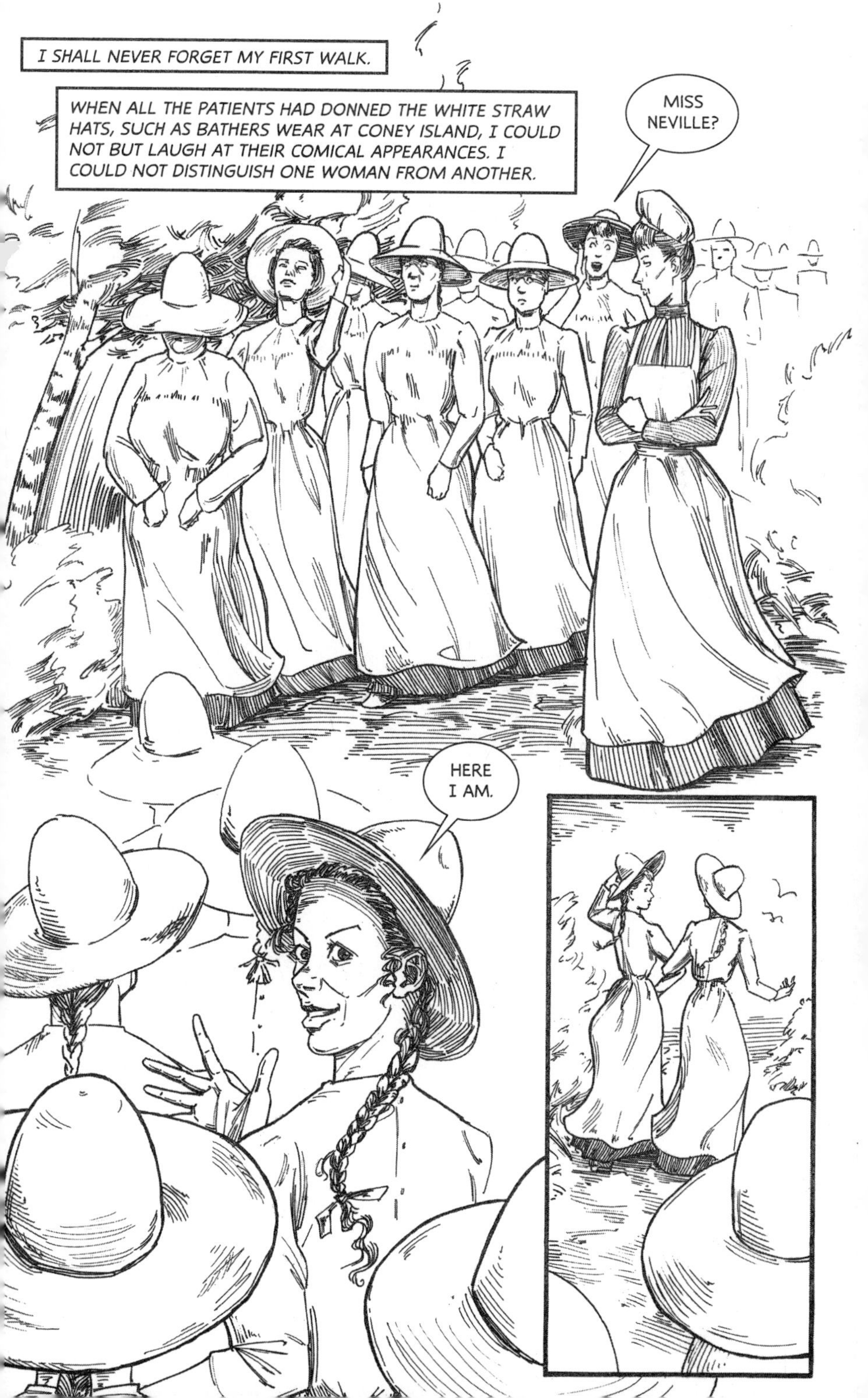
I SHALL NEVER FORGET MY FIRST WALK.
WHEN ALL THE PATIENTS HAD DONNED THE WHITE STRAW HATS, SUCH AS BATHERS WEAR AT CONEY ISLAND, I COULD NOT BUT LAUGH AT THEIR COMICAL APPEARANCES. I COULD NOT DISTINGUISH ONE WOMAN FROM ANOTHER.
MISS NEVILLE?
HERE I AM.

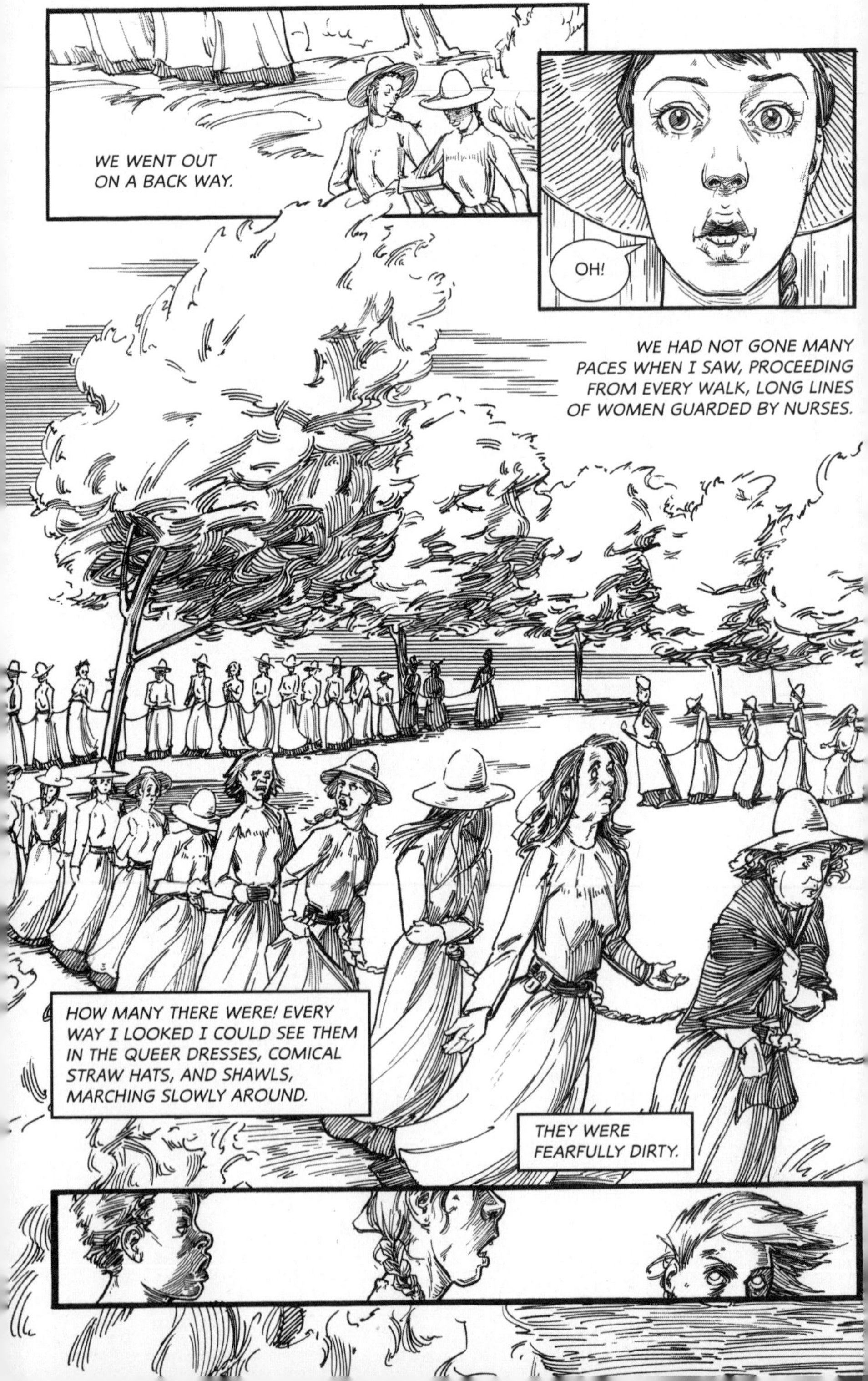
WE WENT OUT ON A BACK WAY.
OH!
WE HAD NOT GONE MANY PACES WHEN I SAW, PROCEEDING FROM EVERY WALK, LONG LINES OF WOMEN GUARDED BY NURSES.
HOW MANY THERE WERE! EVERY WAY I LOOKED I COULD SEE THEM IN THE QUEER DRESSES, COMICAL STRAW HATS, AND SHAWLS, MARCHING SLOWLY AROUND.
THEY WERE FEARFULLY DIRTY.

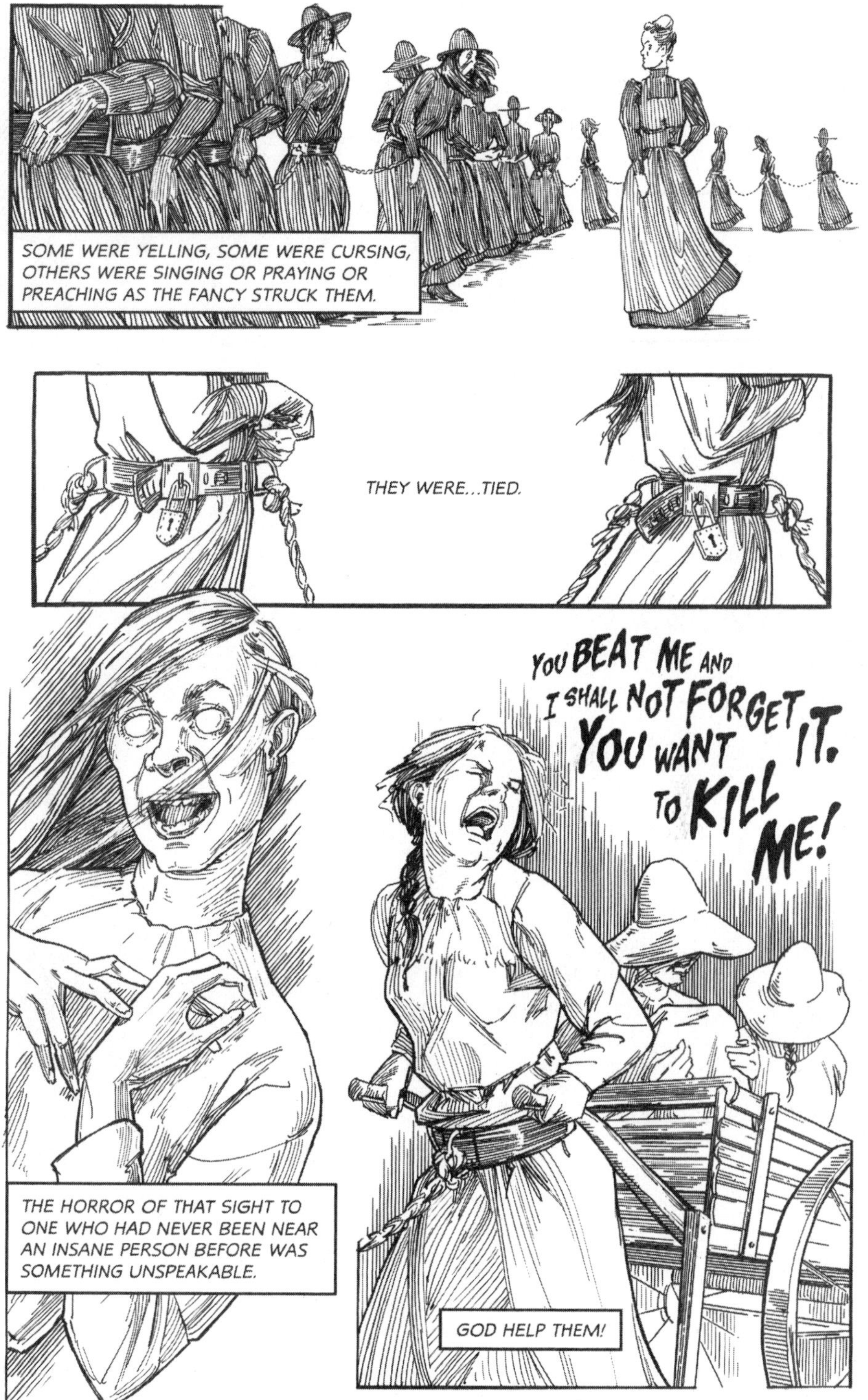
SOME WERE YELLING, SOME WERE CURSING, OTHERS WERE SINGING OR PRAYING OR PREACHING AS THE FANCY STRUCK THEM.
THEY WERE...TIED.
THE HORROR OF THAT SIGHT TO ONE WHO HAD NEVER BEEN NEAR AN INSANE PERSON BEFORE WAS SOMETHING UNSPEAKABLE.
YOU BEAT ME AND I SHALL NOT FORGET IT. YOU WANT TO KILL ME!
GOD HELP THEM!

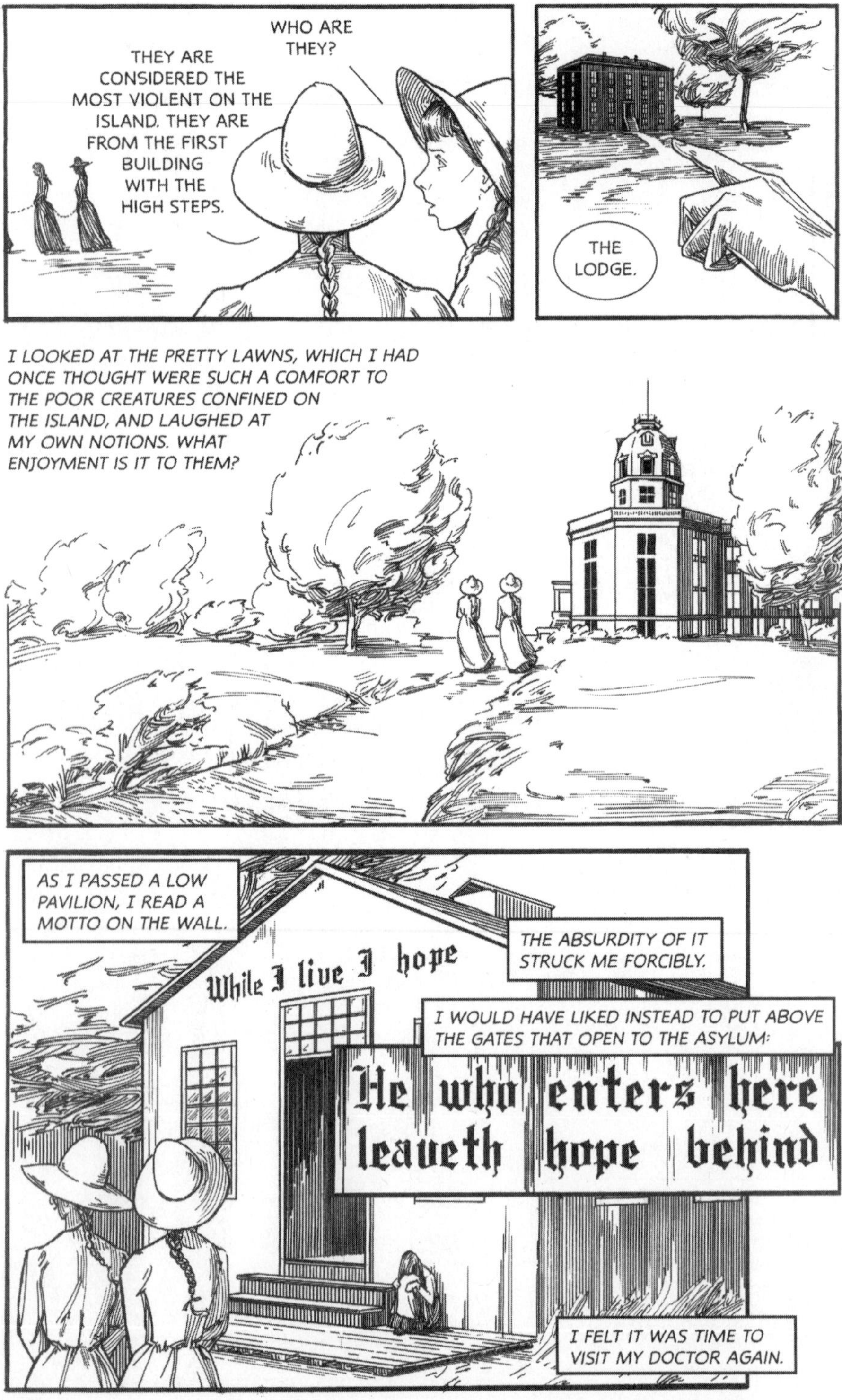
WHO ARE THEY?
THEY ARE CONSIDERED THE MOST VIOLENT ON THE ISLAND. THEY ARE FROM THE FIRST BUILDING WITH THE HIGH STEPS.
THE LODGE.
I LOOKED AT THE PRETTY LAWNS, WHICH I HAD ONCE THOUGHT WERE SUCH A COMFORT TO THE POOR CREATURES CONFINED ON THE ISLAND, AND LAUGHED AT MY OWN NOTIONS. WHAT ENJOYMENT IS IT TO THEM?
AS I PASSED A LOW PAVILION, I READ A MOTTO ON THE WALL.
While I live I hope
THE ABSURDITY OF IT STRUCK ME FORCIBLY.
I WOULD HAVE LIKED INSTEAD TO PUT ABOVE THE GATES THAT OPEN TO THE ASYLUM:
He who enters here leaveth hope behind
I FELT IT WAS TIME TO VISIT MY DOCTOR AGAIN.

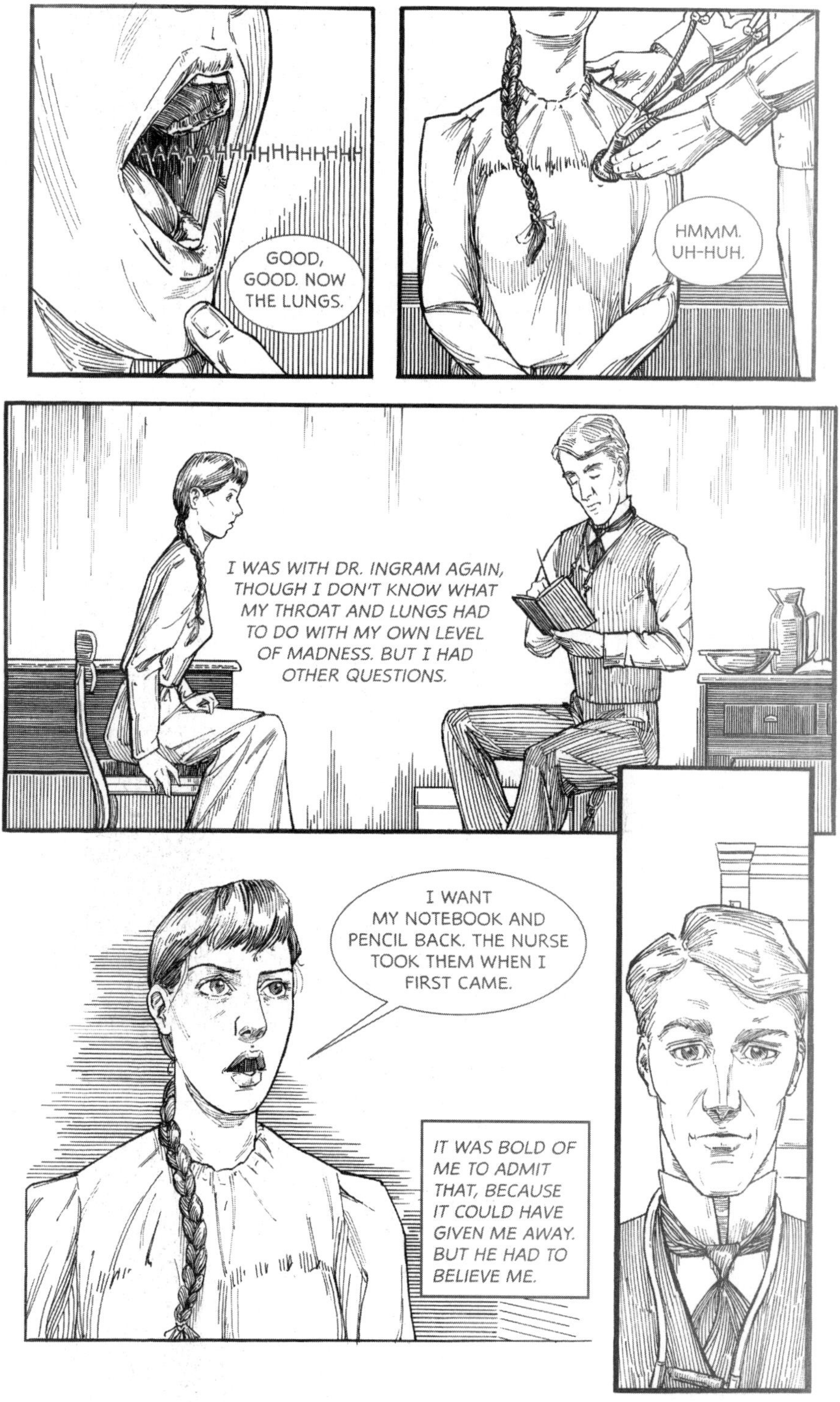
AAAAAAHHHHHHHHHHH
GOOD, GOOD. NOW THE LUNGS.
HMMM. UH-HUH.
I WAS WITH DR. INGRAM AGAIN, THOUGH I DON'T KNOW WHAT MY THROAT AND LUNGS HAD TO DO WITH MY OWN LEVEL OF MADNESS. BUT I HAD OTHER QUESTIONS.
I WANT MY NOTEBOOK AND PENCIL BACK. THE NURSE TOOK THEM WHEN I FIRST CAME.
IT WAS BOLD OF ME TO ADMIT THAT, BECAUSE IT COULD HAVE GIVEN ME AWAY. BUT HE HAD TO BELIEVE ME.

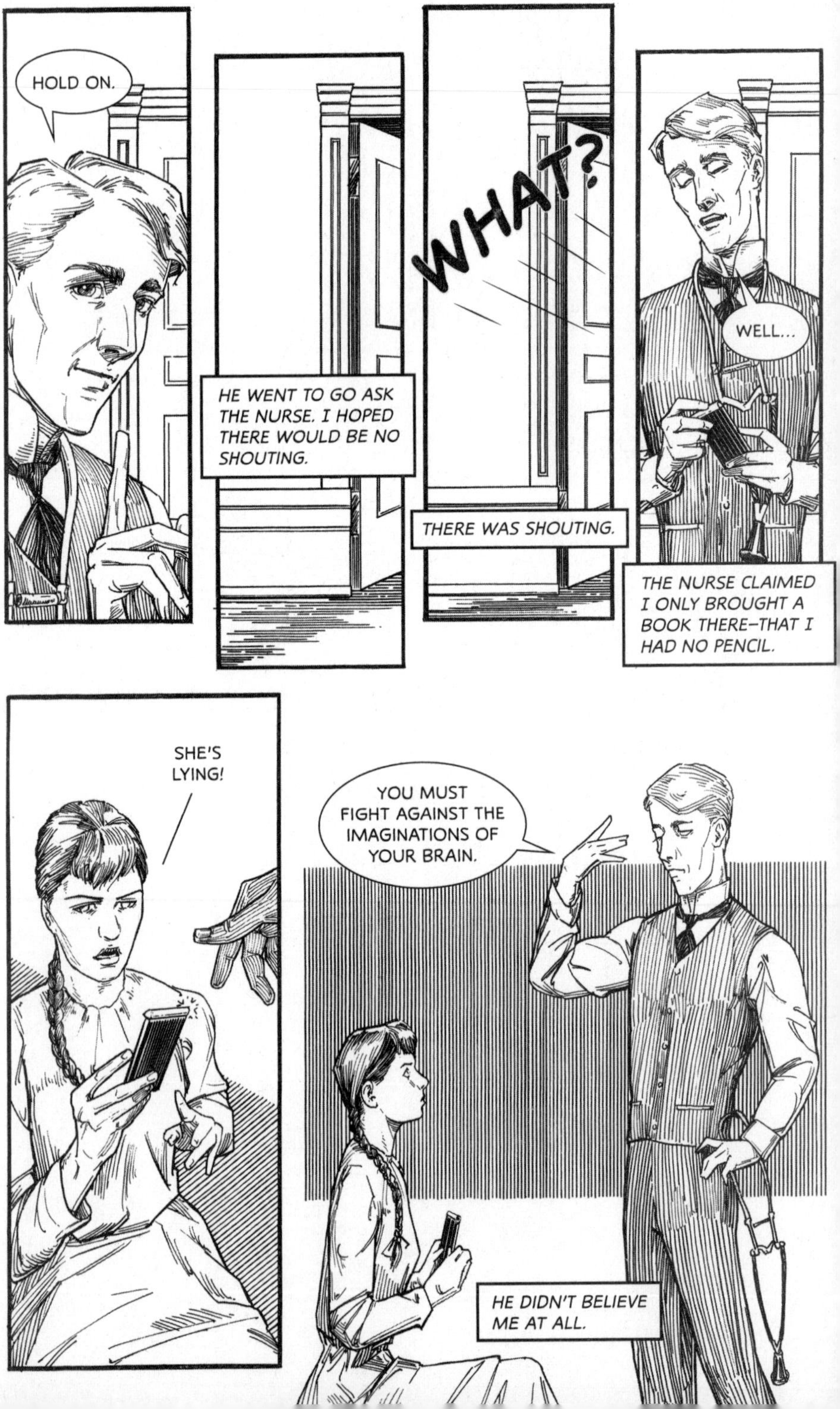
HOLD ON.
HE WENT TO GO ASK THE NURSE. I HOPED THERE WOULD BE NO SHOUTING.
WHAT?
THERE WAS SHOUTING.
WELL...
THE NURSE CLAIMED I ONLY BROUGHT A BOOK THERE—THAT I HAD NO PENCIL.
SHE'S LYING!
YOU MUST FIGHT AGAINST THE IMAGINATIONS OF YOUR BRAIN.
HE DIDN'T BELIEVE ME AT ALL.

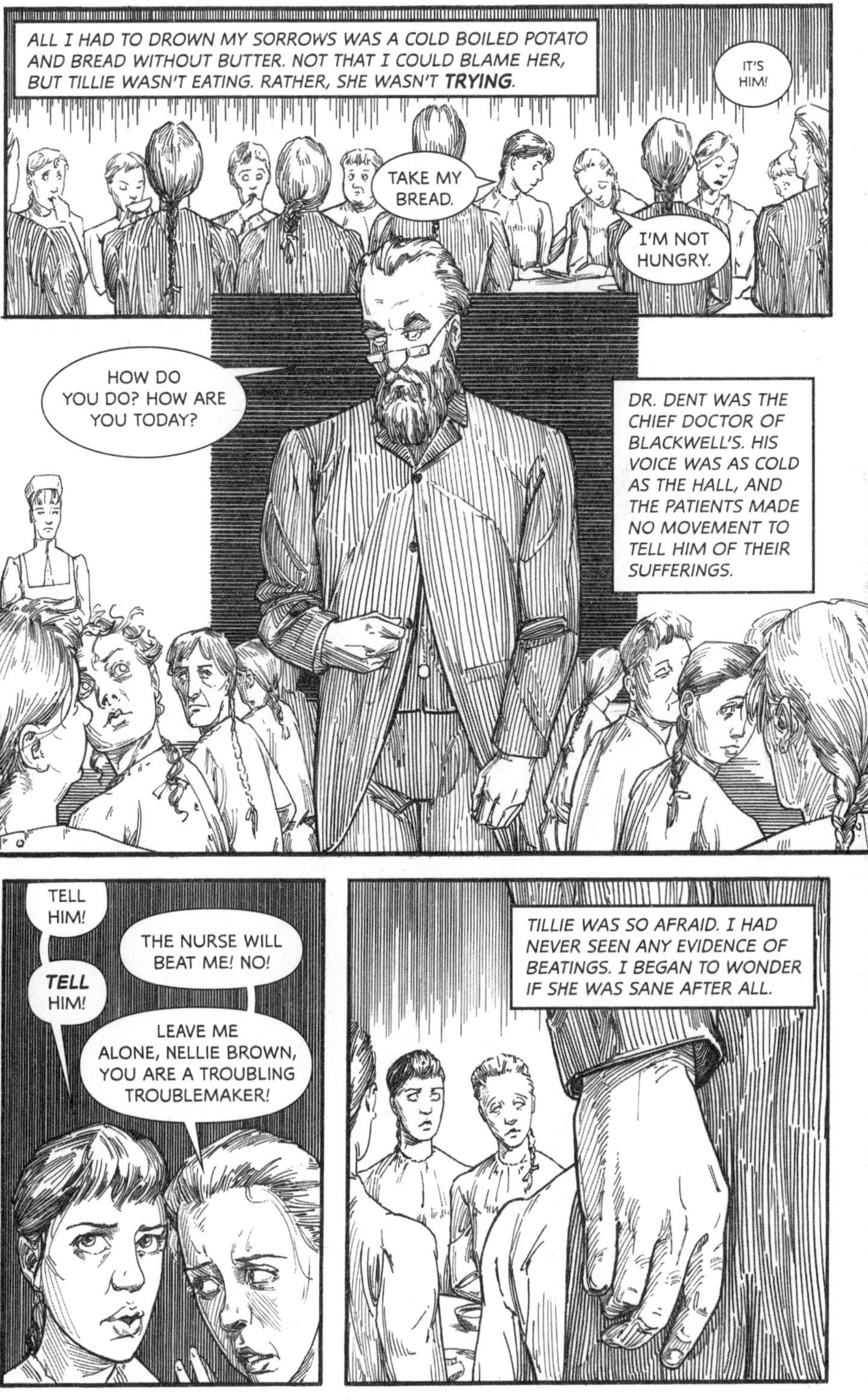
ALL I HAD TO DROWN MY SORROWS WAS A COLD BOILED POTATO AND BREAD WITHOUT BUTTER. NOT THAT I COULD BLAME HER, BUT TILLIE WASN'T EATING. RATHER, SHE WASN'T TRYING.
IT'S HIM!
TAKE MY BREAD.
I'M NOT HUNGRY.
HOW DO YOU DO? HOW ARE YOU TODAY?
DR. DENT WAS THE CHIEF DOCTOR OF BLACKWELL'S. HIS VOICE WAS AS COLD AS THE HALL, AND THE PATIENTS MADE NO MOVEMENT TO TELL HIM OF THEIR SUFFERINGS.
TELL HIM!
THE NURSE WILL BEAT ME! NO!
TELL HIM!
LEAVE ME ALONE, NELLIE BROWN, YOU ARE A TROUBLING TROUBLEMAKER!
TILLIE WAS SO AFRAID. I HAD NEVER SEEN ANY EVIDENCE OF BEATINGS. I BEGAN TO WONDER IF SHE WAS SANE AFTER ALL.

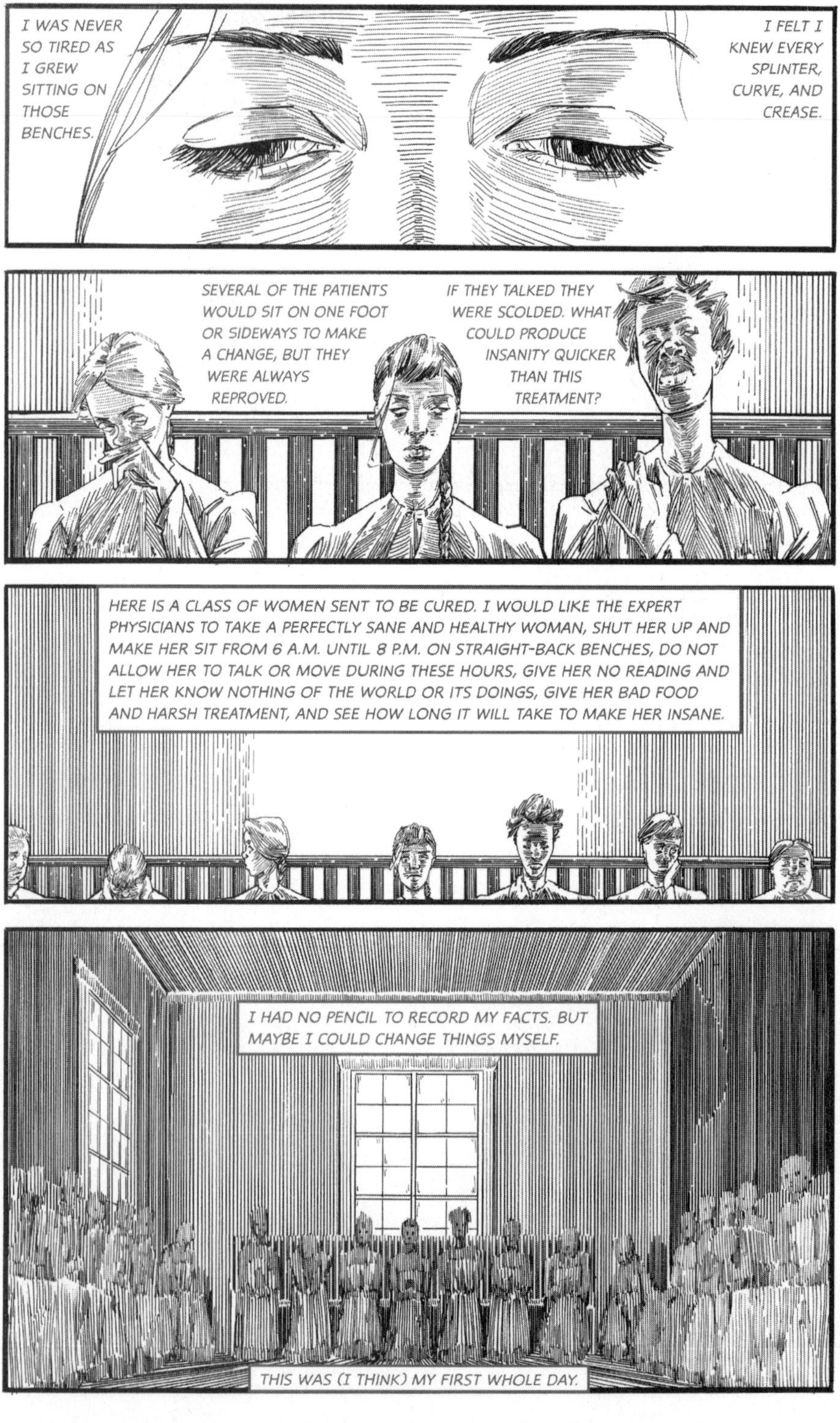
I WAS NEVER SO TIRED AS I GREW SITTING ON THOSE BENCHES.
I FELT I KNEW EVERY SPLINTER, CURVE, AND CREASE.
SEVERAL OF THE PATIENTS WOULD SIT ON ONE FOOT OR SIDEWAYS TO MAKE A CHANGE, BUT THEY WERE ALWAYS REPROVED.
IF THEY TALKED THEY WERE SCOLDED. WHAT COULD PRODUCE INSANITY QUICKER THAN THIS TREATMENT?
HERE IS A CLASS OF WOMEN SENT TO BE CURED. I WOULD LIKE THE EXPERT PHYSICIANS TO TAKE A PERFECTLY SANE AND HEALTHY WOMAN, SHUT HER UP AND MAKE HER SIT FROM 6 A.M. UNTIL 8 P.M. ON STRAIGHT-BACK BENCHES, DO NOT ALLOW HER TO TALK OR MOVE DURING THESE HOURS, GIVE HER NO READING AND LET HER KNOW NOTHING OF THE WORLD OR ITS DOINGS, GIVE HER BAD FOOD AND HARSH TREATMENT, AND SEE HOW LONG IT WILL TAKE TO MAKE HER INSANE.
I HAD NO PENCIL TO RECORD MY FACTS. BUT MAYBE I COULD CHANGE THINGS MYSELF.
THIS WAS (I THINK) MY FIRST WHOLE DAY.

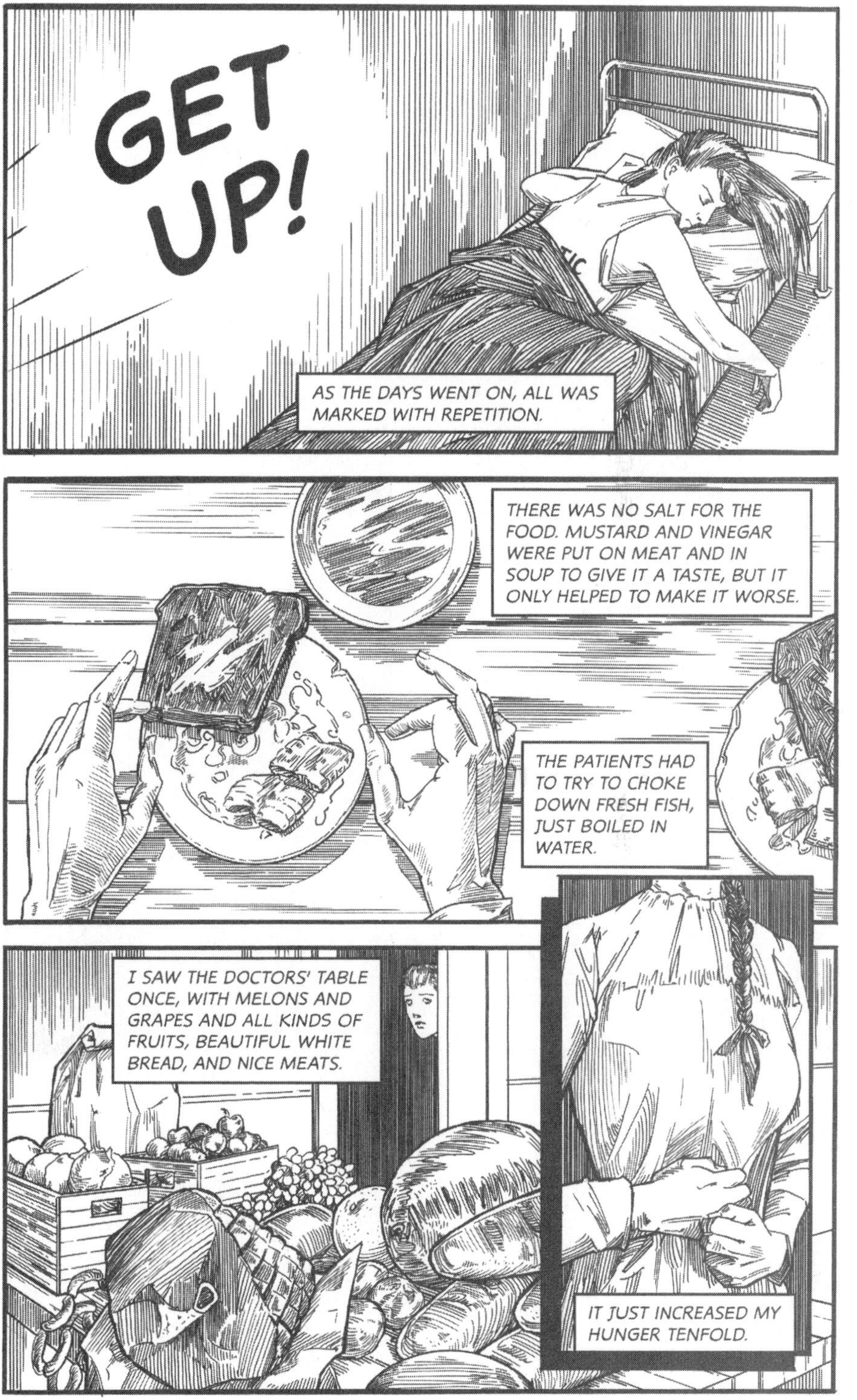
GET UP!
AS THE DAYS WENT ON, ALL WAS MARKED WITH REPETITION.
THERE WAS NO SALT FOR THE FOOD. MUSTARD AND VINEGAR WERE PUT ON MEAT AND IN SOUP TO GIVE IT A TASTE, BUT IT ONLY HELPED TO MAKE IT WORSE.
THE PATIENTS HAD TO TRY TO CHOKE DOWN FRESH FISH, JUST BOILED IN WATER.
I SAW THE DOCTORS' TABLE ONCE, WITH MELONS AND GRAPES AND ALL KINDS OF FRUITS, BEAUTIFUL WHITE BREAD, AND NICE MEATS.
IT JUST INCREASED MY HUNGER TENFOLD.

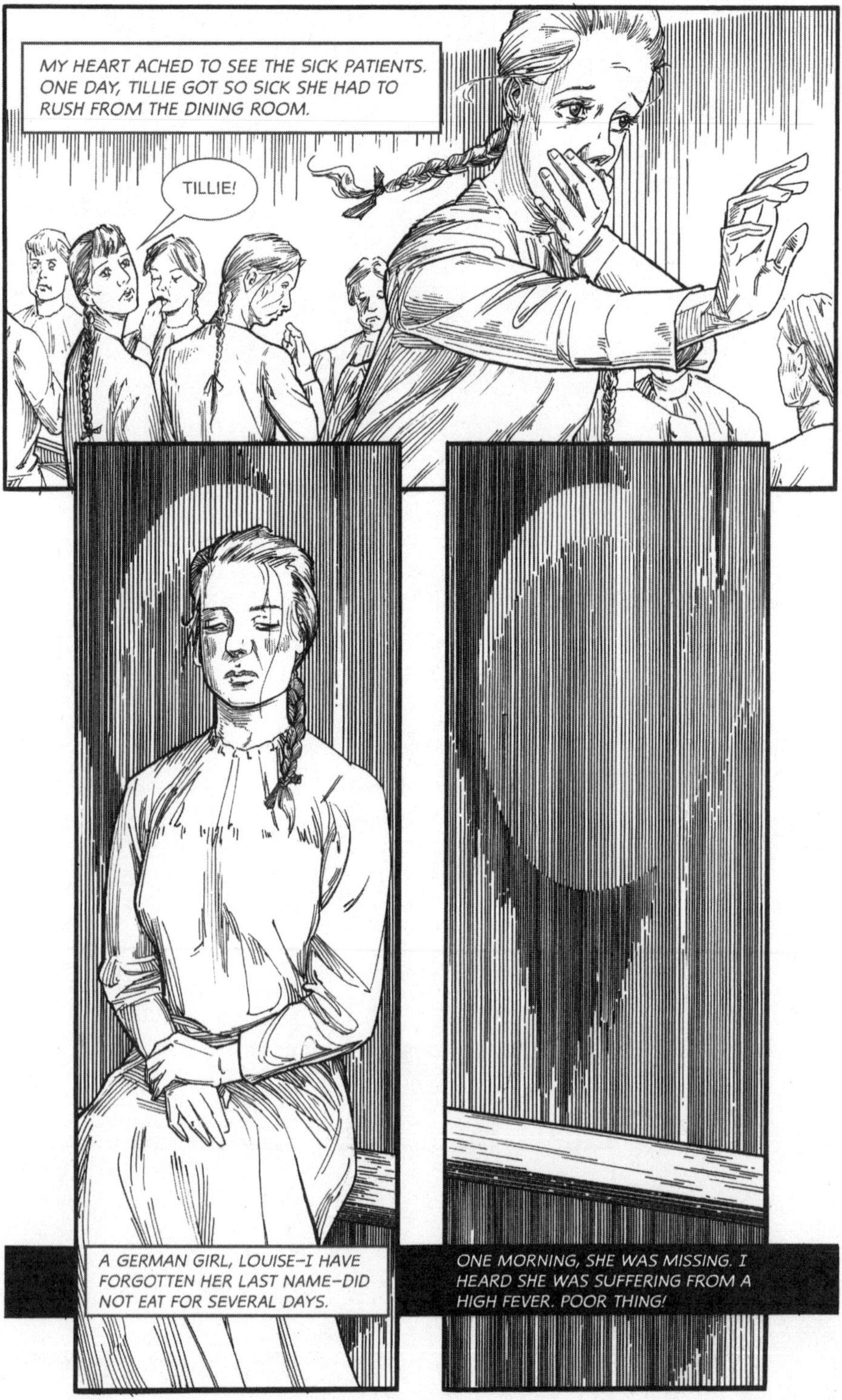
MY HEART ACHED TO SEE THE SICK PATIENTS. ONE DAY, TILLIE GOT SO SICK SHE HAD TO RUSH FROM THE DINING ROOM.
TILLIE!
A GERMAN GIRL, LOUISE–I HAVE FORGOTTEN HER LAST NAME–DID NOT EAT FOR SEVERAL DAYS.
ONE MORNING, SHE WAS MISSING. I HEARD SHE WAS SUFFERING FROM A HIGH FEVER. POOR THING!

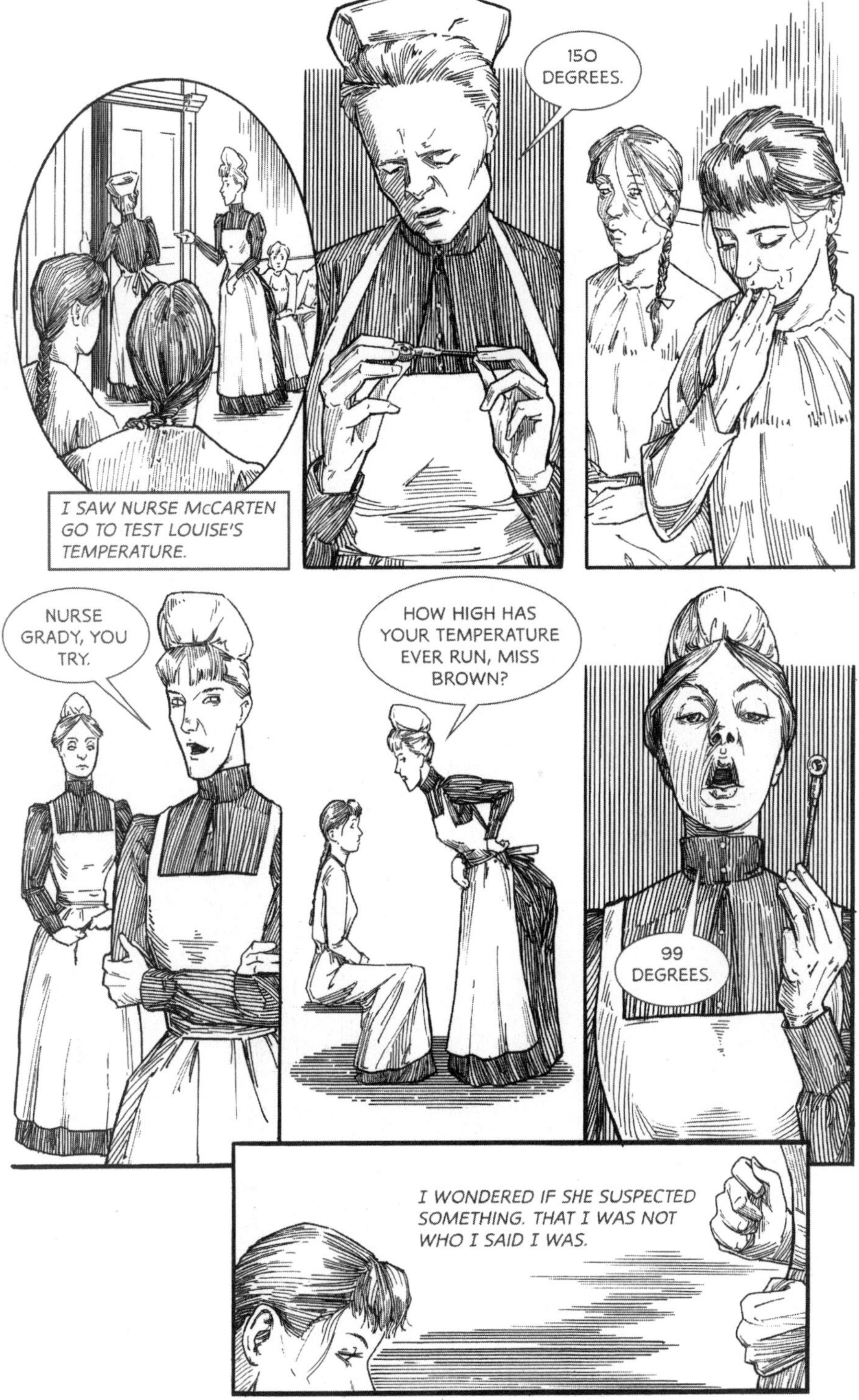
I SAW NURSE McCARTEN GO TO TEST LOUISE'S TEMPERATURE.
150 DEGREES.
NURSE GRADY, YOU TRY.
HOW HIGH HAS YOUR TEMPERATURE EVER RUN, MISS BROWN?
99 DEGREES.
I WONDERED IF SHE SUSPECTED SOMETHING. THAT I WAS NOT WHO I SAID I WAS.

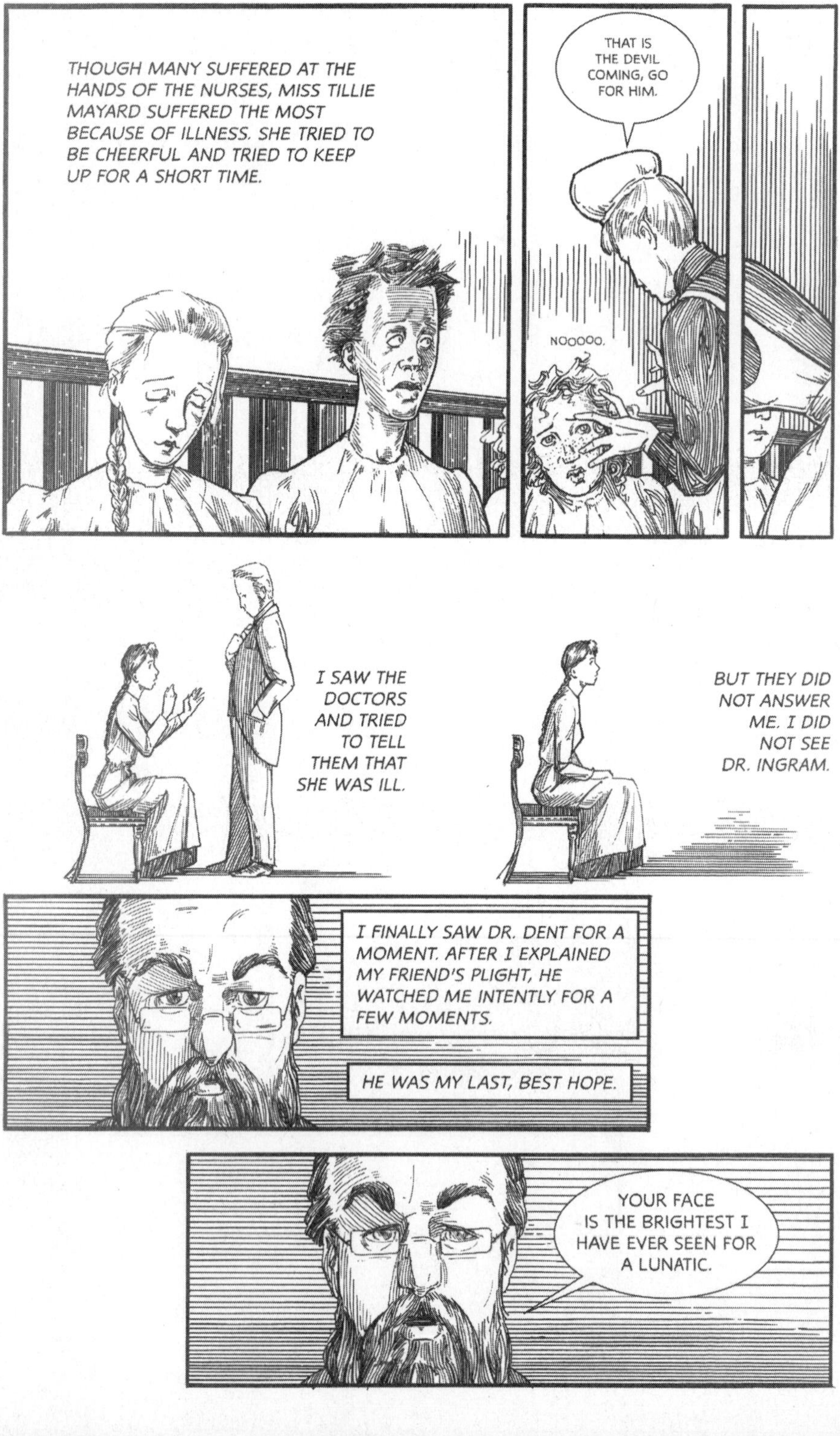
THOUGH MANY SUFFERED AT THE HANDS OF THE NURSES, MISS TILLIE MAYARD SUFFERED THE MOST BECAUSE OF ILLNESS. SHE TRIED TO BE CHEERFUL AND TRIED TO KEEP UP FOR A SHORT TIME.
THAT IS THE DEVIL COMING, GO FOR HIM.
NOOOOO.
I SAW THE DOCTORS AND TRIED TO TELL THEM THAT SHE WAS ILL.
BUT THEY DID NOT ANSWER ME. I DID NOT SEE DR. INGRAM.
I FINALLY SAW DR. DENT FOR A MOMENT. AFTER I EXPLAINED MY FRIEND'S PLIGHT, HE WATCHED ME INTENTLY FOR A FEW MOMENTS.
HE WAS MY LAST, BEST HOPE.
YOUR FACE IS THE BRIGHTEST I HAVE EVER SEEN FOR A LUNATIC.

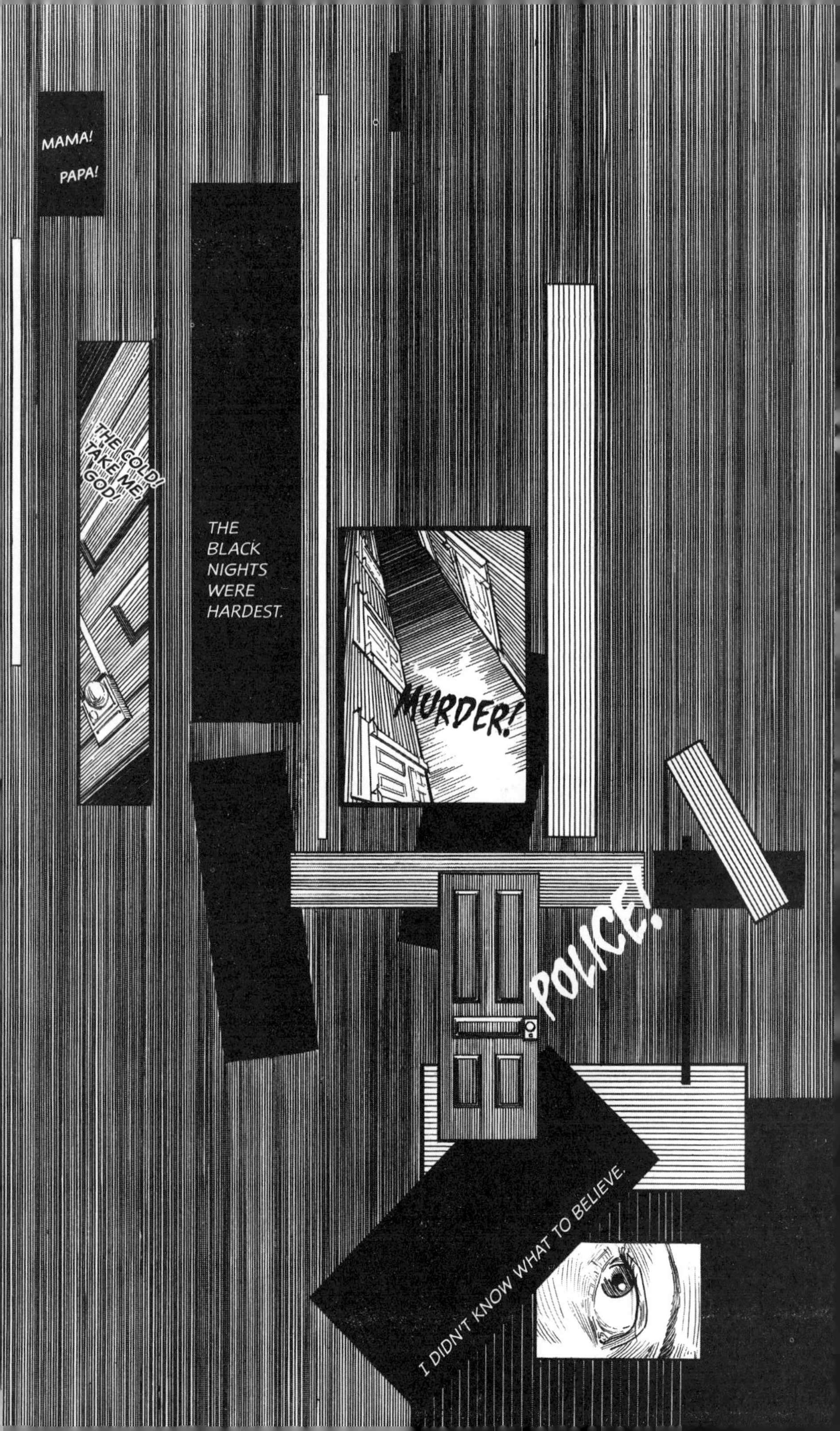
MAMA!
PAPA!
THE COLD! TAKE ME, GOD!
THE BLACK NIGHTS WERE HARDEST.
MURDER!
POLICE!
I DIDN'T KNOW WHAT TO BELIEVE.

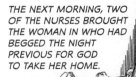

THE NEXT MORNING, TWO OF THE NURSES BROUGHT THE WOMAN IN WHO HAD BEGGED THE NIGHT PREVIOUS FOR GOD TO TAKE HER HOME.

SHE HAD BEEN FREEZING COLD.

WHY CAN'T I STAY IN BED OR HAVE A SHAWL? I AM SO COLD.

SHE WAS BLIND.

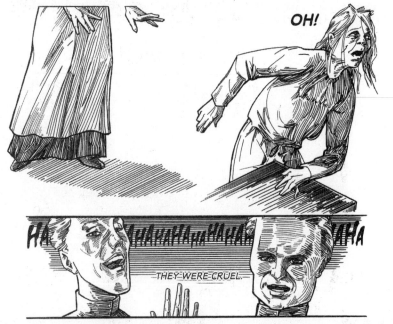

OH!

HAHAHAHAHAHAHAHAHAHA

THEY WERE CRUEL.

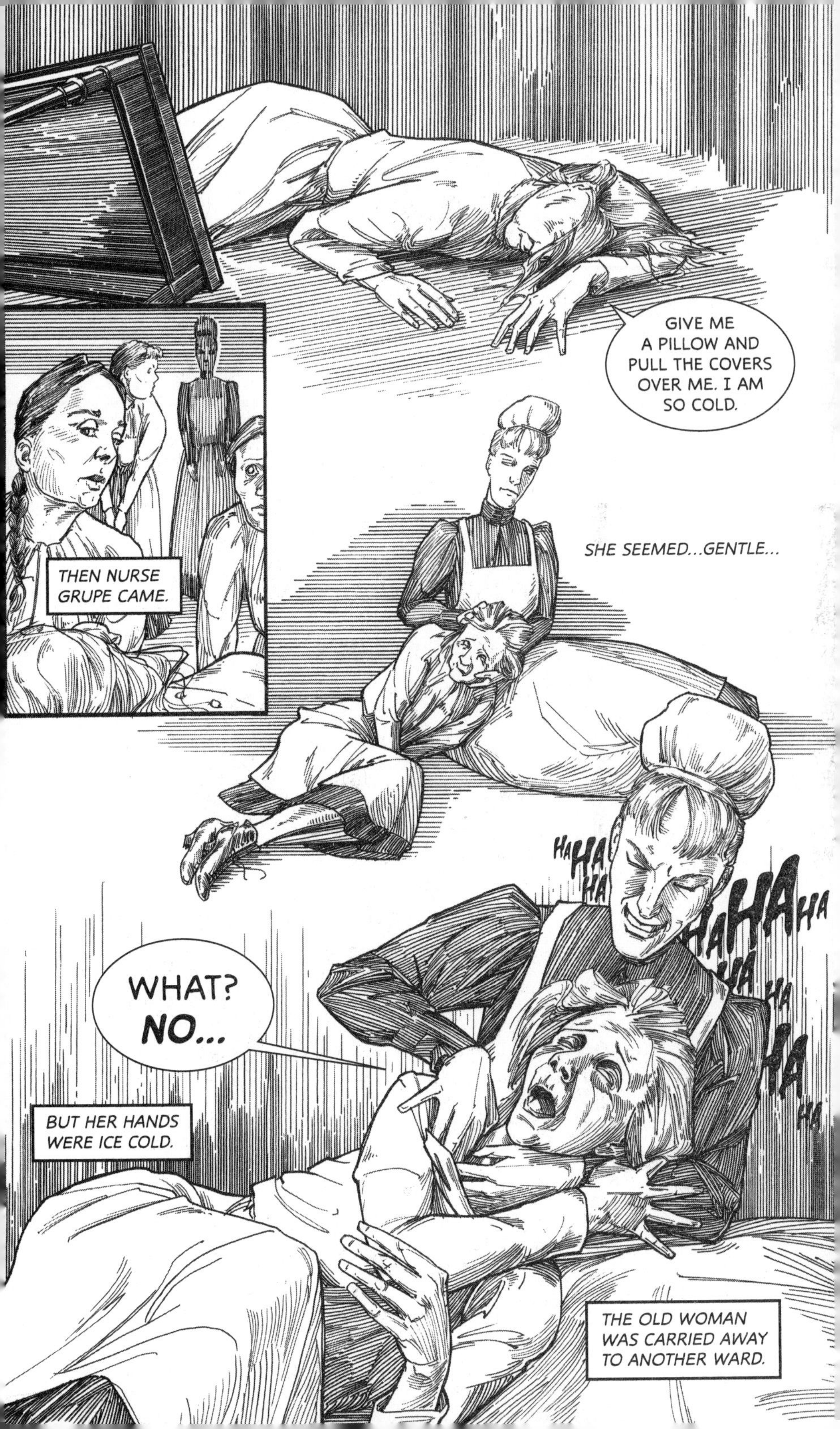
GIVE ME A PILLOW AND PULL THE COVERS OVER ME. I AM SO COLD.
THEN NURSE GRUPE CAME.
SHE SEEMED...GENTLE...
HA HA HA
HAHAHA HA HA HA HA HA
WHAT? NO...
BUT HER HANDS WERE ICE COLD.
THE OLD WOMAN WAS CARRIED AWAY TO ANOTHER WARD.

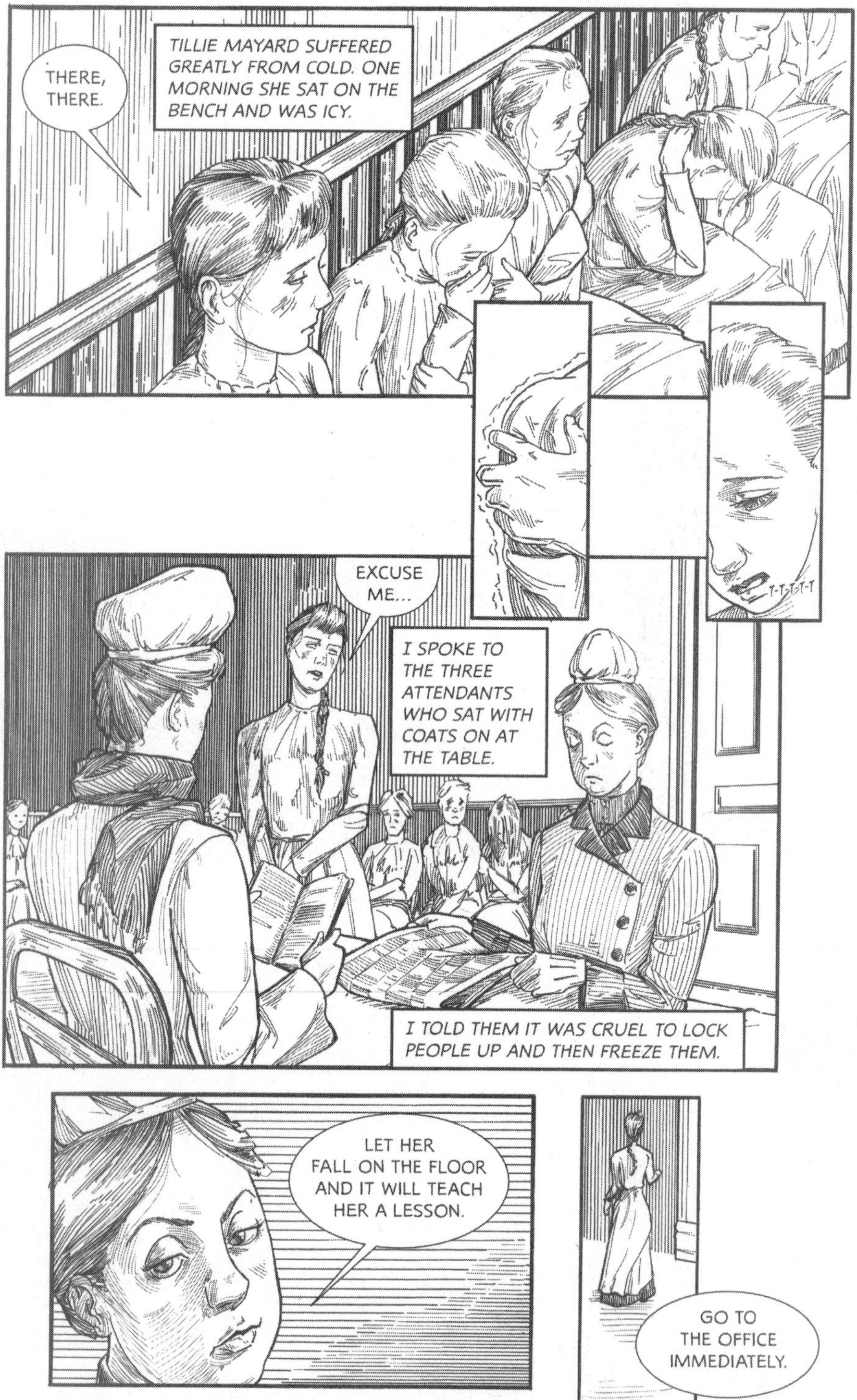
TILLIE MAYARD SUFFERED GREATLY FROM COLD. ONE MORNING SHE SAT ON THE BENCH AND WAS ICY.
THERE, THERE.
T-T-T-T-T
EXCUSE ME...
I SPOKE TO THE THREE ATTENDANTS WHO SAT WITH COATS ON AT THE TABLE.
I TOLD THEM IT WAS CRUEL TO LOCK PEOPLE UP AND THEN FREEZE THEM.
LET HER FALL ON THE FLOOR AND IT WILL TEACH HER A LESSON.
GO TO THE OFFICE IMMEDIATELY.

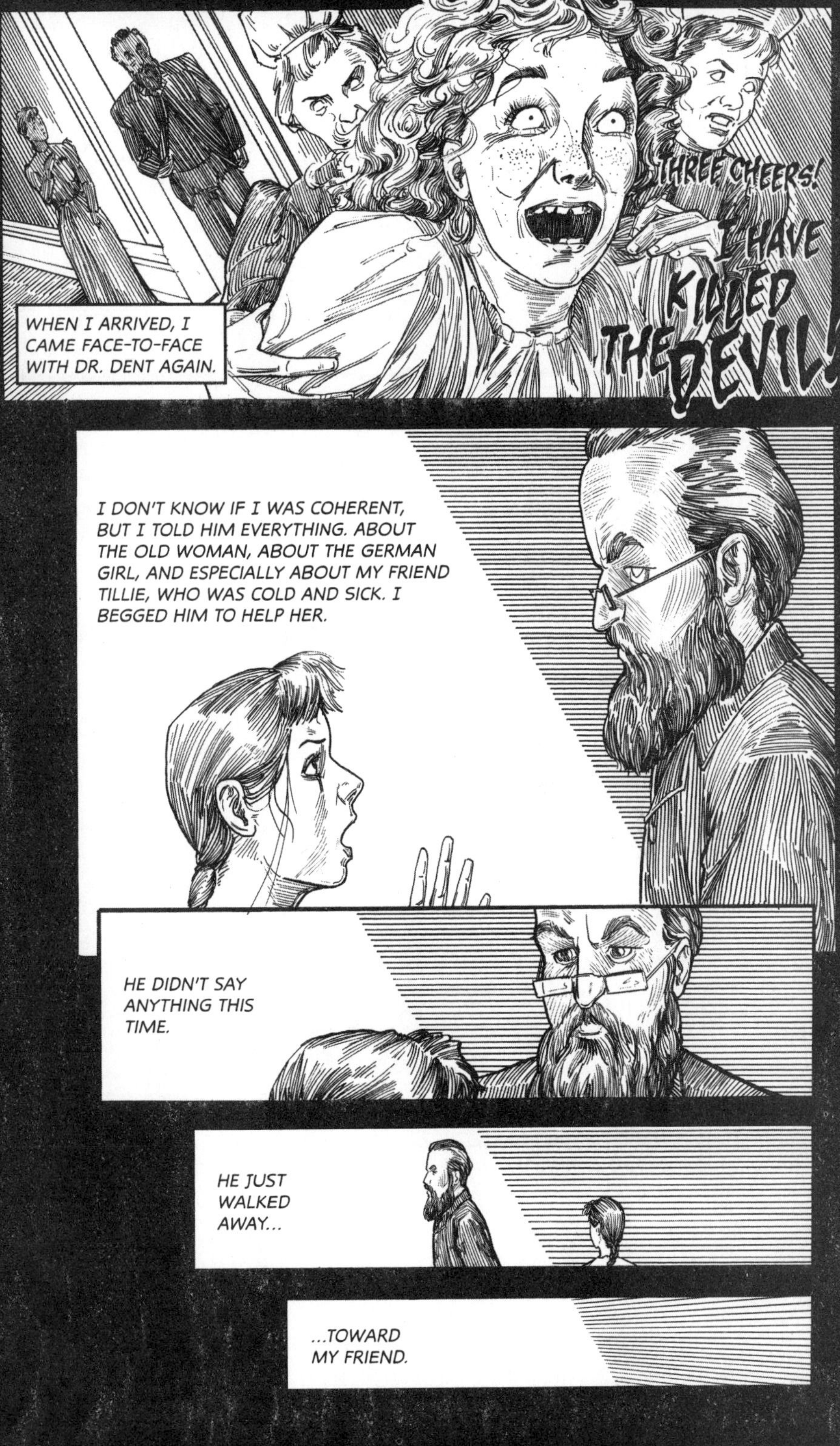
THREE CHEERS!
I HAVE KILLED THE DEVIL!
WHEN I ARRIVED, I CAME FACE-TO-FACE WITH DR. DENT AGAIN.
I DON'T KNOW IF I WAS COHERENT, BUT I TOLD HIM EVERYTHING. ABOUT THE OLD WOMAN, ABOUT THE GERMAN GIRL, AND ESPECIALLY ABOUT MY FRIEND TILLIE, WHO WAS COLD AND SICK. I BEGGED HIM TO HELP HER.
HE DIDN'T SAY ANYTHING THIS TIME.
HE JUST WALKED AWAY...
...TOWARD MY FRIEND.

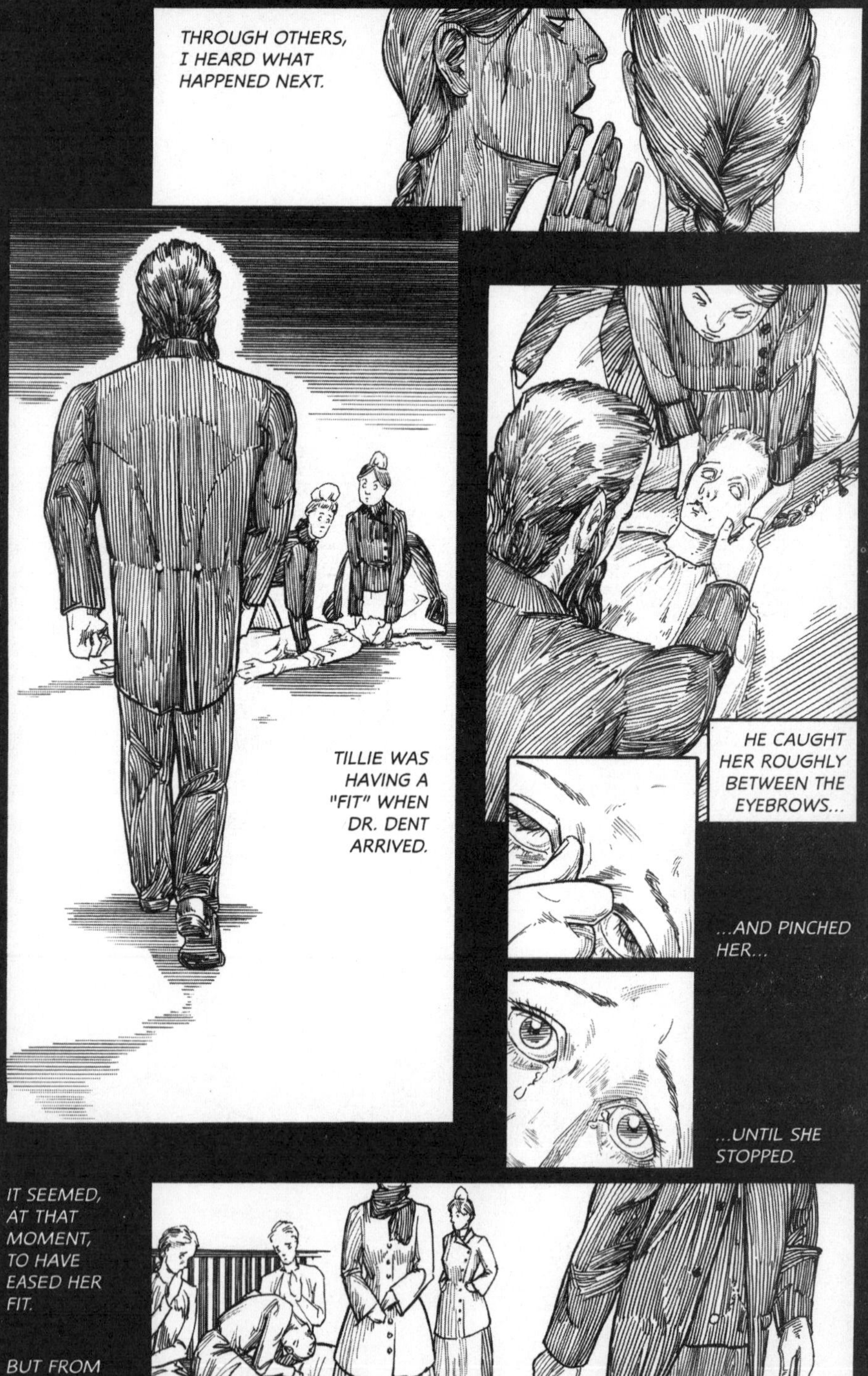
THROUGH OTHERS, I HEARD WHAT HAPPENED NEXT.
TILLIE WAS HAVING A "FIT" WHEN DR. DENT ARRIVED.
HE CAUGHT HER ROUGHLY BETWEEN THE EYEBROWS...
...AND PINCHED HER...
...UNTIL SHE STOPPED.
IT SEEMED, AT THAT MOMENT, TO HAVE EASED HER FIT.
BUT FROM THERE, SHE GREW WORSE.

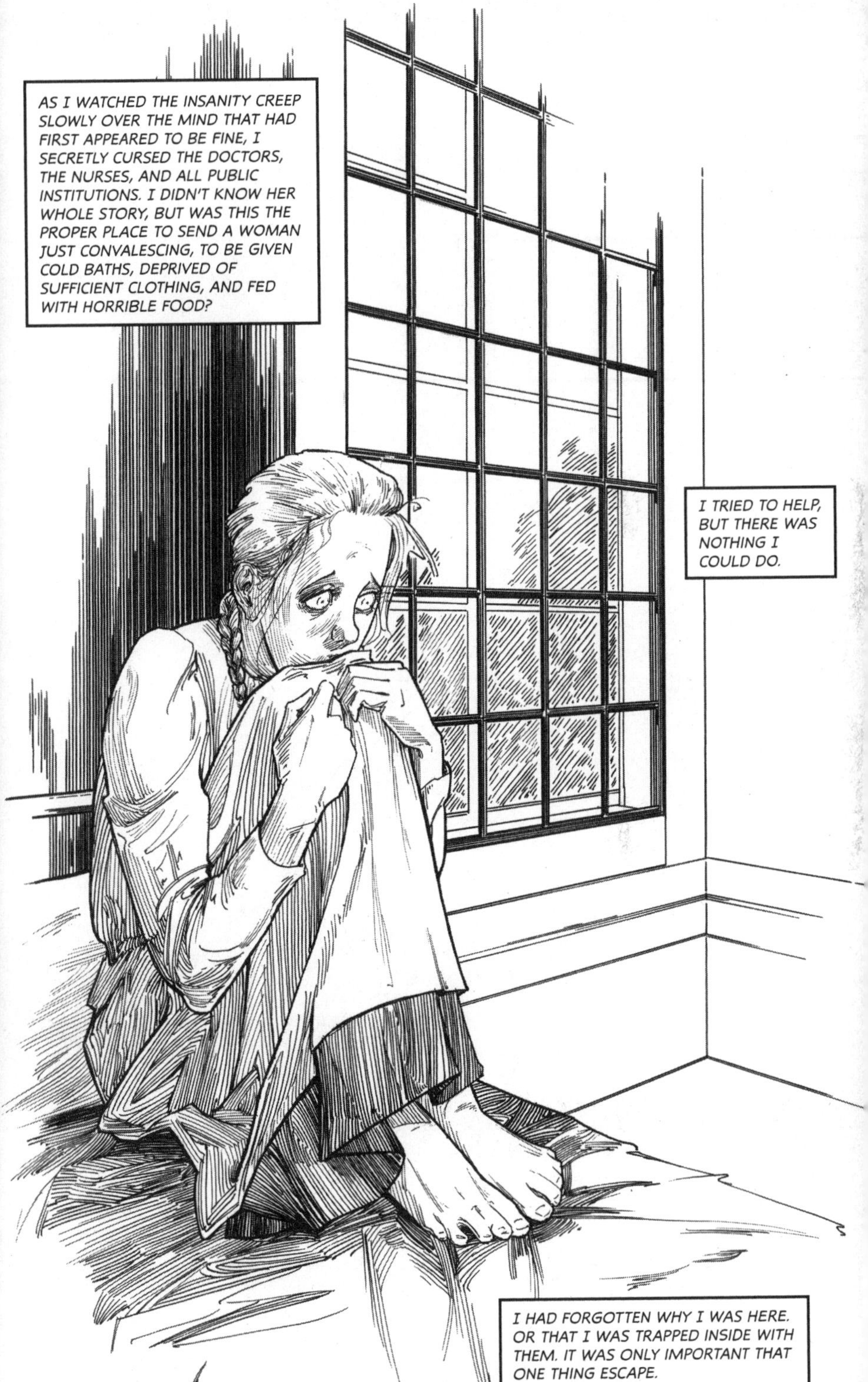
AS I WATCHED THE INSANITY CREEP SLOWLY OVER THE MIND THAT HAD FIRST APPEARED TO BE FINE, I SECRETLY CURSED THE DOCTORS, THE NURSES, AND ALL PUBLIC INSTITUTIONS. I DIDN'T KNOW HER WHOLE STORY, BUT WAS THIS THE PROPER PLACE TO SEND A WOMAN JUST CONVALESCING, TO BE GIVEN COLD BATHS, DEPRIVED OF SUFFICIENT CLOTHING, AND FED WITH HORRIBLE FOOD?
I TRIED TO HELP, BUT THERE WAS NOTHING I COULD DO.
I HAD FORGOTTEN WHY I WAS HERE. OR THAT I WAS TRAPPED INSIDE WITH THEM. IT WAS ONLY IMPORTANT THAT ONE THING ESCAPE.

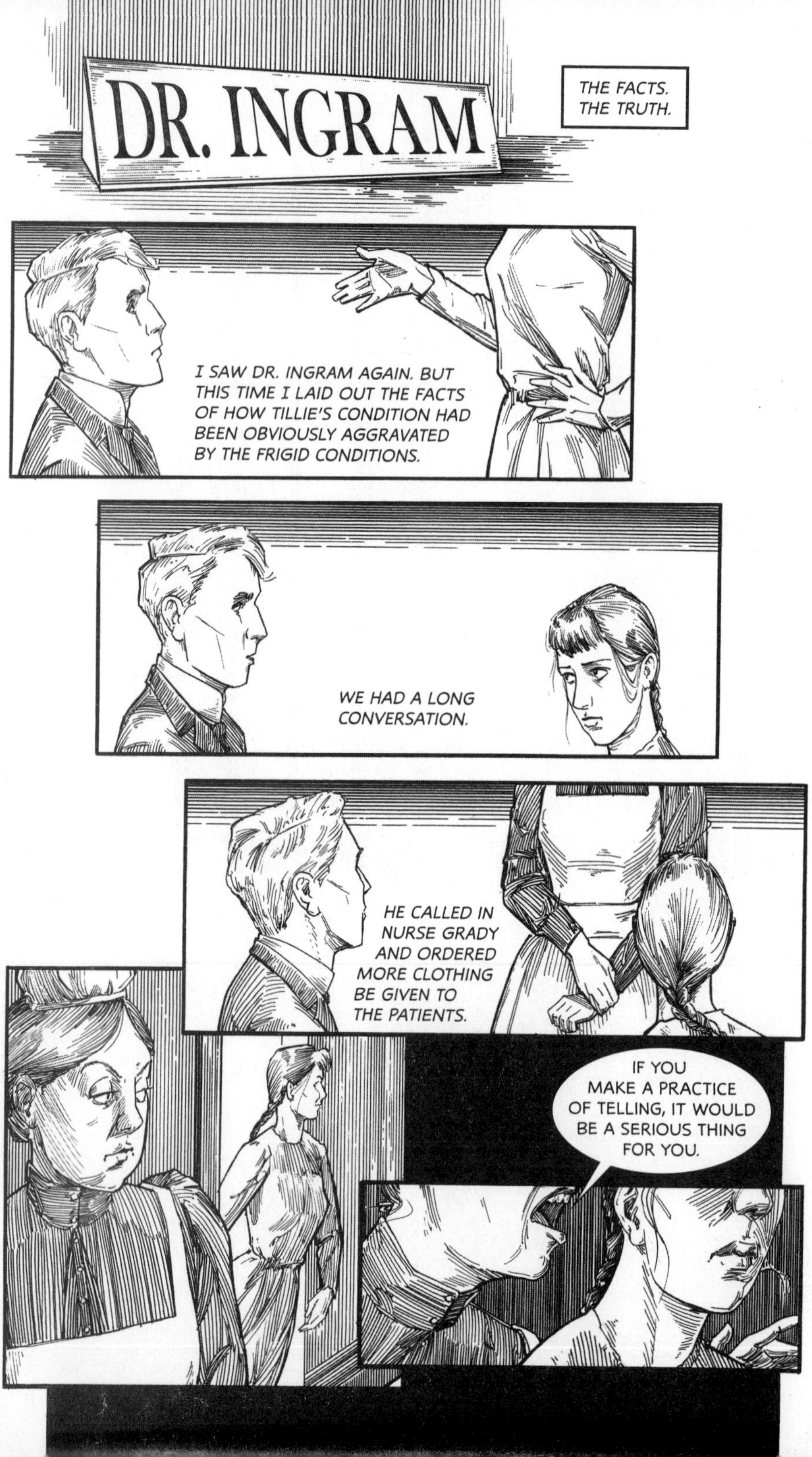
DR. INGRAM
THE FACTS. THE TRUTH.
I SAW DR. INGRAM AGAIN. BUT THIS TIME I LAID OUT THE FACTS OF HOW TILLIE'S CONDITION HAD BEEN OBVIOUSLY AGGRAVATED BY THE FRIGID CONDITIONS.
WE HAD A LONG CONVERSATION.
HE CALLED IN NURSE GRADY AND ORDERED MORE CLOTHING BE GIVEN TO THE PATIENTS.
IF YOU MAKE A PRACTICE OF TELLING, IT WOULD BE A SERIOUS THING FOR YOU.

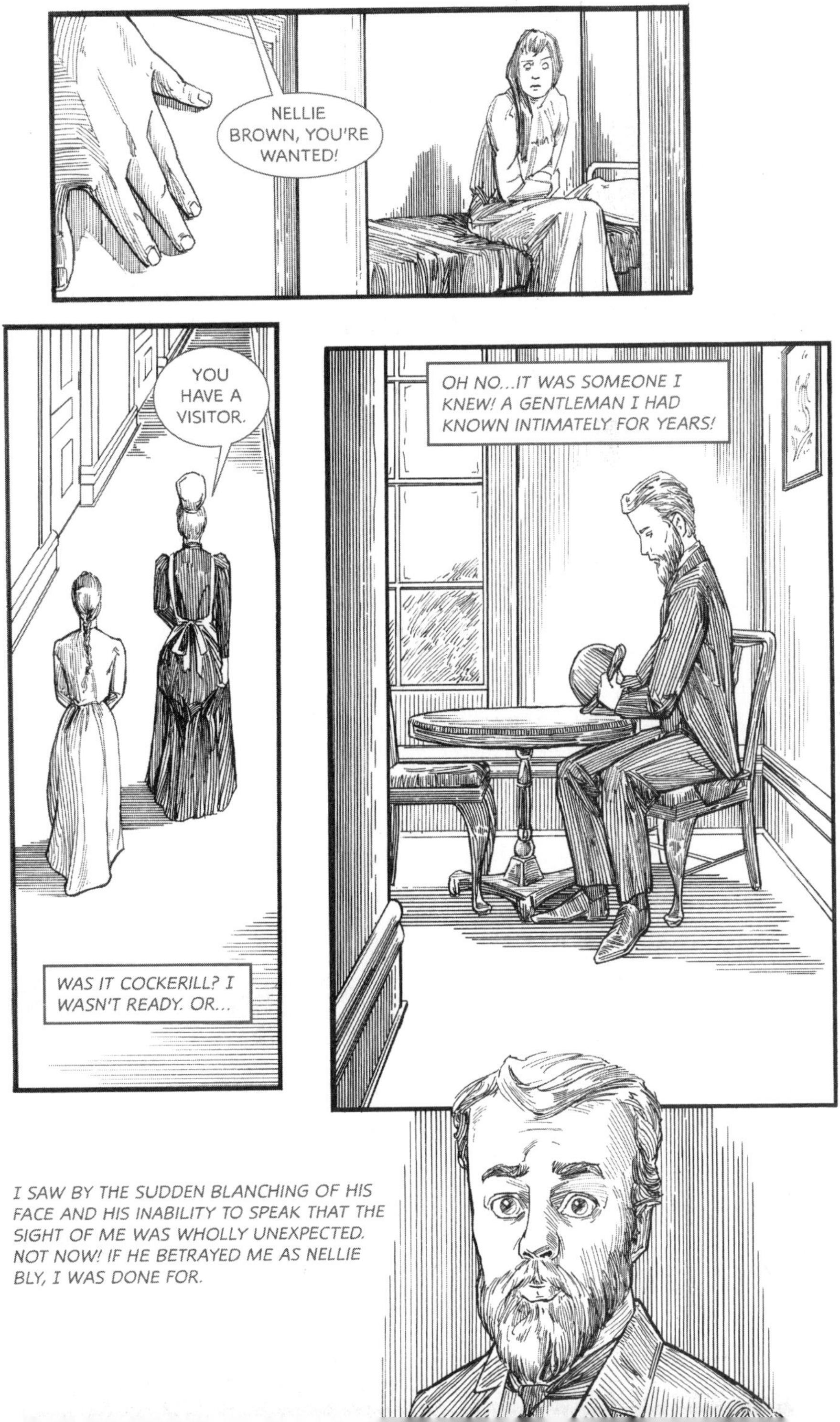
NELLIE BROWN, YOU'RE WANTED!
YOU HAVE A VISITOR.
WAS IT COCKERILL? I WASN'T READY. OR...
OH NO...IT WAS SOMEONE I KNEW! A GENTLEMAN I HAD KNOWN INTIMATELY FOR YEARS!
I SAW BY THE SUDDEN BLANCHING OF HIS FACE AND HIS INABILITY TO SPEAK THAT THE SIGHT OF ME WAS WHOLLY UNEXPECTED. NOT NOW! IF HE BETRAYED ME AS NELLIE BLY, I WAS DONE FOR.

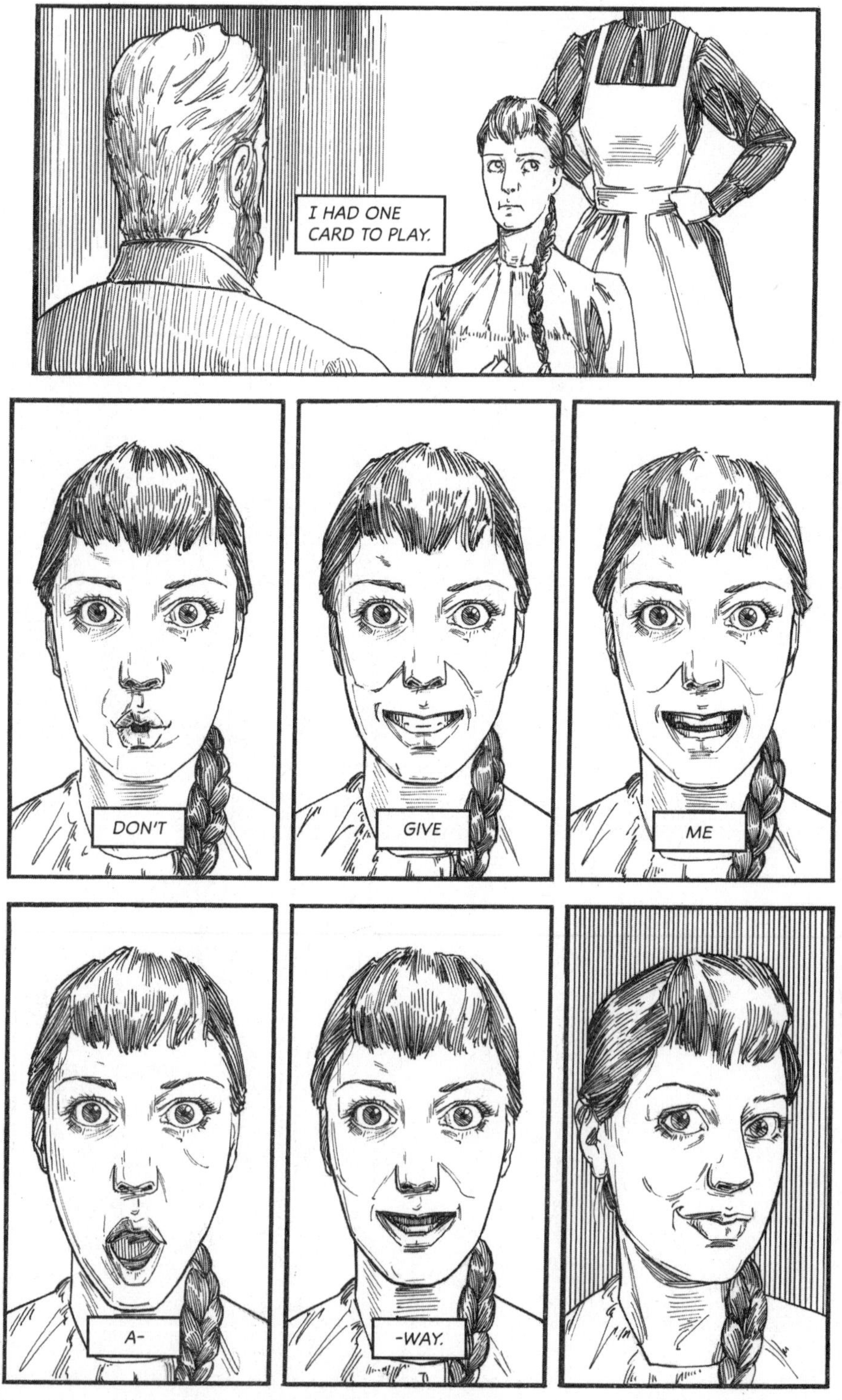
I HAD ONE CARD TO PLAY.
DON'T
GIVE
ME
A-
-WAY.

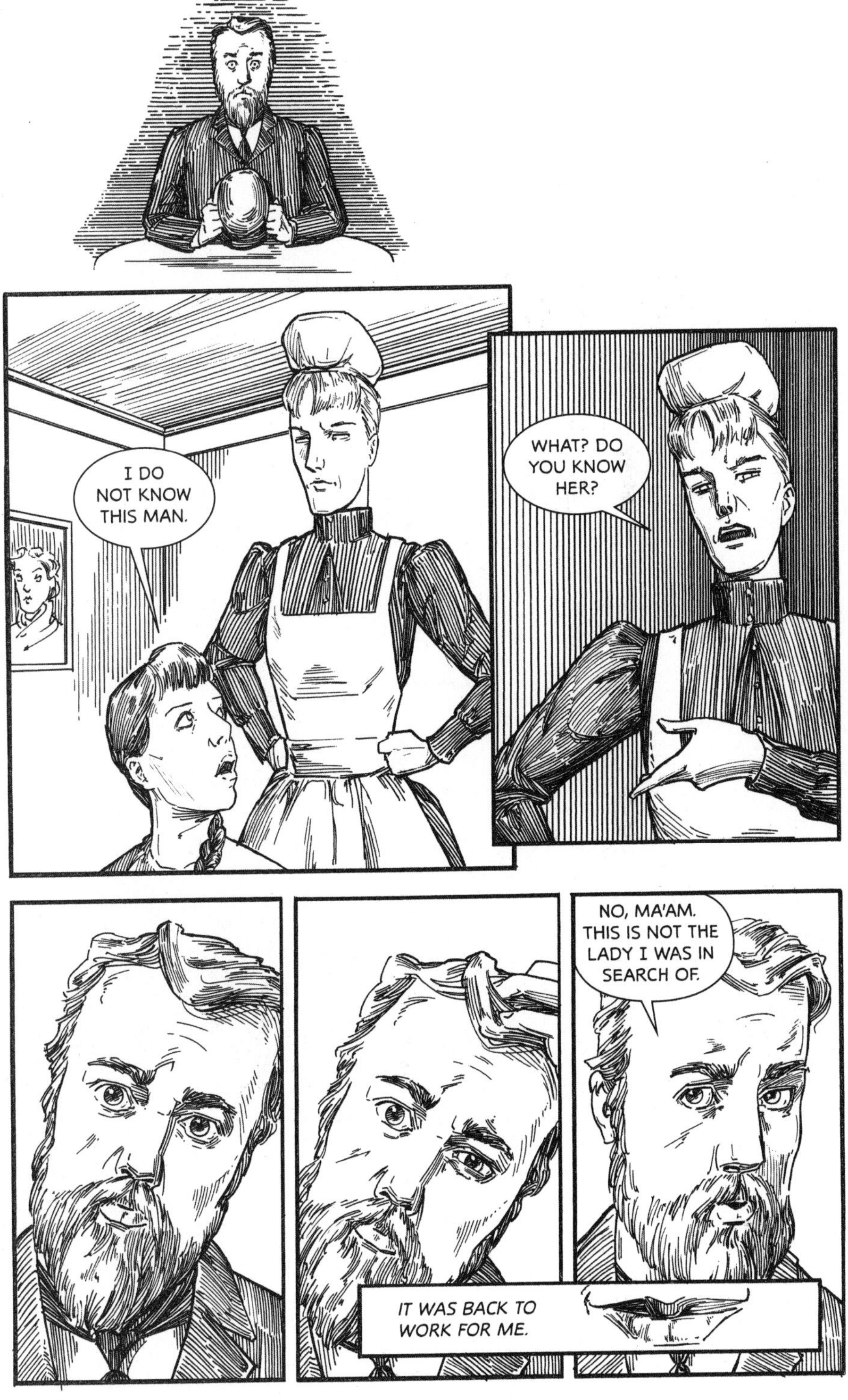
I DO NOT KNOW THIS MAN.
WHAT? DO YOU KNOW HER?
NO, MA'AM. THIS IS NOT THE LADY I WAS IN SEARCH OF.
IT WAS BACK TO WORK FOR ME.

PEOPLE IN THE WORLD CAN NEVER IMAGINE THE LENGTH OF DAYS TO THOSE IN ASYLUMS. THERE IS NOTHING TO READ, AND THE ONLY BIT OF TALK THAT NEVER WEARS OUT IS CONJURING UP THE FOOD THEY WILL GET AS SOON AS THEY GET OUT. WE WELCOMED ANY EVENT THAT MIGHT GIVE US SOMETHING TO THINK ABOUT AS WELL AS TALK OF.

WHEN NEW UNFORTUNATES CAME, IT WAS A SIGNIFICANT EVENT.

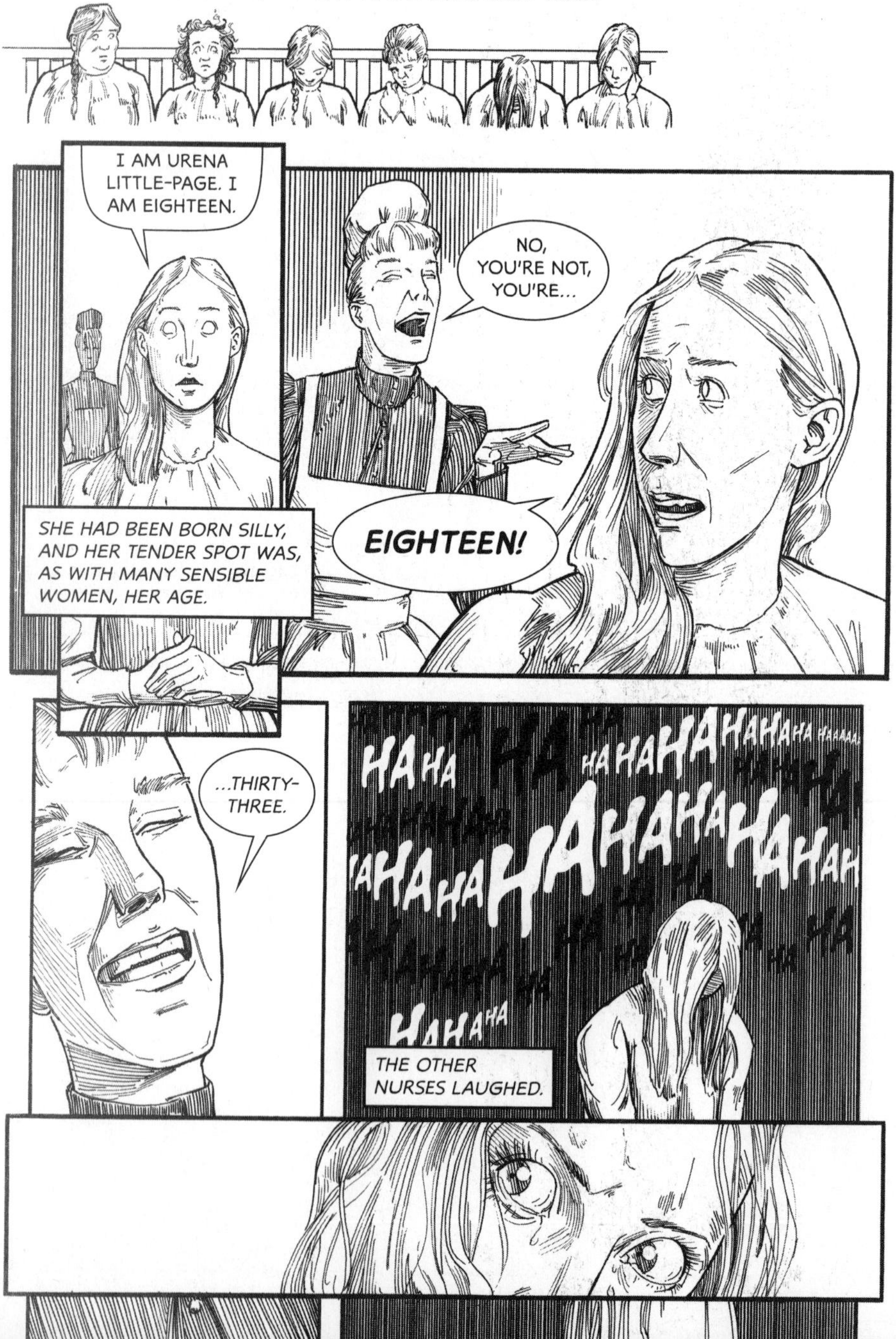
I AM URENA LITTLE-PAGE. I AM EIGHTEEN.
NO, YOU'RE NOT, YOU'RE...
SHE HAD BEEN BORN SILLY, AND HER TENDER SPOT WAS, AS WITH MANY SENSIBLE WOMEN, HER AGE.
EIGHTEEN!
...THIRTY-THREE.
THE OTHER NURSES LAUGHED.

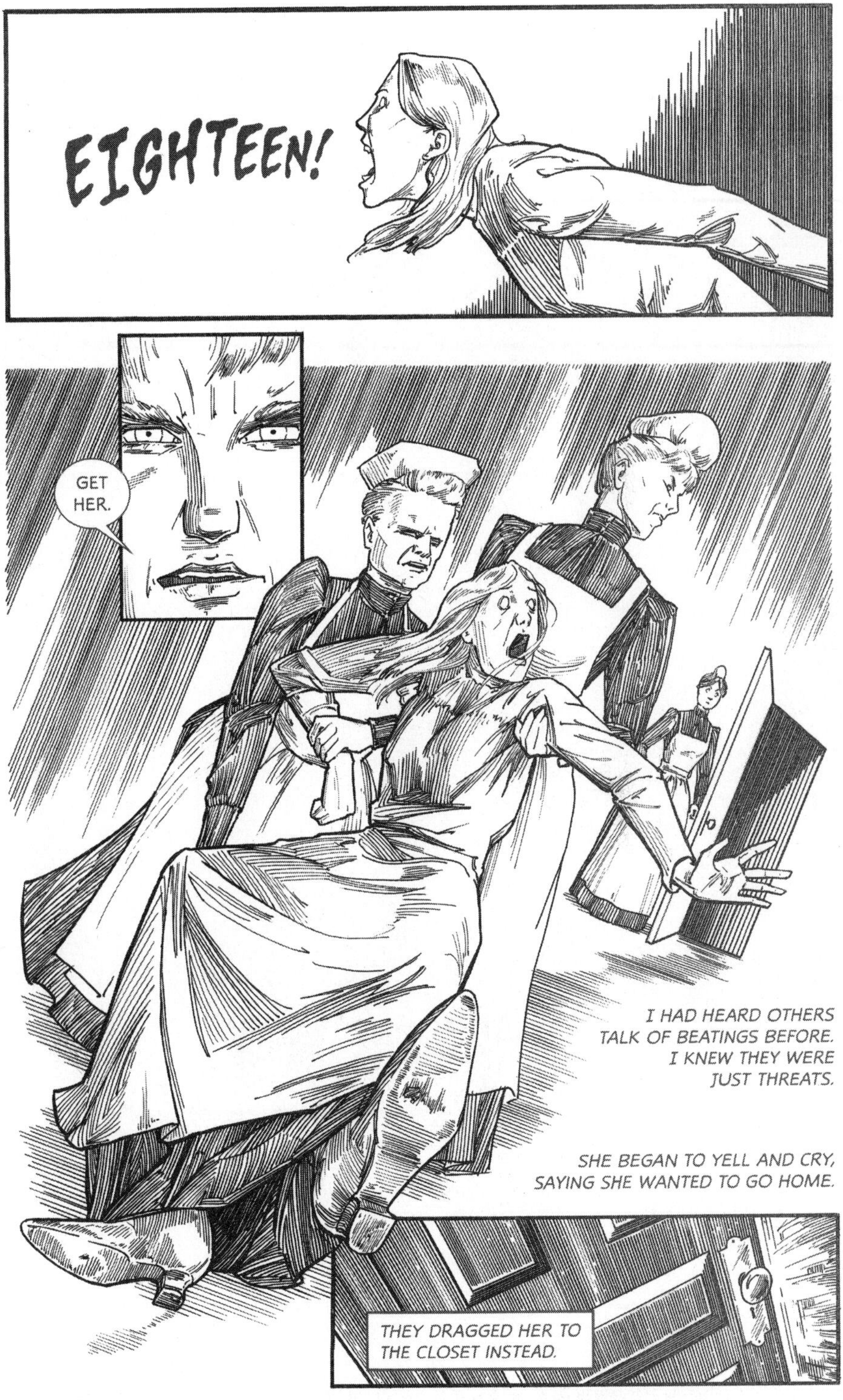
EIGHTEEN!
GET HER.
I HAD HEARD OTHERS TALK OF BEATINGS BEFORE. I KNEW THEY WERE JUST THREATS.
SHE BEGAN TO YELL AND CRY, SAYING SHE WANTED TO GO HOME.
THEY DRAGGED HER TO THE CLOSET INSTEAD.

INSIDE THAT CLOSET, I HEARD HER TERRIFIED CRIES HUSH INTO SMOTHERED ONES.

I SAW THE MARKS OF THEIR FINGERS ON HER THROAT FOR THE ENTIRE DAY.

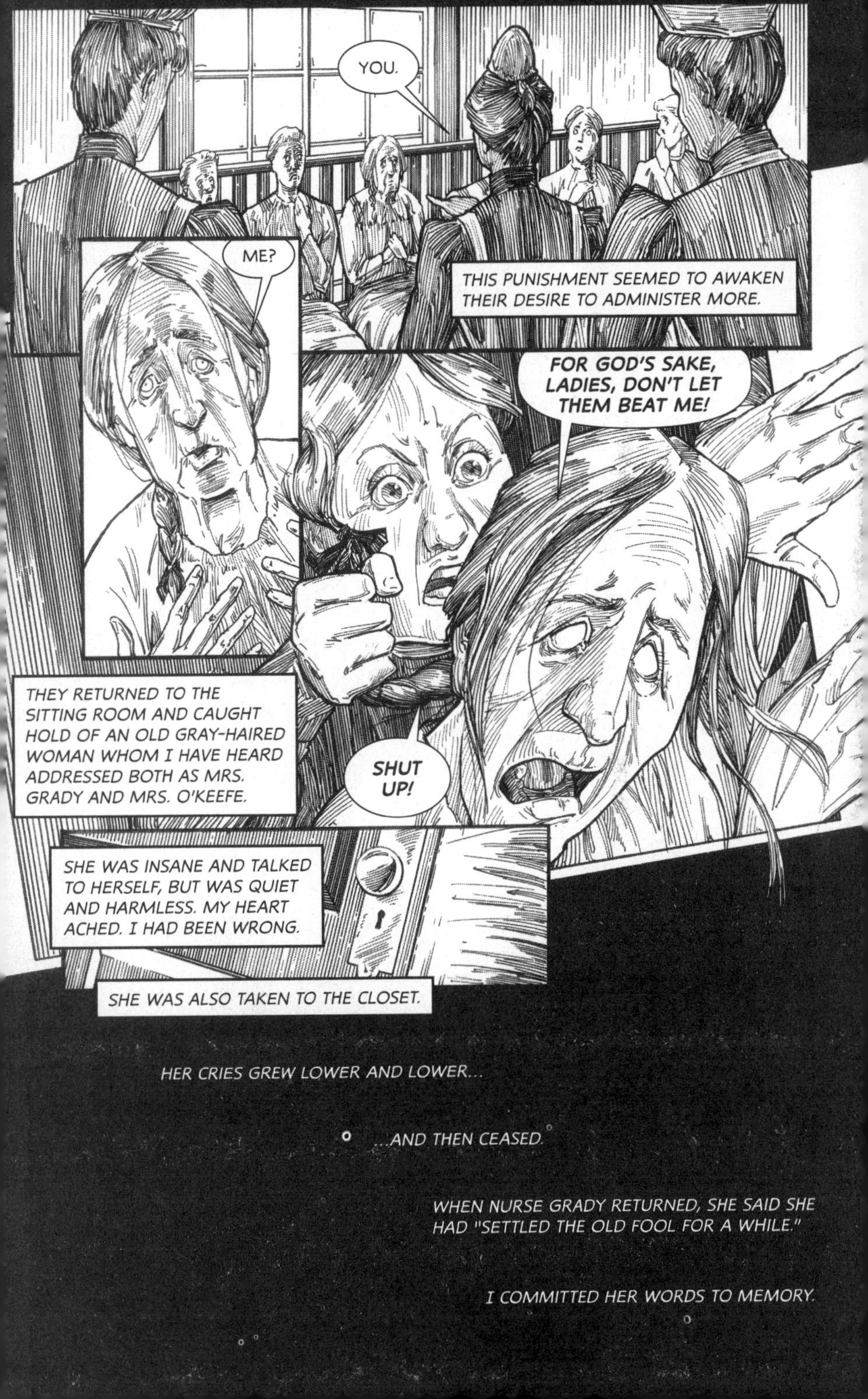
YOU.
THIS PUNISHMENT SEEMED TO AWAKEN THEIR DESIRE TO ADMINISTER MORE.
ME?
THEY RETURNED TO THE SITTING ROOM AND CAUGHT HOLD OF AN OLD GRAY-HAIRED WOMAN WHOM I HAVE HEARD ADDRESSED BOTH AS MRS. GRADY AND MRS. O'KEEFE.
FOR GOD'S SAKE, LADIES, DON'T LET THEM BEAT ME!
SHUT UP!
SHE WAS INSANE AND TALKED TO HERSELF, BUT WAS QUIET AND HARMLESS. MY HEART ACHED. I HAD BEEN WRONG.
SHE WAS ALSO TAKEN TO THE CLOSET.

HER CRIES GREW LOWER AND LOWER...

...AND THEN CEASED.

WHEN NURSE GRADY RETURNED, SHE SAID SHE HAD "SETTLED THE OLD FOOL FOR A WHILE."

I COMMITTED HER WORDS TO MEMORY.

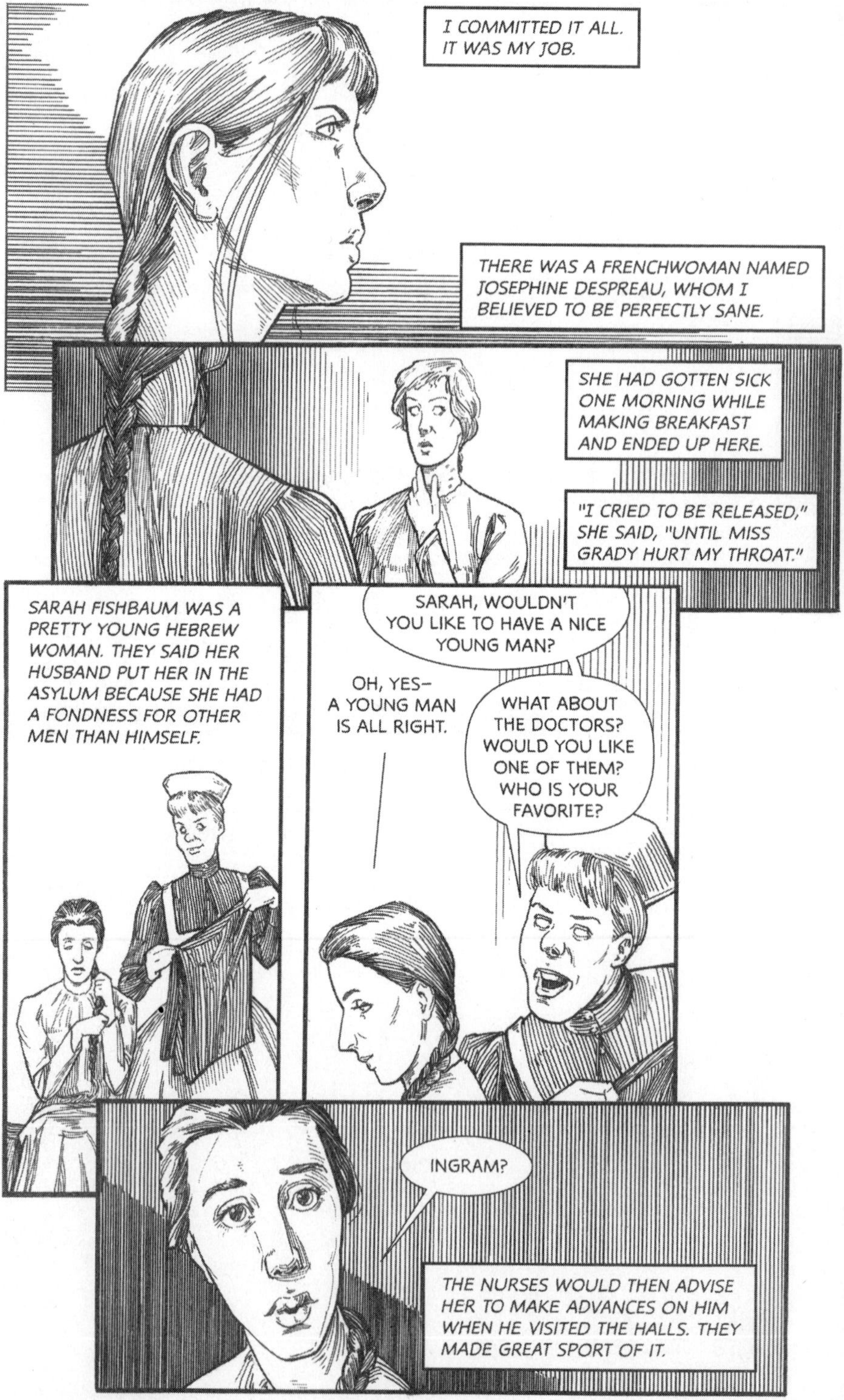
I COMMITTED IT ALL. IT WAS MY JOB.
THERE WAS A FRENCHWOMAN NAMED JOSEPHINE DESPREAU, WHOM I BELIEVED TO BE PERFECTLY SANE.
SHE HAD GOTTEN SICK ONE MORNING WHILE MAKING BREAKFAST AND ENDED UP HERE.
"I CRIED TO BE RELEASED," SHE SAID, "UNTIL MISS GRADY HURT MY THROAT."
SARAH FISHBAUM WAS A PRETTY YOUNG HEBREW WOMAN. THEY SAID HER HUSBAND PUT HER IN THE ASYLUM BECAUSE SHE HAD A FONDNESS FOR OTHER MEN THAN HIMSELF.
SARAH, WOULDN'T YOU LIKE TO HAVE A NICE YOUNG MAN?
OH, YES– A YOUNG MAN IS ALL RIGHT.
WHAT ABOUT THE DOCTORS? WOULD YOU LIKE ONE OF THEM? WHO IS YOUR FAVORITE?
INGRAM?
THE NURSES WOULD THEN ADVISE HER TO MAKE ADVANCES ON HIM WHEN HE VISITED THE HALLS. THEY MADE GREAT SPORT OF IT.

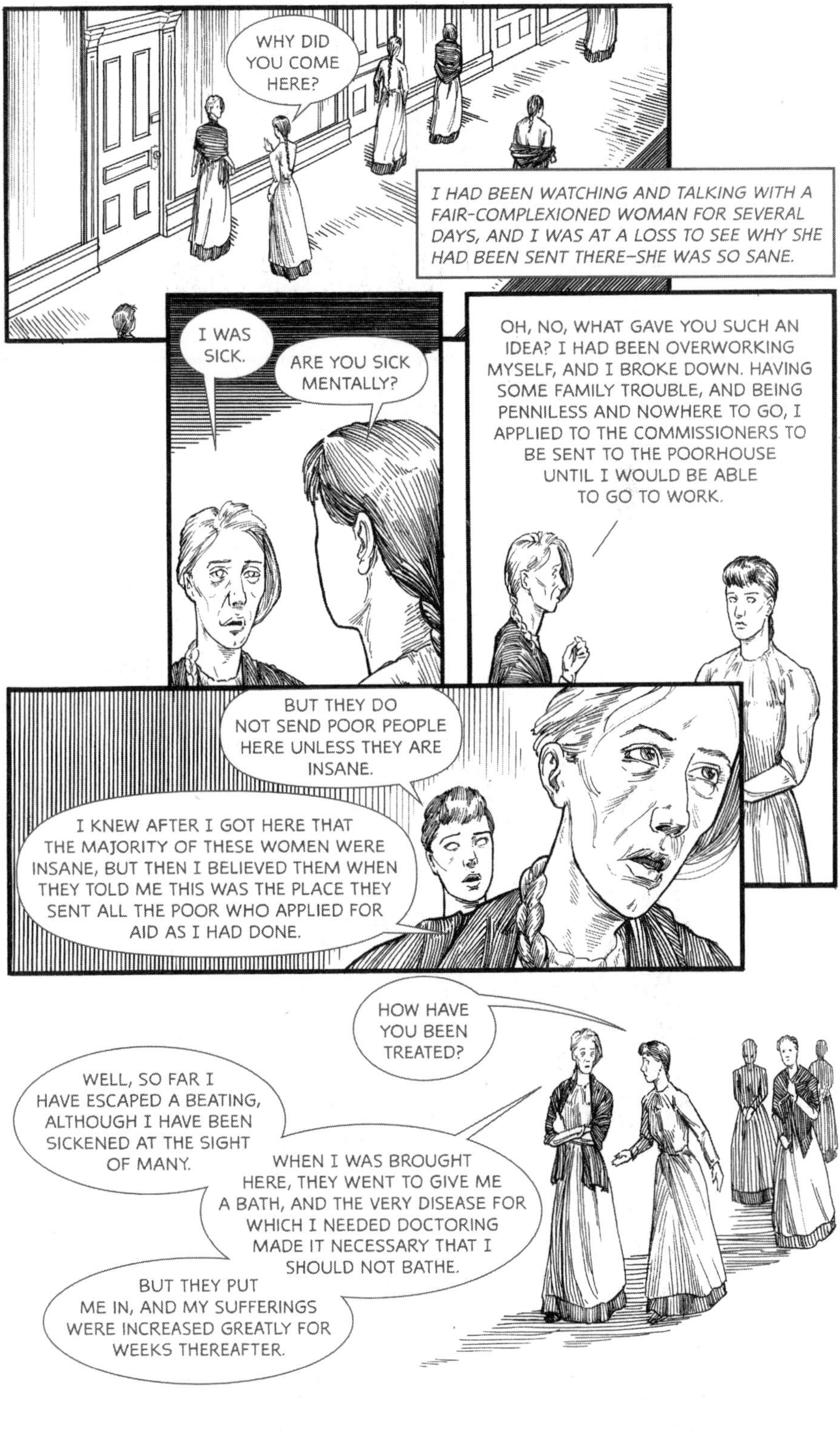
WHY DID YOU COME HERE?
I HAD BEEN WATCHING AND TALKING WITH A FAIR-COMPLEXIONED WOMAN FOR SEVERAL DAYS, AND I WAS AT A LOSS TO SEE WHY SHE HAD BEEN SENT THERE–SHE WAS SO SANE.
I WAS SICK.
ARE YOU SICK MENTALLY?
OH, NO, WHAT GAVE YOU SUCH AN IDEA? I HAD BEEN OVERWORKING MYSELF, AND I BROKE DOWN. HAVING SOME FAMILY TROUBLE, AND BEING PENNILESS AND NOWHERE TO GO, I APPLIED TO THE COMMISSIONERS TO BE SENT TO THE POORHOUSE UNTIL I WOULD BE ABLE TO GO TO WORK.
BUT THEY DO NOT SEND POOR PEOPLE HERE UNLESS THEY ARE INSANE.
I KNEW AFTER I GOT HERE THAT THE MAJORITY OF THESE WOMEN WERE INSANE, BUT THEN I BELIEVED THEM WHEN THEY TOLD ME THIS WAS THE PLACE THEY SENT ALL THE POOR WHO APPLIED FOR AID AS I HAD DONE.
HOW HAVE YOU BEEN TREATED?
WELL, SO FAR I HAVE ESCAPED A BEATING, ALTHOUGH I HAVE BEEN SICKENED AT THE SIGHT OF MANY.
WHEN I WAS BROUGHT HERE, THEY WENT TO GIVE ME A BATH, AND THE VERY DISEASE FOR WHICH I NEEDED DOCTORING MADE IT NECESSARY THAT I SHOULD NOT BATHE.
BUT THEY PUT ME IN, AND MY SUFFERINGS WERE INCREASED GREATLY FOR WEEKS THEREAFTER.

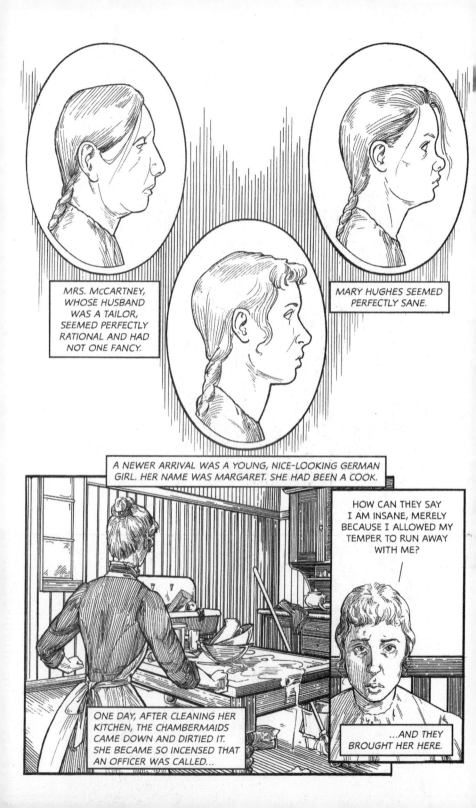

MRS. McCARTNEY, WHOSE HUSBAND WAS A TAILOR, SEEMED PERFECTLY RATIONAL AND HAD NOT ONE FANCY.

MARY HUGHES SEEMED PERFECTLY SANE.

A NEWER ARRIVAL WAS A YOUNG, NICE-LOOKING GERMAN GIRL. HER NAME WAS MARGARET. SHE HAD BEEN A COOK.

HOW CAN THEY SAY I AM INSANE, MERELY BECAUSE I ALLOWED MY TEMPER TO RUN AWAY WITH ME?

ONE DAY, AFTER CLEANING HER KITCHEN, THE CHAMBERMAIDS CAME DOWN AND DIRTIED IT. SHE BECAME SO INCENSED THAT AN OFFICER WAS CALLED...

...AND THEY BROUGHT HER HERE.

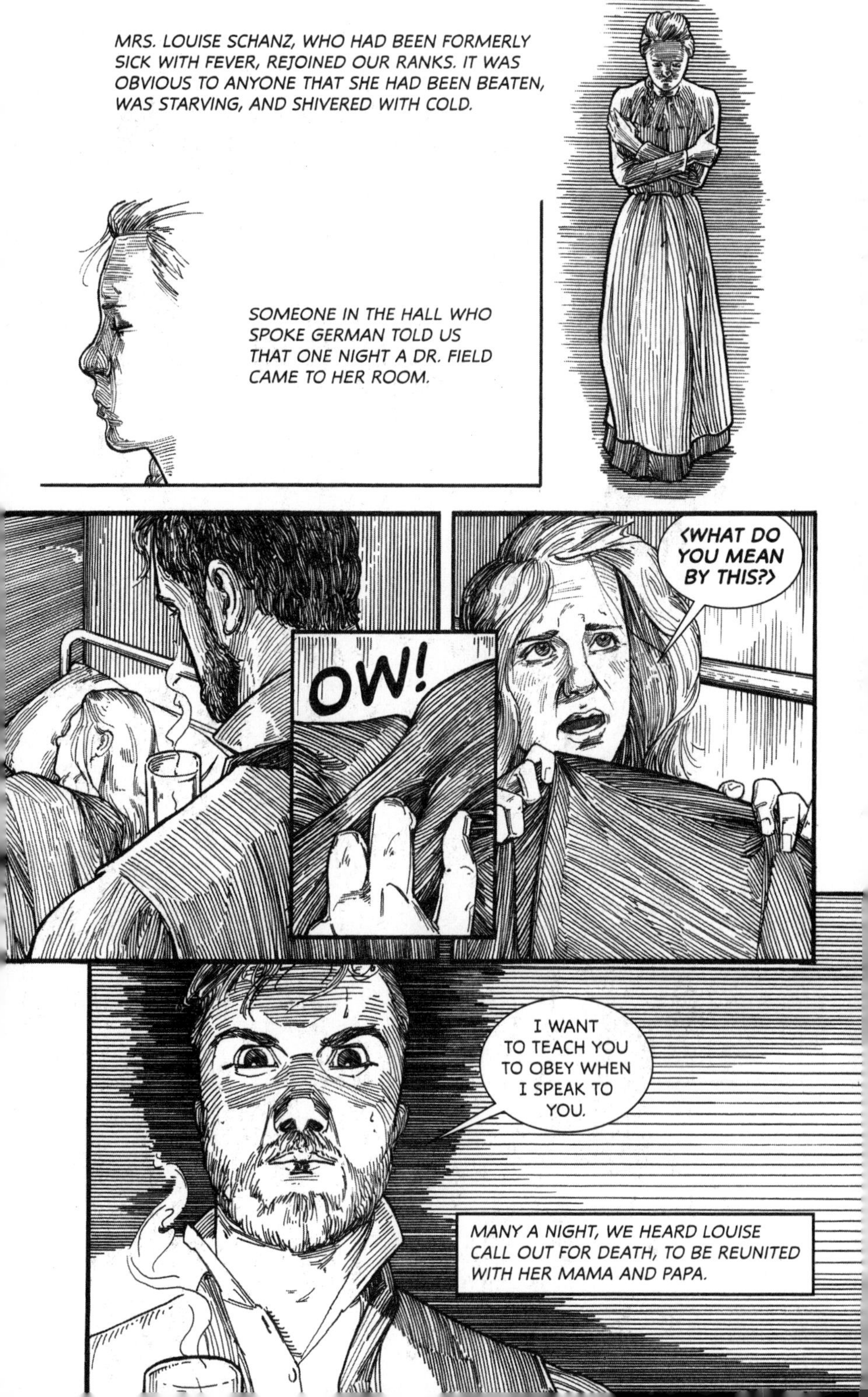
MRS. LOUISE SCHANZ, WHO HAD BEEN FORMERLY SICK WITH FEVER, REJOINED OUR RANKS. IT WAS OBVIOUS TO ANYONE THAT SHE HAD BEEN BEATEN, WAS STARVING, AND SHIVERED WITH COLD.
SOMEONE IN THE HALL WHO SPOKE GERMAN TOLD US THAT ONE NIGHT A DR. FIELD CAME TO HER ROOM.
OW!
‹WHAT DO YOU MEAN BY THIS?›
I WANT TO TEACH YOU TO OBEY WHEN I SPEAK TO YOU.
MANY A NIGHT, WE HEARD LOUISE CALL OUT FOR DEATH, TO BE REUNITED WITH HER MAMA AND PAPA.

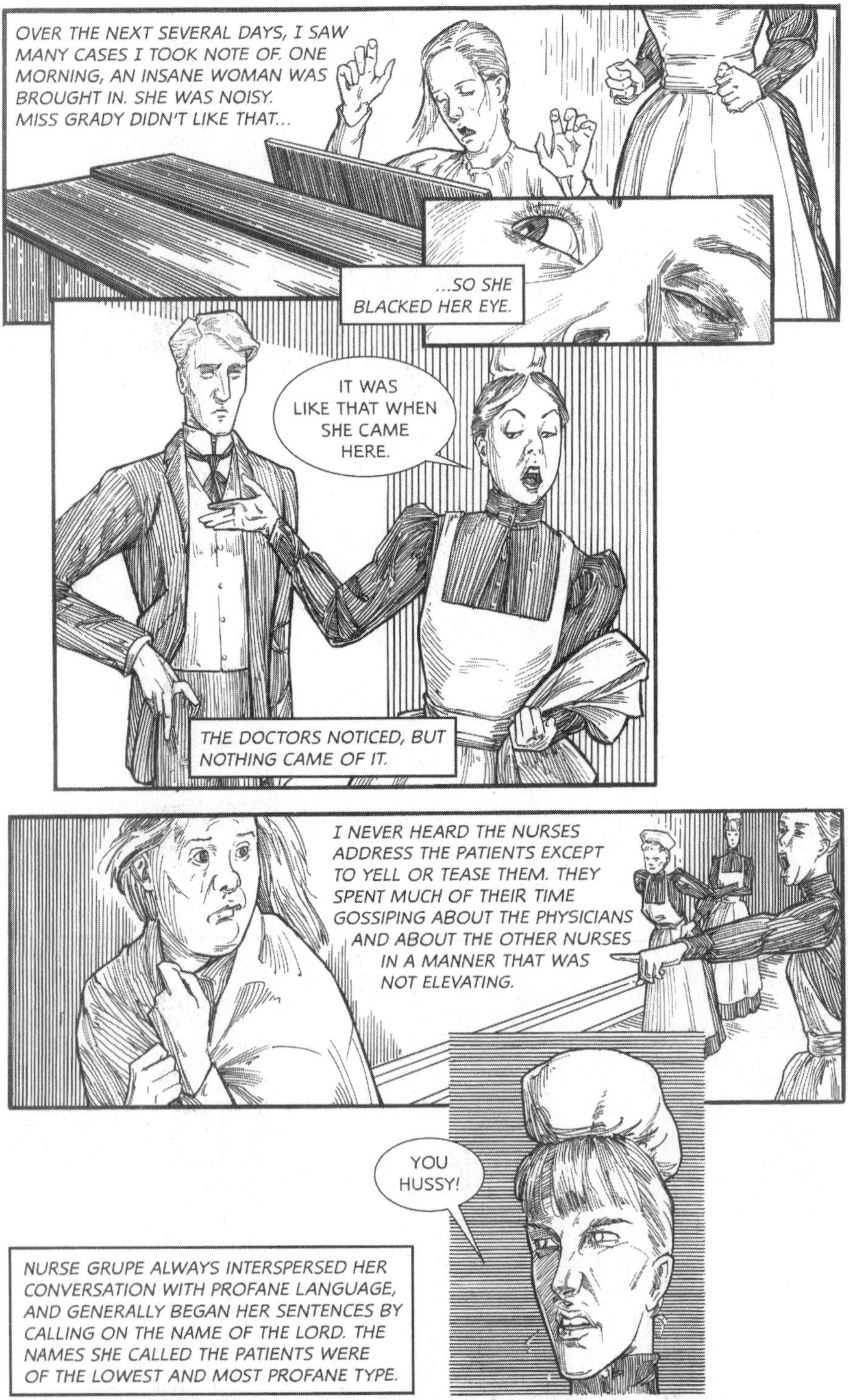

OVER THE NEXT SEVERAL DAYS, I SAW MANY CASES I TOOK NOTE OF. ONE MORNING, AN INSANE WOMAN WAS BROUGHT IN. SHE WAS NOISY. MISS GRADY DIDN'T LIKE THAT...
...SO SHE BLACKED HER EYE.
IT WAS LIKE THAT WHEN SHE CAME HERE.
THE DOCTORS NOTICED, BUT NOTHING CAME OF IT.
I NEVER HEARD THE NURSES ADDRESS THE PATIENTS EXCEPT TO YELL OR TEASE THEM. THEY SPENT MUCH OF THEIR TIME GOSSIPING ABOUT THE PHYSICIANS AND ABOUT THE OTHER NURSES IN A MANNER THAT WAS NOT ELEVATING.
YOU HUSSY!
NURSE GRUPE ALWAYS INTERSPERSED HER CONVERSATION WITH PROFANE LANGUAGE, AND GENERALLY BEGAN HER SENTENCES BY CALLING ON THE NAME OF THE LORD. THE NAMES SHE CALLED THE PATIENTS WERE OF THE LOWEST AND MOST PROFANE TYPE.

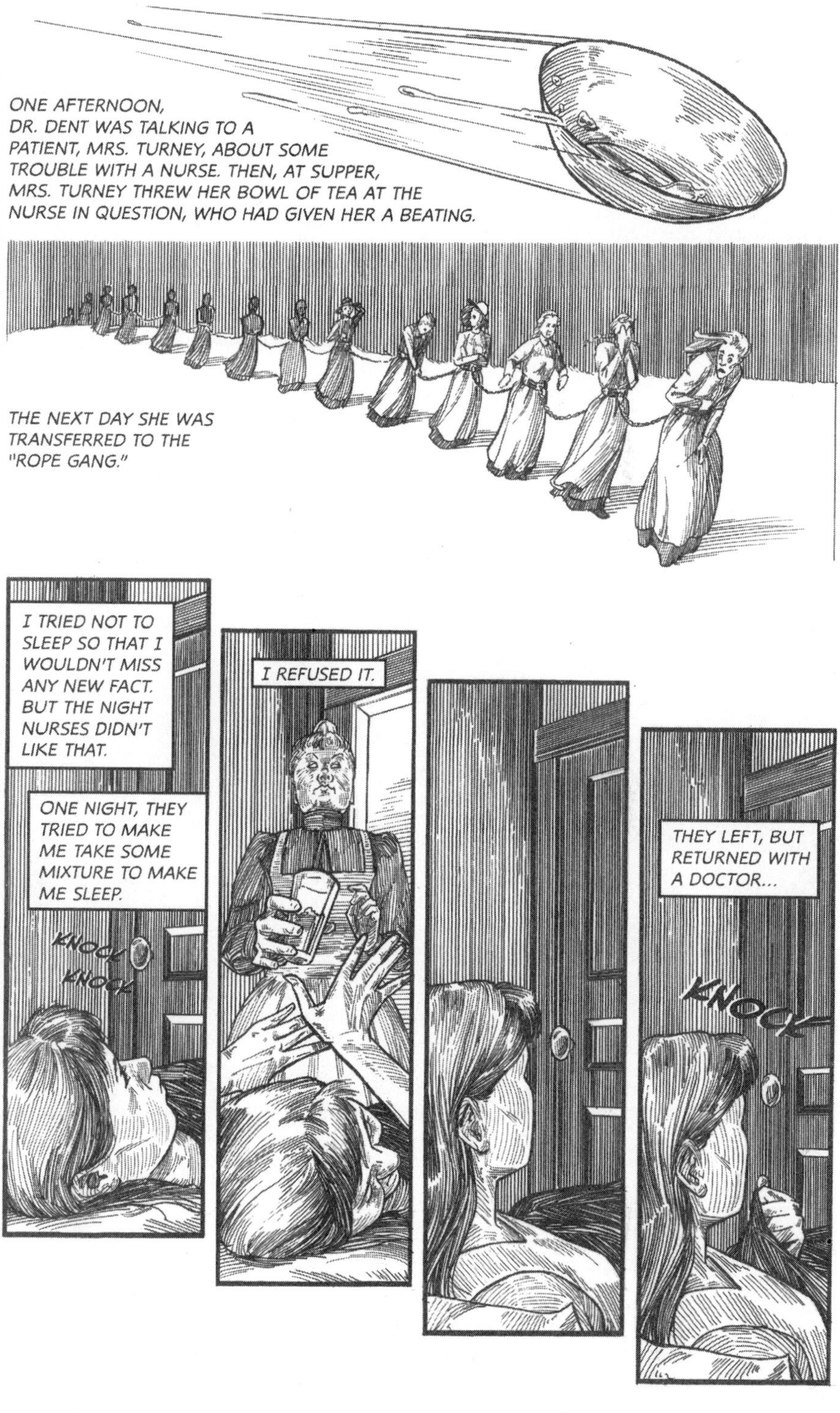
ONE AFTERNOON, DR. DENT WAS TALKING TO A PATIENT, MRS. TURNEY, ABOUT SOME TROUBLE WITH A NURSE. THEN, AT SUPPER, MRS. TURNEY THREW HER BOWL OF TEA AT THE NURSE IN QUESTION, WHO HAD GIVEN HER A BEATING.
THE NEXT DAY SHE WAS TRANSFERRED TO THE "ROPE GANG."
I TRIED NOT TO SLEEP SO THAT I WOULDN'T MISS ANY NEW FACT. BUT THE NIGHT NURSES DIDN'T LIKE THAT.
ONE NIGHT, THEY TRIED TO MAKE ME TAKE SOME MIXTURE TO MAKE ME SLEEP.
KNOCK KNOCK
I REFUSED IT.
THEY LEFT, BUT RETURNED WITH A DOCTOR...
KNOCK

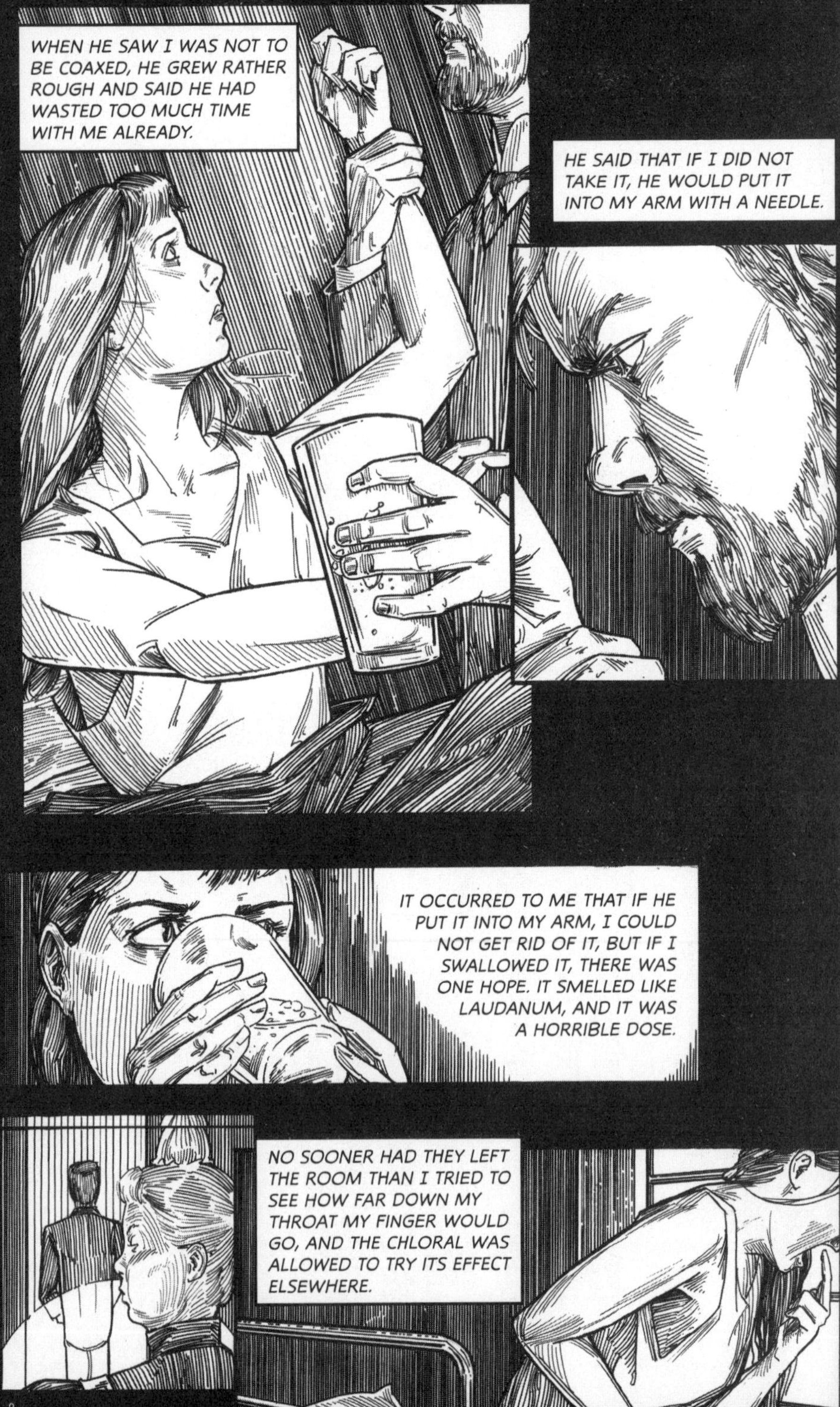
WHEN HE SAW I WAS NOT TO BE COAXED, HE GREW RATHER ROUGH AND SAID HE HAD WASTED TOO MUCH TIME WITH ME ALREADY.
HE SAID THAT IF I DID NOT TAKE IT, HE WOULD PUT IT INTO MY ARM WITH A NEEDLE.
IT OCCURRED TO ME THAT IF HE PUT IT INTO MY ARM, I COULD NOT GET RID OF IT, BUT IF I SWALLOWED IT, THERE WAS ONE HOPE. IT SMELLED LIKE LAUDANUM, AND IT WAS A HORRIBLE DOSE.
NO SOONER HAD THEY LEFT THE ROOM THAN I TRIED TO SEE HOW FAR DOWN MY THROAT MY FINGER WOULD GO, AND THE CHLORAL WAS ALLOWED TO TRY ITS EFFECT ELSEWHERE.

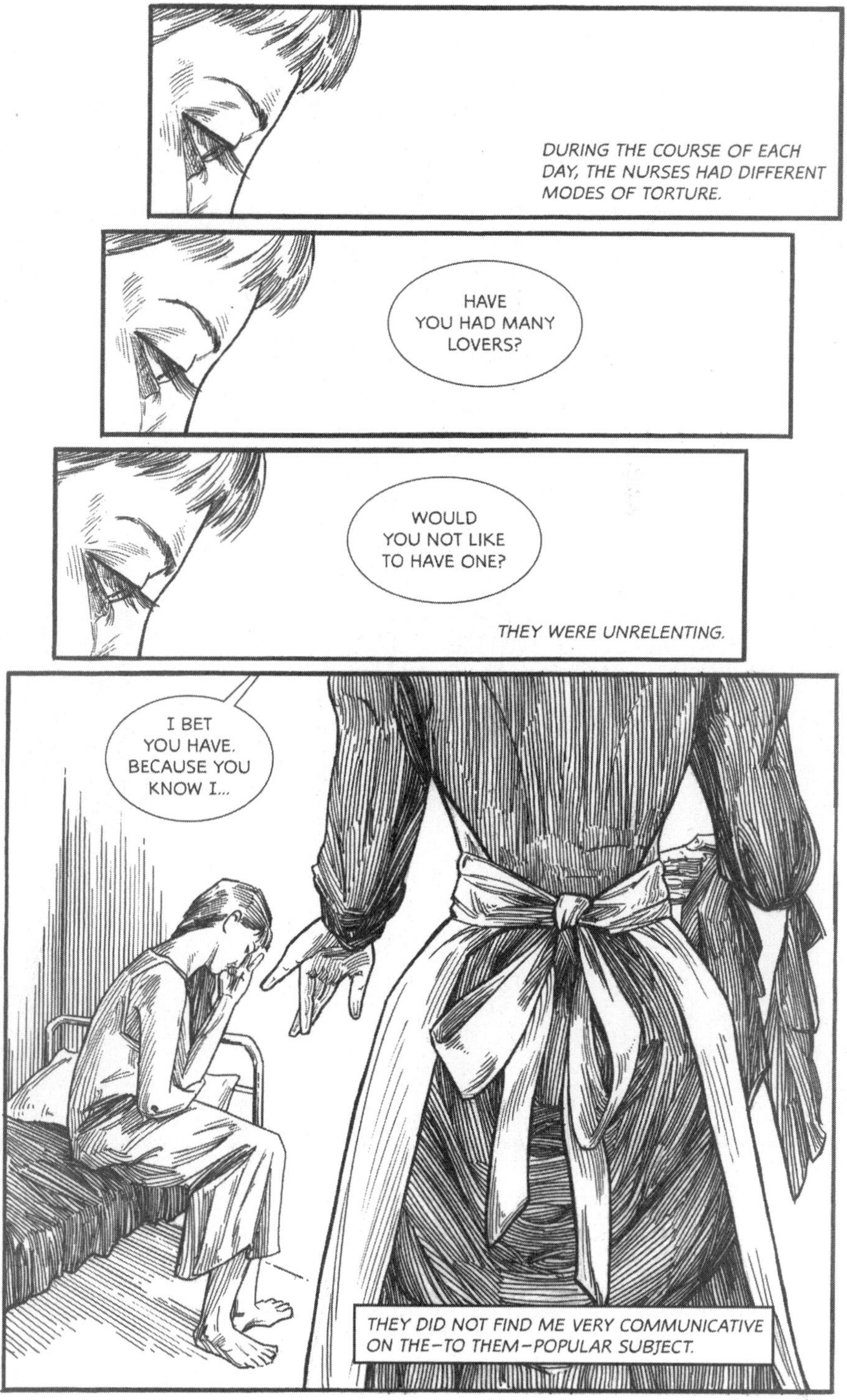
DURING THE COURSE OF EACH DAY, THE NURSES HAD DIFFERENT MODES OF TORTURE.
HAVE YOU HAD MANY LOVERS?
WOULD YOU NOT LIKE TO HAVE ONE?
THEY WERE UNRELENTING.
I BET YOU HAVE. BECAUSE YOU KNOW I...
THEY DID NOT FIND ME VERY COMMUNICATIVE ON THE—TO THEM—POPULAR SUBJECT.

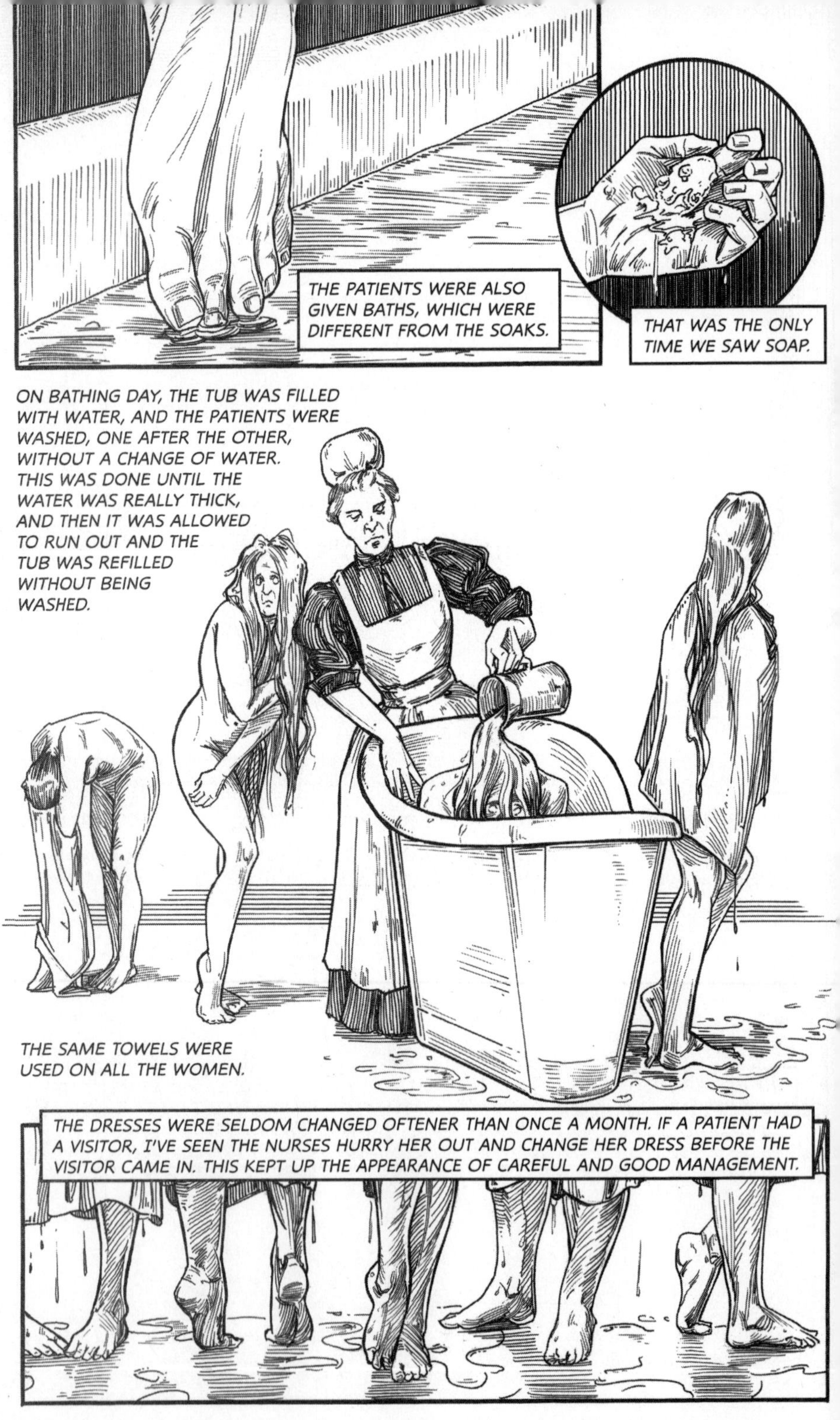
THE PATIENTS WERE ALSO GIVEN BATHS, WHICH WERE DIFFERENT FROM THE SOAKS.
THAT WAS THE ONLY TIME WE SAW SOAP.
ON BATHING DAY, THE TUB WAS FILLED WITH WATER, AND THE PATIENTS WERE WASHED, ONE AFTER THE OTHER, WITHOUT A CHANGE OF WATER. THIS WAS DONE UNTIL THE WATER WAS REALLY THICK, AND THEN IT WAS ALLOWED TO RUN OUT AND THE TUB WAS REFILLED WITHOUT BEING WASHED.
THE SAME TOWELS WERE USED ON ALL THE WOMEN.
THE DRESSES WERE SELDOM CHANGED OFTENER THAN ONCE A MONTH. IF A PATIENT HAD A VISITOR, I'VE SEEN THE NURSES HURRY HER OUT AND CHANGE HER DRESS BEFORE THE VISITOR CAME IN. THIS KEPT UP THE APPEARANCE OF CAREFUL AND GOOD MANAGEMENT.

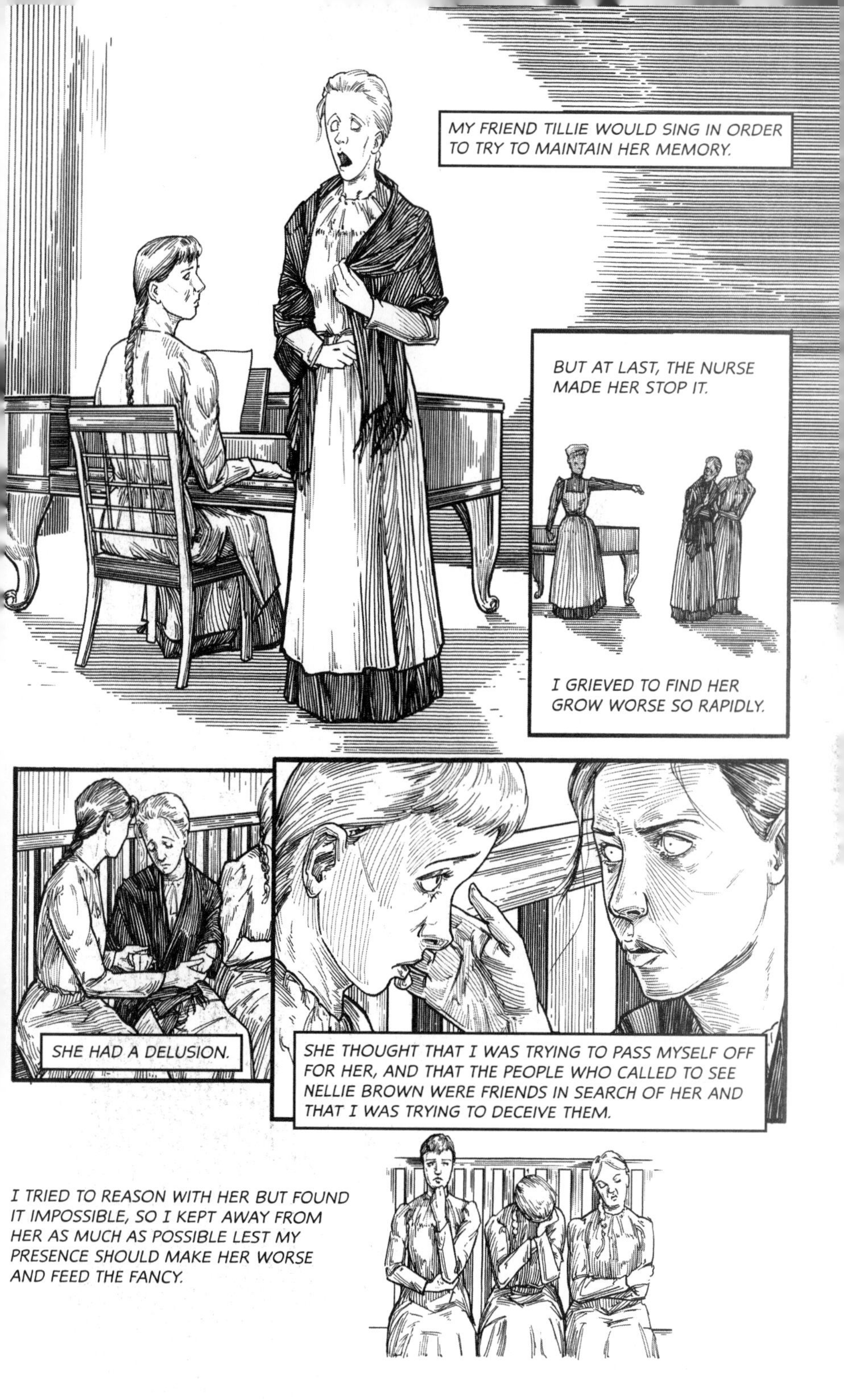
MY FRIEND TILLIE WOULD SING IN ORDER TO TRY TO MAINTAIN HER MEMORY.
BUT AT LAST, THE NURSE MADE HER STOP IT.
I GRIEVED TO FIND HER GROW WORSE SO RAPIDLY.
SHE HAD A DELUSION.
SHE THOUGHT THAT I WAS TRYING TO PASS MYSELF OFF FOR HER, AND THAT THE PEOPLE WHO CALLED TO SEE NELLIE BROWN WERE FRIENDS IN SEARCH OF HER AND THAT I WAS TRYING TO DECEIVE THEM.
I TRIED TO REASON WITH HER BUT FOUND IT IMPOSSIBLE, SO I KEPT AWAY FROM HER AS MUCH AS POSSIBLE LEST MY PRESENCE SHOULD MAKE HER WORSE AND FEED THE FANCY.

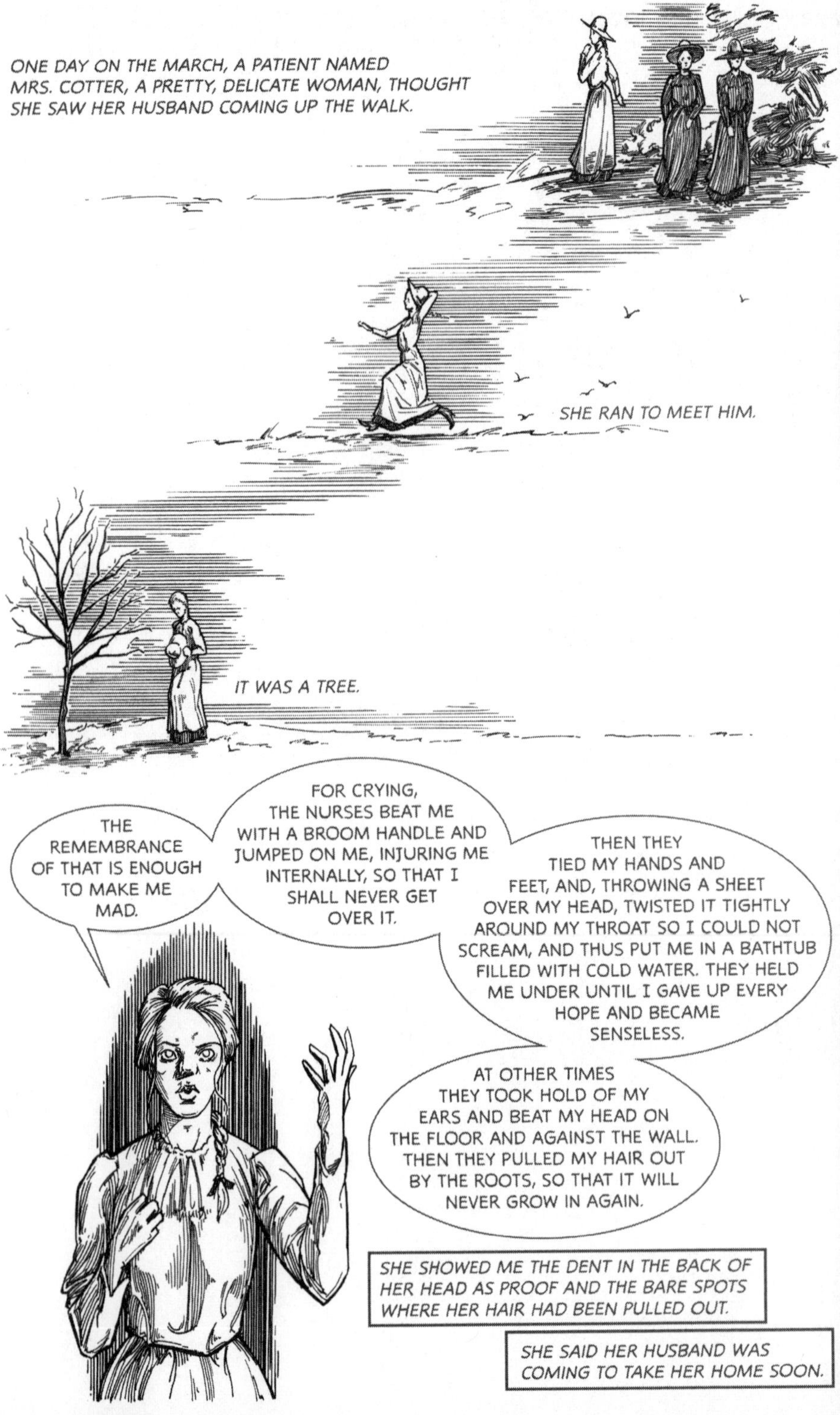

ONE DAY ON THE MARCH, A PATIENT NAMED MRS. COTTER, A PRETTY, DELICATE WOMAN, THOUGHT SHE SAW HER HUSBAND COMING UP THE WALK.
SHE RAN TO MEET HIM.
IT WAS A TREE.
THE REMEMBRANCE OF THAT IS ENOUGH TO MAKE ME MAD.
FOR CRYING, THE NURSES BEAT ME WITH A BROOM HANDLE AND JUMPED ON ME, INJURING ME INTERNALLY, SO THAT I SHALL NEVER GET OVER IT.
THEN THEY TIED MY HANDS AND FEET, AND, THROWING A SHEET OVER MY HEAD, TWISTED IT TIGHTLY AROUND MY THROAT SO I COULD NOT SCREAM, AND THUS PUT ME IN A BATHTUB FILLED WITH COLD WATER. THEY HELD ME UNDER UNTIL I GAVE UP EVERY HOPE AND BECAME SENSELESS.
AT OTHER TIMES THEY TOOK HOLD OF MY EARS AND BEAT MY HEAD ON THE FLOOR AND AGAINST THE WALL. THEN THEY PULLED MY HAIR OUT BY THE ROOTS, SO THAT IT WILL NEVER GROW IN AGAIN.
SHE SHOWED ME THE DENT IN THE BACK OF HER HEAD AS PROOF AND THE BARE SPOTS WHERE HER HAIR HAD BEEN PULLED OUT.
SHE SAID HER HUSBAND WAS COMING TO TAKE HER HOME SOON.

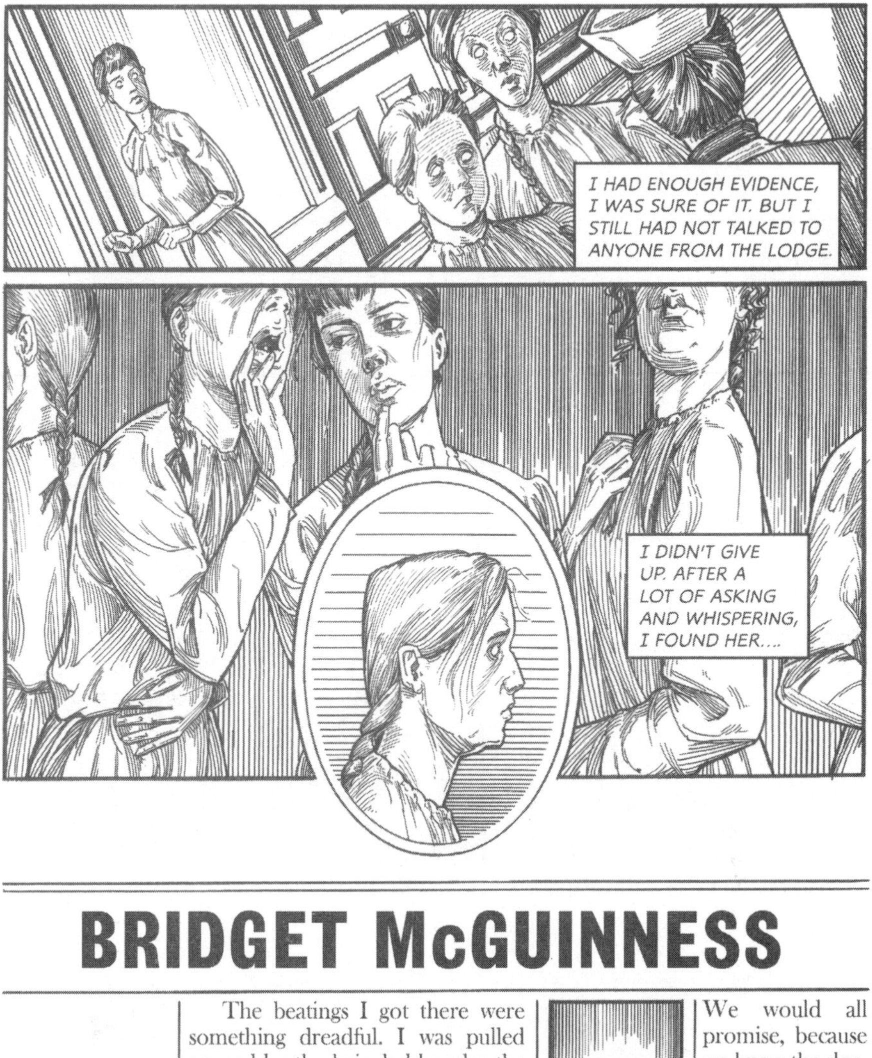
I HAD ENOUGH EVIDENCE, I WAS SURE OF IT. BUT I STILL HAD NOT TALKED TO ANYONE FROM THE LODGE.
I DIDN'T GIVE UP. AFTER A LOT OF ASKING AND WHISPERING, I FOUND HER....

BRIDGET McGUINNESS

THEY SENT ME TO THE RETREAT IN THE ROPE GANG.

The beatings I got there were something dreadful. I was pulled around by the hair, held under the water until I strangled, and I was choked and kicked. The nurses would always keep a quiet patient stationed at the window to tell them when any of the doctors were approaching. It was hopeless to complain to the doctors, for they always said it was the imagination of our diseased brains, and besides we would get another beating for telling. They would hold patients under the water and threaten to leave them to die there if they did not promise not to tell the doctors.

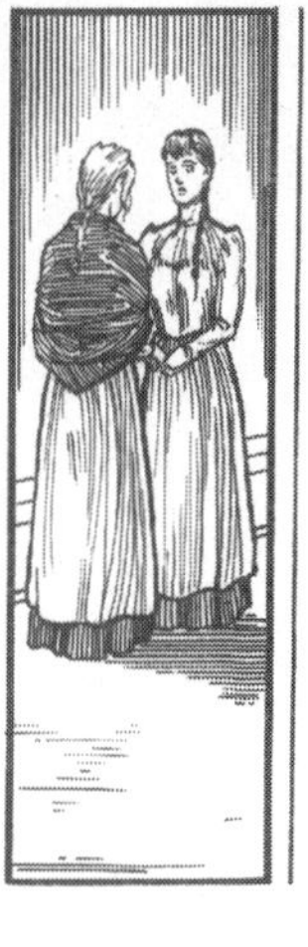

We would all promise, because we knew the doctors would not help us, and we would do anything to escape the punishment.

After breaking a window I was transferred to the Lodge, the worst place on the island.

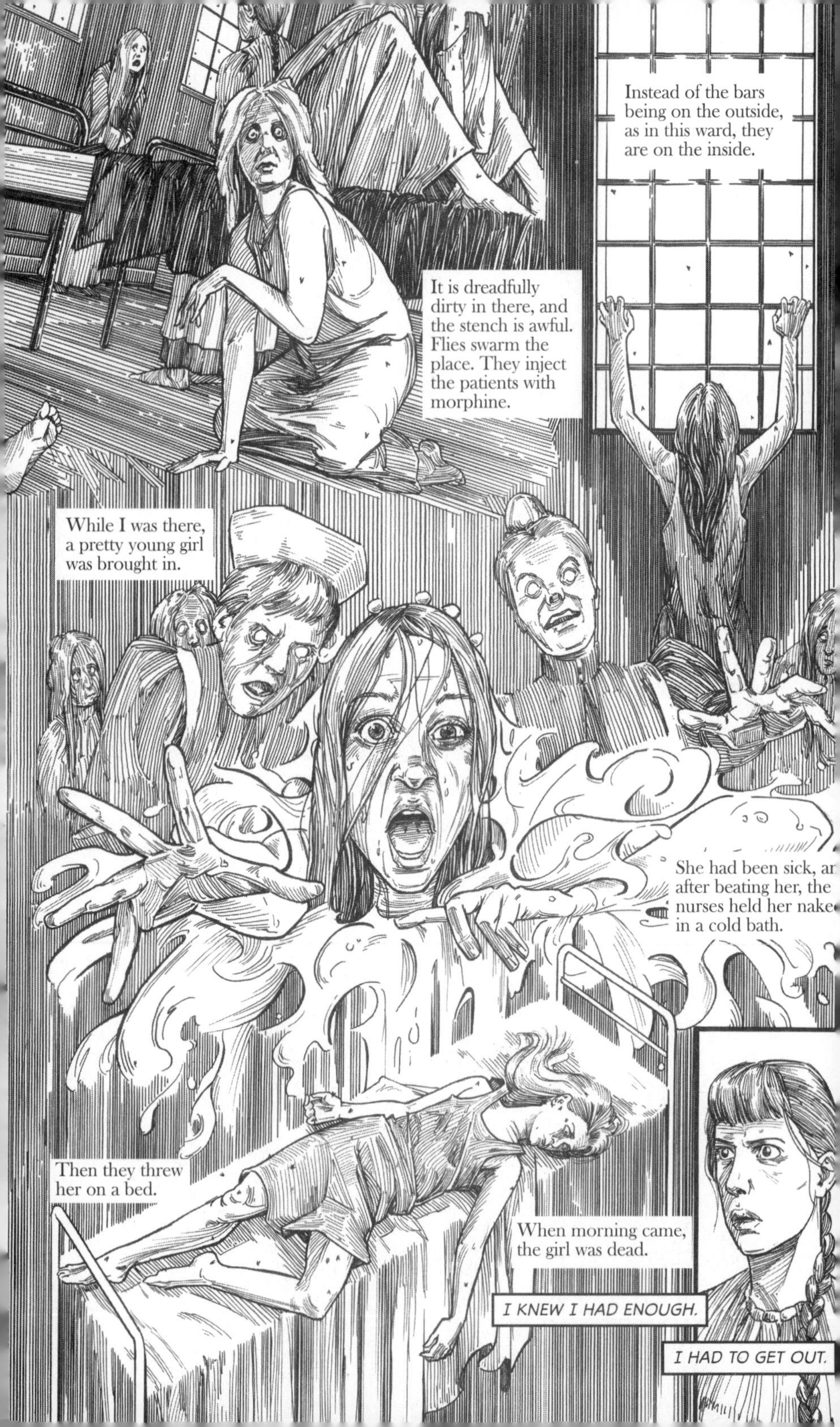
It is dreadfully dirty in there, and the stench is awful. Flies swarm the place. They inject the patients with morphine.
Instead of the bars being on the outside, as in this ward, they are on the inside.
While I was there, a pretty young girl was brought in.
She had been sick, ar after beating her, the nurses held her nake in a cold bath.
Then they threw her on a bed.
When morning came, the girl was dead.
I KNEW I HAD ENOUGH.
I HAD TO GET OUT.

PART III

· THE WAY OUT ·

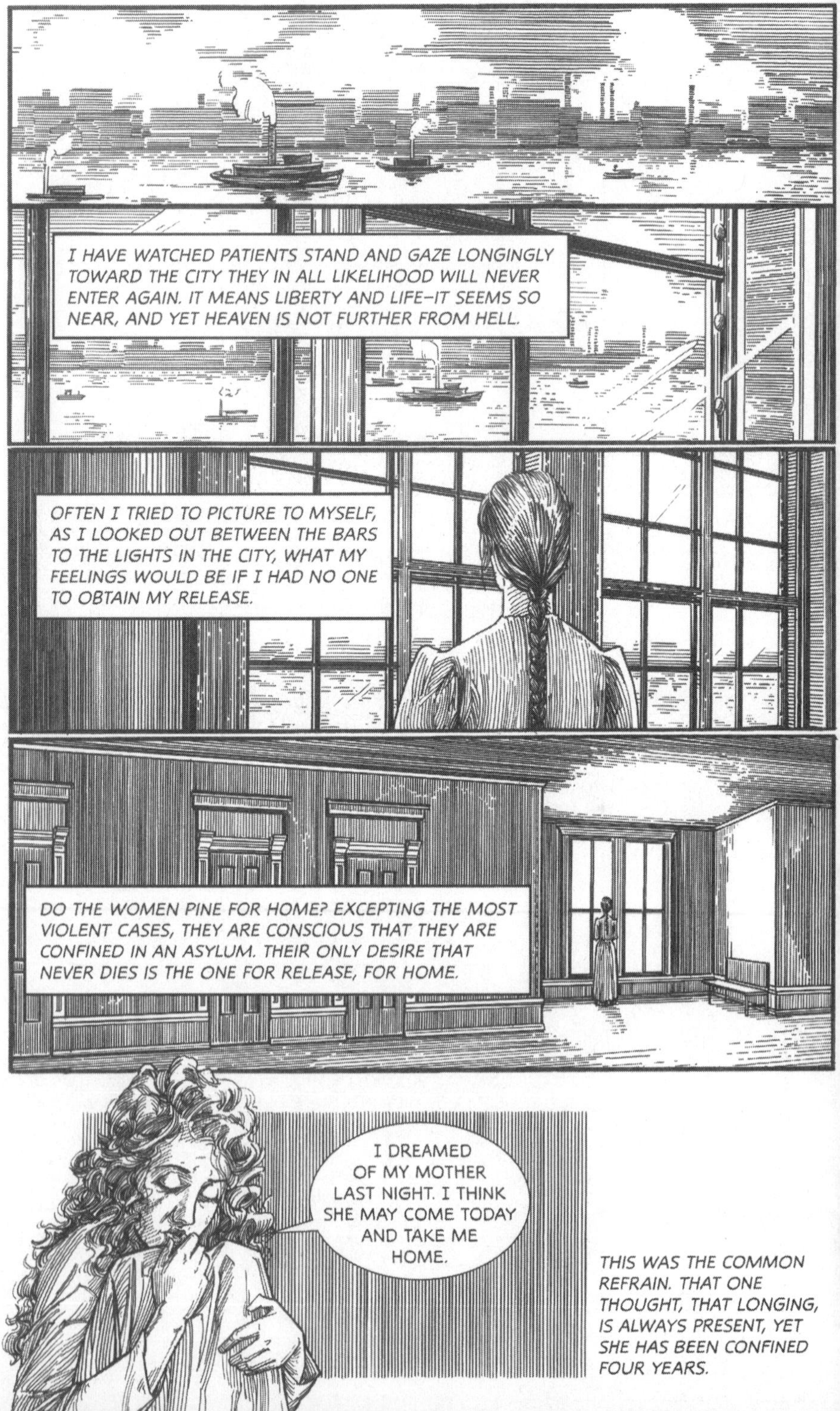
I HAVE WATCHED PATIENTS STAND AND GAZE LONGINGLY TOWARD THE CITY THEY IN ALL LIKELIHOOD WILL NEVER ENTER AGAIN. IT MEANS LIBERTY AND LIFE—IT SEEMS SO NEAR, AND YET HEAVEN IS NOT FURTHER FROM HELL.
OFTEN I TRIED TO PICTURE TO MYSELF, AS I LOOKED OUT BETWEEN THE BARS TO THE LIGHTS IN THE CITY, WHAT MY FEELINGS WOULD BE IF I HAD NO ONE TO OBTAIN MY RELEASE.
DO THE WOMEN PINE FOR HOME? EXCEPTING THE MOST VIOLENT CASES, THEY ARE CONSCIOUS THAT THEY ARE CONFINED IN AN ASYLUM. THEIR ONLY DESIRE THAT NEVER DIES IS THE ONE FOR RELEASE, FOR HOME.
I DREAMED OF MY MOTHER LAST NIGHT. I THINK SHE MAY COME TODAY AND TAKE ME HOME.
THIS WAS THE COMMON REFRAIN. THAT ONE THOUGHT, THAT LONGING, IS ALWAYS PRESENT, YET SHE HAS BEEN CONFINED FOUR YEARS.

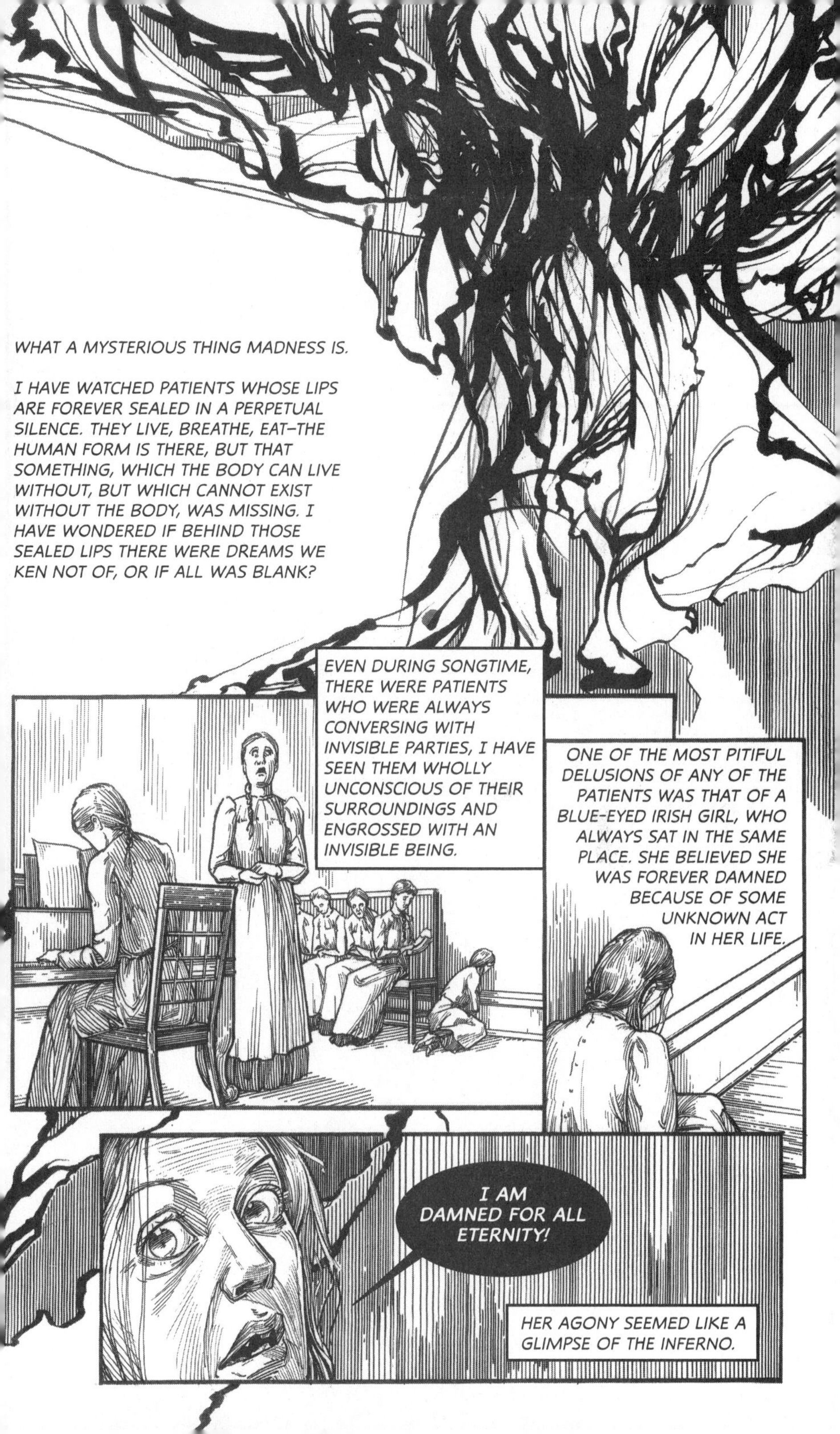
WHAT A MYSTERIOUS THING MADNESS IS.
I HAVE WATCHED PATIENTS WHOSE LIPS ARE FOREVER SEALED IN A PERPETUAL SILENCE. THEY LIVE, BREATHE, EAT–THE HUMAN FORM IS THERE, BUT THAT SOMETHING, WHICH THE BODY CAN LIVE WITHOUT, BUT WHICH CANNOT EXIST WITHOUT THE BODY, WAS MISSING. I HAVE WONDERED IF BEHIND THOSE SEALED LIPS THERE WERE DREAMS WE KEN NOT OF, OR IF ALL WAS BLANK?
EVEN DURING SONGTIME, THERE WERE PATIENTS WHO WERE ALWAYS CONVERSING WITH INVISIBLE PARTIES, I HAVE SEEN THEM WHOLLY UNCONSCIOUS OF THEIR SURROUNDINGS AND ENGROSSED WITH AN INVISIBLE BEING.
ONE OF THE MOST PITIFUL DELUSIONS OF ANY OF THE PATIENTS WAS THAT OF A BLUE-EYED IRISH GIRL, WHO ALWAYS SAT IN THE SAME PLACE. SHE BELIEVED SHE WAS FOREVER DAMNED BECAUSE OF SOME UNKNOWN ACT IN HER LIFE.
I AM DAMNED FOR ALL ETERNITY!
HER AGONY SEEMED LIKE A GLIMPSE OF THE INFERNO.

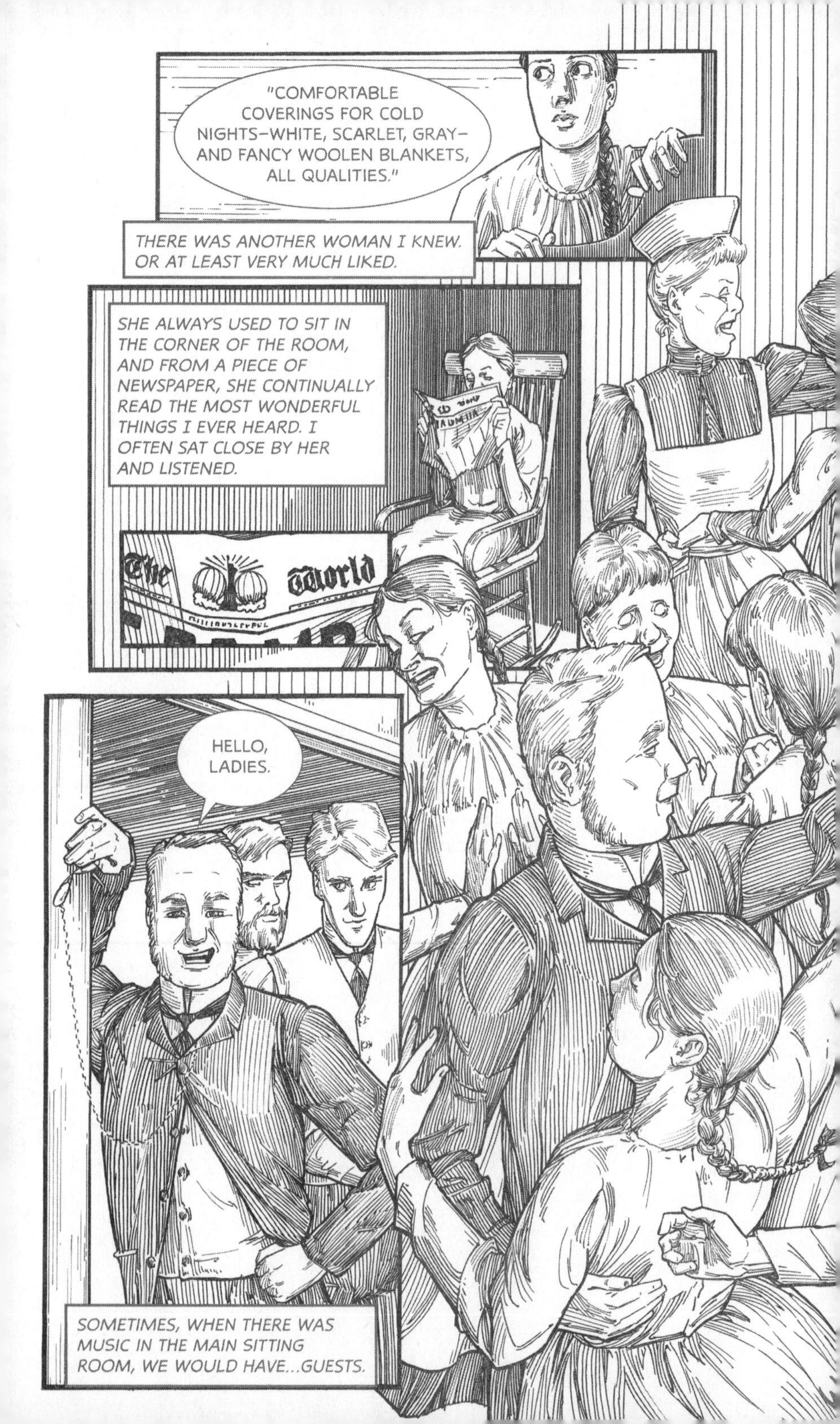
"COMFORTABLE COVERINGS FOR COLD NIGHTS–WHITE, SCARLET, GRAY–AND FANCY WOOLEN BLANKETS, ALL QUALITIES."
THERE WAS ANOTHER WOMAN I KNEW. OR AT LEAST VERY MUCH LIKED.
SHE ALWAYS USED TO SIT IN THE CORNER OF THE ROOM, AND FROM A PIECE OF NEWSPAPER, SHE CONTINUALLY READ THE MOST WONDERFUL THINGS I EVER HEARD. I OFTEN SAT CLOSE BY HER AND LISTENED.
The World
HELLO, LADIES.
SOMETIMES, WHEN THERE WAS MUSIC IN THE MAIN SITTING ROOM, WE WOULD HAVE...GUESTS.

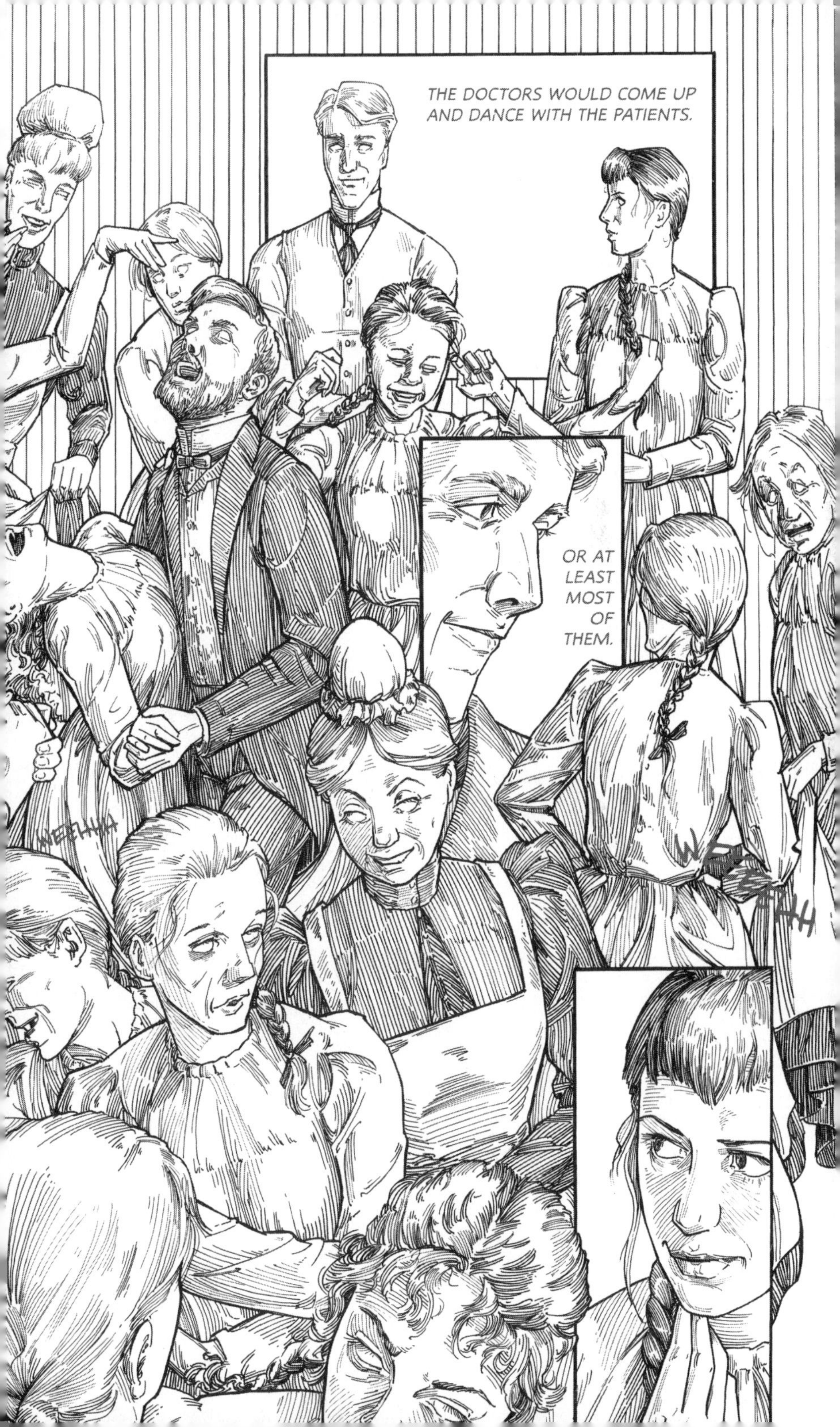
THE DOCTORS WOULD COME UP AND DANCE WITH THE PATIENTS.
OR AT LEAST MOST OF THEM.
WEEHHA

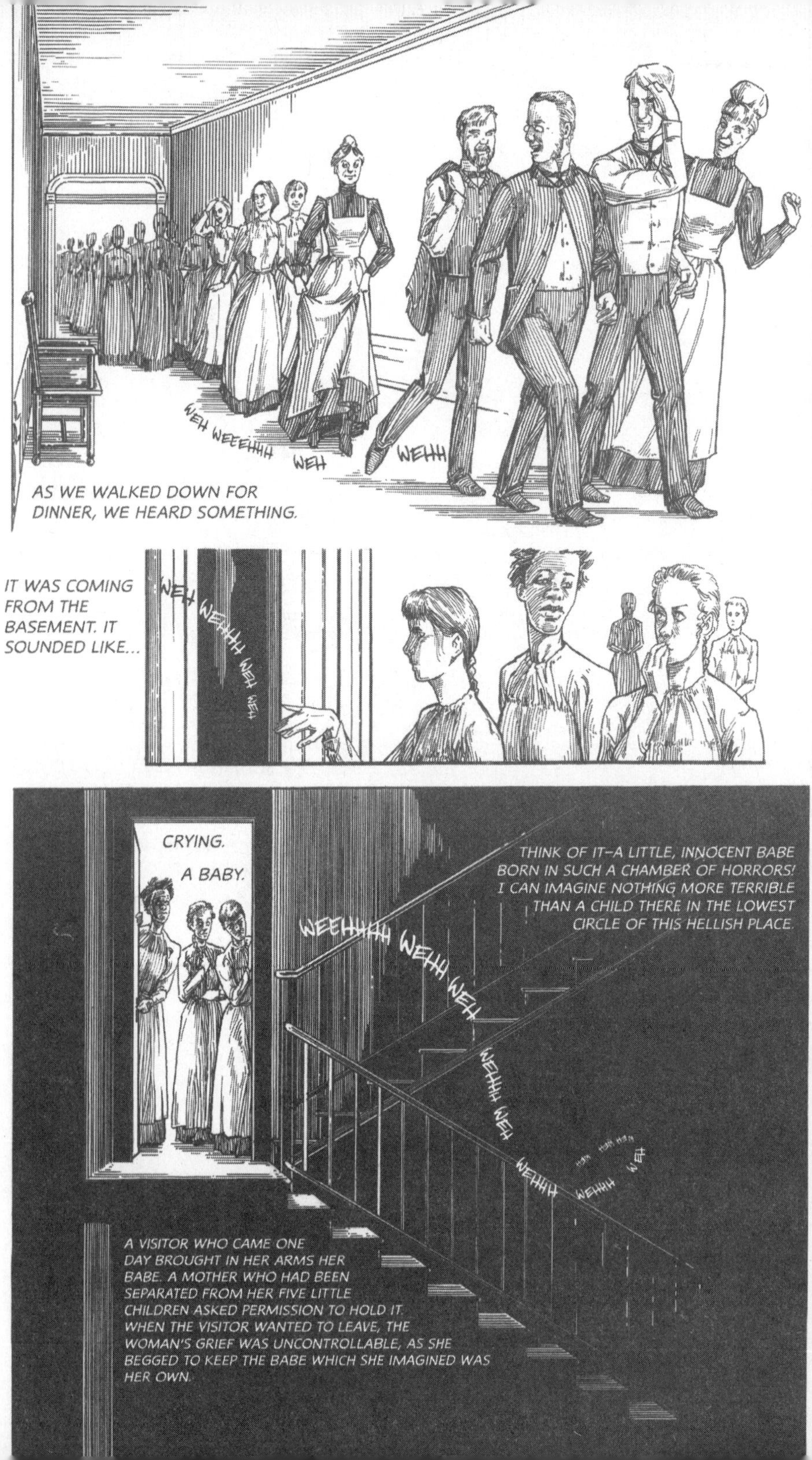
WEH WEEEHHH
WEH
WEHH
AS WE WALKED DOWN FOR DINNER, WE HEARD SOMETHING.
IT WAS COMING FROM THE BASEMENT. IT SOUNDED LIKE...
WEH
WEHHH
WEH
WEH
CRYING.
A BABY.
THINK OF IT–A LITTLE, INNOCENT BABE BORN IN SUCH A CHAMBER OF HORRORS! I CAN IMAGINE NOTHING MORE TERRIBLE THAN A CHILD THERE IN THE LOWEST CIRCLE OF THIS HELLISH PLACE.
WEEHHHH
WEHH
WEH
WEHHH
WEH
WEHHH
WEHHH
WEH
A VISITOR WHO CAME ONE DAY BROUGHT IN HER ARMS HER BABE. A MOTHER WHO HAD BEEN SEPARATED FROM HER FIVE LITTLE CHILDREN ASKED PERMISSION TO HOLD IT. WHEN THE VISITOR WANTED TO LEAVE, THE WOMAN'S GRIEF WAS UNCONTROLLABLE, AS SHE BEGGED TO KEEP THE BABE WHICH SHE IMAGINED WAS HER OWN.

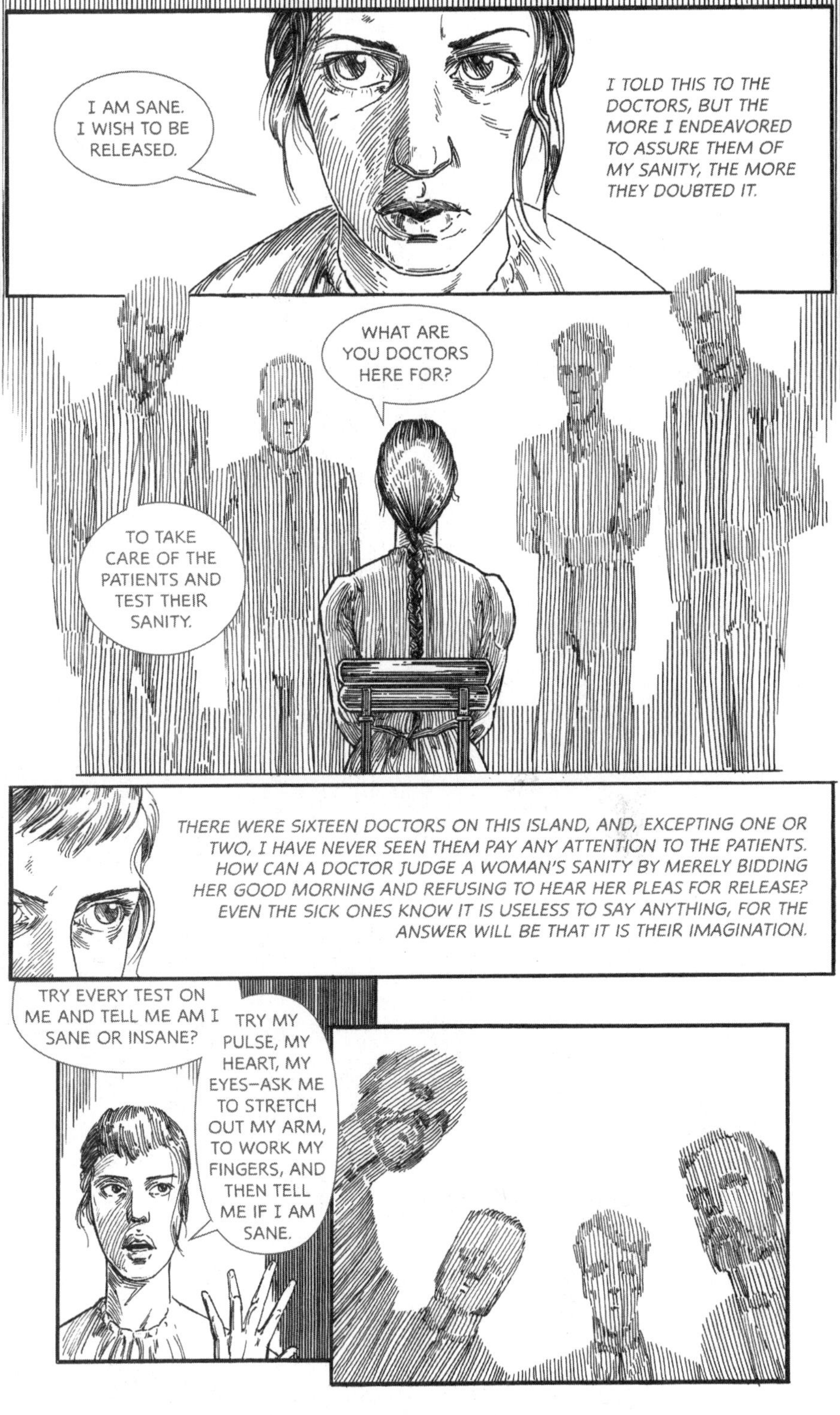
I AM SANE. I WISH TO BE RELEASED.
I TOLD THIS TO THE DOCTORS, BUT THE MORE I ENDEAVORED TO ASSURE THEM OF MY SANITY, THE MORE THEY DOUBTED IT.
WHAT ARE YOU DOCTORS HERE FOR?
TO TAKE CARE OF THE PATIENTS AND TEST THEIR SANITY.
THERE WERE SIXTEEN DOCTORS ON THIS ISLAND, AND, EXCEPTING ONE OR TWO, I HAVE NEVER SEEN THEM PAY ANY ATTENTION TO THE PATIENTS. HOW CAN A DOCTOR JUDGE A WOMAN'S SANITY BY MERELY BIDDING HER GOOD MORNING AND REFUSING TO HEAR HER PLEAS FOR RELEASE? EVEN THE SICK ONES KNOW IT IS USELESS TO SAY ANYTHING, FOR THE ANSWER WILL BE THAT IT IS THEIR IMAGINATION.
TRY EVERY TEST ON ME AND TELL ME AM I SANE OR INSANE?
TRY MY PULSE, MY HEART, MY EYES—ASK ME TO STRETCH OUT MY ARM, TO WORK MY FINGERS, AND THEN TELL ME IF I AM SANE.

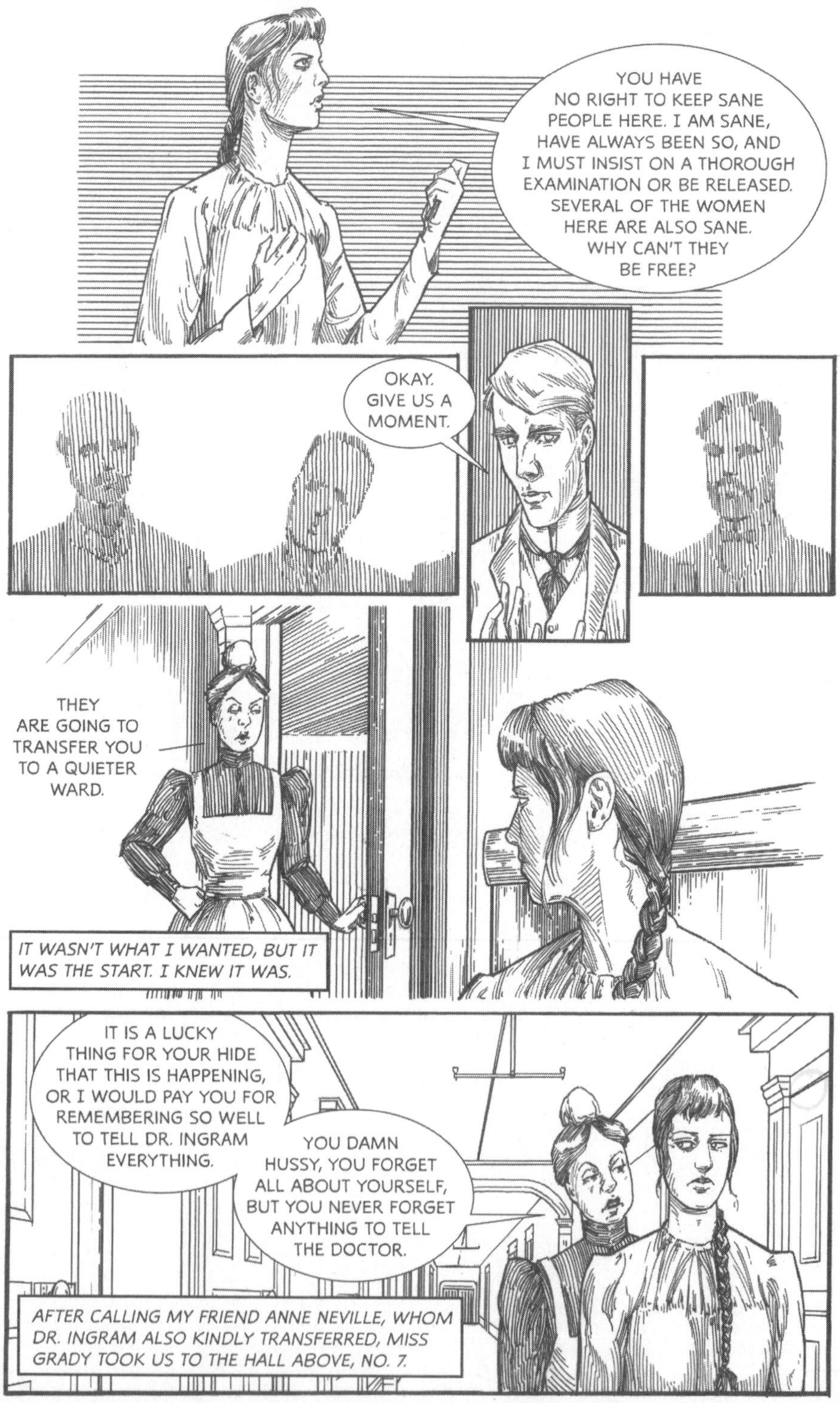
YOU HAVE NO RIGHT TO KEEP SANE PEOPLE HERE. I AM SANE, HAVE ALWAYS BEEN SO, AND I MUST INSIST ON A THOROUGH EXAMINATION OR BE RELEASED. SEVERAL OF THE WOMEN HERE ARE ALSO SANE. WHY CAN'T THEY BE FREE?
OKAY. GIVE US A MOMENT.
THEY ARE GOING TO TRANSFER YOU TO A QUIETER WARD.
IT WASN'T WHAT I WANTED, BUT IT WAS THE START. I KNEW IT WAS.
IT IS A LUCKY THING FOR YOUR HIDE THAT THIS IS HAPPENING, OR I WOULD PAY YOU FOR REMEMBERING SO WELL TO TELL DR. INGRAM EVERYTHING.
YOU DAMN HUSSY, YOU FORGET ALL ABOUT YOURSELF, BUT YOU NEVER FORGET ANYTHING TO TELL THE DOCTOR.
AFTER CALLING MY FRIEND ANNE NEVILLE, WHOM DR. INGRAM ALSO KINDLY TRANSFERRED, MISS GRADY TOOK US TO THE HALL ABOVE, NO. 7.

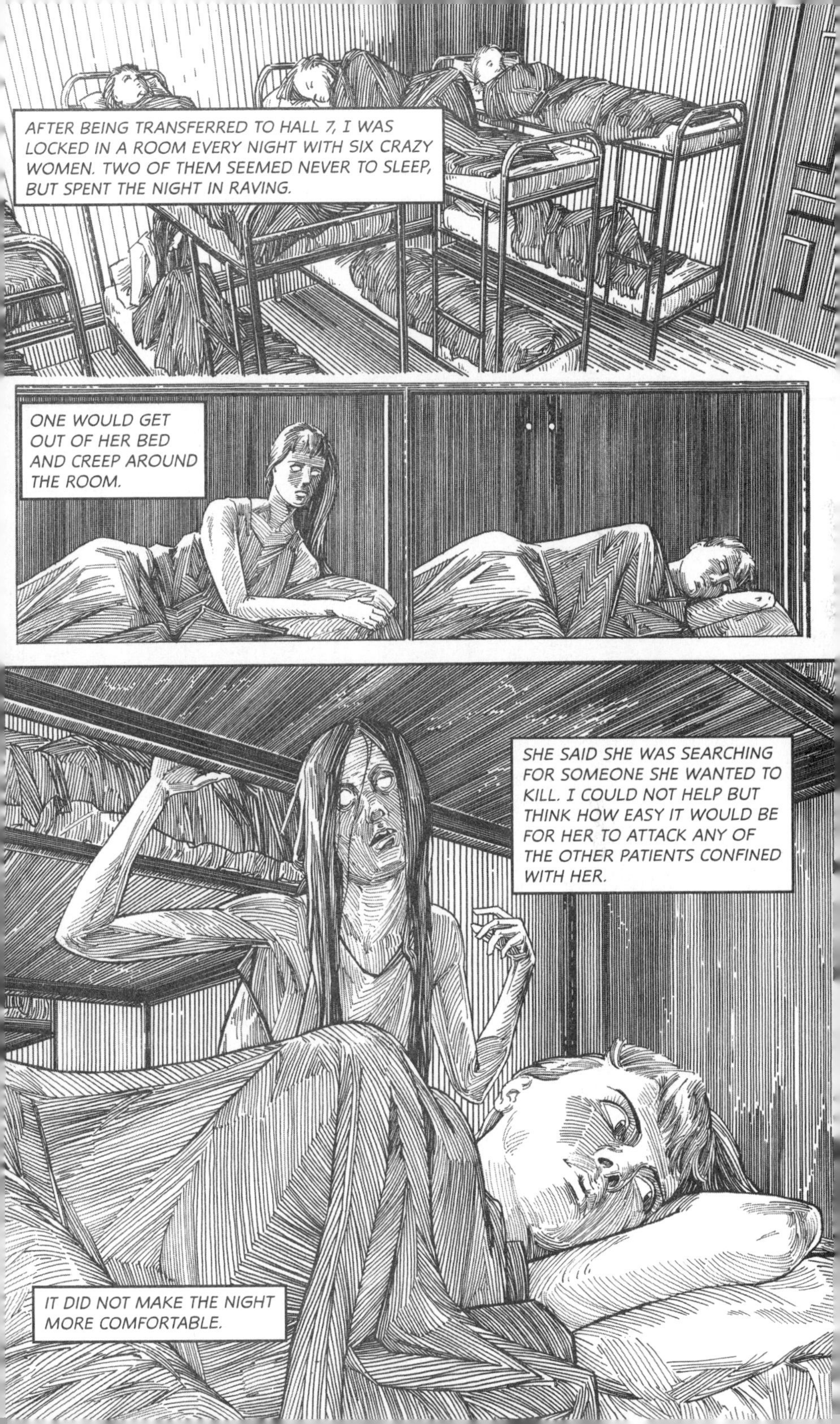
AFTER BEING TRANSFERRED TO HALL 7, I WAS LOCKED IN A ROOM EVERY NIGHT WITH SIX CRAZY WOMEN. TWO OF THEM SEEMED NEVER TO SLEEP, BUT SPENT THE NIGHT IN RAVING.
ONE WOULD GET OUT OF HER BED AND CREEP AROUND THE ROOM.
SHE SAID SHE WAS SEARCHING FOR SOMEONE SHE WANTED TO KILL. I COULD NOT HELP BUT THINK HOW EASY IT WOULD BE FOR HER TO ATTACK ANY OF THE OTHER PATIENTS CONFINED WITH HER.
IT DID NOT MAKE THE NIGHT MORE COMFORTABLE.

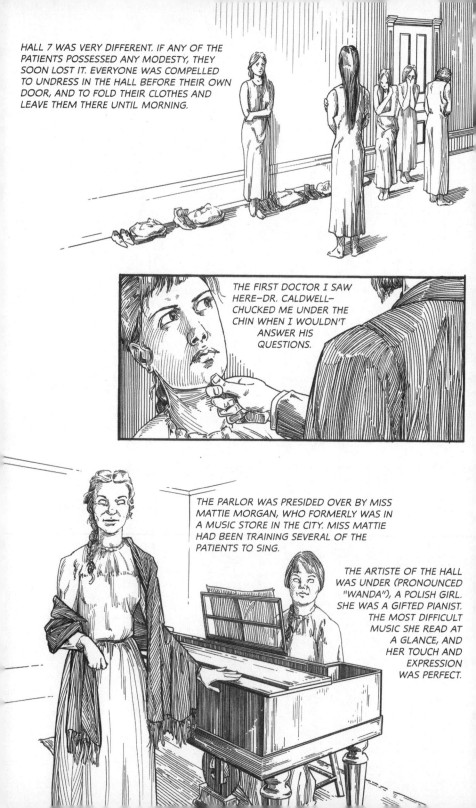

HALL 7 WAS VERY DIFFERENT. IF ANY OF THE PATIENTS POSSESSED ANY MODESTY, THEY SOON LOST IT. EVERYONE WAS COMPELLED TO UNDRESS IN THE HALL BEFORE THEIR OWN DOOR, AND TO FOLD THEIR CLOTHES AND LEAVE THEM THERE UNTIL MORNING.

THE FIRST DOCTOR I SAW HERE—DR. CALDWELL—CHUCKED ME UNDER THE CHIN WHEN I WOULDN'T ANSWER HIS QUESTIONS.

THE PARLOR WAS PRESIDED OVER BY MISS MATTIE MORGAN, WHO FORMERLY WAS IN A MUSIC STORE IN THE CITY. MISS MATTIE HAD BEEN TRAINING SEVERAL OF THE PATIENTS TO SING.

THE ARTISTE OF THE HALL WAS UNDER (PRONOUNCED "WANDA"), A POLISH GIRL. SHE WAS A GIFTED PIANIST. THE MOST DIFFICULT MUSIC SHE READ AT A GLANCE, AND HER TOUCH AND EXPRESSION WAS PERFECT.

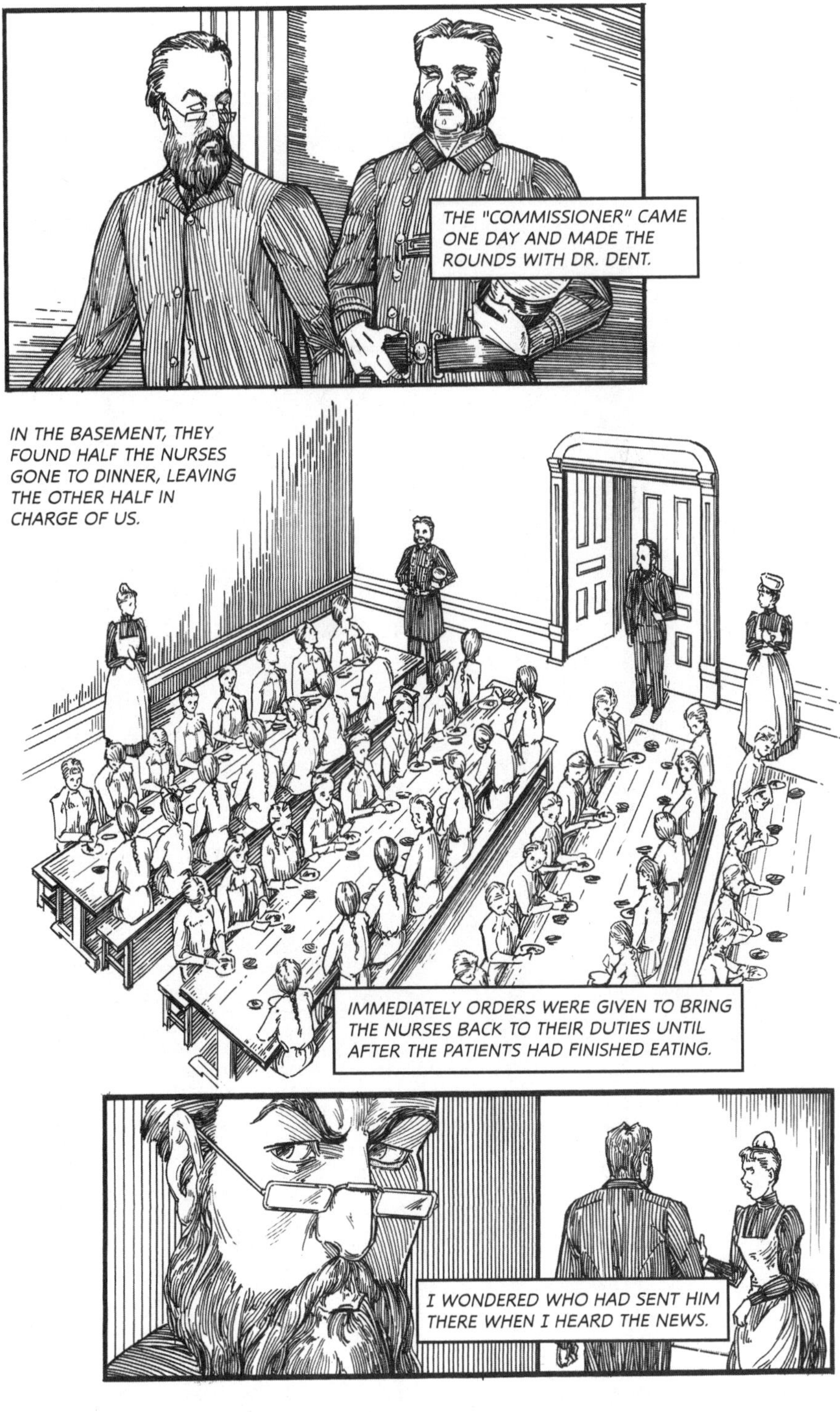
THE "COMMISSIONER" CAME ONE DAY AND MADE THE ROUNDS WITH DR. DENT.
IN THE BASEMENT, THEY FOUND HALF THE NURSES GONE TO DINNER, LEAVING THE OTHER HALF IN CHARGE OF US.
IMMEDIATELY ORDERS WERE GIVEN TO BRING THE NURSES BACK TO THEIR DUTIES UNTIL AFTER THE PATIENTS HAD FINISHED EATING.
I WONDERED WHO HAD SENT HIM THERE WHEN I HEARD THE NEWS.

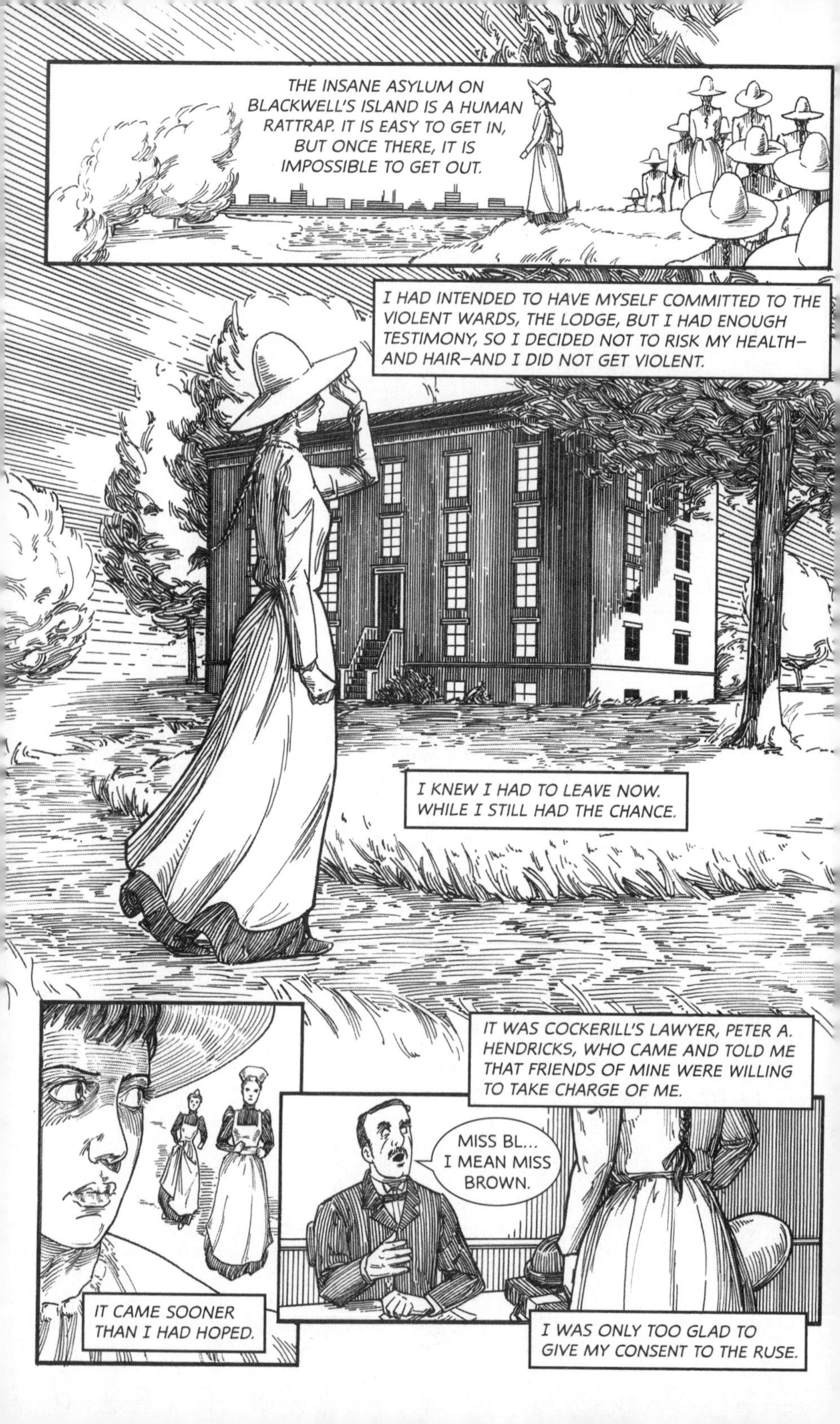

THE INSANE ASYLUM ON BLACKWELL'S ISLAND IS A HUMAN RATTRAP. IT IS EASY TO GET IN, BUT ONCE THERE, IT IS IMPOSSIBLE TO GET OUT.
I HAD INTENDED TO HAVE MYSELF COMMITTED TO THE VIOLENT WARDS, THE LODGE, BUT I HAD ENOUGH TESTIMONY, SO I DECIDED NOT TO RISK MY HEALTH—AND HAIR—AND I DID NOT GET VIOLENT.
I KNEW I HAD TO LEAVE NOW. WHILE I STILL HAD THE CHANCE.
IT CAME SOONER THAN I HAD HOPED.
IT WAS COCKERILL'S LAWYER, PETER A. HENDRICKS, WHO CAME AND TOLD ME THAT FRIENDS OF MINE WERE WILLING TO TAKE CHARGE OF ME.
MISS BL... I MEAN MISS BROWN.
I WAS ONLY TOO GLAD TO GIVE MY CONSENT TO THE RUSE.

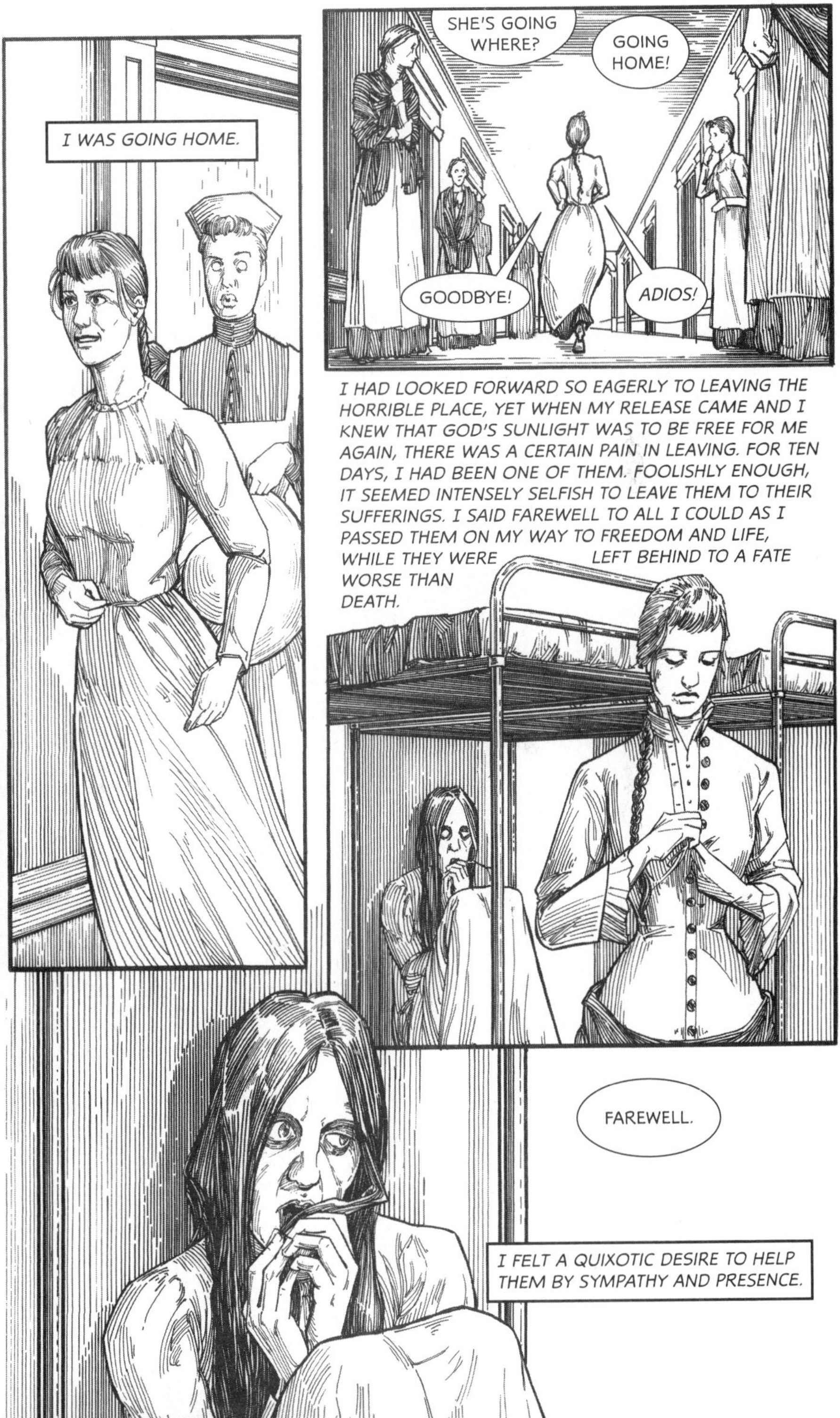
I WAS GOING HOME.
SHE'S GOING WHERE?
GOING HOME!
GOODBYE!
ADIOS!
I HAD LOOKED FORWARD SO EAGERLY TO LEAVING THE HORRIBLE PLACE, YET WHEN MY RELEASE CAME AND I KNEW THAT GOD'S SUNLIGHT WAS TO BE FREE FOR ME AGAIN, THERE WAS A CERTAIN PAIN IN LEAVING. FOR TEN DAYS, I HAD BEEN ONE OF THEM. FOOLISHLY ENOUGH, IT SEEMED INTENSELY SELFISH TO LEAVE THEM TO THEIR SUFFERINGS. I SAID FAREWELL TO ALL I COULD AS I PASSED THEM ON MY WAY TO FREEDOM AND LIFE, WHILE THEY WERE LEFT BEHIND TO A FATE WORSE THAN DEATH.
FAREWELL.
I FELT A QUIXOTIC DESIRE TO HELP THEM BY SYMPATHY AND PRESENCE.

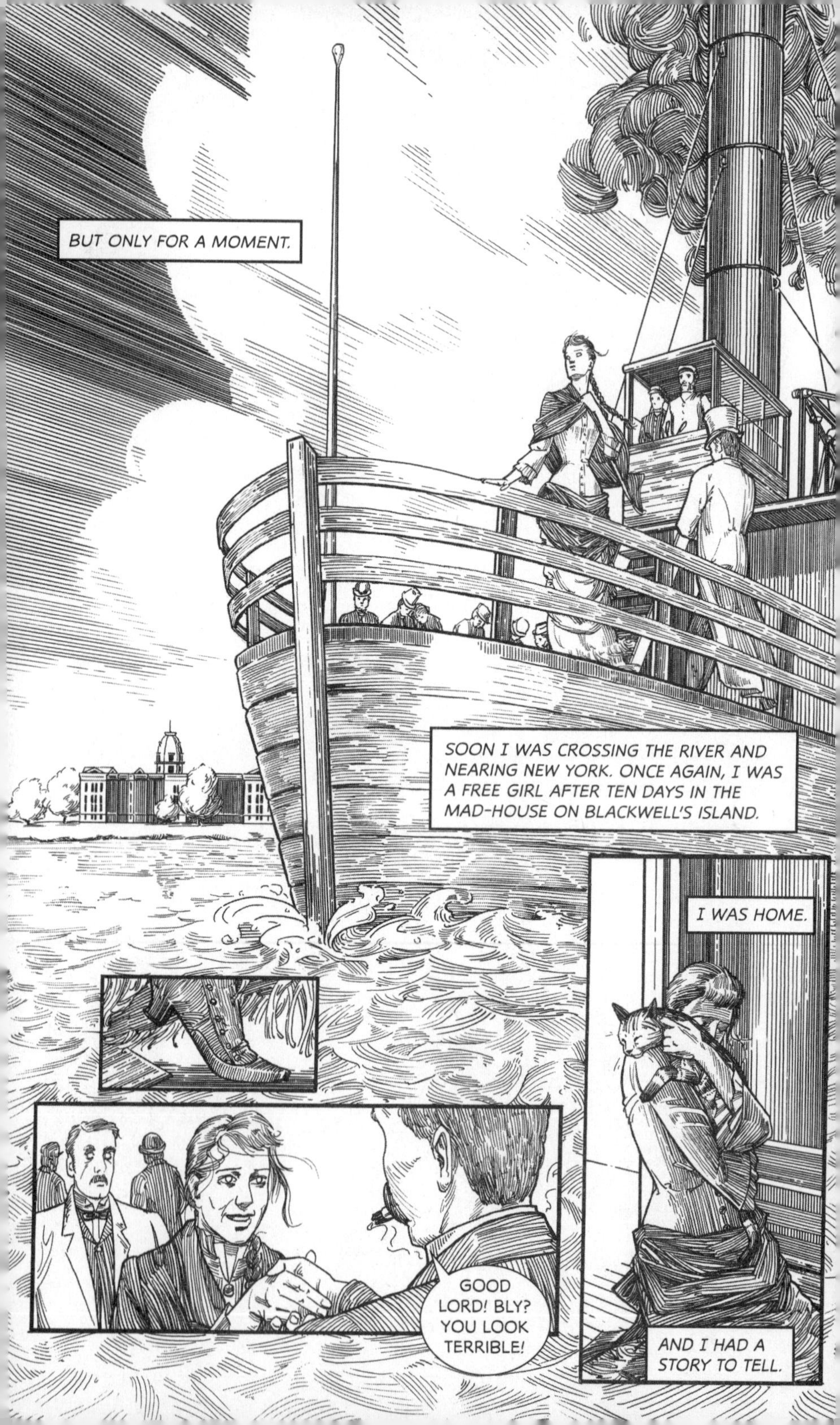
BUT ONLY FOR A MOMENT.
SOON I WAS CROSSING THE RIVER AND NEARING NEW YORK. ONCE AGAIN, I WAS A FREE GIRL AFTER TEN DAYS IN THE MAD-HOUSE ON BLACKWELL'S ISLAND.
GOOD LORD! BLY? YOU LOOK TERRIBLE!
I WAS HOME.
AND I HAD A STORY TO TELL.

THE WORLD.

THE NEW PAPER!
THE
"EVENING WORLD."
Beginning To-morrow.
PRICE 1 CENT.

NEW YORK, SUNDAY, OCTOBER 9, 1887.

BEHIND ASYLUM BARS.

The Mystery of the Unknown Insane Girl.

Remarkable Story of the Successful Impersonation of Insanity.

How Nellie Brown Deceived Judges, Reporters and Medical Experts.

She Tells Her Story of How She Passed at Bellevue Hospital.

Studying the Role of Insanity Before the Mirror and Practicing It at the Temporary Home for Women — Arrested — Brought Before Judge Duffy — Declares She is Some Mother's Darling, and Passes His Sister — Committed to the Care of Physicians for the Insane — The Experts Declare Her Insane — Bellevue — Harsh Treatment — Did Not Complain" — "Charity Hospital Life — How Our Reporter's Contemporaries Have Followed the Trail — Some Things Needed.

the crazier I was thought to be by all except one physician, whose kindness and gentle ways I shall not soon forget.

PREPARING FOR THE ORDEAL.

But to return to my work and my mission. After receiving my instructions I returned to my boarding-house, and when evening came I began to practice the role in which I was to make my debut on the morrow. What a difficult task, I thought, to appear before a crowd of people and convince them that I was insane. I had never been near persons afflicted in my life, and had not the faintest idea of what their actions were like. And then to be examined by a number of learned physicians who make insanity a specialty, and who daily come in contact with insane people! How could I hope to pass these doctors and convince them that I was crazy? I feared that they could not be deceived. I began to think my task a hopeless one but I had to pass...

[column text partially illegible]

I DO.

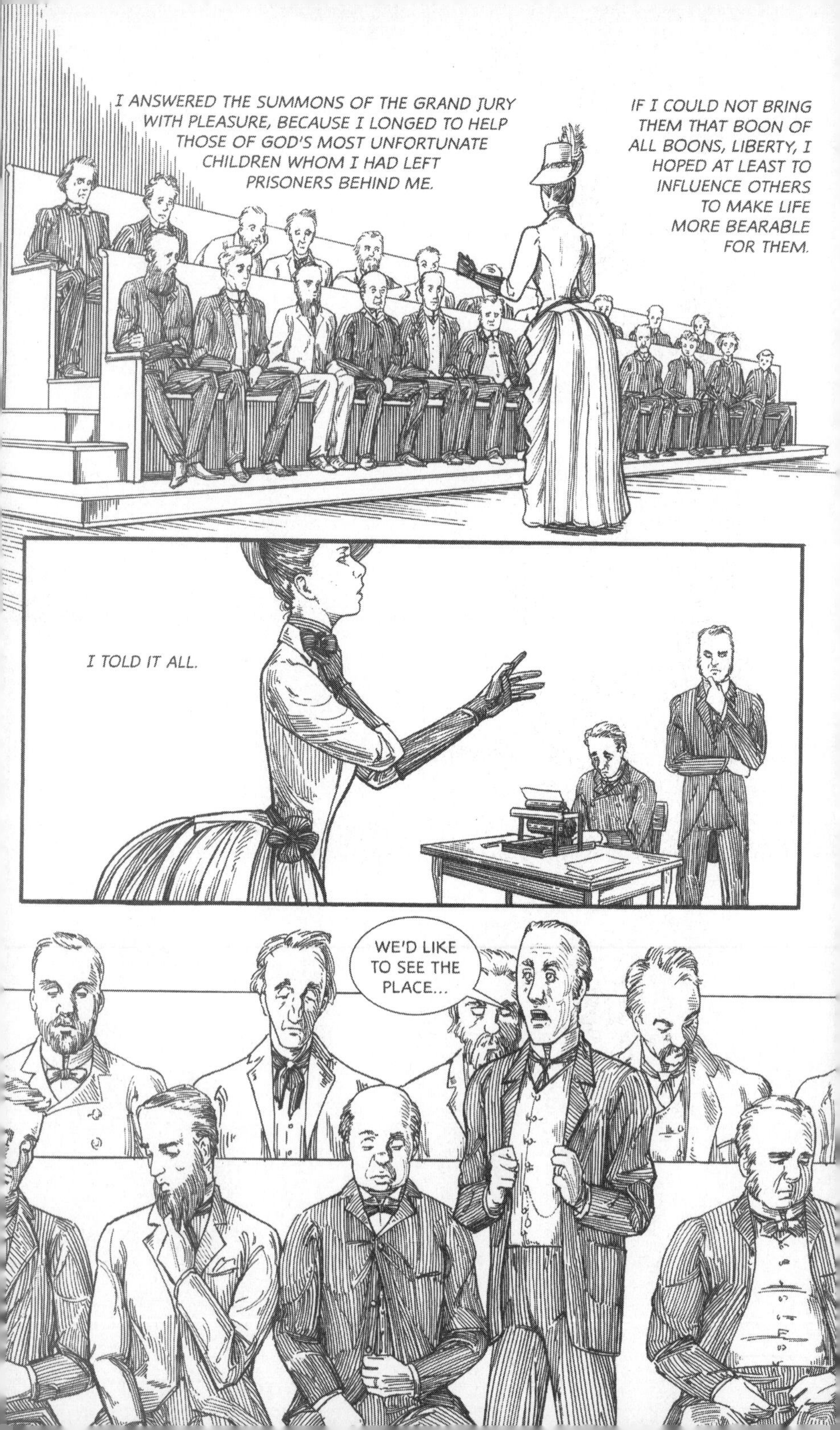
I ANSWERED THE SUMMONS OF THE GRAND JURY WITH PLEASURE, BECAUSE I LONGED TO HELP THOSE OF GOD'S MOST UNFORTUNATE CHILDREN WHOM I HAD LEFT PRISONERS BEHIND ME.
IF I COULD NOT BRING THEM THAT BOON OF ALL BOONS, LIBERTY, I HOPED AT LEAST TO INFLUENCE OTHERS TO MAKE LIFE MORE BEARABLE FOR THEM.
I TOLD IT ALL.
WE'D LIKE TO SEE THE PLACE...

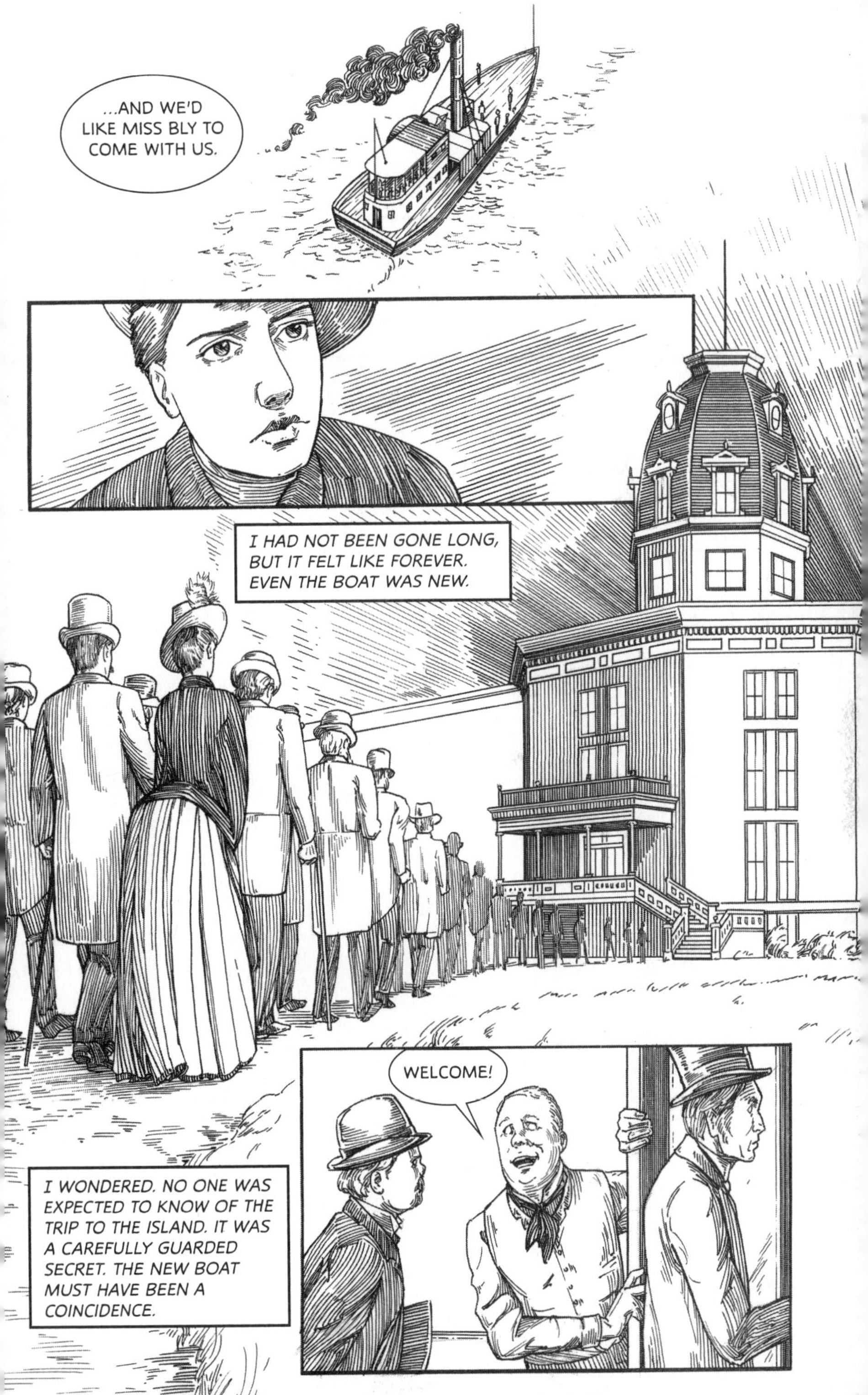
...AND WE'D LIKE MISS BLY TO COME WITH US.
I HAD NOT BEEN GONE LONG, BUT IT FELT LIKE FOREVER. EVEN THE BOAT WAS NEW.
I WONDERED. NO ONE WAS EXPECTED TO KNOW OF THE TRIP TO THE ISLAND. IT WAS A CAREFULLY GUARDED SECRET. THE NEW BOAT MUST HAVE BEEN A COINCIDENCE.
WELCOME!

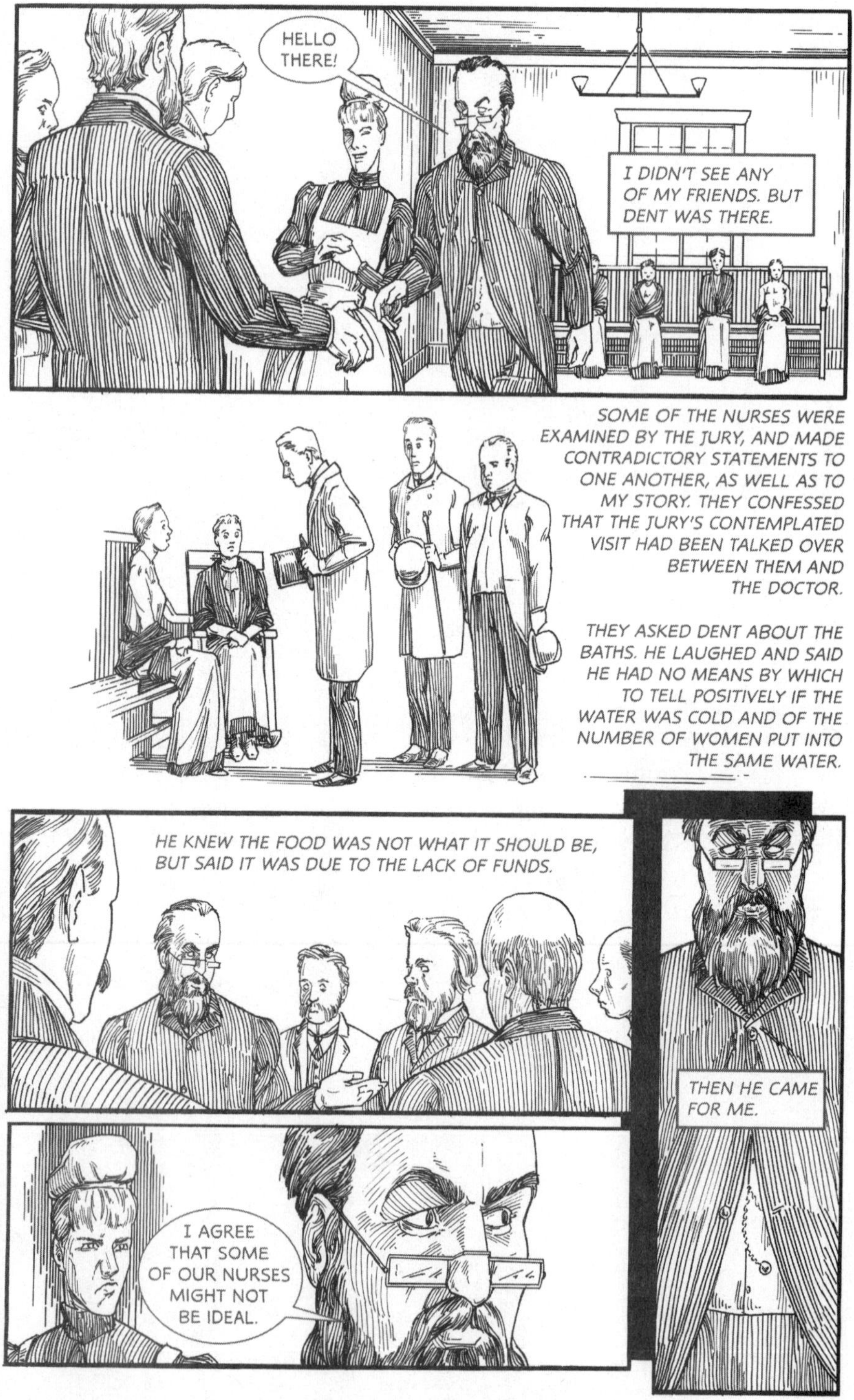
HELLO THERE!
I DIDN'T SEE ANY OF MY FRIENDS. BUT DENT WAS THERE.
SOME OF THE NURSES WERE EXAMINED BY THE JURY, AND MADE CONTRADICTORY STATEMENTS TO ONE ANOTHER, AS WELL AS TO MY STORY. THEY CONFESSED THAT THE JURY'S CONTEMPLATED VISIT HAD BEEN TALKED OVER BETWEEN THEM AND THE DOCTOR.
THEY ASKED DENT ABOUT THE BATHS. HE LAUGHED AND SAID HE HAD NO MEANS BY WHICH TO TELL POSITIVELY IF THE WATER WAS COLD AND OF THE NUMBER OF WOMEN PUT INTO THE SAME WATER.
HE KNEW THE FOOD WAS NOT WHAT IT SHOULD BE, BUT SAID IT WAS DUE TO THE LACK OF FUNDS.
I AGREE THAT SOME OF OUR NURSES MIGHT NOT BE IDEAL.
THEN HE CAME FOR ME.

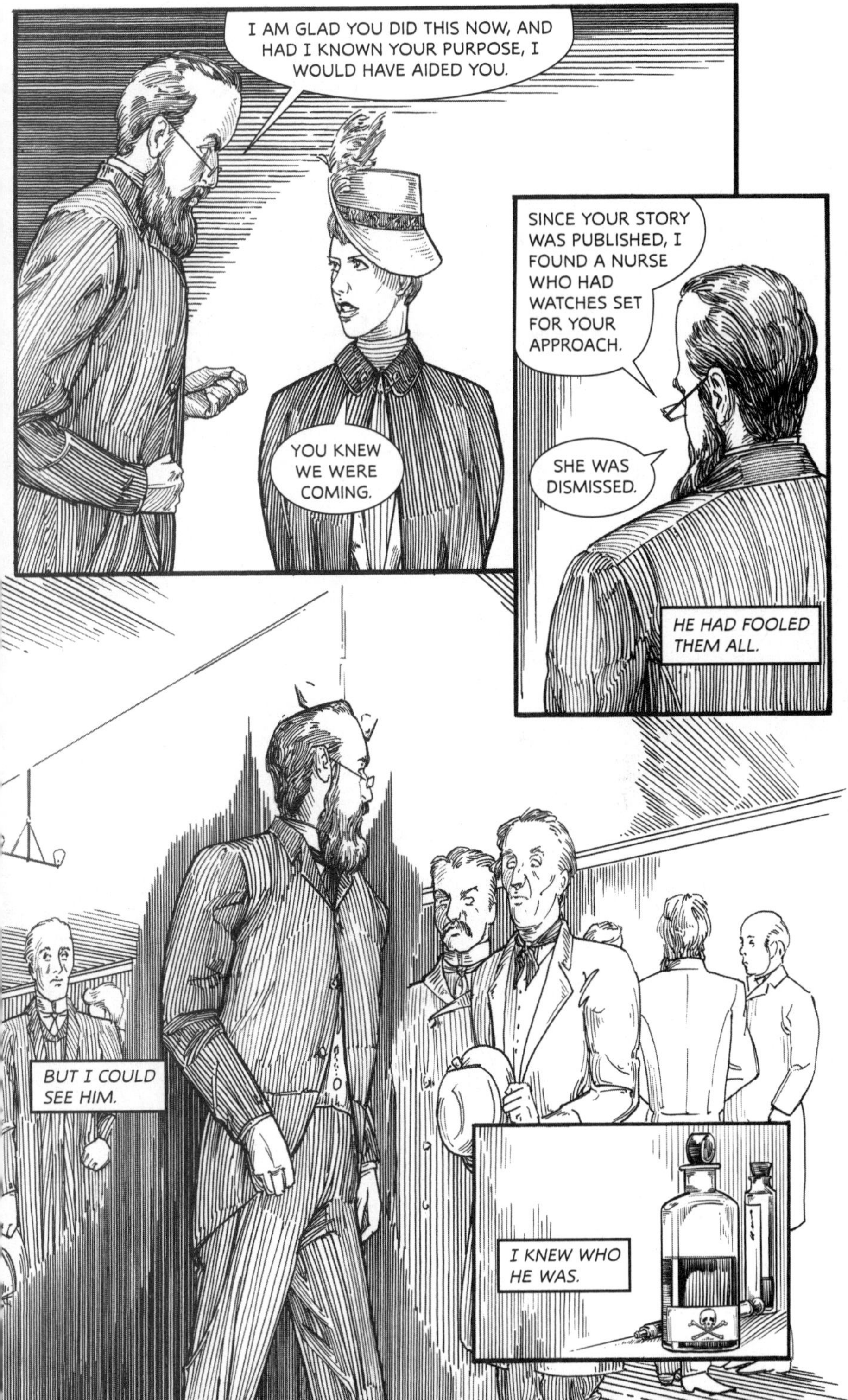
I AM GLAD YOU DID THIS NOW, AND HAD I KNOWN YOUR PURPOSE, I WOULD HAVE AIDED YOU.
YOU KNEW WE WERE COMING.
SINCE YOUR STORY WAS PUBLISHED, I FOUND A NURSE WHO HAD WATCHES SET FOR YOUR APPROACH.
SHE WAS DISMISSED.
HE HAD FOOLED THEM ALL.
BUT I COULD SEE HIM.
I KNEW WHO HE WAS.

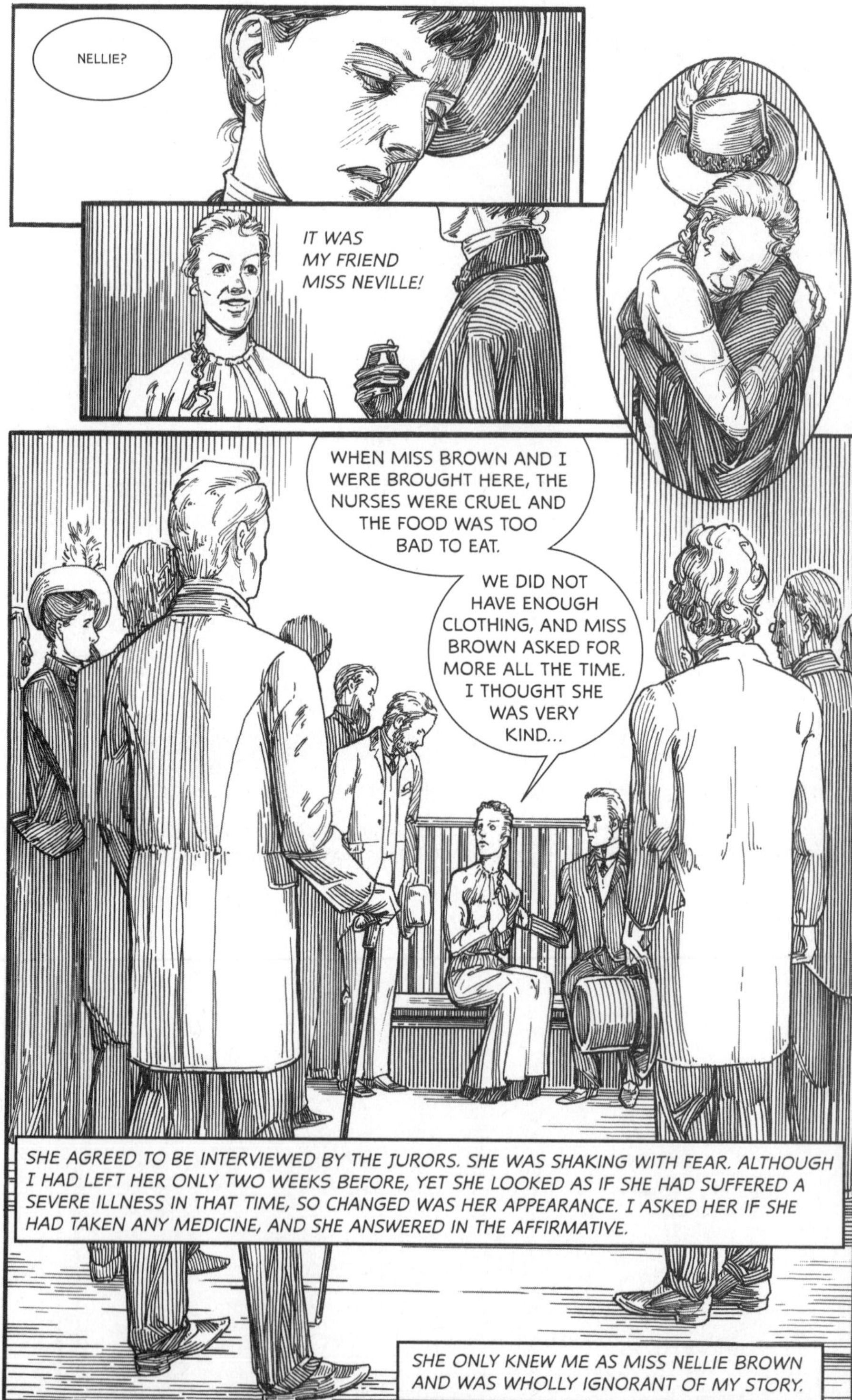
NELLIE?
IT WAS MY FRIEND MISS NEVILLE!
WHEN MISS BROWN AND I WERE BROUGHT HERE, THE NURSES WERE CRUEL AND THE FOOD WAS TOO BAD TO EAT.
WE DID NOT HAVE ENOUGH CLOTHING, AND MISS BROWN ASKED FOR MORE ALL THE TIME. I THOUGHT SHE WAS VERY KIND...
SHE AGREED TO BE INTERVIEWED BY THE JURORS. SHE WAS SHAKING WITH FEAR. ALTHOUGH I HAD LEFT HER ONLY TWO WEEKS BEFORE, YET SHE LOOKED AS IF SHE HAD SUFFERED A SEVERE ILLNESS IN THAT TIME, SO CHANGED WAS HER APPEARANCE. I ASKED HER IF SHE HAD TAKEN ANY MEDICINE, AND SHE ANSWERED IN THE AFFIRMATIVE.
SHE ONLY KNEW ME AS MISS NELLIE BROWN AND WAS WHOLLY IGNORANT OF MY STORY.

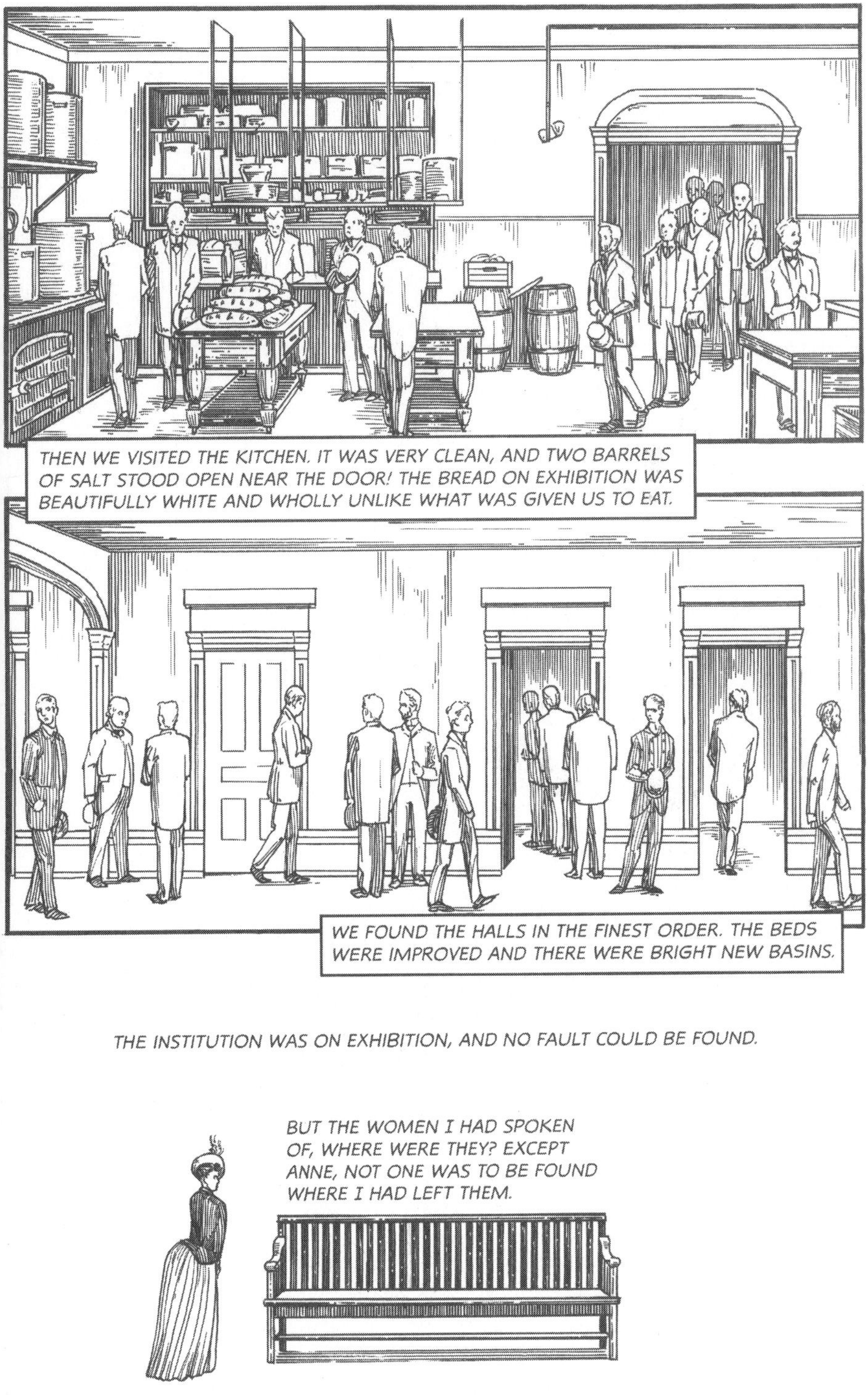
THEN WE VISITED THE KITCHEN. IT WAS VERY CLEAN, AND TWO BARRELS OF SALT STOOD OPEN NEAR THE DOOR! THE BREAD ON EXHIBITION WAS BEAUTIFULLY WHITE AND WHOLLY UNLIKE WHAT WAS GIVEN US TO EAT.
WE FOUND THE HALLS IN THE FINEST ORDER. THE BEDS WERE IMPROVED AND THERE WERE BRIGHT NEW BASINS.
THE INSTITUTION WAS ON EXHIBITION, AND NO FAULT COULD BE FOUND.
BUT THE WOMEN I HAD SPOKEN OF, WHERE WERE THEY? EXCEPT ANNE, NOT ONE WAS TO BE FOUND WHERE I HAD LEFT THEM.

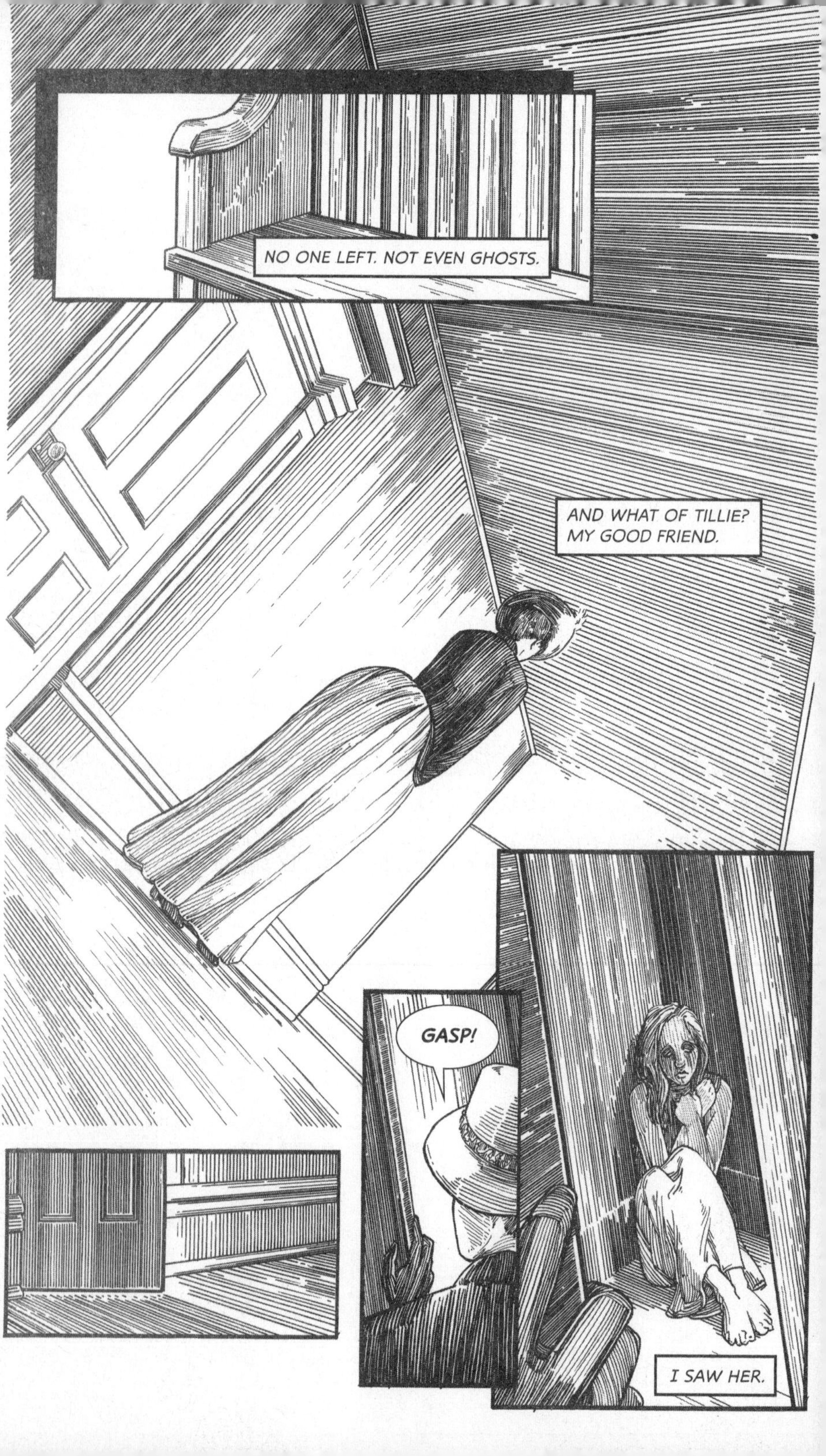
NO ONE LEFT. NOT EVEN GHOSTS.
AND WHAT OF TILLIE? MY GOOD FRIEND.
GASP!
I SAW HER.

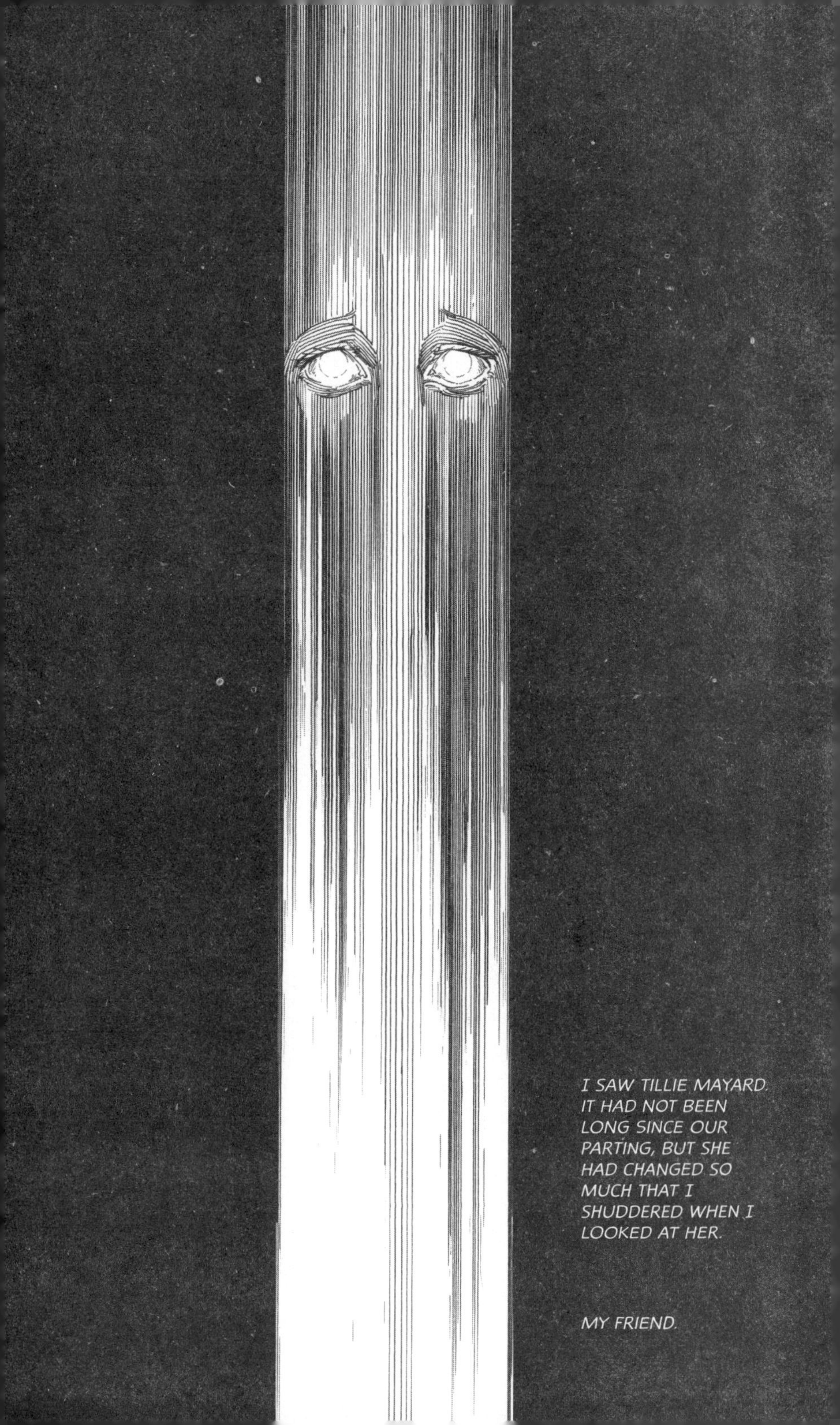
I SAW TILLIE MAYARD. IT HAD NOT BEEN LONG SINCE OUR PARTING, BUT SHE HAD CHANGED SO MUCH THAT I SHUDDERED WHEN I LOOKED AT HER.
MY FRIEND.

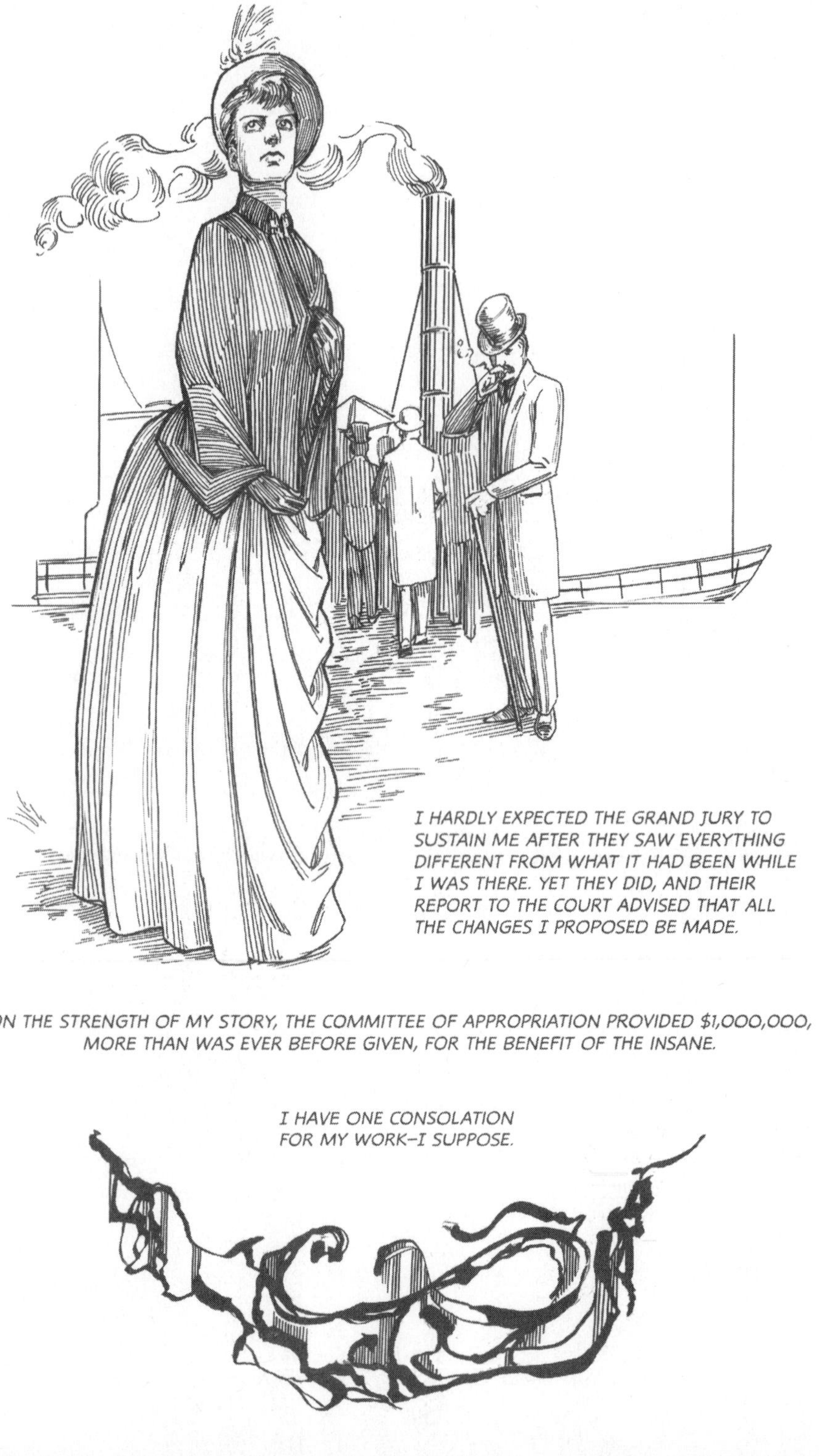
I HARDLY EXPECTED THE GRAND JURY TO SUSTAIN ME AFTER THEY SAW EVERYTHING DIFFERENT FROM WHAT IT HAD BEEN WHILE I WAS THERE. YET THEY DID, AND THEIR REPORT TO THE COURT ADVISED THAT ALL THE CHANGES I PROPOSED BE MADE.
ON THE STRENGTH OF MY STORY, THE COMMITTEE OF APPROPRIATION PROVIDED $1,000,000, MORE THAN WAS EVER BEFORE GIVEN, FOR THE BENEFIT OF THE INSANE.
I HAVE ONE CONSOLATION FOR MY WORK—I SUPPOSE.

Afterword

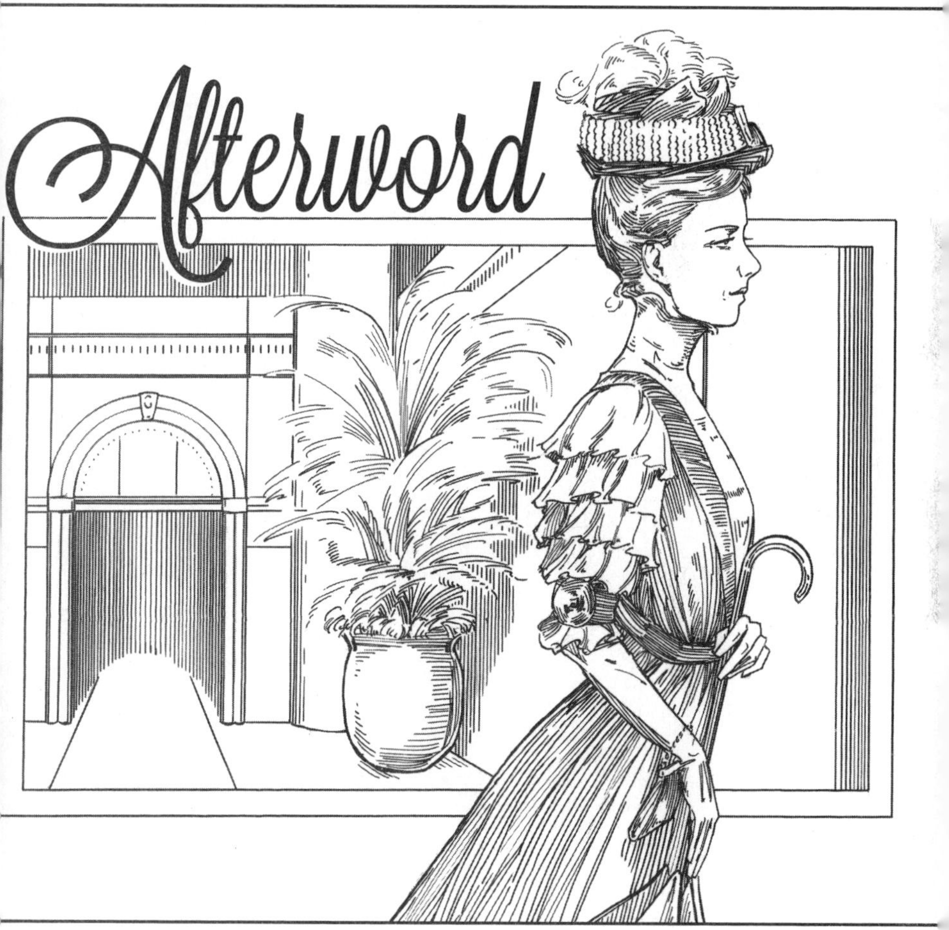

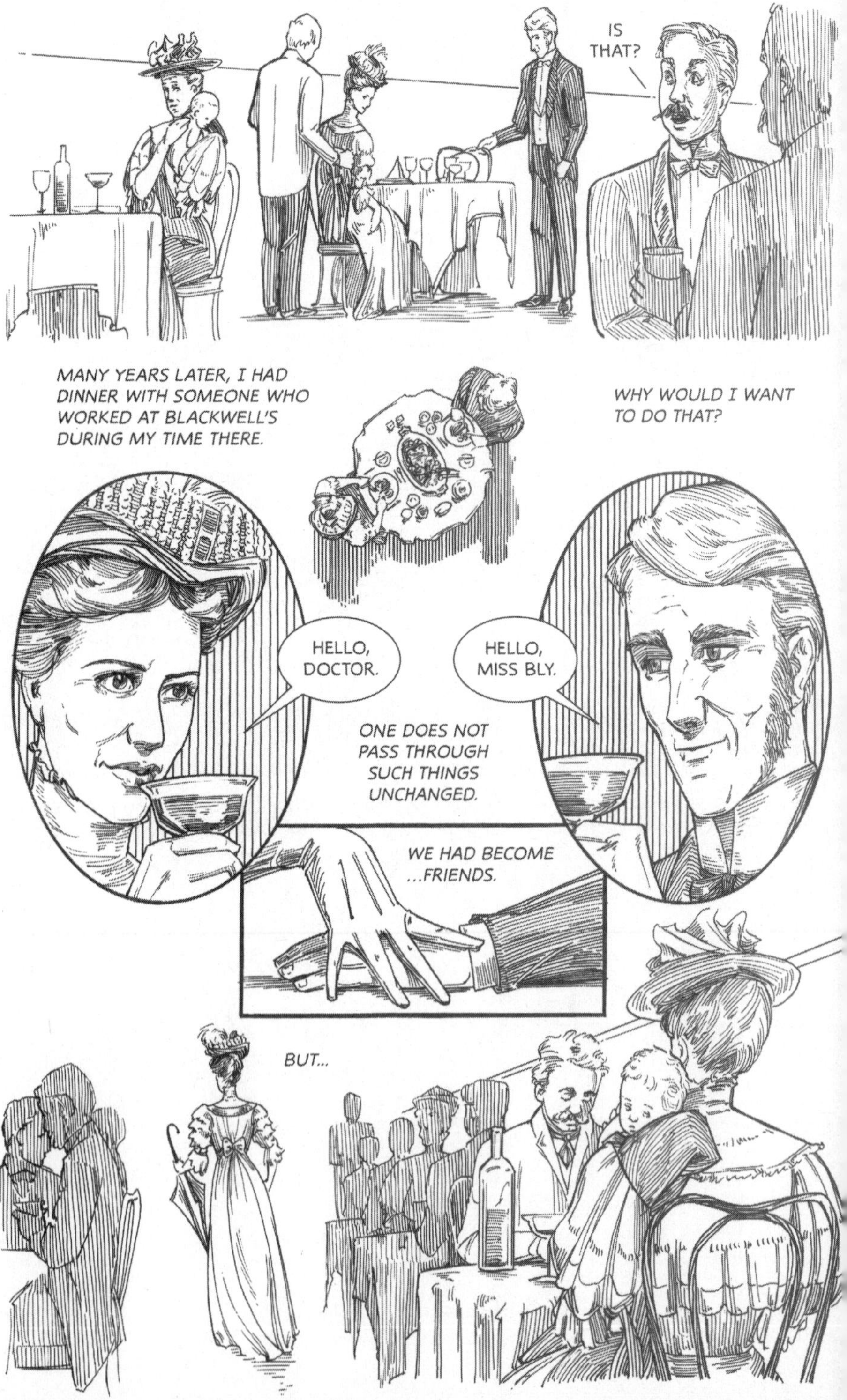
IS THAT?
MANY YEARS LATER, I HAD DINNER WITH SOMEONE WHO WORKED AT BLACKWELL'S DURING MY TIME THERE.
WHY WOULD I WANT TO DO THAT?
HELLO, DOCTOR.
HELLO, MISS BLY.
ONE DOES NOT PASS THROUGH SUCH THINGS UNCHANGED.
WE HAD BECOME ...FRIENDS.
BUT...

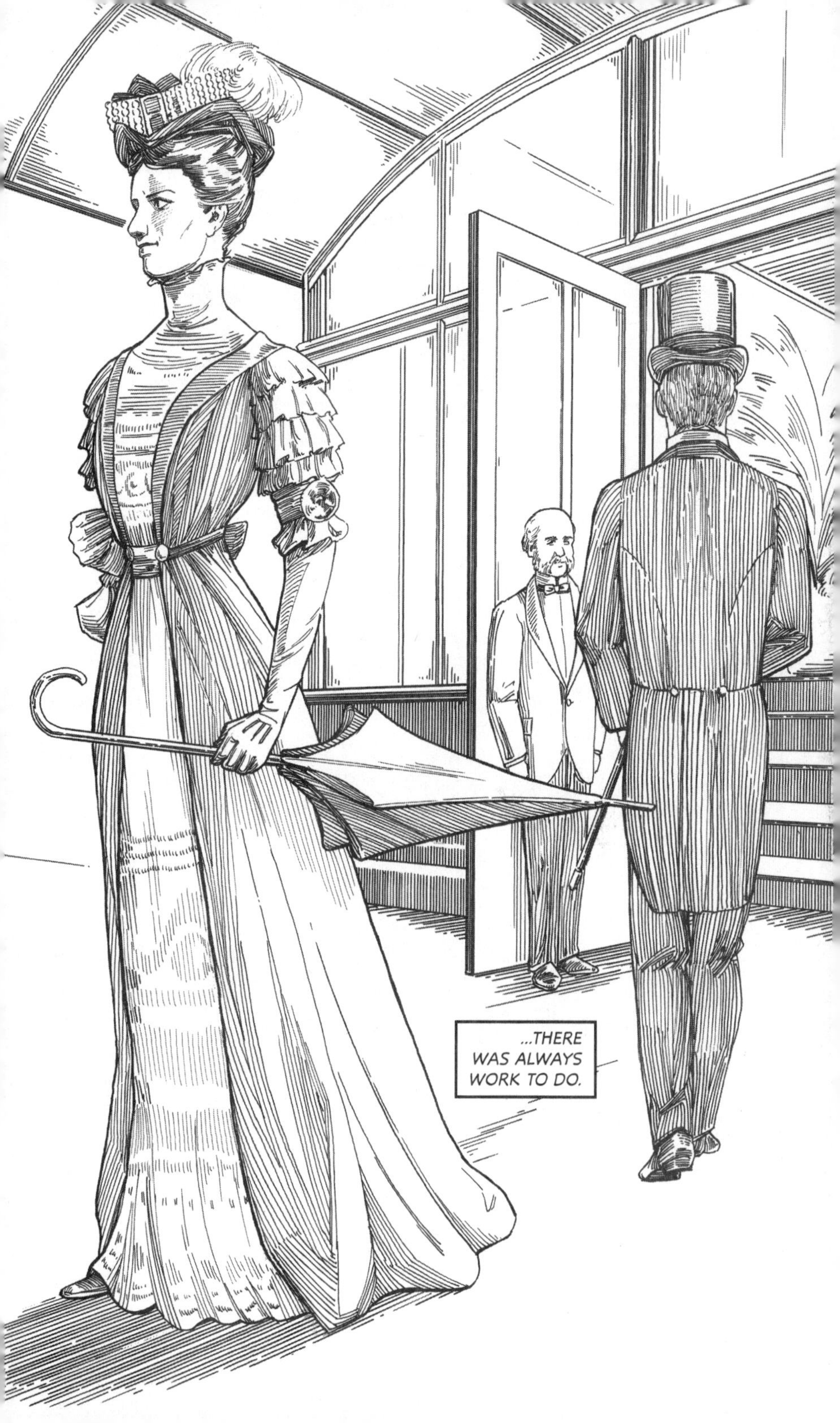
...THERE
WAS ALWAYS
WORK TO DO.

A NOTE FROM THE AUTHORS

When Nellie Bly went undercover in 1887 to expose the evils of institutionalization, the patients she met were probably suffering from illnesses such as anxiety, postpartum depression, and, in some cases, possibly even schizophrenia. Several of the women were there only because their actions in society were considered immoral or unladylike, while others seemed to have had just one bad day. But what they all had in common, these patients who could not leave under any circumstances, was that in the eyes of the law and their male doctors, as well as the state of New York, they were all the same thing: they were mad.

Today, circumstances are thankfully much different. We have life-changing new drugs and more specific diagnoses. Therapy has become commonplace. Mental illness has become more normalized through positive and truthful depictions in the media, and in the way that some celebrities are upfront about their own struggles. We also see it every day in the people we know best—teachers, essential workers, mothers and fathers, friends and acquaintances—and even in ourselves. Though our current system is by no means perfect, especially for the homeless, minorities, the LGBTQ+ community, and those without health care, people are more comfortable seeking knowledge and treatment about their mental health than ever before. It will never be easy, but it is no longer something that is stigmatized or just locked away.

Some of that is because of Nellie Bly. In her exposé, she did the good work of journalism: she investigated a story and reported the facts back to the world. Her methods may not have been conventional (and are maybe even unethical by today's standards), and may have been quick toward stereotyping, but the real truth she reported on (in addition to selling a lot of papers) became a sharp weapon against injustice.

We wanted to tell Nellie's story for those reasons. New readers can be inspired by her work in a hopefully reinvigorated way that shows not only what she did in the asylum but provides the foreground of what she experienced, in her own words, as a "patient" herself: neglected and abused—sympathetic or symptomatic—in the chilling depths of Blackwell's.

Because even though Nellie Bly opened the eyes of the public to the horrors of these places, the doors of the last state mental institution only closed around twenty years ago. More recently, there has been a groundswell of opinion from populist politicians and pundits, even at the highest level of our democracy, who have called for a return to the old system of asylums, where patients can be forcibly removed from society and cared for by the state, without having committed any crime.

History can repeat itself.

Are you mad yet?

Brad Ricca & Courtney Sieh, 2021

ACKNOWLEDGMENTS

The authors would like to thank our editor, Ed Schlesinger, for understanding how much we wanted to tell this story in a very certain way, and for the guidance and patience in helping it get there. Thanks also to our agent, Scott Mendel, for helping a lifelong dream turn into something inked and real.

Brad Ricca: I would like to thank the journalists I know who inspired my interpretation of Nellie and her work. They include Michael Sangiacomo, Joe Sampson, Heidi MacDonald, Andrea Simakis, James Sheeler, Annie Nickoloff, and Nikki Delamotte. And thanks to my parents for encouraging me to read comics. It changed my life.

Courtney Sieh: I would like to thank the New York Public Library, the Museum of the City of New York, and the fine users of Pinterest for all your invaluable visual resources. Thank you to all my supportive friends, especially Gaby. Thank you to professors Dom, John, Lincoln, and Suzie. And a very special thank-you to my mom and dad. You may stop worrying now.

If you are experiencing mental health issues or are in emotional distress,
text "HOME" to 741741 for the Crisis Text Line in the US or Canada
(85258 in the UK and 50808 in Ireland),
or you can message Crisis Text Line on Facebook.

If the situation is potentially life-threatening, get immediate emergency
assistance by calling 911 and asking for a CIT officer
or other specialist in mental health emergencies,
or call the confidential National Suicide Prevention Lifeline
at 1-800-273-TALK (8255). Chat live with a trained counselor 24/7
at suicidepreventionlifeline.org/chat/.

For general mental health questions and to locate local treatment,
call the Substance Abuse and Mental Health Services referral line
at 1-800-662-HELP (4357).

You are not alone.

ABOUT THE AUTHORS

BRAD RICCA is the Edgar-nominated writer of six books, including *True Raiders*, *Mrs. Sherlock Holmes*, and the award-winning *Super Boys*. He lives with his family in Cleveland.

COURTNEY SIEH works out of a swamp near Minneapolis, kept company at her drafting table by her two cats. *Ten Days in a Mad-House* is her debut full-length work.